What is Social Theory?

What is Social Theory?

The Philosophical Debates

Edited by Alan Sica

BLACKWELL
Publishers

Copyright © Blackwell Publishers Ltd, 1998

First published 1998

2 4 6 8 10 9 7 5 3 1

Blackwell Publishers Inc.
350 Main Street
Malden, Massachusetts 02148
USA

Blackwell Publishers Ltd
108 Cowley Road
Oxford OX4 1JF
UK

Library of Congress Cataloging-in-Publication Data

What is social theory?: the philosophical debates / edited by Alan
   Sica.
      p.   cm.
   Includes bibliographical references and index.
   ISBN 0–631–20954–9 (hardback). – ISBN 0–631–20955–7 (paperback)
   1. Social sciences–Philosophy.   I. Sica, Alan, 1949–   .
H61.W496   1998
300′.1–dc21   98–13166
                                                              CIP

British Library Cataloguing in Publication Data

A CIP catalogue record for this book is available from the British Library

Typeset in 10$\frac{1}{2}$ on 12pt Palatino
by Graphicraft Limited, Hong Kong
Printed in Great Britain by TJ International, Padstow, Cornwall.

This book is printed on acid-free paper

Contents

List of Contributors   vii

Introduction: Philosophy's Tutelage of Social Theory:
"A Parody of Profundity"?
Alan Sica   1

1   Mapping Postmodern Social Theory
    Robert J. Antonio   22

2   A Thesaurus of Experience: Maurice Natanson,
    Phenomenology, and Social Theory
    Mary F. Rogers   76

3   From Content to Context: A Social Epistemology of the
    Structure–Agency Craze
    Steve Fuller   92

4   Making Normative Soup with Non-normative Bones
    Stephen Turner   118

5   Criteria for a Theory of Knowledge
    Jennifer L. Croissant   145

6   Examples, Submerged Statements, and the Neglected
    Application of Philosophy to Social Theory
    Stanley Lieberson   177

7   Loosening the Chains of Philosophical Reductionism
    Steven Rytina   192

8   Social Order and Emergent Rationality
    Michael W. Macy   219

9   Theoretical Models: Sociology's Missing Links
    John Skvoretz   238

10 Sociological Models
    Paul Humphreys   253

11 Culture and Social Structure
    Peter M. Blau   265

Name Index   276

Subject Index   282

Contributors

Robert J. Antonio (Ph.D., Notre Dame, 1972) is Professor of Sociology at the University of Kansas. Recent publications include "Nietzsche's Anti-Sociology" and "The Problem of Normative Foundations in Emancipatory Theory" (both in *American Journal of Sociology*). He also co-edited *A Weber–Marx Dialogue* (1986).

Peter M. Blau (Ph.D., Columbia, 1952) is Quetelet Professor of Sociology Emeritus, Columbia University, and Robert Broughton Distinguished Service Professor, UNC/Chapel Hill. His major theoretical books are *Exchange and Power in Social Life* (1964) and *Inequality and Heterogeneity* (1997).

Jennifer L. Croissant (Ph.D., Rensselaer Polytechnic Institute, 1994) is Assistant Professor, Program on Culture, Science, Technology, and Society at the University of Arizona. Her works include "Technoscience or Tyrannoscience Rex," (with Sal Restivo), "Science and Progressive Thought" in S. Star (ed.), *Ecologies of Knowledge* (1995), and "Cyborg Stories" in R. Davis-Floyd and J. Dumit (eds), *Cyborg Babies* (1998). She co-edited *Degrees of Compromise* (1998).

Steve Fuller (Ph.D., University of Pittsburgh, 1985) is Professor of Sociology and Social Policy at the University of Durham, UK. He is the founding editor of the journal *Social Epistemology*, and the author of four books, the latest being *Science* (1997). His forthcoming book is on the origins and impact of Kuhn's *Structure of Scientific Revolutions*.

Paul Humphreys (Ph.D., Stanford University) is Professor of Philosophy at the University of Virginia. Recent publications include "Understanding in the Not-So-Special Sciences" (*Southern Journal of Philosophy*), "Computational Science and Scientific Method" (*Minds and Machines*), and "A Critical Appraisal of Causal Discovery Algorithms" in V. McKim and S. Turner (eds), *Causality in Crisis* (1997).

Stanley Lieberson (Ph.D., University of Chicago, 1960) is the Abbott Lawrence Lowell Professor of Sociology at Harvard University. His best-known works include *A Piece of the Pie* (1980) and *Making it Count* (1985). He is now studying social influences on tastes and fashion, and on questions of evidence in social science research.

Michael W. Macy (Ph.D., Harvard University, 1985) is Professor of Sociology at Cornell University. He studies cooperation in social dilemmas using computer simulation and laboratory experiments with human subjects. Forthcoming works include "Trust and Cooperation Between Strangers," with J. Skvoretz (*American Sociological Review*), and "Dependence and Cooperation in the Game of Trump," with T. Boone (*Advances in Group Processes*).

Mary F. Rogers (Ph.D., University of Massachusetts, 1972) teaches sociology and women's studies at the University of West Florida/ Pensacola. Her most recent book is *Contemporary Feminist Theory: A Text/Reader* (1998).

Steven Rytina (Ph.D., Michigan State University, 1980) is Associate Professor of Sociology at McGill University. His most recent work examines the assumptions of occupational mobility research to yield simpler alternative empirical summaries. His current project is a cross-national comparison of occupational mobility funded by the Social Science and Humanities Research Council.

Alan Sica (Ph.D., University of Massachusetts, 1978) is Professor of Sociology and Director of the Social Thought Program at Pennsylvania State University. For five years editor of the ASA journal, *Sociological Theory*, he is the author of *Weber, Irrationality, and Social Order* (1988) and editor of *Ideologies and the Corruption of Thought* (1997). Among his forthcoming works is *Max Weber and the New Century* (1998).

John Skvoretz (Ph.D., University of Pittsburgh, 1976) is a Carolina Distinguished Professor of Sociology at the University of South Carolina. Current research concerns formal models of social networks, status and participation in discussion groups, and power in exchange networks. He co-edited *Status, Networks, and Structure* (1997) and *Advances in Group Processes, Vol. 15* (1998).

Stephen Turner (Ph.D., University of Missouri, 1975) is Graduate Research Professor of Philosophy at the University of South Florida. His recent books include *The Social Theory of Practices* (1994) and *Max Weber*, with Regis Factor (1994). He co-edited *Causality in Crisis* (1997), which includes chapters by himself and two other contributors to this volume, Paul Humphreys and Stanley Lieberson.

Introduction: Philosophy's Tutelage of Social Theory: "A Parody of Profundity"?

Alan Sica

A Troubled Union

Western philosophy set up shop roughly three millennia ago in Homer's Ionia, or, by Hegel's estimate,[1] with Thales in 640 BC. Yet the quasi-philosophical activity known today as "social theory" is usually dated only from the time of Rousseau or Condorcet – ignoring for the moment Machiavelli, Hobbes, and other worthy "precursors" – thus giving its sister discipline a durational advantage on the order of eleven to one over the infant challenger. This marked disparity of lineage, despite the importance that intellectuals usually attach to such matters, has not always been viewed as troublesome from within the social thought camp. In Durkheim's writing, for example, Kant is invoked so often as almost to prove embarrassing, particularly when one considers the uncertain grasp that the former apparently had on the latter's ideas in their technical sense. Already 45 years ago in a study of comparative mythology, Joseph Campbell chastised "the muddle-headed Durkheim": "Read his confused discussion of Kant's *a priori* forms of sensibility [early in *The Elementary Forms*], and his quackery about the distinction

[1] Georg Wilhelm Friedrich Hegel, *Lectures on the History of Philosophy*, trans. E. S. Haldane [1892] (Lincoln, NE: University of Nebraska Press, 1995), Vol. I, p. 171.

between the Zuni and European experiences of space, and the shallowness of his whole parody of profundity will be apparent!"[2] Whatever the ultimate accuracy or meaning of Campbell's harsh judgment might be, Durkheim himself believed that he was creating what could be termed a "social epistemology" (not exactly in Steve Fuller's sense), and that his theoretical innovations were as fully philosophical as sociological in nature. That he regarded his overall scholarly achievement, even prior to *The Elementary Forms*, as properly philosophical – though sociologically recast – is without question, particularly in texts like *Pragmatism and Sociology*.

Similarly, Marx began academic life with an unpublishable 80-page dissertation that innovatively re-examined a hoary philosophical topic, *[The] Difference Between the Democritean and Epicurean Philosophy of Nature in General*. Anticipating a practice he would follow throughout his life, he assembled for this work more than a hundred printed pages of "preparatory material" in seven *Notebooks on Epicurean Philosophy*. As part of this exercise in textual retrieval and self-edification, he also produced in 1839 (at 21) a schematic diagram of the "philosophy of nature" buried within Hegel's *Encyclopedia*.[3] It is well remembered that in the US and Britain between the mid-1950s and the mid-1970s, by far the most widely studied texts from Marx's bounteous output were *The Economic and Philosophical Manuscripts of 1844*, less formally known as "the early, philosophical Marx." In working out the socio-philosophical significance of alienation and commodification, Marx in these working papers gave careful attention to Hegel, Feuerbach, Fichte, Proudhon, and other figures then impressing themselves on the scholarly identity of Marx's generation.

---

[2] Joseph Campbell, *The Flight of the Wild Gander: Explorations in the Mythological Dimension* (South Bend, IN: Regnery/Gateway, Inc., 1979 [1951?]), p. 45. Campbell substantiates his charge in a footnote: "Durkheim quotes F. H. Cushing to the effect that space in Zuni has seven quarters and declares this to be an essentially different space from ours, which has but four. The seven Zuni quarters are, to wit: north, south, east, west, above, below, and middle. Very different indeed! Durkheim's problems, obviously are semantic and absolutely elementary"; he cites the original edition, *Les formes élémentaires de la vie religieuse*, pp. 15–21; cf. *Elementary Forms of the Religious Life*, trans. Karen E. Fields (New York: Free Press, 1995), pp. 11ff. Campbell also directs the reader to compare Durkheim's remarks on what might be called "comparative epistemology" with Kant's original from *The Critique of Pure Reason*, "Introduction" and "Transcendental Doctrine of Elements," pp. 41–91 in the standard Kemp Smith translation.

[3] All of this material has been translated from Greek, Latin, and German into English in the Karl Marx/Frederick Engels *Collected Works* (London: Lawrence Wishart, 1975), Vol. 1, pp. 25–105, 403–516, plus many accompanying endnotes provided by the international team of editors.

In the unforgettable "Letter from Marx to his Father" (November 10/11, 1837),[4] the 19-year-old college student records at four in the morning his *rite de passage* from adolescent to young man with a mission. His reading by our standards seems astounding in scope and depth, as is the seriousness of his scholarly ambition, much of which turns on historico-philosophical questions. Presaging the concerns of Weber and a succession of later theorists, Marx tries valiantly in this missive to reconceptualize Savigny's historical analysis of legal ownership by means of Hegel's and Fichte's metaphysics, inducing in himself a level of frustration one can well imagine, even for the most precocious youth. Yet it was already evident to Marx, the college boy, that "the grotesque craggy melody" of Hegel's philosophy, initially repugnant as it was, held within it the promise of philosophical and political revitalization so much desired by members of "the Doctor's Club" he had recently been invited to join.[5]

If Durkheim's Kant and Marx's Hegel are symptomatic of philosophy's midwifery at the birth of modern social theory, then it was Dilthey, Rickert, Windelband, Knies, Stammler, and a host of others to whom Weber turned for initial guidance and eventual transcendence in his perfection of *verstehende* sociology. His knowledge of Kant, Hegel, and Goethe was secure enough to serve his purposes. But it was the late nineteenth-century arguments over value, objectivity, nomothetic versus ideographic knowledge – the panoply of neo-Kantian debates that have since been well documented[6] – which caused his analytic and polemical fires to burn their brightest.

If one reads carefully, for instance, *Roscher and Knies* (not, to be sure, one of Weber's more graceful works), it is mostly a linked set of thick philosophical disputations, and can hardly be taken any other way. Weber's hermeneutic labors over now-forgotten texts often erupted into a "veritable fury of irony" – to use Marx's phrase when recording for his father the result of over-studying Hegel's dialectics.[7] Weber's writings about methodology, value-freedom, political versus scientific truths, or ideal–typical social action are each the work of a scholar well-trained in philosophies of social

[4] *Ibid.*, pp. 10–21.
[5] *Ibid.*, pp. 18, 19.
[6] See Thomas Willey, *Back to Kant: The Revival of Kantianism in German Social and Historical Thought, 1860–1914* (Detroit: Wayne State University Press, 1978), and Klaus Christian Kohnke, *The Rise of Neo-Kantianism: German Academic Philosophy Between Idealism and Positivism*, trans. R. J. Hollingdale (Cambridge: Cambridge University Press, 1991).
[7] Marx/Engels, *Collected Works*, Vol. 1, p. 19.

interaction and societal analysis. Naturally, this skilled argumenta-
tion accounts in part for the difficulty novices often have in understanding him the first time through. And that he was also expert
in the philosophy of jurisprudence (documented by Turner and
Factor[8]), welcoming this stream into his social theory, simply adds
to the puzzlement new readers experience with his more epistemological texts.

Once again allowing the all-star troika of social theory to stand
in for another dozen names which could as easily be mentioned
in this context (e.g., Mead's reliance on Hegel, Simmel's devout
Kantianism, or Schutz's sociologization of Husserl) reminds one
of an aged tale. In 1662 John Greenhalgh reported to Thomas
Crompton concerning the delicate symbiosis that he noted abroad
between ascetic friars and their prosperous parishioners:

Some of our English who had lived three or four years in Dunkirk told me
that these [Capuchin monks] do live modestly or meerly upon alms; and
I saw some mendicant friars go into the streets two together, with each a
basket in his arms, and into shops and houses; and I noted how they,
though as beggars, passed along, all people of all sorts take off their hats
and shewing great reverence towards them, as they do strictly observe
towards all their religious. They told me that these friars do each day once
cover their tables with a coarse but a clean cloth, and set on salt only,
there expecting what their providers will bring them (which office they do
by turns), of which be it more or less they make a dinner, and be it never
so short they who beg the next day do not complain; their manner being
not to ask but to stand silent, and to take what is given. But when it falls
out, which sometimes though seldom doth, that they have had many
short meals together, and too sore pinched, they have a bell on the top of
a corner of their House, called the starving bell, which they (having first
covered their empty table, setting on salt only, and setting their hall door
wide open, and have out of modesty retired themselves into their cells out
of sight) they ring out aloud, which being once heard abroad hath the
same effect there that a fire bell being rung hath in a town with us; people
running out into the streets and crying, "Jesu, Maria, the starving bell, wo
and alas for the holy men"; such an hub-bub as though the judgement of
Sodom were ready to fall upon the town, for their neglect of the holy men.
So of the richer sort, the mistresses do in all hast send out each their maid,
running one with a cheese, another with a loaf, another with a dish of
butter, one carries half a great pastie, another runs with a standing piece
of roast beef, &c. all which entring the monastery hall, they lay down

[8] Stephen P. Turner and Regis A. Factor, *Max Weber: The Lawyer as Social Thinker*
(London: Routledge, 1994).

upon the table, and get them out again; one monk peeping through a hole sees when the table is soundly furnished, then comes out and shuts the hall door of modesty, so as they who come after that go back again with their meat, saving both it and their credit; when all are gone the hungry friars, creeping out of their holes, do fall aboard.[9] [archaisms in original]

Does not the seventeenth-century monks' infrequent but urgent need for local help bear a reasonable relation to our own condition, when late twentieth-century social theorists irregularly but inevitably turn for aid to their philosophical brethren? Does not the social theory mansion have its own "starving bell," which rings every so often in the form of one or another manifesto, and to which philosophers, some of them at least, respond by laying fresh nutrients at the door?

The Dialogue of Late

In 1970 when Dorothy Emmet (emerita philosopher from Manchester) and Alasdair MacIntyre (then "professor of sociology" at Essex) issued Sociological Theory and Philosophical Analysis,[10] they included chapters by a group of philosophically oriented theorists whose names have since become standard in a way they were not at the time, including Habermas, Tom Burns, Steven Lukes, Gellner, Victor Turner, plus Schutz and several others. Because the book was published in London, one-third of its pages were given to anthropological theory, reflecting a tradition more important there than in the US. Still, the volume was noticed in the States because of the unique title, and because the editors' introduction persuasively hinted that the future of social theory lay in developing a renewed relationship to philosophical traditions, whether phenomenological, Marxian, neo-Kantian, or others. If models from physics, biology, and math had inspired functionalists during the 1950s and 1960s while they worked up their theoretical programs, it seemed time for such enthusiasms to be reconsidered, particularly in view of political and cultural events during the late 1960s. The hope for eventual maturation as a credible intellectual pursuit, so Emmet

[9] Sir Henry Ellis (ed.), Original Letters, Illustrative of English History; including Numerous Royal Letters: From Autographs in the British Museum, The State Paper Office, and One or Two Other Collections (London: Richard Bentley, 1846), Vol. IV, pp. 281–2.

[10] Dorothy Emmet and Alasdair MacIntyre (eds), Sociological Theory and Philosophical Analysis (London: Macmillan, 1970).

and MacIntyre implied, would oblige social theorists to remain alert to developing trends in philosophy in a way that they had not for some decades. If, for instance, Mead had profitably cut his teeth on Hegel, the same could not be said for his direct theoretical descendants in the mid-twentieth century.

Needless to say, a sea-change has occurred in the ensuing quarter-century which surely would have astonished Emmet and MacIntyre in their role as editors of this heterodox anthology. Where their book stood practically alone in trying to bring together serious philosophy and equally serious social thought, dozens of others have by now consigned theirs to oblivion. Though no one to my knowledge has yet assembled a full-scale bibliography of such materials, even a brisk electronic search (which omits most of what preceded 1985 or so) turns up enough reading for a lifetime. By my provisional count, books in English which somehow intermingle sociology or social theory with philosophical concerns now exceed several hundred, and pertinent articles, of course, number well into the thousands.[11]

---

[11] This is not the place even to outline what such a bibliography might take in, but a few items might be mentioned to give a sense of what for the alert reader already exists pertaining broadly to the philosophy–social theory nexus. To begin with, the State University of New York Press has thus far issued no fewer than 16 titles in a new "Series in the Philosophy of Social Sciences." These volumes deal at length with Marx, Von Hayek, Habermas, hermeneutics, narrative, utopianism, nihilism, computer simulation of cognition, pragmatism, habit, and video icons, among a number of topics. Meanwhile, Pennsylvania State University Press has published a number of "feminist rereadings" in its "Re-reading the Canon" series, thus far providing separate volumes that treat Plato, Arendt, Hegel, Wollstonecraft, Foucault, de Beauvoir, and Derrida. Neither of these series is substantively unique in the scholarly publishing trade, and both could be interpreted as bellwethers for a confluence of interests that link social theory, philosophy, and historical change, along with "race, class, and gender" – the latest academic mantra.

Other recent books which, through the diversity of their approaches and contents, might prove instructive for social theorists attuned to philosophical argument include: Margaret S. Archer, *Realist Social Theory: The Morphogenetic Approach* (Cambridge: Cambridge University Press, 1995); James Bohman, *New Philosophy of Social Science: Problems of Indeterminacy* (Cambridge, MA: MIT Press, 1993); Paul A. Bové, *In the Wake of Theory* (Hanover, NH: Wesleyan University Press, 1992) and *Mastering Discourse: The Politics of Intellectual Culture* (Durham, NC: Duke University Press, 1992); Brian Fay, *Contemporary Philosophy of Social Science* (Cambridge: Blackwell, 1996); Andrew Feenberg, *Alternative Modernity: The Technical Turn in Philosophy and Social Theory* (Berkeley: University of California Press, 1995); Peter A. French et al., eds, *The Philosophy of the Human Sciences/Midwest Studies in Philosophy, Vol. XV* (Notre Dame, IN: University of Notre Dame Press, 1990); Robert F. Goodman and Walter R. Fisher, eds, *Rethinking Knowledge: Reflections Across the*

The reasons for this efflorescence are many. For example, during the last decade feminism's quest to transform all disciplinary inquiry has met with conspicuous success in the broad realm of social thought – if "success" is adequately measured by the sheer amount of material that has found its way into print. From rereadings of Plato to the latest cultural studies manifestoes, no method or style of analyzing social life or mental processes has escaped feminist recalibration. There are by now two parallel and often mutually uncommunicating canons, one for men, the other for women, as pointedly exemplified (to cite only one example) by Genevieve Lloyd's *The Man of Reason: "Male" and "Female" in Western Philosophy*.[12] And whereas the "male reading" of, say, Machiavelli or Kant now numbers in the thousands, another 50 years of feminist investigation will probably tip the scales. For some years it has seemed that for every "traditional" (i.e., male) hermeneutic appraisal of a canonical figure or concept which manages to find a publisher, a dozen rejoinders by and for women come onto the

Disciplines (Albany, NY: State University of New York Press, 1995), Alvin I. Goldman, *Liaisons: Philosophy Meets the Cognitive and Social Sciences* (Cambridge, MA: MIT Press, 19091); Scott Gordon, *The History and Philosophy of Social Science* (New York: Routledge, 1993); Michael Haas, *Polity and Society: Philosophical Underpinnings of Social Science Paradigms* (Westport, CT: Praeger Publishers, 1992); David K. Henderson, *Interpretation and Explanation in the Human Sciences* (Albany, NY: State University of New York Press, 1993); Martin Hollis, *Reason in Action: Essays in the Philosophy of Social Science* (Cambridge: Cambridge University Press, 1996); Martin Kreisworth and Thomas Carmichael, eds, *Constructive Criticism: The Human Sciences in the Age of Theory* (Toronto: University of Toronto Press, 1995); Elizabeth Long, ed., *From Sociology to Cultural Studies* (Malden, MA: Blackwell, 1997); Michael Martin and Lee C. McIntyre, eds, *Readings in the Philosophy of Social Science* (Cambridge, MA: MIT Press, 1994); Paul Rabinow and William M. Sullivan, eds, *Interpretive Social Science: A Second Look* (Berkeley: University of California Press, 1987); H. P. Rickman, *The Adventure of Reason: The Uses of Philosophy in Sociology* (Westport, CT: Greenwood Press, 1983); R. H. Roberts and J. M. M. Good, eds, *The Recovery of Rhetoric: Persuasive Discourse and Disciplinarity in the Human Sciences* (Charlottesville: University Press of Virginia, 1993); Gillian Rose, *The Broken Middle: Out of Our Ancient History* (Cambridge: Blackwell, 1992); Ronald Schleifer, *Culture and Cognition: The Boundaries of Literary and Scientific Inquiry* (Ithaca, NY: Cornell University Press, 1992); Theodore R. Schatzki, *The Social and Political Body* (New York: Guilford, 1996); Frederick F. Schmitt, ed., *Socializing Epistemology: The Social Dimensions of Knowledge* (Lanham, MD: Rowman & Littlefield, 1994); Quentin Skinner, ed., *The Return of Grand Theory in the Human Sciences* (New York: Cambridge University Press, 1990); Piotr Sztompka, ed., *Agency and Structure: Reorienting Social Theory* (Amsterdam: Gordon Breach, 1994).
12 Genevieve Lloyd, *The Man of Reason: "Male" and "Female" in Western Philosophy*, 2nd ed. (Minneapolis: University of Minnesota Press, 1993; 1st ed. 1984).

market.[13] (Whither the academic monograph in general is another question, of course, yet feminist studies are often pitched at a wider market than was the case 20 years ago for works covering like terrain, so they may weather the coming storm better than "traditional" studies will.)

Yet the continuing cross-fertilization that fructifies between philosophical notions and social theory is not exhausted by reference to feminism. Introducing a book of essays which challenges conventional methodology across disciplines, Stephen Toulmin claims that the "Received Program of epistemology and human sciences" that remained supreme for 300 years after Descartes has finally entered its "death throes." Its primary tenets – that knowledge is personal and individual, that Locke's *camera obscura* is a useful metaphor for perception, and that apodictic knowledge must be deductive in nature – no longer persuade enough of its intended constituency to hold up.[14] Part of this failure to convince has sprung from questions of personal, political, and sexual identitities that have loomed large for some time, as have related macro-issues bearing on nationality and ethnic affiliations. The ancient but renamed debate attempting to define how "action" interacts with "structure" (what Gerth and Mills 45 years ago termed "character" versus "social structure"[15]) naturally slides onto philosophical terrain, especially regarding the precise nature of "the self" (the history of which goes back at least to the Scottish and French Enlightenments). To

---

[13] See, among many, Robin May Schott, *Cognition and Eros: A Critique of the Kantian Pradigm* (Beacon Press, 1988; reissued in paperback by Pennsylvania State University Press, 1993), pointing out ten years ago that Kant's "reason" was more fundamentally male than female – that, in fact, "Kant's Fetishism of Objectivity" had become "a problem" for female philosophers. In due course other feminist Kantians critically examined his fascination with analytical and substantive "purity" as opposed to the putative "messiness" of everyday life, wherein most women existed during the eighteenth century. Similar observations regarding other canonical thinkers, as they have accumulated, set in motion a reconstruction of Western philosophizing from top to bottom, a kind of intellectual/political excavation (for a variety of examples, see Nancy Sorkin Rabinowitz and Amy Richlin, eds, *Feminist Theory and the Classics* [New York: Routledge, 1993], Roslyn W. Bologh, *Love or Greatness: Max Weber and Masculine Thinking – A Feminist Inquiry* [London: Unwin Hyman, 1990], or Victoria Lee Erickson, *Where Silence Speaks: Feminism, Social Theory, and Religion* [Minneapolis: Fortress Press, 1993]). Social theory has obviously not been immune from this kind of recasting, though the thoroughgoingness has not yet matched works produced by philosophers.

[14] "Foreword" to Goodman and Fisher, eds, *Rethinking Knowledge*, pp. ix–x.

[15] Hans Gerth and C. Wright Mills, *Character and Social Structure: The Psychology of Social Institutions* (New York: Harcourt, Brace, & World, 1953).

say, then, that social theory in its highest reaches remains married to philosophy – most obviously in writers like Habermas, Derrida, or Rorty – requires no great insight.

But having admitted this, a puzzling condition becomes apparent. The most casual student of social theory, as promulgated over the last quarter-century in the West, sees constant references to canonical figures of philosophy, from Plato and the Sophists forward. Overt and protracted theorizing by means of Nietzsche's ideas, for instance, as carried out by social theorists rather than philosophers, has become unexceptionable. Novices with hope of contributing noticeably to the manifold discourses of theorizing must now face the time-consuming necessity of learning about various streams of philosophy, a task which their predecessors in mid-century did not take very seriously. At that time logical positivism sang the siren's melody for many theorists, which obviated any need to possess philosophy's past. And even for those not in thrall to "Carnap and Co.," it seemed enough to accede, for instance, to Schutz's version of Husserl without having to deal with Husserl's thorny phenomenology itself. Neither did accepting Durkheim's or Simmel's Kantianized social theory, during the 1950s and 1960s, seem to require a critical return to original sources, even in translation. While not absolutely changed, there has occurred enough of an alteration since about 1970 or 1975 (when, say, Hans-Georg Gadamer's *Truth and Method*[16] or the major works of Foucault and Derrida were first translated) of which the more committed students of social thought have taken careful note, adjusting the scope and breadth of their apprenticeship readings accordingly.

The puzzle mentioned above lies in the nature of graduate education within sociology and related fields, where future theorists are expected to be "nurtured." While no end of methods and statistics courses proliferate in the higher-status programs, no similar thought is given to the special pedagogical needs that increasingly impinge on turning a beginner into a practicing expert in the history and contemporary elaboration of theory. It is almost axiomatic that among today's theorists of note, none has been able to leave philosophy out of their intellectual make-up. One might even say that the more at home in philosophical texts a given theorist has become, the more likely they now are to reach the most catholic audience – one which lies at the crossroads of social and political thought, history, philosophy, feminism, comparative studies, and

[16] 2nd revised translation by Joel Weinsheimer and Donald G. Marshall (New York. Continuum, 1989).

certain forms of literary criticism. Yet the difficult background that must be assimilated by the student before venturing with confidence into these discussions is typically picked up haphazardly and strictly at the initiative of the aspiring theorist. The entire burden for recapturing the philosophical past lies with the individual, without any formal institutional support. Yet if it seems to make sense that apprentice survey researchers learn about sampling design and statistical manipulation through arduous coursework, why is it not equally prudent for theorists to invest themselves in formal study of philosophy, given the intimate relationship that continues to obtain between the two fields? For educators to pretend that this kind of labor is not a prerequisite to sociocultural theorizing comes close to pedagogical negligence – not unlike prohibiting students from learning statistics, while insisting that they publish in the better journals.

My argument, to repeat, is simple. With the exception of certain "formal" models, relatively few in number, which take their lead more from the graphical representations common to natural science than to the abstract linguistic formulations of philosophy, all theorists today are indebted to their sister discipline – often more so than they realize – and remain in continuing need of her tutelage. The chapters that follow seek to illuminate and exemplify selected aspects of this condition, and the heritage which gave rise to it, without pretending to offer a complete survey of the issues that could be addressed under the general title, "How Philosophy and Social Theory Are Currently Related."

This Book's Multifaceted Offering

The reigning custom pertaining to books of this type calls for the editor at this point to make kindly, hyperbolic observations about each of the chapters that follow and, if possible, to summarize the achievements of each, if for no other reason than to lighten the burden of potential reviewers. I cannot be trusted to do this adequately for at least two reasons. At my invitation, the venerable Peter Blau (among many honors, President of the American Sociological Association in 1973–4) agreed to oversee with me the "miniconference" that gave rise to earlier versions of these chapters. As nearly everyone in sociology knows, ever since the early 1960s Blau has helped create a quasi-positivistic branch of theorizing that in textbooks falls under the rubric of "exchange" or "network" theory. Though Blau's later work has become more structural in nature,

moving away from the actor-centered theorizing common to predecessors in this tradition (e.g., George Homans), a proposition central
to this general way of theorizing holds that social actors (individual and aggregated) behave "rationally" as they try to maximize
their rewards while minimizing costs. At its simplest level – as the
backbone of marginal utility theory, for instance – this is very nearly
a platitude. Yet social life, it seems to me, is seldom experienced at
its simplest level, despite the need for theorists to conceptualize
about it at a reduced level of activity and complexity.

Inasmuch as my main interest in general questions of social theory
has long revolved around how "irrationality" is apprehended and
"tamed" in various strands of theorizing,[17] it might "reasonably"
be argued that I am congenitally incapable of appreciating the route
that Peter Blau's theory has taken since the early 1960s, when he
first proposed it in *Exchange and Power in Social Life*.[18] Thus, the
first reason I cannot in good conscience champion everything that
follows in this book is that I do not believe all of the schemes
put forth offer plausible accounts of social reality. However, that
each chapter has been produced with a high level of competence
and imagination I can guarantee, which is perhaps sufficient for
the occasion. The second reason I am not the ideal introducer for
everything that follows is that my tastes and training have not
prepared me to appreciate all the contributions which Blau inspired at our mini-conference, at least to the most sympathetic level.
This is especially the case in the works of the sociologists Steven
Rytina, Michael Macy, John Skvoretz, and the philosopher, Paul
Humphreys, all of whom work along lines that could roughly be
identified with formal modeling. This still developing area of theory
seems to me too much infused with the chill wind of "objectivity"
to prove satisfying, though it is clear that some of theory's brightest lights have taken to it with gusto. Though in a perfect publishing world Blau might well have been called upon to canvass these
chapters himself, his schedule did not allow it, and given that he
will turn 80 years old in the year this volume appears, his preference for elaborating his own ideas is understandable.

[17] Among others, see "What is Rational, What is Not: Reply to Münch," *American
Journal of Sociology* 90 (2) (1984): 432–4; *Weber, Irrationality, and Social Theory* (Berkeley:
University of California Press, 1988); "Reasonable Science, Unreasonable Life: The
Happy Fictions of Marx, Weber, and Social Theory," in Robert Antonio and Ronald
Glassman, eds, *A Weber–Marx Dialogue* (Lawrence, KS: University Press of Kansas,
1985), pp. 68–88; "The Social World as a Countinghouse: Coleman's Irrational
Worldview," *Theory and Society* 21 (2) (1992): 243–62.
[18] New York: Wiley, 1964.

So it is left to me to speak, as best I can, on behalf of some authors whose notion of theorizing is quite distinct from my own, and who would likely be as hard-pressed to make complimentary remarks about my work as I am about theirs. However, since theory has always been a contentious business, this is hardly surprising, nor necessarily unfortunate. In fact, one might argue quite the contrary. The very strength of this collection may well lie in its marked heterodoxy, both from the field at large and internal to itself. By my count there are no fewer than seven or eight distinct theoretical vantage points represented in what follows, each argued with passionate regard for its own merit, yet none so dogmatically as to rule out the efficacy of other approaches. It is this happy confusion, this Babel-like quality, that will make the book valuable for those interested in theory's immediate prospects, particularly as it positions itself with regard to philosophical problems.

Robert Antonio's long opening chapter could easily become a standard source for novices wishing to enter the uneven terrain of the postmodern fray at the side of a trusty guide, as well as serving as a sound checkpoint for more seasoned readers. In characteristic fashion Antonio offers not only a measured and reasonable analysis of how postmodern theory has affected social thought over the last 15 years or so, but also connects his remarks in thorough detail to a first-class bibliography, around which his argument is built. Refusing to bow either to the louder proponents or critics of "the postmodern," understood as cultural event(s) or theoretical "intervention," he shows just which elements of this new stream are likely to benefit the development of social thought as it slowly detaches itself from classical, nineteenth-century roots. Especially interesting is Antonio's connecting of Nietzschean themes to contemporary interests, an elaboration of his own recent work, and one that ties his theorizing to that of writers in literary criticism, cultural studies, political thought, and philosophy proper. Earlier in the century Husserl, Heidegger, Scheler, Plato, and other speculative figures made their way more or less thoroughly into social theory. Yet today if there is one iconic character bridging social theory and philosophy, it is surely Nietzsche – with all the uncertain baggage that attaches to his person and reputation. Evidencing the same sort of balanced assessment of Lyotard, Jameson, or Baudrillard, Antonio points out the indispensability of Nietzsche's ideas today, without obscuring its anti-sociological drawbacks.

With Mary Rogers's chapter we encounter an interesting attempt to link phenomenological sociology, which thrived between about

1965 and 1980, with very current expressions of the need to speak about subjectivity with a new voice. The writers Rogers names – Sedgwick, Bartky, Bordo, Connell, Dorothy Smith, and others – do not hail from the world of Husserl, Ricoeur, or Schutz, yet their interest in experience as a central category of theorizing ties in well with those of their famous predecessors. Rogers's renewed phenomenology celebrates the ideas of Maurice Natanson (who died the very day she presented the paper on which the chapter is based), for the last 30 years a central resource for social theorists wishing to pursue the phenomenological current, but lacking the patience to learn from Husserl himself. Rogers perpetuates Natanson's own characterization of Robert Burton's immortal meditations on melancholy (1621) as a "thesaurus of human experiencing," as she pulls the reader rapidly through Natanson's ideas by means of nine interlinked terms: consciousness, intentionality, constitution, sedimentation, then mundane, expression, enclave, horizon, and madness. As in her previous work, Rogers combines imaginative theorizing with an acute sense for the everyday that ties in well with current concerns of feminists, postmodernists, and other cultural critics who remain suspicious of theory when it wanders too far from experience as commonly known to the "uninitiated." With Rogers's chapter – a fitting tribute to Natanson at his passing – phenomenological theorizing is given a new lease on life.

Ever since bursting onto, or into, the theory scene in 1988 with *Social Epistemology* (the book and then the journal), Steve Fuller has been throwing conceptual hand grenades into the backyards of social theorists, sociologists of science, and philosophers of social scientific method. A practiced disparager of theorists who have "become world-class sociologists simply by engaging" in exegesis (he names Parsons and Giddens in particular), he prefers to recast what theory and theorists ought to be doing in terms of his own construct, social epistemology. Ranging from Plato to Nietzsche to Searle, Darwin to Elster, Kuhn to Joas, he uses whatever literature he finds to make his points in an eclectic performance that is always bracing and sometimes precarious. In this chapter his target for demolition is the fetish that has been made (more in England than in the US) over the putative dichotomy, God-given one might assume from the literature, between "structure" and "agency" – what in the States many decades back was called the "personality and social structure" problem. Fuller's way of attacking this pseudo-distinction is by returning to ancient debates over translation techniques – literal versus contextual – and applying these found differences to the ideas of classical social theory versus the contexts of their invention. To use his opening example, it may be as important to understand Plato's reaction to Athens's political condition when reading the *Dialogues* as to comprehend the fine points of Greek grammar. By extension, Fuller believes that nineteenth-century theorists can still teach us, not with their conceptual apparatuses and endless elaborations of same, but by our consideration of what prompted them to say what they did in the way they did. Though Mannheim is conspicuously absent from Fuller's creatively assembled bibliography, it could be argued that his sociology of knowledge from the 1920s is more than casually related to this newer project. Fuller also manages to bring in an arresting analogy between social theory's agency/structure mantra versus the ancient theological distinction of worldly and other-worldly. His three figures summarize the argument and, as always, promise either to disturb or enchant readers depending on their preconceptions of what theory is supposed to achieve.

Closely allied with Fuller in spirit and sharing certain bibliographical enthusiasms, Stephen Turner uses Robert Brandom's *Making it Explicit* as a launching pad for a technically demanding run through questions of normativity, legal reasoning, and Wittgenstein's theory of language, with related observations about Carl Schmitt, Weber, and other noteworthy theorists. In this chapter Turner expands on his innovative monograph, *The Social Theory of Practices*, which holds the field in terms of philosophically anchored criticism of how social theorists have misconstrued and under-theorized the vexing question of normativity – of how taken-for-granted knowledge is created and then analyzed. Turner forces us to reconsider what is meant by "norm," probably the most common and least well analyzed concept in the sociological lexicon. By criticizing Brandom's argument for "implicit norms," and then tracing this confused position back to Kant's epistemology and forward to Kripke, Pufendorf, and others, Turner is able to illustrate by means of tight philosophical reasoning and example – a style rarely seen in sociological argument – that typical defenses of normative justifications are hollow, and need to be reshaped. The virtues of Turner's chapter include bringing philosophical texts into immediate contagion with those of Weber and other social theorists, to the enrichment of both sides. Though often enough invoked as a worthwhile activity, this kind of virtuoso performance seldom occurs, even in an intellectual climate which in principle warmly endorses the need of each zone of critical activity to inform the other.

From an entirely different perspective and scholarly generation, the newcomer, Jennifer Croissant, contributes a feminist examination of social theory, but from the special sector known as Science, Technology, and Society (STS) studies. Working from her recent dissertation as well as pregnant material from the *Oxford English Dictionary*, she carries out a simultaneous interrogation of classical and contemporary theory. The tone of her complaint has become familiar during the last dozen years as the voice of women previously excluded from the theoretical enterprise for no other reason than their gender. This string of connected objections to the *status quo ante* revolves around gross disparities in representation that women have endured while "the canon" was being assembled, while also, more subtly, bringing up matters concerning definitions of objectivity, truth, and the value of knowledge about which men and women seem to differ along very fundamental lines. Her sources of inspiration – de Beauvoir, Hartsock, Dorothy Smith, Haraway, Harding, and others – now form a counter-canon, as it were, to which feminists turn with the same sort of enthusiastic attention that men have in the past brought to *their* "classical" texts. The general objection that unifies these otherwise disparate thinkers turns on how knowledge is experienced and then codified. Their apparent consensus joins them in the realization that the male worldview, particularly as expressed by nineteenth-century originators of theory, goes about its tasks in ways that violate or trivialize the knowledge of the social world more common to women. Croissant also brings STS work into her critical ken, showing that what is defined as important or unimportant intellectual labor within this subfield too often revolves around gender-related matters, most of them too far beneath the conscious surface of discourse to be noticed. Her request for a more inclusive and gender-sensitive study of science/society connections is surely indicative of the road ahead for serious scholars in this area of work.

With Stanley Lieberson's chapter, we move to the senior reaches of the discipline. Like Blau, Lieberson is a former president of the American Sociological Association, and the author of several works which are close to the hearts of many practitioners, e.g., *A Piece of the Pie* (1980) and *Making It Count* (1985). His work is known for its wit, concision, continuous wedding of careful methods with plausible theory, and perhaps most of all, for its steady refusal to be awed by tradition or received wisdom as he pursues empirical matters with theoretical verve. His persistent common sense, quintessentially American in flavor, seems to have been "designed" to infuriate those who confuse pretentious formulation – whether quantitative or linguistic – with sophisticated practice. Lieberson is sociology's "man from Missouri," never failing to remind the inattentive or sluggardly that proving hunches by means of careful technique is how sociology, and its theories, will improve, and not through mere numerical or terminological legerdemain. His tidy chapter is interesting because it is more speculative than much of what he has published, and because formally philosophical matters are given a warmer welcome than is usually the case in his work. Here he points out that certain forms of philosophy – although not necessarily, so he remarks several times, those most often called upon today by social theorists – can benefit the construction of good theory. By explaining precisely what an "example" is and is not, what an example can do to help prove or disprove an hypothesis or theory, formal philosophizing can clarify otherwise muddy waters. And by illuminating those aspects of theoretical and empirical claims which lie beneath the surface, philosophy might also open up aspects of research that otherwise hide from examination – not so much because researchers wish to ignore reality, but more because they are unaware that the "submerged" is there to exhume. In crisp terms, then, Lieberson turns the book away from emphasis upon European ideas and the cognate concerns that dominate the first chapters, and moves it toward the speculative tradition of formal theorizing and linguistic analysis with which he and the subsequent authors are more at home.

It is fortunate that a Penn State professor, Werner Pluhar, recently created a new English translation of Kant's *Critique of Pure Reason* with much more illuminative apparatus (at 1,100 pages in length) than was provided by Norman Kemp Smith in 1929, when he published what became the favored version for nearly 70 years.[19] I say this having read both Fuller's chapter, as well as Steven Rytina's, in which Kant's general way of going about epistemology – using something Rytina calls "the Kantian pyramid" – is respectfully dismantled at length in the interest of improving today's goals for social theory. It seems we are not yet free of the sage of Königsberg in quite the way that some theorists finally feel they are rid of Hegel, now that Marxism is out of fashion. Rytina's purpose, though, is not simply to rectify Kant's latent control upon how social theory has been carried out in the past, distant[20] or more

---

[19] Immanuel Kant, *Critique of Pure Reason (Unified Edition)*, trans. Werner S. Pluhar and intro. Patricia W. Kitcher (Indianapolis, IN: Hackett, 1996).
[20] Talcott Parsons, *The Structure of Social Action* (New York: McGraw-Hill, 1937).

recent.[21] He uses Kant's "domain assumption" (as Alvin Gouldner would have called it), his belief that a discoverable, logical chain extends from sensory data to the transcendental apparatus of cognition and evaluation, to argue against this pronounced logocentrism. He prefers an openness in epistemological matters that concedes from the outset the unlikelihood of establishing purely logical relations between data, concepts, and theoretical axioms, and pays attention instead to something Rytina calls "granularity." He adopts this term from the jargon of computer programmers, implying by it the fact that reality is multilayered, and that solutions to the problems it poses are often "nested" and therefore very "messy" in a distinctly unKantian, and nonlogical way. He also introduces a few observations about the role of rhetoric in social science explanation, a field of inquiry that over the last ten years has become a cottage industry unto itself.[22] His chapter, in sum, is philosophical in a useful and sharply reasoned sense.

Shoring up some of the less plausible assumptions behind "rational choice/rational action theory," Michael Macy puts to use an array of game-theoretic and logical distinctions that flow from a philosophical bailiwick closer to the hearts of Fuller and Rytina than to Antonio and Rogers. His chapter is less friendly to novices than those which preceded it, jumping into debates that have swirled for years around a number of concepts and ideas which he ties together: rationality, altruism, evolutionary change, pragmatism, norms/rules, game theory, and so on. He regards rational *choice* theory as debilitated by its fascination with the given social

---

[21] Jeffrey C. Alexander, *Theoretical Logic in Sociology*, Vol. 1 (Berkeley: University of California Press, 1982).

[22] Among dozens of pertinent works, see Michael Billig, *Arguing and Thinking: A Rhetoric Approach to Social Psychology* (Cambridge: Cambridge University Press, 1987); Richard H. Brown, *Society as Text: Essays on Rhetoric, Reason, and Reality* (Chicago: University of Chicago Press, 1987); Ricca Edmondson, *Rhetoric in Sociology* (London: Macmillan, 1984); A. G. Gross, *The Rhetoric of Science* (Cambridge, MA: Harvard University Press, 1990); Jeff Mason, *Philosophical Rhetoric: The Function of Indirection in Philosophical Writings* (London: Routledge, 1989); Donald McCloskey, *The Rhetoric of Economics* (Madison: University of Wisconsin Press, 1985); J. S. Nelson et al., eds, *The Rhetoric of the Human Sciences* (Madison: University of Wisconsin Press, 1987); L. Prelli, *A Rhetoric of Science: Inventing Scientific Discourse* (Columbia: University of South Carolina Press, 1989); Herbert W. Simons, *Rhetoric in the Human Sciences* (London: Sage, 1989); Herbert W. Simons, ed., *The Rhetorical Turn* (Chicago: University of Chicago Press, 1990); Stephen Tyler, *The Unspeakable: Discourse, Dialogue and Rhetoric in the Post-modern World* (Madison: University of Wisconsin Press, 1987); Susan Wells, *Sweet Reason: Rhetoric and the Discourses of Modernity* (Chicago: University of Chicago Press, 1996).

actor's motivation and action, and finds that rational *action* theory, emphasizing as it does aggregated rather than individual resource usage, is the better bet for theoretical refinement. He also makes a "rules-eye view" argument to explain why people can be kind to others without apparently rational motivation or likely payoff: "Altruistic rules are those that have learned how to replicate by transferring influence (or reproductive chances). . . ." Macy is willing to pay a high theoretical price for such insights, for he indulges in a stark form of reification, even personification of concepts, that seemed to have gone out of style with the late Parsons. As I explained earlier, my predilections move decidedly away from this sort of analysis, so it is likely I cannot represent it so well as it might be. I wonder, for instance, how Macy's theorizing might stand up in the context of a book I recently edited which links processes of mental illness with those that give rise to false consciousness.[23] He admits that "expressive behaviors . . . fall outside the theoretical scope of rational choice," so perhaps instances of the truly "irrational" would become a non-problem for theory of this kind by definitional fiat. Macy also invokes an evolutionary vocabulary of human adaptation to phenomena related to what he calls "emergent rationality" (with a nod of thanks to pragmatism). The calm with which he still uses sociobiology's lexicon (particularly Dawkins's) does not reflect recent acrimonious debates among experts who are much less sure of the validity evolutionary thinking will ultimately be shown to have regarding human behavior.[24] Still, Macy's chapter is full of brisk intelligence, and will encourage its careful readers to pursue several modes of theorizing which are not often brought under one roof.

As was the case with Rytina's chapter, John Skvoretz's falls under the influence of Peter Blau's theory of social structure, which he works at improving by means of an alternative theoretical

---

[23] Joseph Gabel, *Ideologies and the Corruption of Thought*, ed. and intro. Alan Sica (New Brunswick, NJ: Transaction, 1997); see especially my introduction, pp. 1–59.
[24] There is no shortage of debate about the proper use to be made of evolutionary thought when applied to human behaviors of the more complex types, much of it set off by the publication of Richard J. Hernstein's and Charles Murray's *The Bell Curve: Intelligence and Class Structure in American Life* (New York: Free Press, 1994) several years ago. Particularly enlightening and cautionary are Stephen Jay Gould's two recent essays, "Darwinian Fundamentalism," *New York Review of Books* 44 (10) (June 12, 1997): 34–7, and "Evolution: The Pleasures of Pluralism," *New York Review of Books* 44 (11) (June 26, 1997): 47–52, plus the heated exchange they aroused between the evolutionary psychologist, Steven Pinker, and Gould: "Evolutionary Psychology: an Exchange," *New York Review of Books* 44 (15) (October 9, 1997): 55–8.

model. Skvoretz for some time has been working with his mentor, Thomas Fararo, in promoting what they call "biased net theory," which they believe is superior to linear regression models for the proof or disproof of various theoretical claims. Skvoretz approves of Randall Collins's observation that the unreflective use of statistics and probability in social research is *itself* a theoretical statement – that regression analysis is not a neutral method of investigation, but embodies an entire set of presuppositions about an imagined relationship between randomness and social action. Though from different parts of the theory playing-field, Skvoretz and Collins are in accord that most social research fails to test theory as precisely as it should. It is Skvoretz's goal to introduce a superior way of going about the task. He argues for a theory-driven mode of social research in which a theoretical model is specified along formal, falsifiable lines *before* data are computed, rather than *post facto*, which has become the conventional style during the last 40 years or so, following the dictates of logical-positivism. He illustrates the superiority of his approach by subjecting certain aspects of Blau's theory of interracial marriage to test, and shows that Blau's ideas, when tested conventionally, are actually weaker than when retested following Skvoretz's alternative technique. Moreover, according to Skvoretz, his way of carrying out research allows him to build into his preliminary theorizing precise ideas about how humans actually behave, rather than having to come up with *post hoc* hypotheses to "explain" correlations that are the fruits of standard research. This is not completely orignal to him, but if enough readers agree with the argument, it could prove to be revolutionary.

Paul Humphreys's chapter is, as one would expect from a philosopher, dense, concise, and rigorously argued. Whereas Humphreys shares Skvoretz's approval of Blau's ideas, he differs with him markedly in his estimate of Randall Collins's notions about the relationship between statistical and linguistic modes of analysis, accusing the latter of "an astonishing degree of ignorance" vis-à-vis the real limitations of formal modelling. He also agrees with Skvoretz that "top-down," theory-driven models ought to be the future of sociological theory and research. Yet he seems sensitive enough to various critiques of this approach that have surfaced over the last decade to offer correctives for skeptics, particularly the notion that both major types of theorizing might profitably be combined to form a new hybrid. By using Newton's Second Law – apparently a favorite in the literature for these sorts of exercises – Humphreys illustrates how *formal* definitions of theory, models, data, and systems could be used in social research. He argues that models can bring abstract theory to data by serving as intermediary devices. Humphreys then uses coin-tossing probability theory (and a good story about Las Vegas dice) to advance his argument into the everyday world of social research. While his conclusions and suggestions about how to improve theorizing may seem arid to readers more attuned to the sort of theorizing that appears earlier in the book, a cold dose of analytic precision, free of any conceptual or historical undergrowth, might nevertheless prove beneficial, particularly as some social researchers try harder each year to ape the precision and goals of the physical sciences.

Peter Blau's elegantly concise concluding chapter reveals some surprises for those who think of his long and much lauded record of research as being strictly "scientific" in the hypothesis-testing format. Most of the chapter recounts the way major theorists – Weber, Marx, Pareto, and Durkheim – dealt with "the problem" of culture within the works for which they are remembered. While admitting that "cultural theories" are "more profound than structural ones," the latter "can be more easily formulated rigorously," which is why he has favored them in his own work. He also accepts the need for testability for *all* theories. Yet he admits that "Despite my preference for structural theories, my favorite theory, an imaginative gem, is a cultural one and one that cannot be tested to boot": Weber's Protestant ethic thesis. In the end, though, Blau awards the laurels to Marx and Durkheim, leaving his admiration for Weber's "idealistic" theorizing in another zone of consciousness that does not lend itself either to elaboration or "testing." Blau believes that the structuralist arguments first promoted by Durkheim in his *Division of Labor* as well as *Suicide*, along with Marx's understanding of structure in *Capital*, should serve as the foundation on which modern structuralist analysis ought to erect its more ornate edifices. Blau concludes this trot through the early period of social theory by saying that "I consider it [Durkheim's *Division*] to be emblematic of structural sociology, *the only truly sociological approach*" [my emphases]. This is a strong position, for which, of course, he is famous. If it turns out in the long run that his theory of structure can be supported 15 out of 16 times by means of data-driven tests, as he reports it has been to date, then the next century may become the intellectual property of Durkheimians as much as the waning one belongs more to Weber.

I cannot second some of Blau's strongest preferences – except in his closet devotion to *The Protestant Ethic* – but an elaborated explanation for our difference of opinion must await another opportunity. For the time being, it is wonderful to conclude the book with the frankly conciliatory statement of a sociological elder famous for his bold structuralism who says, in "a personal statement," "My own recent work has been structural, but this was not the case for my earlier work." In recalling a youthful love without blushing, he illustrates the sort of humility and honesty that typifies the best from social theory's past, and encourages its future creators to put to use the same strength of character that has given his own work its longevity and promise.

1 Mapping Postmodern Social Theory

Robert J. Antonio

What is it? Everyone who has written a book or article on postmodernism begins with an apology for the inability to define the term. This is understandable, for if one could define it, it would not be postmodernism, since it would then have an identifiable referent. (Daniel Bell [1976] 1996: 297)

I . . . get just as tired of the slogan "postmodern" as anyone else, but when I am tempted to regret my complicity with it, to deplore its misuses and its notoriety, and to conclude with some reluctance that it raises more problems than it solves, I find myself pausing to wonder whether any other concept can dramatize the issues in quite so effective and economical a fashion. (Fredric Jameson 1991: 418)

Introduction: Postmodern Cacophony and Sociology

New philosophically oriented theories have had a major impact on a growing number of sociologists.[1] Interdisciplinary thinkers

Many thanks to Steve Best, Doug Kellner, and Mara Miele, who probably do not agree, but who have contributed to this essay though our many conversations. Also, thanks to Alessandro Bonanno and Bill Staples for their critical comments on an earlier draft of this essay. I map a different terrain than Andreas Huyssen's (1984) classic "Mapping the postmodern"; I dwell less on aesthetics and deal analytically with a broad range of more recent issues and work from social theory.
[1] The influence of nonsociologists is growing in the discipline. Five of the ten books on *Contemporary Sociology's* list of the most influential books for sociologists during the last 25 years are by nonsociologists. Moreover, four of the ten have influenced the postmodernism debates (i.e., by Michel Foucault, Edward Said, Clifford Geertz, and Pierre Bourdieu), and several others address broad theoretical themes (i.e., by Nancy Chodorow, Theda Skocpol, and Immanuel Wallerstein; see

from outside of sociology, such as Michel Foucault, Nancy Fraser, Jürgen Habermas, Fredric Jameson, and Cornel West, have much wider audiences than sociological theorists. French philosophers (e.g., Foucault, Derrida, Lyotard), who read Nietzsche through a Heideggerian lens and fused his ideas with a variety of other heterodox approaches, have had especially powerful impact. Their poststructuralist alternatives to modern theory, especially Marxist variants, helped give rise to "postmodernism" – a most intensely debated topic in philosophically oriented social theory circles.[2] Postmodernist discourses criticize rationalism, embrace the aesthetic dimension, and displace "structure" and "society" with very broad concepts of "culture."

For over twenty years, postmodernism has helped stimulate new academic programs (e.g., "cultural studies"), new journals, and new debates that extend beyond academe. Fueling broader interest in interdisciplinary social theory, postmodernist ideas have been prominent in feminism, multiculturalism, and the new social movements.[3] But social scientists are often bemused and frustrated by postmodernism. As Pauline Marie Rosenau (1992: 3) asserts, postmodernism "haunts social science today"; it "rejects epistemological assumptions, refutes methodological conventions, resists knowledge claims, obscures all versions of truth, and dismisses policy recommendations." Unsurprisingly, North American sociologists generally have been hostile to postmodernism. Although seldom appearing in the most important sociology journals, they see it as a looming threat or dangerous distraction. For example, in

Clawson 1996a; also, pp. 293–325 of this journal issue). In a second inquiry, asking sociologists to list a favorite book from the same period, which has not received due recognition, two-thirds of the works selected were by nonsociologists (Clawson 1996b).

[2] Postmodernism's ambiguities will be a major theme of this essay, but a few initial qualifications are in order. The more delimited concept of "poststructuralism" overlaps with and is usually treated as a root and branch of postmodernism. Because postmodernism has very porous, ill-defined borders, I include poststructuralist approaches in my analysis, without providing hairsplitting justifications. Postmodern theories are usually pitched against "modern" approaches, but the borders of modern thought are just as unclear as the borders of postmodernism (e.g., modern thought ranges from libertarianism to Marxism, ethnomethodology to demography, and mechanistic forms of positivism to highly reflexive conceptions of science and knowledge). On the modern and postmodern, see Calinescu 1987.

[3] By contrast to recent sociological theory, postmodernism has been influential in the arts and mass culture and in political debates over the state of American culture. Barnes and Noble's and Borders's well-stocked shelves of cultural studies and postmodernist works attest to nonacademic interest in the topic.

a state of the discipline essay honoring the centennial of *American Journal of Sociology*, Joan Huber (1995: 204–5) alleges that postmodernists' relativist, antirationalist, and antiscientific views are the source of an "unbridgeable" disciplinary divide that threatens to undermine sociology's institutional legitimacy. And Dan Clawson (1996c), editor of *Contemporary Sociology*, asserts that "postmodernism . . . may be the most contested issue in sociology today – even more likely than Marxism to raise sociologists' blood pressure."[4]

At the start of a now classic essay, Ihab Hassan (1985: 119) stated that "postmodernism has shifted from awkward neologism to derelict cliché without ever attaining the dignity of a concept." More than a decade later it remains an ambiguous, polarizing term. As Bell implies above, the postmodern split between signifiers and referents precludes unambiguous definitions. Even thinkers stressing postmodernism's plurality and complexity, often fail to address the haphazard manner in which the term is employed. Thus, different sides in the postmodernism debate speak past one another.[5] Heated exchanges are complicated by the term's multiple meanings and conflation of fundamentally different usages. For example, critics often fail to specify whether they are addressing normative or analytical arguments about postmodern theory or historical claims about postmodernization, and they usually fail to distinguish radical departures from the modern tradition from positions at its borders. Although a "full" portrayal of postmodernism is beyond my scope, I will map some major themes, which are often confused, and then reflect on their historical context and meaning for "social theory."[6]

---

[4] In a telling introduction ("Taking postmodernism – seriously?") to featured, postmodernist review essays, Clawson (1996c: ix) charges postmodernists with "academic self-absorption" and a perceived "air of superiority, even smugness." But his own condescending comments and decision to publish sharp critiques (van den Berg 1996; Demerath 1996) of the featured essays and overall postmodernism with no response from the reviewers or other postmodernists manifest the hostility he sees elsewhere in the discipline. Similarly, Huber's (1997) overheated response to a tough, but respectful, critique from postmodernist Norman K. Denzin (1997) exhibits the same dismissive inclination. Postmodernists sometimes embrace irrationalist views, but "defenders" of the discipline greatly exaggerate this tendency.

[5] See, e.g., the debate over postmodernism in *Sociological Theory* 9: 131–90; 10: 231–58; 11: 241–2.

[6] For some broad efforts to map or criticize postmodern thought, see, e.g., Habermas 1981; Lyotard 1984; Huyssen 1984; Hassan 1985; Denzin 1986; Kellner 1988; Fraser and Nicholson 1988; Nicholson 1990a, 1990b; Jameson 1991; Best and Kellner 1991; Rosenau 1992; Bertens 1995; Nicholson and Seidman 1995a, 1995b.

Nietzschean Perspectivism: Culture, Power, and Legitimacy

Framing the problem of the entwinement of knowledge and power, Nietzsche held that culture's epistemological and normative foundations ultimately shape society; they give rise to values, norms, and ideas that channel bodily drives into enduring patterned actions and structures. In his view, the consequent normative "orders of rank" and broader "cultural complexes," operating at the macroscopic level of civilization, reproduce similar types of people and social relations for millennia.[7] In particular, he argued that, while "noble cultures" nurture healthy, imaginative, and independent types of persons, capable of creative self-assertion and vital social life, modern or "Socratic culture" treats bodily drives as evil and sanctifies mediocrity. He saw the modern West as a prototypic "culture of *ressentiment*"; its leading strata of cunning "ascetic priests" attain power by legimating suffering and manipulating hostility. They turn drives inward, generating guilt and resentfulness and redirecting pent-up aggression toward marginal and brilliant people, who operate beyond or defy the "herd's" rigid normative boundaries. Equating modern culture with "slave morality" and "sickness," Nietzsche held that strict repression of the instincts, bottomless guilt, and stultifying conformity produce a paradoxical fusion of passivity to authority and viciousness to "outsiders" (Nietzsche [1886] 1966, [1887] 1969, [1883–8] 1968a).

Nietzsche argued that modern culture originated with Socratic philosophy, was rationalized and spread by Christianity, and was later secularized by modern philosophy, science, and emergent mass media. He decried western thought's unnatural inwardness and weakened personalities, deriving from its core emphasis on the rule of soul, mind, and truth over the body (Nietzsche [1873–6] 1983: 83–7). Seeing these foundations as "decadent," he held that modern culture was in an epochal crisis. Nietzsche heralded the end of modernity, calling for the creation of a less inward, more uninhibited, more creative, and noble culture. He contended, however, that sociologists, focusing too narrowly upon society and failing to problematize culture, internalize modern culture's "decadent" presuppositions and employ them as "the norms of sociological judgement." Nietzsche argued that, under the very misleading

---

[7] Nietzsche saw the rise of modernity to be rooted in Socratic philosophy, which he believed marked the end of ancient Greece's earlier, more "noble" and uninhibited "tragic culture."

sign of enlightenment, they reproduce unwittingly modernity's "nihilistic" culture and herd-type personality.[8]

Nietzsche posed a "perspectivist" attack on modern culture's representational theory of truth, which treats knowledge as a kind of picture of "external" reality and its producer as a neutral or disembodied eye motivated purely by cognitive or ethical aims. His perspectivism opens all knowledge to suspicion, challenge, and discussion, treating the borders between "facts" and "interpretations" as ambiguous and subject to contestation; it frames a partial, uncertain, plural, contextual, experimental approach to knowledge that anticipated postmodern positions. In Nietzsche's view, philosophy and science cannot be autonomous sources of values; their meaning and direction depend on the broader culture's diverse spheres of life and, especially, its aesthetic features. He rejected all-encompassing theories of history and theodicies, and treated modern culture's core legitimacy claims about the truthfulness and emancipatory thrust of scientific knowledge as masks for power. Because he problematized fundamentally the presuppositions of modern culture and society, his thought has had multiple directions and impacts. Today's postmodernists, like earlier Nietzscheans, pose heterodox fusions; i.e., fresh critiques of science, reflexive sociologies of knowledge, and anti-authoritarian cultural critiques as well as relativist, irrationalist, and even protofascist positions.[9]

In *The Postmodern Condition*, Jean-François Lyotard (1984: 39) portrayed an "internal erosion of the legitimacy principle of knowledge."[10] In the post-World War Two era, he held, the great western

[8] See Nietzsche [1883–8] 1968a: 33. He spoke primarily of the early sociological traditions rooted in Comte and Spencer. He also stated: "In place of 'sociology,' a theory of the forms of domination. In place of 'society,' the culture complex, as my chief interest. . . . In place of 'epistemology,' a perspective theory of affects . . ." (Nietzsche [1883–8] 1968a: 255; see also pp. 156, 231–47 on Socrates and modernity; and p. 33 on decadence and sociology; on the same topic, see [1888] 1968b: 91–2).
[9] See Nietzsche [1883–8] 1968a: 267, 272–6, 339–40, on perspectivism ("a complex form of specificity"]). On Nietzsche's perspectivism and science, see Babich 1994; on the relationship of his ideas to poststructuralism and postmodernism, see Foucault 1980; Schrift 1990, 1995; Koelb 1990; and on his contribution to social theory and politics, see Hughes 1977; Aschheim 1992; Antonio 1995.
[10] This essay was written for a North American audience and had much impact here; its programmatic style made it more accessible to English-speaking readers than the more philosophical works of French poststructuralism. Although Lyotard (1984: xxv) claimed to be reporting generally "on knowledge in the most highly developed societies," the essay reflects distinctive French cultural and sociopolitical conditions (e.g., the wake of a long dialogue with Cartesianism and more recent impacts of the French Communist Party, Marxist Humanism, Heidegger's

"metanarratives," which formally legitimated science (i.e., the "love of truth" and "emancipation of humanity") and were attacked by Nietzsche, have been replaced by a purely instrumental emphasis on optimal or profitable performance and system maintenance. Because the defunct metanarratives were a source of alternative political visions (e.g., Marxism) as well as legitimation, he implied, the instrumentalist regime depleted the Left's critical resources. In this regard, the Enlightenment ideals of freedom, justice, and science have become identified with "the system," neutralizing the Left's chief method of ideology critique or immanent critique (which formerly turned Enlightenment ideals against dominant institutions and spurred radical social movements). Against Marx and Habermas, Lyotard asserted that the Left's ideas of emancipatory subjectivity and uncoerced consensus now justify domination and terror.[11] This perceived cultural exhaustion of left politics opened the way for a postmodern move in the tracks of Nietzschean perspectivism. Instead of new metanarratives, Lyotard called for a "postmodern science" to deconstruct the prevailing forms of pseudoconsensus and cultural homogeneity and generate system instabilities.[12]

Lyotard's postmodern science scuttles modernist presuppositions about exposing distorted surfaces, detecting hidden truths, and guiding emancipation. Emphasis is shifted to "language

---

Nietzsche, Althusserian Structuralism, the May 1968 worker–student revolt, the Gaullist normalization, Eurocommunism, and hyperradical 1970s movements). For important precursors to Lyotard, see Lefebvre [1962] 1995 and Dubord [1967] 1983; and for the intellectual–political context, see Jameson 1984a; Hirsh 1981; Ferry and Renaut 1990; Plant 1992.

[11] Like other poststructuralists, Lyotard saw Marx as the master-theorist of bankrupt modernism and recent Marxism as conformist, repressive, and devoid of critical force. Speaking of its "totalizing model and its totalitarian effect," he held that: "Everywhere, the Critique of political economy (the subtitle of Marx's *Capital*) and its correlate, the critique of alienated society, are used in one way or another as aids in programming the system" (Lyotard 1984: 13). He also rejected Habermas's effort to save Marx's Enlightenment critique through a consensual theory of communicative action (Lyotard 1984: 46, 60–7).

[12] Lyotard argued that his new science would stress "such things as undecidables, the limits of precise control, conflicts characterized by incomplete information, '*fracta*,' catastrophes, and pragmatic paradoxes . . . theorizing its own evolution as discontinuous, catastrophic, nonrectifiable, and paradoxical. It is changing the meaning of the word *knowledge*, while expressing how such a change can take place. It is producing not the known, but the unknown. And it suggests a model of legitimation that has nothing to do with maximized performance but has its basis in difference understood as 'paralogy'" (Lyotard 1984: 60).

games" and "little narratives" and the effort to cancel the new forms of epistemological and normative truth claims underpinning the instrumentalist cultural regime. Moreover, Lyotard hoped that understanding of language games would provide insight into the plural types of "local" knowledge that foster genuine social bonds, new free spaces, and difference. Arising from the climate of French Nietzscheanism, Lyotard's postmodern perspectivism was aimed at countering and providing alternatives to exhausted Marxist rationalism and workerism and expressing sensibilities of a younger generation of radicals. Poststructuralist works became widely available in English in the 1970s and 1980s, shortly after European Marxism made substantial inroads into North American academe. Their perspectivist themes of plurality, locality, and difference and critiques of totality, consensus, and science left a deep imprint on North American postmodernism. Overall, these ideas captured the imagination of many younger, left-leaning intellectuals, especially those who were born after the New Left generation and who were active in the new forms of identity politics and social movements.

By contrast to Lyotard's argument about a recent shift in the foundations of science and knowledge, instrumentalism has held sway in the US, at least, since the professionalization of science and its connection to corporate culture in the 1920s (Ross 1991). The great legitimating metanarratives have never been as important here as they have been in Europe; Western philosophy and theories of modernity have had a much less significant role in US cultural life. Also, in the post-World War Two era, the US did not adopt scientifically legitimated planning characteristic of European-style, social democratic and Marxist politics. Although extremely important in the US, science did not have the same historical–ideological meaning as it did in Europe. Yet confidence in science was high; generally it was seen as an impartial producer of reliable, valid, and useful knowledge. Today, postmodernists question these views; their perspectivism challenges tacit presuppositions about scientific knowledge's capacity to "represent" the world "neutrally" and "objectively."

The much publicized "Sokal affair" dramatizes the continued importance of this representational theory of knowledge as well as the perceived threat posed by perspectivism and postmodernism. Physicist Alan Sokal's (1996a, 1996b, 1996c) totally bogus essay on "quantum gravity" fooled the editors of *Social Text*, a leading "cultural studies" journal, employing politically correct jargon and sycophantic references to their favorite writers. On its publication, the media reported gleefully that suspicion about postmodern thought had been confirmed; in addition to its pretentiousness and elitism, they charged, Sokal proves it to be muddled, and even fraudulent.[13] The "constructionist" views expressed in the issue's featured "science studies" essays constitute an intense battleground, because they hold that sociocultural conditions shape scientific practices, opening them to external interpretations, challenges, and debates. Sokal implies that they share an extreme perspectivism verging on solipsism; i.e., they treat the physical world solely as a social construct and its laws as mere interpretations rather than real properties of external reality. Invoking "the search for truth," "fearless analysis of objective reality," and "scientific objectivity," he attacks their supposed "epistemic relativism" and disregard for scientific methods and declares that "a scientific world-view, based on a commitment to logic and standards of evidence and to the incessant confrontation of theories with reality, is an essential component of any progressive politics."[14]

Yet even Sokal's opponents defer to science. Justifying their decision to publish the bogus essay, the editors of Social Text, Robbins and Ross (1996), assert that their journal is not a scientific

[13] Writing for socialist In These Times, Tom Frank's (1996: 22) biting commentary about this affair manifests sentiments, typical of a broad spectrum of critics. He stated that:

Almost from its inception the playful practice of poststructuralism has been dogged by a curious sense of its own absurdity. The high theorists of the genre often veer toward – and sometimes beyond – high silliness. There's something about the field's combination of nearly incomprehensible jargon, its grand claims of subversiveness and its practitioners' air of self-importance and professorial correctness that makes it a natural, even obligatory, target of parody and farce. A discipline that makes much of puns and cleverness, it issues a standing challenge to the prank-inclined: I dare you to outwit me. So formulaic does the real academic article sometimes seem . . . using the same buzzwords, performing the same readings, striking the same pseudo populist poses and reaching the same predictable conclusions – that critic Meaghan Morris once wondered whether "somewhere in some English publisher's vault there is a master-disk from which thousands of versions of the same article about pleasure, resistance, and the politics of consumption are being run off under different names with minor variations."

The mass media and right-wing journals were also jubilant and made similar points.

[14] Although cultural studies and science studies are too diverse (much more so than Sokal implies) to be considered postmodernist per se, postmodern sensibilities and ideas have been central to their development. George Levine (1996a, 1996c) charges that Sokal's claims about eliding the obdurate nature of physical reality ignore completely the "complexity" of constructionism and imply an "imperial" view of science closed to interpretation. He claims that Sokal mystifies science, and supports the anti-intellectual forces that he and the constructionists oppose. Also see Keller 1996; Albert 1996a, 1996b. On constructionism, see, e.g., Knorr-Cetina 1981; Latour and Woolgar 1986; Latour 1993.

organ, but a forum of opinion and cultural commentary. Moreover, they claim to reject the "sectarian postmodernism" or radical constructionism parodied by Sokal, and assert that they chose to publish his essay merely to present the position for debate (i.e., the journal had not yet published a piece by a physical scientist on postmodern science). Stanley Fish (1996), leading cultural critic and executive director of Duke University Press, which publishes the journal, also argues that its contributors do not try "to do science," but focus on the social conditions that shape or make it possible. Like the editors, he held that they are not antiscience and do not reject science's presuppositions. Speaking warmly of "scientific procedure" and science's culture of "communal effort," Fish clumsily tries to turn the tables, charging that it was Sokal, rather than the editors, who transgressed scientific norms (i.e., his "fraud" violated the "trust" undergirding all scientific "inquiry"). Although not revealing much about the nature of science, the sanctimonious claims and counterclaims in the Sokal affair do imply that scientific values are far from moribund and that their luster remains even in some postmodern circles. Because the legitimacy of modern knowledge claims and intellectuals are entwined with these presuppositions, even critics appeal to them when they are threatened (Antonio 1991). The perceived intense threat of postmodernism, mentioned above, arises in this context.

Social Theories of Postmodernism and Postmodernization

My focus is on social theory and work in or close to sociology (i.e., the huge "cultural studies" and aesthetics literatures are not covered). Five types of discourses about the postmodern are discussed below. I distinguish "moderate" postmodernist positions from "strong" and "radical" ones (i.e., more uncompromising perspectivist presuppositions and sharper departures from modern theory) and distinctly postmodernist theories from even more diverse theories of postmodernization. Moreover, my selection of discourses to be discussed is based on analytical and substantive convergences rather than on whether or not the authors made direct references to postmodernism or postmodernization. The deceptiveness of these labels is exemplified below in borderline positions and by individuals that express "postmodernist" views in some instances and "modernist" ideas in others. Finally, examples are drawn primarily from positions that either address the North American context or are widely debated here.

Postmodernism: polysemy, diversity, and situated knowledge

Epistemological perspectivism[15] "Moderate perspectivists" criticize "strong" truth claims. Posing conditional ideas of "objectivity," they argue that "facts" are culturally constituted, and they reject exaggerated claims about the certainty and sweeping scope of knowledge. In particular, they attack reified views, which ignore the impact of social location, power, and values in shaping scientific problems and interpretive practices. Moderate perspectivists believe that crude objectivism conceals sociocultural power and homogenizes the conditions of divergent strata. However, they neither see social knowledge in a purely textualist, constructed fashion nor reject scientific methods per se. Rather, they aim to strengthen science by clarifying its limits and increasing its specificity. Their epistemological "modesty" follows in the tracks of Weber's highly qualified, punctuated idea of "objectivity."

From within the border of the modern camp, Cornel West (1993: 119–41) embraces postmodernist "difference" and "otherness," which he argues favor realization of the post-World War Two tendency toward inclusion.[16] Although still incomplete, he sees the opening of academe and science to minorities, women, and the working class to have had fruitful epistemological consequences, increasing the range of perspectives, reducing intellectual rigidity, and enriching knowledge. West (1993: 121), however, wants "to historicize and pluralize and contextualize the postmodernism debate." He is critical of what he sees as "the narrow linguistic idealism" and overall subjectivist, textualist, and ahistorical tendencies of the radical perspectivist followers of Derrida, Foucault, and Lyotard. In his view, their "austere epistemic skepticism" undermines the ability to link "rhetorical" expressions of power to its organizational and material forms.[17] West supports "new openings"

---

[15] Because of the lack of a readily identifiable alternative, I employ "epistemology" with reservations. In this context, the term is contradictory, because it has been entwined with the West's representational theory of knowledge (i.e., "philosophy of the subject" or "spectator theory") stressing the subject–object dichotomy, primacy of theory, external truth, and knowledge producers as disembodied, neutral eyes.

[16] Especially with borderline approaches, as in West's case, the labels of modernist or postmodernist are often haphazardly employed and reveal little about the nature of the positions.

[17] West (1994: 15–17) holds that poststructuralism had critical impact in its original French context, reframing left theory in response to a dominant, rigid, Marxist structuralism. But he attacks uncritical appropriations of the tradition in North America, where Marxism and class politics have always been marginal. In particular, he sees Lyotard to be an "excessively overrated theorist" (West 1993: 122–3; also see 87–105).

for minorities and women, and embraces the aspects of postmodernism that overlap with John Dewey's scathing critique of the
"spectator theory of knowledge" and of the passivity that he
held follows from its disembodied subjectivity and false sense
of certainty. Arguing that North America has largely "evaded"
European metanarratives, West wants to recover perspectivist resources within a critical tradition stretching from Emerson to Rorty
and to deploy them with selected facets of British cultural studies
and Continental postmodernism. Like Dewey, he embraces science,
but calls for a more inclusive, pluralistic, and historical mode of
inquiry sensitive to location, power, and nonrational forces (West
1993: 87–104; 1989: 69–111, 211–39; 1994; Dewey [1929] 1988a).

Many North American feminists share West's affirmation of
moderate perspectivism and an opening of science and academe.
But they usually reject radical perspectivist moves that would undermine the privileged status of their own critiques of domination
and patriarchy. For example, self-identified "postmodern feminists,"
Nancy Fraser and Linda Nicholson (1988: 390–1), make a perspectivist turn, but reject emphatically Lyotard's tendency to lump
"large historical narratives" and portrayals of "societal macrostruc-
tures" with the defunct philosophical metanarratives. In their view,
he discards the very tools for analyzing and responding politically to macroscopic domination (e.g., transnational violations of
women's rights). By contrast, they call for "explicitly historical"
theory capable of "representing" accurately "the cultural specificity of different societies and periods." Recognizing cross-cutting
patterns of domination based on race, ethnicity, and class as well
as gender, they aim at "a broader, richer, more complex and multilayered feminist solidarity." Beyond their moderate perspectivism, they retain direct links to modern social theory and, especially,
to Marxian critical theory (e.g., their claims that the local and global
can be meshed in "big" historical narratives and that broad social
solidarities can still be forged).[18]

---

[18] Fraser (1989: 13 n. 2) declares: "In general, I am not persuaded that poststructuralist suspicions of 'totality,' certainly well founded when it comes to ahistorical
philosophical 'metanarratives,' tell against attempts to devise 'big' empirical theories
about historically specific social formations. Rather I assume a big diagnostic picture
is both epistemically possible and politically useful." See Fraser 1989, 1992, 1993,
1995a, 1995b, 1996. For more on modern and postmodern elements in feminism, see
Sandra Harding 1990: 99–101; Benhabib 1990; Bordo 1990; Nicholson and Seidman
1995a; for exchanges over Marxist feminism and modernism–postmodernism; Ebert
1995; Stabile 1994; Kaufman and Martin 1994; Bat-Ami 1993; Wood 1986, 1995; and
on "differences among women," Farganis 1994a, 1994b; Fraser 1996.

Although seeing "disembodied scientific objectivity" as a key-stone of masculinism, Donna Haraway's perspectivism stops far short of radical constructionism's "fully textualized and coded world."[19] She calls for "radical historical specificity" and a "successor science" that provides "richer," "better" and more "critical" and "reflexive" accounts of the world. She does not abandon "rational knowledge" or the "real," but stresses their socially mediated, plural nature. Sounding like earlier reflexive modernists, she calls for an "embodied," "feminist objectivity" stressing "particular" conditions, "specific" locations, "mobile positioning," "passionate detachment," and "partial" knowledge open to "contestation" (Haraway 1988: 576–9, 581–5, 590, 593). She is a good example of why Sokal's generalizations about science studies' subjectivism are exaggerated. Haraway also admits that her views are "not new" in Western thought (parallels between her arguments and those of thinkers, such as Nietzsche, Weber, and Dewey, are easy to detect).

Conversely, stronger postmodernist moves pose more "radical perspectivist" critiques of modernist presuppositions about representation, truth, and objectivity. Often they suggest a pure textualism that withholds epistemological privilege from all narratives, suspending completely all judgments based on representational grounds or on the relative truth or falsity of depictions of "realities" beyond the text. Rather, they focus on "language games" or "discursive practices." This move should not be equated with solipsistic denial of the existence of obdurate materiality or the "external" dimension of human experience. By contrast, radical perspectivists usually imply that complex cultural mediation and diffuse power blur so seriously the already ambiguous borders between interpretations and "facts" that more radical versions of perspectivism and constructionism are required to problematize the exceptionally reified cultural sphere, probe the deceptive workings of all-pervasive power, and reactivate quiescent cultural politics.

Providing a rationale for this sharper postmodernist break, Nicholson (1990b: 3–4) argues that science's "very criteria" of truth

---

[19] Haraway occupies a kind of middle ground between modernism and postmodernism. Although attacking "strong social constructionist" positions, she employs postmodern ideas and charges that feminist standpoint theory implies an epistemologically privileged, common subjectivity (i.e., marginality affords women special access to and understanding of reality), retaining objectivist taints of vulgar Marxism (Haraway 1988: 576–7, 583–7; also see Bat-Ami 1993; Hartsock 1984, 1987; Clough 1993a, 1993b; Smith 1993).

and falsity and core ideas of objectivity and reason reflect the "values of masculinity at a particular time in history." If these core presuppositions are seen to be completely perverted by patriarchy or other forms of power, science is inextricably entwined with modernist sociocultural reproduction and is, thus, beyond revision and must be discarded or rebuilt *in toto*. This postmodern equivalent to Nietzsche's dictum that sociologists assimilate the norms of decadent social orders and use them as standards treats moderate perspectivist inclusivity, reflexivity, and specificity as merely providing more nuanced justification for intractable domination and repression. Laurel Richardson (1991: 173) states: "Once the veil of privileged truth is lifted, feminism, Afro-American, gay, and other disparaged discourses rise to the same epistemological status as the dominant discourse. With the monotone of power interests exposed a multitude of voices speaks." Radical perspectivists argue that putting normally excluded and dominant positions on equal epistemological footing removes privilege, makes power relations transparent, and opens the way for more diverse types of knowledge production (Kaufman and Martin 1994).

Similarly, Steven Seidman (1995: 125–8) points out that "queer theorists" opt for textualism in order to establish a radical "cultural politics of knowledge" that undermines the very deeply embedded and pervasive hetero/homosexual binary. In an earlier essay, he called for purely narrative or storytelling "social theory" to subvert such presuppositions and escape "sociological theory's" metatheoretical navel-gazing. He believed that dumping the epistemological dead weight and canceling all claims about representation would enliven "social theory." By contrast to West, he embraced the radical "epistemic suspicion" he saw "at the core of postmodernism." In this view, modern knowledge is shaped so powerfully by its ties to specific locations, such as "class, gender, race, and sexual orientation" that it is wed, at its very "epistemological" foundations, to racism, homophobia, and sexism. Thus, all truth claims and efforts to privilege knowledge epistemologically universalize "local prejudices" and justify elite dominance. Like Richardson, Seidman (1991a: 134–5) hoped that a textualist move would give minority voices parity with mainstream positions, provide richer and more diverse knowledge, and enliven moribund sociological theory. In this regard, their break with modernism is not an absolute one.

Recently, Seidman (1996a, 1996b), moving towards West's borderline position, adopted a fuller pragmatic view that averts pure textualism, yet retains the emphasis on postmodern plurality. Stressing "consequentialist" justification of knowledge, Seidman (1996a: 757) argues emphatically and rightly that his view is neither anti-science nor irrationalist. Rather he calls for careful empirical work and "thick, dense, elaborated critical reasoning." Although his pragmatism borders modernism, his Foucaultian view that *"science is power"* still expresses a stronger Nietzschean "suspicion" than those, like West, who stand on the modern side of the divide.[20] Haraway has argued that radical perspectivists believe that scientists hardly ever act according to their espoused values of objectivity and scientific method.[21] Perhaps this suspicion animates Seidman's tendency to embrace the pragmatists' antifoundationalism and views about science's rootedness in everyday practices and power, yet to put aside their suggestion to employ its normative content (i.e., as a communication community) and methods in radical politics.

Jean Baudrillard, who focuses on American culture and is more widely read in the US than in his native France, breaks much more sharply with modern theory than the North American postmodernists mentioned above. In a radical perspectivist rejection of representational theory, he holds that symbolic "codes" are entirely autonomous and contingent; "signs" are self-referential, lacking any connection to conceptual or external referents. All-pervasive "simulation," or infinite production of copies without originals, obliterates distinctions between real and illusory conditions or events and evaporates the possibilities for genuine communication and agency. Baudrillard sees culture as a flat "surface" of floating, aleatory media signifiers that dissolve history, society, and the self. Signs represent nothing and have no meaning, but their "codes" still shape desire and experience. Arising from very diverse locations and from consumption and fascination, domination cannot be terminated by simple revolution against elites and is impervious to active resistance (Baudrillard 1983a, 1983b, 1987, 1988a, 1988b, 1989, 1990).

Baudrillard implies that the sociocultural bases of modern epistemology have been demolished by postmodern media culture.

---

[20] However, as suggested by Clough's (1996), Richardson's (1996), and Denzin's (1996) emphatic postmodernist critiques of Seidman, he probably stands closer to West than to radical postmodernism.

[21] Haraway (1988: 576) says:

According to these tempting views, no insider's perspective is privileged, because all drawings of inside–outside boundaries in knowledge are theorized as power moves, not moves toward truth. So, from the strong social constructionist perspective, why should we be cowed by scientists' descriptions of their activity and their accomplishments; they and their patrons have stakes in throwing sand in our eyes.

Coordination by codes means the "end of the political" and "end of the social." Postmodern micropolitics as well as Marxian emancipatory politics are reduced to mere simulations, upholding the sign system and moribund reality principle. Intersubjective capacities that Durkheim, Mead, and other modern social theorists once saw as vital social resources for forging solidarities and culturally integrated groups, communities, and societies are dissipated. By contrast to the other postmodern theorists' taints of modernism and democratic hopes about inclusion, Baudrillard portrays complete exhaustion of modern politics and culture.

Normative perspectivism   Normative affirmations of "difference," stressed in the recent cultural or identity politics of race, gender, sexual preference, and ethnicity (e.g., Gutmann 1994; Calhoun 1994) are prominent threads in postmodernist positions. As should be evident from the above discussion, the epistemological view that diverse values from divergent locations give rise to richer "knowledges" is entwined with the "normative perspectivist" embrace of value diversity *per se* and suspicion about broader value consensus. These views are posed against the supposedly homogenizing force of modern theory and, especially, Marxian concepts of class-consciousness, class politics, and universal emancipation. For example, Nicholson (1990b: 11) charges that Marxist emphases on: "production and class . . . delegitimize demands of women, black people, gays, lesbians, and others whose oppression cannot be reduced to economics. Thus, to raise questions now about the necessarily liberating consequences of universalizing categories is to open spaces for movements otherwise shut out by them."

Normative perspectivism encourages an appreciative stance toward diverse movements and groups with divergent identities, lifestyles, and politics. From this standpoint, postmodernists challenge the normative foundations or cultural significance of dominant theory and research programs, questioning the value of knowledge or why certain matters are "worth knowing" and others are ignored. They hold that functionalist claims about emergent universal consensus around modern values and expert management justify domination and exclusion. They stress diverse values and publics, discursive mediation of conflict, recognition of minority cultures, and entry of minorities into spheres where they have been historically excluded. As exemplified by West and Fraser, however, moderate perspectivists believe that, albeit with difficulty and struggle, diverse groups, even with highly conflictive pasts, can still reach understandings through communication and cooperation and form solidarities based on mutual recognition. Thus, they embrace difference, but neither reject consensus *in toto* nor imply value relativism. They revise, update, and broaden modern theory.

One reason for distinguishing normative from epistemological perspectivism is that some thinkers take different stances toward each matter. For example, Seidman's earlier epistemic relativism contrasted sharply with his nonrelativist normative position; he thought a purely textualist antiepistemology could counter sociological theory's all-too pervasive abstract methodological, metatheoretical ruminations, which, he held, dulled its normative purview. He hoped that a radical, "postmodern" epistemological move would close the gap between social theory and political practice; revive the ethically engaged side of modern social theory (e.g., its "broad social narratives," "expansive political hopes," and "radical democratic" ideals) by making it more plural (i.e., bringing suppressed normative issues concerning sexuality and marginality to the center of discourse). Although expressing strong suspicion about science and of the old politics of solidarity, Seidman believes that social theory can make a difference and that readers will be receptive to his arguments for inclusion.[22] His normative views converge strongly with reflexive modernism, especially since his pragmatist turn.[23]

Expressing a strong normative perspectivism, Richard Rorty, a prominent US philosopher, combines facets of analytic philosophy, Deweyan antifoundationalism, and poststructuralism into his own distinctive postmodernism. He argues that the "moral self" is a "centerless web" of shared beliefs and feelings with "nothing

[22] See Laclau and Mouffe (1985: 153) on identifying "the discursive conditions for the emergence of a collective action, directed towards a struggling against inequalities and challenging relations of subordination." By contrast to Lyotard, they employ textualism to reformulate modernist ideas of "socialism." Like Seidman, they are normatively committed to radical democracy. See Nicholson's and Seidman's (1995b: 1–7) biographical statements about their drift from Marxism.

[23] Compare Seidman's views (1991a, 1991b, 1996a, 1996b; Nicholson and Seidman 1995a: 35) with Immanuel Wallerstein's (1997) critique of abstract metatheory or with Weber's ([1904–17] 1949: 7, 21–8, 68–104) critiques of orthodox Marxist monism and "pseudo-ethical neutrality" and support for inclusion into academe of Jews, women, and even political radicals he opposed bitterly. Much more disjunctive fusions of postmodernism and modernism abound. For example, Denzin (1994: 185–7, 195, 197) combines the directly conflictive approaches of Baudrillard, Althusser, and Goffman. He embraces textualism, but still speaks of "underlying ideological presuppositions" and "artificially constructed needs, desires, feelings, and ideas"; his depth model, distinguishing distorted surfaces from underlying realities and suggesting epistemological privilege, is cancelled by his textualism.

behind" and that "loyalties" and "convictions" lack "grounds" beyond a group's shared history, sentiments, and ideas. At least formally, he agrees with Dewey's and Mead's view that moral selves arise from the dynamic relations between human organisms and their culturally and linguistically mediated environments. But Rorty holds that "ethnocentricism," inherent to solidarities, prevents genuine communication from extending beyond the borders of "*ethnos*" or circles of believers (Rorty 1991: 30–1, 192, 199–200). He does not share Dewey's view that the sweeping mechanical interdependencies of modern corporate organizations and states, in addition to fragmentation and disaffiliation, produce shared consequences and ties at the regional, national, and even global levels, which make possible broader communities.[24] If one accepts Dewey's view that culture has a macroscopic associative substrate, the dominant types of selves and ultimate values are neither as local nor as arbitrary as Rorty implies. Thus, they can be debated in terms of their "fit" for different structural contexts. This macrosociological vision, tacit in much modern theory, opens space for discourse, stressing consequentialist, social justification of normative matters. By contrast, Rorty draws sharp boundaries between nations and their divergent values, which put strict limits on communication, ethical agency, and responsibility in mediating sociocultural differences.

Employing irony, Rorty argues that antiethnocentrism or active openness to other cultures and tolerance of difference at the heart of North America's ethnocentric liberalism can go too far. His "anti-anti-ethnocentrism" and emphasis on the strict borders of "ethnos" are posed against openness to antiliberal visions. But the consequent view that basic value differences are beyond discourse precludes wider consensus or solidarity and implies that pluralistic mass societies, such as the US, are composed of monadic or cellular solidarities, which, given the futility of efforts to forge wider consensus, are best governed by already reigning liberal proceduralism. Thus, Rorty's perspectivism can easily be construed as a defense of the status quo. Likening liberal mass society to "a bazaar surrounded by lots and lots of exclusive private clubs," his "postmodernist bourgeois liberalism" favors quick retreat to private spheres at the end of daily transactions and requires minimal

---

[24] For Dewey, rugged individualism and corporate social structure were contradictory. His critique of American culture amplified a historical tension between ideology, rooted in the pioneers' independent production, and advanced capitalism's complex cooperation and organization (e.g., Dewey [1929–30] 1988b).

consensus or mutual responsibility. This view has affinity for the neoliberal position that relationships among the general citizenry are best limited to individualistic, market-like exchange.[25] Rorty's move counters cultural right and communitarian moralism, but offers little guidance with respect to the burning intergroup conflicts over substantive justice (e.g., economic equality). By contrast, hopes for "stronger" or egalitarian democracy presume capacities to forge wider, deeper social bonds, mutual obligations, and consensus and to accept the costs for the greater public good and relief of human suffering. Although a self-proclaimed Deweyan, Rorty departs sharply from his mentor's Civic–Republican values and ideal of "renascent liberalism" – a radically democratic "fighting faith" stressing a "socialized economy," "cultural liberation," and "great community" (Dewey [1935] 1987, [1929–30] 1988b).

Lyotard's "incredulity to metanarratives" and stress on "local knowledge" suggest an even stronger normative perspectivism. By contrast to Rorty's affirmation of liberalism, Lyotard's radical deconstructive equation of solidarity–consensus with oppression–domination precludes virtually any broader normative standpoint beyond his own antiauthoritarian gestures and references to abstract difference. Consequently, the political significance of his postmodernist move is ambiguous (Lyotard 1984: xxiv; Ferry and Renaut 1990: 228–9; Dews 1987: 242). But Baudrillard's (1983b) radical split between signs and referents and end of the social suggest a complete evaporation of the cultural resources and communicative capacities presumed by all imaginable versions of liberal and radical democracy. Although playful, ironic, and good-natured, Baudrillard implies an aestheticized, anything-goes relativism, celebrating "seduction," "implosion," "indifference," and re-enchanted life on culture's surface, that has affinity for protofascism's virulently antiliberal radicalism.

Perspectivism is a defining feature of postmodernist theory. Stronger versions presume enormous differences between groups,

---

[25] Rorty (1991: 209) states that:

You cannot have an old-timey *Gemeinschaft* unless everybody pretty well agrees on who counts as a decent human being and who does not. But you *can* have a civil society of the bourgeois democratic sort. All you need is the ability to control your feelings when people who strike you as irredeemably different show up at City Hall or the greengrocer's, or the bazaar. When this happens, you smile a lot, make the best deals you can, and, after a hard day's haggling, retreat to your club. There you will be comforted by the companionship of your moral equals.

Also see Rorty 1991: 21–34, 175–222; and for his response to critics and the Foucaultian Left (e.g., their "wasted" literary efforts), see Rorty 1991: 1–17; Saatkamp 1995.

precluding wider communication, social bonds, or solidarities. Abandoning truth and falsity, their textualist moves equate knowledge with politics. They see power/knowledge to be all-pervasive, and treat all claims about substantive consensus transcending local solidarities to be inherently contrived and repressive. Moreover, treating societal-level ties as "thin" connections based on minimal mutual understanding and obligation, they subvert the sociological bases of strong visions of societal-wide democracy.[26] By contrast, moderate perspectivists share conditional views of power/ knowledge, less suffused with coercion and exclusion. Although they see science to be rife with worldly imperfections, they imply that it still has the capacity to distinguish conditional "truth" from falsity and create "valid," albeit transitory, knowledge of the world. In this regard, they argue that its effectiveness depends on adoption of a modest epistemology, stressing transitory, uncertain, partial, plural, discursive, and embodied knowledge. Believing that the normative resources for strong democracy are not yet depleted, they hold that nurturance of wider, intergroup consensus and social bonds requires moderate perspectivist understandings of values and communicative practices as well as of science.

Postmodernization: progress, crisis, or rupture?

Even if one rejects postmodernist theory, perspectivism's recent widespread resurgence in the social sciences and humanities and related trends in the arts, design, built environments, cinema, and other areas of mass culture and social structure still cry out to be addressed. Thus, modernists as well as postmodernists analyze postmodernization. Regardless of philosophical splits, divergent thinkers portray surprisingly similar trends, stressing pastiche, radical pluralism, eroded standards, disjunction, decenteredness, uncertainty, indeterminacy, immediacy, nostalgia, ahistoricism,

[26] Strong perspectivists' views about the impossibility of consensus and thin relationships among the general citizenry have an affinity for minimalist liberalism. Like classical liberals, they are skeptical of larger solidarities, see the state as the center of power and oppression, presume conflictive communities of local interest, emphasize individual rights, and stress countervailing forces and shifting alliances. On the other hand, they often favor group rights rejected by liberal individualism, celebrate the virtues of difference and marginality rather than embrace mere liberal tolerance, and reject liberal beliefs about the harmonizing force of the market. On postmodernism and the liberal "ideology of difference," see Jameson 1991: 340–56.

floating signifiers, blurred sociocultural borders, and restructuring of post-World War Two organizational and political economic arrangements. They also raise the question of "culture" in a manner that makes deeply problematic consensual naming, judging, analyzing, and planning of social conditions and changes. But a major split exists between those thinkers that see postmodernization pessimistically as fragmentation and exhaustion and others who interpret it as a liberating rupture heralding a nascent, post-traditional order much more open to difference.

Cultural postmodernization   Recall Baudrillard's radical perspectivist view that truth discourses are obliterated by mass media simulation. The split between sign and referent and complete absorption of the viewer into the cultural text erases the distinction between reality and illusion. Thus, claims that signs are representations or even ideological distortions of "reality" become "deterrents" masking the "*absence* of basic reality." Baudrillard contends that we live at "the decisive turning point" after which signs will be grasped as "pure" simulacra bearing "no relation to any reality." From this viewpoint, he castigates futile, "panic-stricken" efforts to cling to epistemological and normative life rafts. In his view, for example, the Watergate hearings merely simulated a sense of "scandal," drawing attention away from the fact that political morality is dead and the same types of surveillance, control, and dirty tricks are employed pervasively elsewhere. He holds that only abandoning the reality principle and representational presuppositions and embracing the aleatory "play of infinitesimal signifiers" will break the semiotic code's all-embracing control (Baudrillard 1983a: 11–13, 26–37, 83–6, 109, 119; 1987).

Some modern theorists make parallel arguments, but see the eroded reality principle to be rooted in conditions outside the text. Daniel Bell ([1976] 1996: xi–119) argued that Puritan character structure once constrained desires unleashed by the acquisitive, market-side of capitalism. But he claimed that these constraints were soon eroded by avant-garde culture; hedonistic cultural modernism was later fused with consumer culture, neutralizing the bourgeois values of work, saving, prudence, and responsibility. Bell held that the commercialization of the 1960s counterculture made the artistic pose all-pervasive and modernism hegemonic. By contrast to the Marxian primacy of production, he argued, the overall course of US society is now shaped by mass consumer culture and a media-based, "cultural class" of transmitters and vendors, or vanguard of the now dominant "new class" of knowledge and communication

workers, who make "everything permissible." The resulting uninhibited individualism expands consumer demand and profits, but
lacks the resources to sustain capitalist work or organization (Bell
1980: 154–64).

Bell sees modernism as originally a creative force that tempered
bourgeois moralism and infused its austere individualism with
aesthetic sensibilities. But he is scathingly critical of its current
hegemonic power and all-pervasive emphasis on irrational impulse,
immediacy, and "eclipse of distance," which eradicate the border
between observer and events. Absorbed into the action, the individual cannot stand back and judge and, thus, loses his/her
critical capacities, bearings, coherence, and agency. For Bell, "postmodernism" is merely hypertrophic modernism, free of genuine
traditionalist opposition and, consequently, bereft of creative force.[27]
Accordingly, postmodern hedonism neither shocks nor liberates;
rather, it merely justifies the acquisitive–consumerist facets of
capitalism and fosters overall sociocultural disintegration. In Nietzschean style, moreover, Bell implies that cultural exhaustion opens
the way for simulated tradition, fundamentalist religion, reactionary politics, and ethnic–nationalist retribalization (Bell [1976] 1996:
99–119, 295–339).

Bell states that his notion of contemporary cultural dissolution
was foreshadowed by Marx's and Engels's idea of the capitalist
wrecking-ball (i.e., "All that is solid melts into air, all that is holy is
profaned"). But Bell's somber vision of an epochal ending is more
Nietzschean than Marxist. While Marx and Engels held that incessant change and evaporation of tradition will cause humanity
to finally come to terms with its "real" life conditions, Bell detects
a different sort of "clearing": "The exhaustion of modernism, the
aridity of Communist life, the tedium of the unrestrained self, and
the meaninglessness of the monolithic political chants all indicate
that a long era is coming to a slow close." Against Hegelian–Marxian
historicism, he declares that: "All hopes have seemingly been
betrayed. The Owl of Minerva which once flew at dusk has folded
its wings, . . . the direction of History has been lost, and it knows
not what to tell us" (Bell [1976] 1996: xxix, 16–17; 1990a: 43).

---

[27] In Bell's recent "Afterword, 1996," he distinguishes "postmodernism" (i.e., "a
somewhat serious" architectural style or method of literary criticism) from "PoMo"
(i.e., "vulgar" forms of postmodern jargon and culture). However, he now stresses
severe dislocations of global economic restructuring, increased socioeconomic inequality, and unregulated capitalism. Moreover, he is critical of the postmodernist
tendency to overstate the role of culture and ignore class (Bell [1976] 1996: 284–5,
297, 333).

But believing that cultural exhaustion or postmodernization should be resisted, Bell wants to restore community and the shared sense of the past that once regulated desire, located individual lives and deaths in meaningful collective narratives, and integrated culture. In his view, a revived, but substantively refashioned, "sacred" would answer existential questions, justify liberal institutions, regenerate "*Civitas*" (i.e., self-constraint in the public good), and provide consensual means to cope with socioeconomic polarization, the corroded public sphere, and gross violations of human rights. Bell's position is reminiscent of Durkheim's view that democracy needs a normative foundation or civil religion. Bell embraces human rights, but, seeing himself as a "conservative in culture," he equates postmodernization and increased tolerance for marginal lifestyles with cultural fragmentation. Thus, he contradicts, at least implicitly, the postmodernist values of difference and inclusion (Bell 1980: 324–54; 1990a, 1990b, [1976] 1996: xi, 25, 116–19, 245, 283–5, 334–9).[28]

Leading North American cultural theorist, Fredric Jameson, portrays postmodernism as the "cultural logic" of a "purer," decentered, global, and thoroughly commodified "late capitalism" (i.e., as described by the Marxist, Ernest Mandel). Paralleling Bell's view of postmodernism as detraditionalized modernism, Jameson argues that the new phase of capitalism drastically speeds up and diversifies production of disjunctive fashions and integrates aesthetic creation more completely than ever before into mass commercial culture, colonizing the last domains of precapitalist "traditionalist space" (Jameson 1984b: 77–82; 1984c: 206–7). For Jameson, today's schizophrenic fragmentation, pastiche, disorientation, and dehistoricization all manifest the hyperextension and hyperacceleration of capitalist tendencies. Because culture has lost its former "relative autonomy," Jameson holds, "every" postmodern cultural position is "an implicitly or explicitly political stance on the nature of multinational capitalism today" (Jameson 1984b: 55, 87). Accordingly, he sees postmodernist textualism or claims about culture's "absolute self-referentiality" (e.g., signs circulating totally separately from referents) to be rooted in a transformation of the mode of production (Jameson 1984b: 82, 87; 1984c: 197–201). Although providing one of the richest, most nuanced analyses of postmodern culture, Jameson implies a Marxist epiphenomenalism opposed emphatically by virtually all postmodernist cultural theorists.

---

[28] Bell's views overlap with communitarian positions, which are sometimes criticized for opposing indirectly minority values and lifestyles (Bellah et al. 1986; Etzioni 1995; Bauman 1996a).

But Jameson's position is more complicated and ambivalent than it appears initially. Firstly, he sees the Marxist ideas of base-superstructure and ideology to have been, from the start, contested, ambiguous, and plural categories. In his view, they simply make problematic the relationship of "culture" to "its socioeconomic context." Theorized this loosely, he believes, Marxian materialism remains useful and can even shed light on postmodernist claims about culture's "mysterious autonomy" and role as a "determinant" (Jameson 1996: 45–8). Secondly, admitting his "great debt" to Baudrillard, Jameson holds that culture's transformation into a flat plane of detached, aleatory signifiers undermines distinctions between distorted "surfaces" and underlying "realities" and, thus, neutralizes the "critical distance" needed for modern "depth models" (e.g., Marxism, empiricism, hermeneutics, psychoanalysis, phenomenology). He holds that poststructuralist textualism or shift to "practices, discourses, textual play" and "intertextuality" is a "surface" strategy to cope with depthlessness and consequent inability to forge "representations of our own current experience." Similarly, his yet to be refined method of "cognitive mapping" is also a surface move to replace Marxist ideology critique. However, his portrayal of postmodern culture as a logic of late capitalism still presumes depth (Jameson 1984b: 60–2, 68, 83, 85–6; 1991: 399).[29] He formally preserves sociocultural space for his depth model and for resistance by arguing that postmodernism is a "cultural dominant" rather than an all-encompassing cultural complex, but his claims about multinational capitalism's nearly total colonization of social life implies a sweeping coextension of postmodern culture that eliminates alternative space. In this light, his cognitive mapping seems to be a *deus ex machina* or prop to save Marxism (Jameson 1984b: 89–92; 1988; 1991: 409–18).

At the end of *Postmodernism*, Jameson (1991: 418) refers elliptically to his "rhetorical strategy" or his effort to see if "by systematizing something that is resolutely unsystematic, and historicizing something that is resolutely ahistorical, one couldn't outflank it and force a historical way of at least of thinking about that." By contrast to earlier Marxism, he does not equate hypercommodification with cultural decline. Rather he holds that it

[29] Jameson's (1984b: 79) points about depthlessness undercut the epistemological and normative presuppositions of his assertion that "faulty representations of some immense communicational and computer network are themselves but a distorted figuration of something even deeper, namely the whole world system of present-day multinational capitalism."

is experienced as "a prodigious expansion of culture" making "everything in our social life . . . 'cultural' in some original and as yet untheorized sense." He implies a mutual penetration of culture and the market that is neither purely culturalist nor materialist; postmodernist textualism is a distortion of some sort, but also expresses a "fundamental mutation" or change in cultural experience that should not be dismissed as mere reification (Jameson 1984b: 86–7). But the unresolved theoretical tensions that flow from Jameson's straddling the line between Marxism and post-Marxism and modernism and postmodernism manifest the blurred sociocultural borders mentioned above and the sensibility that radical cultural change transforms the very meaning of theory and interpretation. He points beyond Marxism in the same move that he embraces it.[30]

Jameson's ambivalence about postmodern culture contrasts with Bell's despairing portrayal of its profound contradictions with capitalism and with Baudrillard's claims about a fundamental aesthetic break. However, Jameson's (1984c: 195–6) emphasis on postmodernism's "social functionality" (i.e., as the "hegemonic aesthetic of consumer society" and late capitalism's "laboratory of new forms and fashions) clashes even more sharply with those who equate it with new free spaces and new social movements. This multicultural branch of postmodernism sees the blurred borders and floating signifiers as eroding modern domination, empowering marginalized groups, pluralizing sociocultural life, and enlivening radical democratic politics (e.g., Nicholson and Seidman 1995b: 34–5). Contra Jameson, Bell, and Baudrillard, they celebrate the demise of postwar liberalism and Marxism as a dawning of inclusive tendencies, envisioning postmodern culture as an affirmative, oppositional force. To cover new ground, I will focus on European theories, which, like North American multiculturalists, embrace difference and treat the new social movements as an alternative to the old Left.

But these European positions arose in contexts where the labor movement, social democratic parties, and Marxist social theories dominated the postwar Left. Multiple waves of new immigration, following the collapse of European colonialism, as well as the more recent fall of Eastern European communism and erosion of postwar political parties, opened new political possibilities, undercut

---

[30] Jameson's (1991: 417–18) ambivalence is visible in his point that "cognitive mapping" is "nothing but a code word for 'class consciousness,'" but that it implies "a new and hitherto undreamed of kind" bearing the imprint of postmodern culture.

the dominant class-based positions, and made way for fresh theories. In the new discourses, "detraditionalization" is often seen as the core process in the rise of a new modernity or postmodernity; a move from "traditional authority" (i.e., collective, ritualized, hierarchical, monovocal, and closed) to "post-traditional authority" (i.e., individual, reflexive, discursive, polyvocal, and open) (Heelas 1996). Postmodern themes of locality, plurality, and uncertainty abound. Like North American multiculturalism, however, these theories hold that today's dispersed, fragmented cultures and selves enhance, rather than diminish, capacities for responsibility and "agency." In an emphatic post-Marxist move, they shift the main institutional locus of problems from capitalism to the state and culture, treating corporatist planning models and scientism as the last phase of traditionalism. By contrast, many of them treat consumer choice as a core basis of post-traditional identity building, and imply a deeper optimism than their North American counterparts. I will refer to these positions as "new openings" theories.[31]

Anthony Giddens (1990: 21, 175–6; 1994a) holds that a nascent "reflexive" stage of modernization is radicalizing the earlier, modern "turn from tradition." He contends that abstract codes and specialized expertise facilitate global "disembedding of social systems" or " 'lifting out' of social relationships from local contexts of interaction" and "restructuring" them "across indefinite spans of time–space." Because abstract norms cannot be specific guides to action in particular locations, individuals must interpret and apply them reflexively, choosing the precise contexts where they are employed. By contrast to traditionalism's uncritical approach to received knowledge, they must treat information discriminately and think for themselves. Implying that postwar scientism and technocracy were deceptive variants of traditionalism, Giddens holds that breaking with their "formulaic truth" opens the way for much more diverse types of information and perspectives from dispersed sources. False certainty gives way to soberness about the many-sidedness of problems inherent in technical and political interventions. Giddens believes that participation by diverse social movements and publics, outside normal bureaucratic channels, multiplies perspectives, requires discursive mediation of differences, and improves qualitatively the employment of knowledge

---

[31] At least guardedly optimistic US thinkers, such as West, Fraser, and Seidman, support the new social movements, and can be viewed as a North American wing of new openings theory. But their approaches vary, reflecting a different historical situation (e.g., see Anderson and Camiller 1994; Cerullo 1994).

in sociocultural life. He also holds that the self becomes a "reflexive project" and center of a new "life politics"; plural struggles over self-actualization, identity, and lifestyle supersede "emancipatory" or class politics. Top-to-bottom authority, homogeneity, and ideology of the postwar parties and unions are replaced by decentered types of reflexive authority, nurturing autonomy, choice, tolerance, discursivity, and agents capable of forging and sustaining radical democracy (Giddens 1991: 20, 214–17; 1994a: 64, 106–7).[32]

Conversely to Bell or Baudrillard, new openings theorists do not see the eroded legitimacy of parties and state administration and exhausted liberal-left ideology as a decline of public life and meaning. Rather, they stress a post-traditional break with the politics of power, interest, and class. They suggest a shift from the technocratic culture of "first modernity" to a decentered "subpolitics" of "second modernity." For example, Beck argues that "reflexivity" arises from "self-confrontation" about "risks" and their costs. Increased awareness of risk opens development and growth to public debate, encourages input from diverse points of view (including effected populations), and leads to more sensible, measured approaches to public problems and policies (Beck 1996: 19; 1994: 5–8). Alberto Mellucci (1996a: 197–8) argues that the new social movements constitute "a qualitative leap in the nature of collective action" and a new "public space of representation" superior to labor-centered politics. He sees these new subpolitics to manifest a broader "culturalization of conflicts" forging "postmaterial" ends and "more autonomous, more self-reflexive, more responsible, and more resourceful" agents.[33] Central themes of the European postwar Left (i.e., "organization," "interest," and "structure") give way to "the importance of the individual and subjective dimensions of social life." New openings theorists believe that consequent increased diversity, openness, and participation herald a more inclusive, freer, and sustainable democracy (Mellucci 1989, 1996a: 100–17, 211–25; 1996b: 145–50; also see Beck 1992a, 1992b, 1994, 1996; Beck and Gernsheim 1996; Touraine 1992, 1995; Piccolomini 1996).

[32] For the overall argument that is too complex to do justice to here, see the texts cited above and Giddens 1990, 1992, 1994b.

[33] For example, the 300,000-person march in Brussels (October 1996), protesting a pedophile scandal and murder of several small children, was a spontaneous action of mostly first-time protesters. According to Mellucci and other new openings theorists, such events break fundamentally with interest group politics (i.e., involving conflicts of material interests, organized parties, and state bureaucracies) and supplant old left strategies with fresh types of critical, cultural politics.

Although the emphases on the primacy of culture and identity express well sensibilities of important social movements, their relationship to the politically gridlocked, polarized, and garrison-state features of the current US scene is ambiguous. Claims about future "coalitions" moderating splits are contradicted by the fractious politics of identity (e.g., rampant intergroup struggles over ideal and material interests and uncompromising views of essentialist "differences"). Divergent thinkers, such as Daniel Bell, Richard Sennett ([1974] 1992), Christopher Lasch ([1979] 1991), Todd Gitlin (1995), and Michael Sandel (1996), have held that the new politics foster narcissism, centrifugal haggling, and corroded community and public life. The most unsympathetic critics hold that they serve the clientalistic interests of a "new class" and privileged minority fragment of the professional middle class, who benefit from bureaucratically entrenched status and ignore the growing marginalization of the underclass (e.g., Piccone 1988, 1995; Lasch 1995).

New openings theorists counter the postwar Left's structuralist and poststructuralist "antihumanism" by reviving the "subject" in the form of very plural, active "agents." However, like earlier evolutionary theorists, they can be taken to task for not situating adequately their theories in specific space, time, and strata. For example, Mellucci (1996a: 92, 190, 198) declares the "end of historicism" and of its "linear," progressive view of history, yet also speaks very generally about a "qualitative leap" in "autonomy and self-realization" and in capacities for radical democratic action. By anchoring theory again in claims about developmental tendencies and social movements, these theories revive, at least indirectly, left historicism and critical theory. But they do not explain sufficiently or specify their claims with regard to divergent life-chances and strata in materially polarized late capitalism (i.e., especially in the US). Also, these approaches lack Nietzschean sensibilities about power/knowledge *within* their own politics, and, thus, fail to provide a lens to grasp intense US "culture wars," battles over "political correctness," and internecine splits between and within the different new social movements. Although the politics and theories of new openings generate fresh ideas and help carve out new free spaces for certain marginal groups and lifestyles, the question of whether their new "radical" politics really "goes beyond" or simply breaks with the postwar Left is an open one.

Another European, Zygmunt Bauman, portrays postmodernism as a "radical victory" of "modern culture" over "modern society" that flattens "power-supported structures" and "hierarchies" (Bauman 1992: viii–ix, 34). Arguing that capital has been "emancipated" from labor, he describes a paradigm shift from production to consumption

that erodes traditional authority. In his view, the new postmodern order relies mainly on market "seduction"; i.e., regulation
by consumer choice and pleasure rather than by ideology, surveillance, or force. He also sees an end of the central life projects and
"immutable" idea of the self, which served workaday existence,
mass political projects, "legislated" knowledge, centralized control,
and bourgeois discipline. Bauman argues that decentered, post-
traditional, multiple, postmodern identities embrace uncertainty,
plurality, and change, justify goals and means discursively, and
nurture choice, responsibility, and agency. Although suggesting a
new openings scenario, he also argues that postmodernization does
not "increase the total volume of individual freedom," but redis-
tributes it "in an increasingly polarized fashion." Thus, while the
middle and upper classes gain increased autonomy, marginal
people are deprived of "resources for identity building and . . .
tools for citizenship." Beyond the market's passive postmodern regulation, these outsiders remain targets of panoptical surveillance
and coercion. Bauman cannot imagine a substantial reduction of
polarization and inequality or a postmodern alternative to what he
sees as the exhausted politics of class and redistribution. Therefore,
he embraces postmodernity ambivalently (Bauman 1992: 49–53,
97–8, 191–204; 1993; 1995a: 6, 27–9; 1995b: 14–16; 1996a, 1996b).

Organizational and political–economic postmodernization   In a modern
voice, Bauman speaks of a cultural transformation to an "interpretive" or "postmodern" paradigm as part of a shift from production-
centered capitalism, rooted in work and coercion, to consumer
capitalism, based on leisure and seduction. Although this position
underlines the need for continued structural analysis, Bauman also
holds that the sociological concepts of "structure" and "society"
originate from bankrupt "legislative reason" and justify top-to-
bottom rule. Thus, his dominant postmodernist voice favors textualist strategies that privilege culture and diminish the significance
of organization and power (Bauman 1992: viii–ix, 48–65, 97–100,
125–30). Extreme culturalist stances treat organization and political
economy as epiphenomena or ignore them completely. But even
Bell stresses the primacy of culture, and the "Marxian" Jameson
(1996: 46–7) reframes the "base-superstructure" idea so radically
that it accommodates postmodernist views about the complete
autonomy of culture. Thus, "structural" facets of postmodernization
usually have to be teased out of cultural arguments or be drawn
from work on the borders or outside of postmodernist thought.
    The splits, implied above, over the meaning of postmodernization
and detraditionalization for democracy are central to matters of

organization and political economy. For example, new openings theorists portray a democratizing culturalization of structure deriving from flexible, inclusive social networks emerging below the hollowed-out remains of postwar technocracy. For example, Mellucci (1996b: 114–15) sees the new social movements' "hidden networks of groups, meeting points, and circuits of solidarity" as stealing impetus from "the politically organized actor." Beck's (1994: 22) views about the rise of the "subpolity" and Giddens's (1994a: 107) points about nascent "dialogic democracy" imply a similar scenario. Although holding that bureaucracy cannot be eliminated immediately, they see new self-regulating, informal networks to be increasingly shaping the direction of administrative action and posing basic challenges that decenter and democratize top-to-bottom structure.

The changes from below supposedly erode patriarchy, radically pluralize the public sphere, weaken the authority of mainstream parties, and diminish expert planning monopolies. Substituting multiple, inclusive, decentered, goal-setting agencies for central-ized structures activates heretofore underutilized social resources, empowers diverse agents, and employs more effectively and demo-cratically a much wider range of knowledge, information, and communication than ever before. Complex, dynamic, nonlinear net-works, composed of reflexive individuals, losely coupled groups, single-issue campaigns, and multifaceted alliances, manifest a nearly hegemonic, culturally driven pattern of collective action. New open-ings theorists believe that departure from the former all-pervasive authoritarian hierarchy has been already substantial enough to constitute a new order than can no longer be grasped by Marxian categories of exploitation and socialism, Weberian conceptions of bureaucratization and rationalization, or postwar models of demo-cracy stressing public administrative power and planning. In their view, the shift to a "centerless" social topography requires new sub-structural theories (e.g., Bauman 1992: 50–3, 97–100, 187–204; Beck 1992b, 1994, 1996; Giddens 1994a, 1994b; Mellucci 1996a: 207–28).[34]

[34] Certain North American thinkers pose similar conditions arising in the wake of corporate restructuring – a move from centralized, rigid hierarchy to centerless, flexible networks. For example, see Leinberger's and Tucker's (1991) portrayal of a move from the domain of "organization men" (and spouses) to a new world of socially sensitive, "artificial" men and women governed by a highly individualistic "enterprise ethic." The structural side of their very optimistic postmodernist scenario portrays a fundamental shift from vertically integrated companies and concentrated postwar suburbs to leaner, wired, constantly shifting, nonlinear, information era "network organizations." See Ashley (1997: 184–209) for treatment of changes in complex organization and the professions.

The new decentered, processual views of organization and sociopolitical life are not entirely new. They were prefigured by classical liberal ideas of "spontaneous order," which pitted the market's supposedly decentralized power, individual choice, local autonomy, and tacit knowledge against the regulatory–redistributional state's bureaucracy, collectivism, central planning, and universalistic rationalism (e.g., Mises, Hayek, and Oakeshott). Rejecting libertarian economism, however, the new positions also parallel Durkheim's critique of unregulated markets and idea that fresh democratic possibilities are latent in new forms of complex sociocultural interdependence.[35] But departing Durkheim's emphases on normative consensus and civil religion, the new theories' antifoundationalist, discursive ideas of pluralism, uncertainty, and democracy are reminiscent of Dewey. Yet they do not share Dewey's ideas that corporate power is still firmly in the saddle and that resistance requires "scientific" state planning and state-managed redistribution as well as local cultural strategies and interventions (Dewey [1929] 1988a, [1929–30] 1988b). Giddens expresses these ambiguities; employing classical liberal ideas in his version of "radical politics" and repeating the mantra that "left and right" are exhausted, he declares that: "We should all become conservatives now . . . but not in a conservative way" (Giddens 1994b: 49, 51–77, 104–33, 151–73).

Foucault earlier shifted emphasis from Marxian–Weberian power to processes operating below centralized organization. But rather than increased democratization, he saw, starting in eighteenth-century Europe, a massive diffusion of power that greatly diversified and increased the constraints on human multiplicity. An inspiration for thinkers stressing the erosion of agency, he treated the new "human sciences" as the leading edge of a multifaceted rationalization that disciplines the body more thoroughly than ever before. In his view, "normalizing" practices are diffused widely by training, examination, and treatment in numerous institutional locations. For Foucault, power is not a fixed property of a few leaders in central administrative and penal offices, but inheres in modern knowledge, education, and therapy, and flows through all local networks. He held that replacing "monarchical 'super-power'" and

[35] Durkheim heralded a nascent stage of modernity that promises to bridge the gulf between "unorganized individuals" and the "hypertrophied state," loosen "collective surveillance," and forge very plural, "supple" or "elastic" social relations that cultivate enhanced autonomy and responsibility. However, the new theories highly optimistic views also have affinity for Parsons's postwar claims about new evolutionary breakthroughs overcoming early modernity's hierarchical authority and bureaucracy. See Durkheim [1893] 1964: 28, 275–303, 329–50; Parsons 1971: 86–143.

hyperviolent public cruelty with a new, "innocent," dispersed "micro-physics of power" gave rise to a "panoptical" regime where an all-pervasive emphasis on "minute," "meticulous" discipline and continuous surveillance cultivates exact, self-regulated control (Foucault 1979: 80, 139).[36] Following Nietzsche, Foucault suggests that modernization pluralizes and culturizes control mechanisms. Being less directly coercive, they are more economical and effective.

Using Bentham's "panopticon" as a metaphor for modernity, Foucault saw "micro-power" to be a self-reproducing feature of virtually every niche of social life. Like Nietzsche, however, he recognized that power has diverse purposes and consequences.[37] Thus, he did not imply a completely homogenous, sociocultural terrain (Foucault 1979: 16–31, 201–50). Following Foucault, many postmodernists and borderline modernists stress the disciplinary and normalizing effects of today's explosion of new computer, informational, and security technologies, pointing to the threats and costs of consequent testing, surveillance, and information-gathering. Yet these thinkers stop far short of implying a "Brave New World" scenario or end of individuality (e.g., Hanson 1993; Staples 1997). Also, gay/lesbian, feminist, and other minority writers often temper their optimistic hopes about postmodern inclusivity with references to Foucault and continued panoptical controls (e.g., Seidman 1991a, 1996a). These thinkers emphasize constraints on agency, but suggest neither seamless control nor complete erosion of countervailing power and resistance. But others express more extreme dedemocratization. According to Baudrillard (1987), Foucault's claims about a micro-physics of power operating as a formative force beneath the surface of culture obscures all-encompassing simulation by preserving illusions about bygone depth, the reality principle, and modernity. Declaring an end of panopticism, he envisions complete semiotic control and evaporation of all agency; his idea of total depthlessness opens the way for his textualist reduction of organization, political economy, and power to simulations.

Although appropriating some ideas from Foucault, William Bogard (1996: 54) follows Baudrillard's vision, arguing that the

---

[36] Foucault does not argue that centralized power disappears. For example, he held that the scientific and therapeutic arms of the state remain fundamentally important institutional matrixes of normalizing practices and coercive force (Foucault 1979).

[37] For example, rationalization of disciplinary techniques has given rise to elaborate, well-coached ballet and micropolitics as well as more exact military training and Taylorism.

"forces of surveillance which once served the integration and reproduction of Capital in the industrial period are everywhere today in the process of disappearing." Portraying his book as an "imaginary" verging on "science fiction," he sees a rising "telematic" order based on digital technology and "simulated surveillance."[38] Marxian–Foucaultian discipline is surpassed by a system that makes workers "one more switch or relay in a growing cybernetic assemblage." Regulated by "codes, models, programs, chips," and other elements of computerized systems, "programmed" or "simulated" work is controlled much more effectively than that based on direct surveillance (e.g., "cameras, microphones, and . . . supervisors"). Bogard claims that this shift spreads "monumental sameness and repetitiveness" relentlessly across all sectors of "the postindustrial economy." He sees organized political efforts to resist simulated surveillance as deterring the fall of the reality principle and feeding the control system.[39] Like Baudrillard, Bogard awaits implosion to end the "excruciatingly boring" and "endlessly dull fantasy" of totally homogenized, virtual life (Bogard 1996: 4, 99, 104, 116–17, 182–3).

Recall Bauman's point that seduction regulates the classes wealthy enough to participate widely in consumer markets, while surveillance and coercion regulate the poor and marginalized. Mike Davis's (1992) lucid study of accelerating use and dispersion of surveillance in Los Angeles's postmodern built-environments provides a detailed portrait of the radically divided world mentioned more passingly by Bauman. In the chilling tone of the best postmodern science fiction, Davis describes "Fortress LA" and its sweeping advances in disciplinary controls and "Star Wars"-like security and police technology. Quoted on the book's back cover, leading postmodern science fiction writer William Gibson describes it as

[38] Bogard provides a very simple illustration of simulated surveillance (i.e., an empty vehicle painted to look like a sitting police-car causing speeding drivers to slow down). But his prolix "definition" exemplifies, in the extreme, the postmodern blurring and ambiguity that maddens modernists. He states: "I cannot, unfortunately, give a simple definition of this, at least one that doesn't almost immediately contradict or deconstruct itself." The term can refer to "introducing discipline into the very heart of an operation" as well as the "opposite." And "both descriptions are right and both are wrong, yet both are inescapable"; simulated surveillance "is a fantasy of absolute control and the absence of control at the same time, total control and the end . . . of control" (Bogard 1996: 22, 25).
[39] Although claiming that worker organization and rebellion are fruitless, Bogard (1996: 122–3) implies that workers can resist by simulation (i.e., "hacking and viral strategies, recodings, doublings, . . . simulated readouts, electronic decoys").

"more cyberpunk than any work of fiction could ever be." But Davis's complex mapping of LA's Foucaultian transfiguration of space and of the regime's all-too-real multilayered, differentiated, political–economic and police forces constitute much more than a postmodern "imaginary."

Davis locates postmodern cultural trends within explicit, albeit very disjunctive, temporal–spatial and organizational contexts, and shows how the old types of control and readiness to offer or withdraw political–economic support or employ instant coercive force are combined with simulated power.[40] Careful observers, especially from the target populations, detect "real" from "hyperreal" types of control. Davis's nuanced historical accounts and appreciation of difference render highly segmented social spaces, "gated" by race, class, and ethnicity and by very different mixtures of simulation, surveillance, and brute force. The control systems vary greatly between downtown areas, the upscale Westside suburbs in the Hills or on the Coast, ghettos and barrios of South and South–Central LA, and the Valley's middle-class suburbs and nearby working-class towns. Moreover, extreme variations exist between microenvironments in the various areas (e.g., downtown hotels and shopping centers versus adjacent minority or homeless areas). Davis portrays a much more complex, "post-liberal" topography than the homogenous landscape described in Bogard's hyperculturalized vision of simulated surveillance.

Modern theorists, operating more directly in the Marxian tradition, attribute political–economic factors much stronger, unambiguous causal power, and usually see postmodernism as a cultural manifestation of a major acceleration and globalization of capitalist commodification. Arguing that the old types of power and organization are still ascendent and, in some way, "behind" the new cultural forms, they challenge culturalism and textualism and see organizational and cultural postmodernization to be mostly an erosion of democracy. By contrast to Bell and Jameson, they revise earlier Marxist ideas of structure and materialism much more modestly, suggesting shifts in capitalist "regulation" or in capitalism's

---

[40] By contrast to Bogard's scenario, Davis describes how the Los Angeles Police Department increased employment of cutting-edge, computer-based technologies in underclass, minority areas at the same time that it escalated (i.e., rather than replacing) the use of direct surveillance and police paramilitarization. The widespread use of high-tech, aerial surveillance, enormous roundups of black youths in operation HAMMER, pervasive employment of physical and verbal intimidation (police spouting racist slogans while making the youths "kiss the pavement"), and police brutality constituted something more than simulated surveillance.

"structures of accumulation" (i.e., the institutional and cultural matrixes of capitalist finance, exchange, and production). Whether suggesting a sharper transformation from "Fordism" to "post-Fordism" or a milder shift to "neo-Fordism," they focus primarily on political–economic and organizational factors rather than on culture, and see current conditions as continuous with a long-term materialist pattern of change originating in early modernity and early capitalism.[41]

For example, in *The Condition of Postmodernity*, David Harvey (1989) suggests a transparent primacy of political economy and a Marxian historical logic implying a much less substantial shift in the relationship of culture and society than contended by postmodernists, post-traditionalists, or borderline theorists. He holds that capitalists, coping with severe accumulation crises or system-wide profit squeezes, explore new strategies of "time–space compression" to speed up the turnover time of capital and expand profit. Thus, they periodically reorganize capitalism. Harvey argues that capitalism's recent crises generated a global wave of restructuring of firms, high finance, and urban space. Consequent modes of instant exchange, information, communication, and entertainment, in his view, manifest postmodern sensibilities and styles. Harvey speaks scathingly of postmodernists dismissing "out of hand any suggestion that the 'economy' (however vague the word is understood) might be the determinant of cultural life even . . . 'in the last instance,'" even though the "odd thing about postmodern cultural production is how much sheer profit making is the determinant in the first instant" (Harvey 1989: 336).

Neo-Marxians stress an approximately 25-year shift from nationally based, state-guided capitalism to globalized, free-market capitalism. They see a break from the postwar era's vertically integrated, national firms to more decentralized, transnational, "network" organizations, characterized by much more "flexible" operations (e.g., a smaller core of permanent employees, globally outsourced manufacturing and assembling processes, reduced wages and benefits, weaker workplace and environmental regulation, and hyper-rationalized finance and research capacities concentrated in global cities). Eroding organized labor and the state's regulatory and welfare arms, heightened capital mobility means a "disembedding" of

---

[41] Summarizing the debate over the degree of divergence from postwar capitalism and over the issue of whether a genuine capitalist regime change has occurred requires another essay, e.g., see Kumar 1995: 6–65; Amin 1994, 1997; Ashley 1997: 95–183.

economic activities from their former local and regional modes of social, political, and cultural regulation. Instant finance transactions, highly abstract credit, unregulated deal-making, and very divergent, rapidly changing, and deeply polarized forms of organization, work, and consumption parallel cultural postmodernization. Decentered, individuated, fragmented, and liquid features of the nascent form of global capitalism blur the line between reality and illusion (e.g., Harvey 1989, 121–97; Harrison 1994; Antonio and Bonanno 1996).[42]

Although stressing material factors, neo-Marxian arguments converge, at some points, with postmodernist positions. For example, Harvey (1989: 156) sees post-Fordism generating "ferment, instability, and fleeting qualities of a postmodernist aesthetic that celebrates difference, ephemerality, spectacle, fashion, and the commodification of cultural forms." From this vantage point, contemporary capitalism's core emphasis on "flexibility" permits and even "causes" more varied, disjunctive, and globally dispersed organizational forms. Its diverse markets and firms, new regulatory environments, and increased globality decenter the postwar era's homogenous mass markets and national regulation systems. John Myles (1992: 171) suggests parallel changes in the micro-organization of the life-course; a shift from "order, predictability, and homogeneity" to post-Fordist "fragmentation, individualization, and dechronologization." But the emphases on centralized power, class polarization, and depth models diverge sharply from postmodernist and other culturalist positions. Neo-Marxists often concede the sociopolitical importance of the new social movements, but see them as primarily middle-class events. In their view, postmodernization's democratizing features are outweighed by its polarizing aspects, especially the increasing imbalance of power between labor and capital. Growing commodification of public goods means that increased "choice" is "gated" by class and that widely celebrated "democratic" innovations (i.e., access to the World Wide Web, cablevison, niche markets, and free spaces) sharpen the vast material and cultural gaps between the strata.

Postmodernization as endings: epochal or conjunctural rupture?

And if we are now at a point where we cannot imagine a world substantially different from our own, in which there is no apparent or obvious

---

[42] See Gordon's (1996) Marxist critique that downsizing arguments exaggerate the degree of capitalist restructuring.

way in which the future will represent a fundamental improvement over our current order, then we must also take into consideration the possibility that History itself might be at an end. (Francis Fukuyama 1992: 51)

Fukuyama's (1989) widely covered (in the US media) essay about "the end of history" celebrated the collapse of Soviet communism and declared an end of fundamental alternatives to neoliberalism. He suggested sensibilities inscribed elsewhere as "postmodern." Similarly, Jameson (1984b: 53) speaks of "inverted millenarianism" or the obsession with "the end of this or that," Bell ([1976] 1996: xxix) of "a long era . . . coming to a slow close" and "groping for a new vocabulary," and Baudrillard (1992: 3–4) of "History" coming "to an end . . . by deceleration, indifference, and stupefaction" ("The masses neutralized . . . by information, in turn neutralize history . . ."). Popular expressions of postmodern endings abound in media visions of apocalyptic dedemocratization (e.g., *Blade Runner, Robocop*), sweeping cultural exhaustion and disintegration (e.g., *Pulp Fiction; Trainspotting*), and highly ambiguous postliberal or protofascist imagery (e.g., cyberpunk comics or Laibach's music). Millenarian themes also run rampant in the "paranoid" fringe and talk radio; conspiratorial blathering about black helicopters, UN takeovers, Internal Revenue Service plots, and dreamingly absurd New Age schemes. One is tempted to dismiss all these tendencies summarily for their silliness or as mere *fin de siècle* epiphenomena, but their prevalence, intensity, and refracted taints of reality make them disturbingly problematical. "Endings" themes appear often above and are transparent in the ideas of *post*-traditionalism, *post*-Fordism, and *post*modernism, Thus, a detailed account of the topic would be redundant.

Claims about "the end of modernity," especially frequent in culturist discourses, are not framed in light of comparative knowledge of past epochal transformations. Although the scope of the ongoing transition is an empirical matter requiring inquiry, it is very unlikely that life will be altered nearly as radically as it was, let us say, by the agricultural revolution or by capitalist industrialism. My point is that the tacit meaning of the endings discourses is other than "the end of modernity," but this does not imply that the changes are insignificant. Nascent sea-changes are either overlooked or overstated, because their nature and scope are contingent, inquiries about them are often stymied by the lack of adequate categories and methods, and the prospects may be too new, too speculative, or too extreme to be addressed by academic journals, "responsible" media, and mainstream politics. Thus, confusion is likely to reign over such issues. Contrast, for example, postmodern cinema's thinly sublimated dystopian scenarios of an emergent garrison state of gated suburbs, urban security zones, and armed rural areas with the nightly news's good tidings about the growth of wealth, low inflation, inexpensive labor, deregulation, and welfare "reform."

It still can be argued, with some veracity, that much in the endings discourse is a recycling of Bell's ([1960] 1988: 402–7) *End of Ideology*, which contended, nearly 40 years ago, that the big political ideas of the time were "exhausted" and that "blueprints" and "social engineering" could not guarantee "social harmony." Regardless of convergent rejections of evolutionary historicism (especially of Marxist variants), Bell's argument is fundamentally different from the new positions. He stated emphatically that he was *not* suggesting an "end to utopia," but was attacking the "terrible simplifiers" and reifications that sap the life from utopian visions. Moreover, he posed his position during a sweeping expansion of material well-being, where optimism about unplanned and planned progress was high and disagreements over economic polarization and immiseration were largely over the method, pace, and scope of reductions (see Hodgson 1978: 67–98). By contrast, today's endings discourses suggest a nearly reversed context where ideas about the absence of resources and intractability of problems preclude such changes and imply, urge, or celebrate the end of utopian vision. Even Fukuyama fears that neoliberalism's prosaic nature opens contemporary capitalism to threats from the right. Putting claims of epochal rupture aside, the endings discourses suggest a terminus of the postwar era; especially its leading normative aspirations, sociopolitical bases, and left, social democratic, or centrist–right visions of modernization.[43]

Generally, endings discourses either hold that ennui, cacophony, and simulation undercut capacities to deal with the most serious social problems and institute change or that major planned changes are ruled out by their complexity and costs and by a new sobriety about large-scale interventions. The endings discourses imply a

[43] Aesthetically inclined critics often discuss determinate breaks with postwar styles of aesthetic modernism (e.g., in architecture, design, or cinema), but postmodernists seldom engage adequately the ebullient modernism of postwar Western society and socioeconomic thought. Their theorizing about today's conditions would benefit substantially if they attended much more closely at the backdrop of postwar "modernization" theories and political economy (e.g., see Hodgson 1978; Chandler 1977) than highly generalized conceptions of "modernity" or late nineteenth- and early twentieth-century "modern theories."

demise of postwar beliefs in progressive modernization; i.e., rationalization and inclusion, led by the state and other big institutions, will overcome the most severe social problems and create a more pacified, freer social order. Most thinkers see macroscopic interventions by public agencies to be moribund strategies, and the most pessimistic positions declare that even progressive social movements are doomed to fail. Baudrillard (1992: 4) holds that the "mass" absorbs and evaporates all "social, historical, and temporal transcendence"; Bauman (1992: 175–86), speaking of "living without an alternative," sees citizenship to be so closely identified with consumerism that seduction blunts all serious critique and reform (despite extreme "polarization of well-being and life chances"); and Fukuyama, equating the end of Soviet communism with the cusp of global neoliberalism, applauds the decline of misguided egalitarian impulses.[44] Even the "optimistic" new openings theorists criticize big state interventions, imply "solutionless" problems, and treat the demise of historicism as a positive event. Largely, postmodern endings discourse is the death bell of the "faith" that liberalism, social democracy, or socialism can be renewed to create a much more just, pacified, radical democratic future.

Even neo-Marxist, Claus Offe (1996: 36–7) holds that, today, socialism "is operationally empty" and the Left has no "concrete final ends." He sees these views to arise from a broader collapse of former beliefs in progress, planning, and "modernity" as a "desirable endpoint." Unhappily convergent with neoconservative Fukuyama, Offe holds that people now feel that public actions must fail and that minimalist proceduralism (i.e., only *formal* equality/rights) is inevitable. He charges that "'postmodernist' social and political trends" paralyze "collective agency" and pave the way for a major erosion or collapse of the European welfare states (Offe 1996: viii, ix, 3–4, 19, 33–54, 171–9).[45] Seeing the paralysis to be much more than an ideological reflex, however, Offe and other

---

[44] See Fukuyama's later (1996) fusion of his minimalist, elitist of vision of democracy, with a quasi-Durkheimian or communitarian antidote for the growing fragmentation of American society.

[45] Offe (1996: viii) states that

Membership densities, voter turnout, elite support, and trust in political institutions are all sharply declining . . . , while volatility, fragmentation, localism, fluctuation, and the rapidity of succession of issues and themes are all increasing. A widespread cult of difference leads individual actors to believe that other individual actors are insufficiently "similar" . . . to join forces with them in . . . robust, durable, and large-scale collective actors. Social classes at the point of production do not coincide anymore with "consumption classes," . . . What remains is informal association on the basis of ascriptive "passport identities" (such as gender, generation, territory, ethnicity).

neo-Marxists believe that the current political economic problems have no easy solutions and require new visions. Habermas (in Habermas and Michnik 1994: 11) states:

scarcely anyone . . . wants to criticize capitalism. And yet in the European Union alone we have seventeen million unemployed and no one knows . . . how to get out of this *jobless growth*. In other words we have to imagine something new to criticize this system. But the standard criticism can only be the realization of radical democracy, which naturally involves taming capitalism by means of a social state to a degree as yet unknown.

If these thinkers are correct, glaring inequalities are likely to worsen substantially and the endings discourses would become the harbinger of foundational threats to liberal democracy.

Conclusion: Postmodernism and the Renewal of "Social Theory"

The need for large and generous ideas in the direction of life was never more urgent than in the confusion of tongues, beliefs, and purposes that characterizes present life. (John Dewey [1929] 1988a: 248)

Postmodern perspectivism: end or renewal of social theory?

The primacy of culture as an analytical category and historical culturalization of the various spheres of life are major themes in the discourses discussed above, affirming Scott Lash's (1994: 214) view that cultural theories "rule the roost today." But critics argue that the concept of culture is now so inflated in value and used so indiscriminately that its analytical power is sharply diminished (see Kumar 1995: 112–21). In this regard, radical textualism, combining both of the above tendencies in the extreme, collapses society into culture, undercuts empirical and prudential judgments about divergent representations of obdurate realities, and, consequently, undermines the very bases of social theory. This radical perspectivism cannot address the lack of alternatives that postmodernism itself problematizes, especially in the current North American climate, where simulation, soundbites, and conspiracy theories abound as well as confusion and dissension about substantive democratization (which requires consensual rankings of needs, problems, and strategies). In these times, exclusively deconstructive aims and limpid ideas of diversity cannot inform the reconstructive projects we now face or even contest the reigning minimalist proceduralism. Total subversion of modern epistemological and normative criteria neutralizes the very "ideals" that must be nurtured (e.g., seeking agreement about pressing social problems, cultivating honest inquiry, and creating reliable knowledge) if our practices are ever going to be ruled less imperiously than they are now by self-interest, emotion, and power (Antonio 1991).

But radical textualism aside, perspectivist "suspicion" and deconstruction are still needed in addition to constructivist methods. The line between modernism and postmodernism is often hard to draw, because moderate perspectivists belong to the reflexive side of the Enlightenment. Each major wave of criticism further conditions, situates, and limits rationality, becoming the new borderline region (i.e., reflexive modernism) to be engaged and transformed by a later generation of critics. Open borders and appropriation of formerly opposing themes gives the Enlightenment more than nine lives and makes the efforts of the most ardent antirationalists maddeningly futile. Technocrats as well as antimodernists ignore the Enlightenment's radically skeptical side (e.g., see Levine 1996b). Science's legitimating metanarratives and broader Cartesian rationalism have been eroded at least as much by successive waves of internal criticism as by outside attacks. Critiques have periodically renewed Enlightenment thought in the face of major social changes and crises of representation (Hughes 1977; Kloppenberg 1986). It is still premature to tell if the current generation will do the same, but many of the postmodernist critics engage modern theory reflexively and carry on social theory in new form.[46]

Concluding his famous "Objectivity" essay, Max Weber ([1904] 1949: 112) stated that specialized researchers would eventually lose sight of the normative bases of their work and "consider the analysis of data as an end in itself." But he also asserted that "there comes a moment when the atmosphere changes" and the meaning "of the unreflectively utilized viewpoints becomes uncertain and the road is lost in the twilight." In these times, "the great cultural problems" shift, and scientists too prepare "to change . . . standpoint

---

[46] See e.g., Fraser 1989; Best and Kellner 1991; Brown 1993, 1995; Gottdiener 1993, 1994, 1995; Farganis 1994a, 1994b; Dickens 1994; Hollinger 1994; Ashley 1994, 1997; Seidman 1996a, 1996b.

and analytical apparatus and . . . view the streams of events from the heights of thought." In other words, the previously ignored foundational questions about the value of knowledge, or "what is worth knowing," are once again brought to the foreground, and science's presuppositions, problems, methods, and theories are debated and reshaped in light of new conditions and aspirations. Living in the context of the Second Industrial Revolution's multiple ruptures and nascent age of specialization, Weber theorized the basis of his own complex metatheoretical reflection. Seeing earlier programmatic ideas of social science to be too linear and naive for the new day, he called for perspectivist "objectivity" and more particular, complex, situated knowledge.[47] If today's endings discourses manifest a real transition, then the recent philosophical turn in social theory and return to the issues of "culture" and "modernity" herald the type of moment that Weber predicted. In this frame, postmodernism is a renewal of periodic efforts to readjust intellectual practices in light of major sociocultural change.

The need for social theory: mediating science and politics

Although the scope of the recent changes remains a topic of intense debate, postmodern discourses about the matter afford an opportunity to reflect on the nature of "social theory." Scientific or empirical–analytical methods and theories can shed light on value conflicts, but their legitimacy is entwined with the ideal of "objectivity" and, thus, do not provide an appropriate language for debating the value of knowledge or other normative matters. Also, in an age of disenchantment, where intellectuals and public figures, usually share, or pretend to share, the ideals of respecting value diversity and subjecting contested issues to undogmatic debate, public discourses about normative matters must go beyond religion and philosophy. If socio-political life is to be democratic and

[47] Usually heralded or attacked as the root of modern sociology's objectivist canon, Max Weber's "Objectivity" essay poses a highly conditioned perspectivism that is usually forgotten; in his view all sociocultural knowledge comes "from *particular points of view*" (i.e., each of us sees what is in our "own heart") and is partial and value-relevant. Stressing "the hair-line which separates science and faith," Weber mused about the West's "peculiar" cultural "belief" or "optimistic faith" in science, the "discursive," transitory nature of sociocultural knowledge, and the need for "many-sidedness" or "participation" in social science by different types of people with conflicting points of view (Weber [1904–17] 1949: 62, 81, 85, 94, 105, 107, 110–12).

not merely left to raw power or tradition, such issues must be discursively mediated and, thus, oriented to contestable historical claims and evaluated according to their consequences for conjoint life.

By contrast to sociological theory, "social theory," lay or professional, is an alternative language for debating normative issues, replacing transcendental and absolutist approaches as well as technocratic or scientistic positions. Although social theories raise analytical issues (i.e., epistemological questions follow from shifts in normative foundations) and are argued on empirical–historical grounds, they are "primarily" normative in thrust, constituting a systematic, discursive, and, therefore, public means for justifying socio-cultural practices or ways-of-life and the forms of knowledge and knowledge production that perpetuate them or help bring them into being.[48] Social theories pose world-pictures, societal regimes, and trajectories of change in response to nascent problems and possibilities. They do not escape ultimate theological or philosophical presuppositions, but their core substantive stances (e.g., about the virtues of gender equality, markets, redistribution, or democracy) are open to debate, riding largely on claims about actual or potential social consequences, rather than on ontological and ethical beliefs.

Although many later nineteenth- and early twentieth-century "theorists of society" prefigured social theory, they were too eager to justify their "new science of society" and too tied to the early Enlightenment dream of a self-justifying "science of morality" to clarify the nature of the new knowledge they were creating. Thus, normative issues were often masked as "truths" reflecting the inevitable direction of history or epistemological verities of "real" science. Secularizing earlier absolutism, these positions obscured their normative thrust and diminished, somewhat, the distinctive discursivity and public features that distinguish social theory from other intellectual practices. In the worst cases, "science" merely provided a new ultimate warrant for matters that were still closed to inquiry and debate.

[48] The key word here is "primarily," because the line between social theory and sociological theory is often thin (all types of theory, at least implicitly, have normative content and are put to diverse uses – predictive, interpretive, analytical, or normative). Thus, formal theories, employed to analyze market behavior, may also affirm it, and normative theories critical of capitalism may generate useful empirical hypotheses. But even if the borders of the two types of theorizing are hazy, attempting to clarify their general outlines is an important task, because they have different properties, call for different types of argument, and constitute different forms of knowledge.

The early social theories never had as much impact in the US as in Europe (Ross 1991). Secularization proceeded rapidly here without much mediation between the older theological standpoints and specialized science. Thus, during the post-World War Two height of the professionalization and institutionalization of sociology, American sociologists lacked a distinct discourse space for debating foundations and averting conflation of empirical–analytical approaches with normative positions. They generally saw the earlier European theories as a historical canon and source of empirical hypotheses, but considered theorizing in the classical ("armchair") style to be a defunct practice and its obsolescence as prima facie evidence of US sociology's arrival as a "real" science. The shelving of value questions fit well the postwar, US liberal consensus and popular versions of its "end of ideology" ideology (i.e., society without fundamental conflicts) (Hodgson 1978). Although today's conditions and theories break with the postwar climate, neopositivists still neglect the issue of normative foundations, ideologues still masquerade their views as science, and confusion still reigns about the meaning of social theory. Diverse sociologists criticize the metatheoretical tendencies in contemporary sociology (e.g., Turner 1990; Seidman 1991a, 1991b; Wallerstein 1997), but even critiques of navel-gazing do not diminish the need for undogmatic debate over foundations.

Given today's ominous global problems, cacophonous splits, and erosion of the old political models, the legitimacy of the most important ideals and institutions can no longer be taken for granted. In this context, it would be foolish to expect too much from sociology, especially given its discredited status among elite US decision-makers and a large portion of the general public. Yet if we are to retain the discipline's integrity and promise, however circumscribed by current culture and politics, we need social theory to help us clarify the meaning of our practices, take responsibility for their normative directions, and enhance their limited "autonomy" from other institutional spheres and powers. The point above made by Dewey still holds for these "postmodern" times; social theory is needed more than ever. In this light, Lyotard's (1984: 82) command to "wage war on totality" is dated as is Rorty's (1991: 191) view that Western liberals should declare thinkers, such as Loyola and Nietzsche, "crazy" and simply ignore basic challenges to liberal ideals.

Social theory cannot substitute for specialized research or empirical–analytical theory. In an age of specialization, it also depends on technical knowledge to grasp effectively its own limits, take account of possible consequences, and enjoy wider legitimacy distinct from philosophy and religion. There is also a need to go beyond Weber's limited hope for foundational discourse in times of crisis; competing social theories should help mediate between "science" and plural public spheres in good times as well as bad. The very appearance and wide popularity (beyond academe) of postmodern theories points to a possible renewal and fuller development of social theory. The burning problems of the day are all substantive ones, but success in these all-important concrete matters requires first clarifying what we are doing and why.

References

Albert, Michal. 1996a. Science, postmodernism, and the left: lessons from Alan Sokal's parody in *Social Text*. *Z Magazine* 9 (7–8): 64–9.

——. 1996b. Science wars. *Z Magazine* 9 (9): 12–14.

Amin, Ash, ed. 1994. *Post-Fordism: A Reader*. Oxford and Cambridge, MA: Blackwell.

——. 1997. Placing globalization. *Theory, Culture and Society* 14 (2): 123–37.

Anderson, Perry and Patrick Camiller, eds. 1994. *Mapping The West European Left*. London and New York: Verso.

Antonio, Robert J. 1991. Postmodern storytelling versus pragmatic truth-seeking: the discursive bases of social theory. *Sociological Theory* 9: 154–63.

——. 1995. Nietzsche's antisociology: subjectified culture and the end of history. *American Journal of Sociology* 101: 1–43.

Antonio, Robert J. and Alessandro Bonanno. 1996. Post-Fordism in the United States: the poverty of market-centered democracy. *Current Perspectives in Social Theory* 16: 3–32.

Aschheim, Steven E. 1992. *The Nietzsche Legacy in Germany 1890–1990*. Berkeley and Los Angeles: University of California Press.

Ashley, David. 1994. Postmodernism and antifoundationalism. In David Dickens and Andrea Fontana, eds, *Postmodernism and Social Inquiry*, 53–75. New York: Guilford.

——. 1997. *History Without a Subject: The Postmodern Condition*. Boulder, CO: Westview Press.

Babich, Babette E. 1994. *Nietzsche's Philosophy of Science: Reflecting Science on the Ground of Art and Life*. Albany: State University of New York Press.

Bat-Ami, Bar On. 1993. Marginality and epistemic privilege. In Linda Alcoff and Elizabeth Potter, eds, *Feminist Epistemologies*, 83–100. London and New York: Routledge.

Baudrillard, Jean. 1983a. *Simulations*, trans. Paul Foss, Paul Patton, and Phillip Beitchman. New York: Semiotext(e).

——. 1983b. *In the Shadow of the Silent Majorities or, The End of the Social and Other Essays*, trans. Paul Foss, John Johnston, and Paul Patton. New York: Semiotext(e).

——. 1987. *Forget Foucault*, trans. Nicole Dufresne, and *Forget Baudrillard*, intro. Slyvere Lotringer and trans. Phil Beitchman, Lee Hildreth, and Mark Polizzotti. New York: Semiotext(e).

——. 1988a. *The Ecstasy of Communication*, trans. Bernard and Caroline Schutze and ed. Slyvere Lotringer. New York: Semiotext(e).

——. 1988b. *America*, trans. Chris Turner. London and New York: Verso.

——. 1989. The anorexic ruins. In Dietmar Kamper and Christoph Wulf, *Looking Back on the End of the World*, trans. David Antal, 29–45. New York: Semiotext(e).

——. 1990. *Fatal Strategies*, ed. Jim Fleming and trans. Philip Beitchman and W. G. J. Niesluchowski. New York and London: Semiotext(e) and Pluto.

——. 1992. *The Illusion of the End*, trans. Chris Turner. Stanford, CA: Stanford University Press.

Bauman, Zygmunt. 1992. *Intimations of Postmodernity*. London and New York: Routledge.

——. 1993. *Postmodern Ethics*. Oxford and Cambridge, MA: Blackwell.

——. 1995a. *Life in Fragments: Essays on Postmodern Morality*. Oxford and Cambridge, MA: Blackwell.

——. 1995b. Making and unmaking of strangers. *Thesis Eleven* 43: 1–16.

——. 1996a. On communitarians and human freedom: or, how to square the circle. *Theory, Culture and Society* 13 (2): 79–90.

——. 1996b. Morality in the age of contingency. In Paul Heelas, Scott Lash, and Paul Morris, eds, *Detraditionalization: Critical Reflections on Authority and Identity*, 49–58. Oxford and Cambridge, MA: Blackwell.

Beck, Ulrich, 1992a. From industrial society to the risk society: questions of survival, social structure and ecological enlightenment. *Theory, Culture & Society* 9 (1): 97–123.

——. 1992b. *Risk Society: Towards a New Modernity*. London: Sage.

——. 1994. The reinvention of politics: towards a theory of reflexive modernization. In Ulrich Beck, Anthony Giddens, and Scott Lash, eds, *Reflexive Modernization: Politics, Tradition and Aesthetics in the Modern Social Order*, 1–55. Stanford, CA: Stanford University Press.

——. 1996. World risk society as cosmopolitan society? Ecological questions in a framework of manufactured uncertainties. *Theory, Culture & Society* 13 (4): 1–32.

Beck, Ulrich and Elisabeth Beck-Gernsheim. 1996. Individualization and "precarious freedoms": perspectives and controversies of a subject-centered sociology. In Paul Heelas, Scott Lash, and Paul Morris, eds, *Detraditionalization: Critical Reflections on Authority and Identity*, 23–48. Oxford and Cambridge, MA: Blackwell.

Bell, Daniel. [1960] 1988. *The End of Ideology: On the Exhaustion of the Political Ideas of the Fifties*. Cambridge, MA and London: Harvard University Press.

——. [1976] 1996. *The Cultural Contradictions of Capitalism*. New York: Basic Books.

——. 1980. *The Winding Passage. Essays and Sociological Journeys 1960–1980*. Cambridge, MA: ABT Books.

——. 1990a. Resolving the contradictions of modernity and modernism. *Society* 27 (3): 43–50.

——. 1990b. Resolving the contradictions of modernity and modernism (Part Two). *Society* 27 (4): 66–75.

Bellah, Robert N., Richard Madsen, William M. Sullivan, Ann Swidler, and Steven M. Tipton. 1986. *Habits of the Heart: Individualism and Commitment in American Life*. New York: Perennial Library.

Benhabib, Seyla. 1990. Epistemologies of postmodernism: a rejoinder to Jean-François Lyotard. In Linda Nicholson, ed., *Feminism/Postmodernism*, 107–30. London and New York: Routledge.

Bertens, Hans. 1995. *The Idea of Postmodernism: A History*. London and New York: Routledge.

Best, Steven and Douglas Kellner. 1991. *Postmodern Theory: Critical Interrogations*. London: Macmillan.

Bogard, William. 1992. Postmodernism one last time: a comment on Seidman et al. *Sociological Theory* 10: 241–3.

——. 1996. *The Simulation of Surveillance: Hypercontrol in Telematic Societies*. Cambridge and New York: Cambridge University Press.

Bordo, Susan. 1990. Feminism, postmodernism, and gender-scepticism. In Linda Nicholson, ed., *Feminism/Postmodernism*, 133–56. London and New York: Routledge.

Brown, Richard Harvey. 1993. Modern science: institutionalization of knowledge and rationalization of Power. *The Sociological Quarterly* 34: 153–68.

—— ed. 1995. *Postmodern Representations: Truth, Power, and Mimesis in the Human Sciences*. Urbana: University of Illinois Press.

Calhoun, Craig, ed. 1994. *Social Theory and the Politics of Identity*. Oxford and Cambridge, MA: Blackwell.

Calinescu, Matei. 1987. *Five Faces of Modernity: Modernism, Avant-Garde, Decadence, Kitsch, Postmodernism*. Durham, NC: Duke University Press.

Cerullo, John J. 1994. The epistemic turn: critical sociology and the "Generation of '68." *International Journal of Politics, Culture and Society* 8 (1): 169–81.

Chandler, Alfred D. 1977. *The Visible Hand: The Managerial Revolution in American Business*. Cambridge, MA and London: The Belknap Press of Harvard University Press.

Clawson, Dan. 1996a. From the editor's desk: influential decisions. *Contemporary Sociology: A Journal of Reviews* 25 (3): ix.

——. 1996b. From the editor's desk: a loose canon. *Contemporary Sociology: A Journal of Reviews* 25 (4): x.

——. 1996c. From the editor's desk: taking postmodernism seriously? *Contemporary Sociology: A Journal of Reviews* 25 (1): ix.

Clough, Patricia T. 1993a. On the brink of deconstructing sociology: critical reading of Dorothy Smith's standpoint epistemology. *The Sociological Quarterly* 34: 169–82.

——. 1993b. Response to Smith's response. *The Sociological Quarterly* 34: 193–4.

——. 1996. A theory of writing and experimental writing in the age of telecommunications: a response to Steven Seidman. *The Sociological Quarterly* 37: 721–33.

Davis, Mike. 1992. *City of Quartz: Excavating the Future in Los Angeles*. New York: Vintage Books.

Demerath, N. J., III. 1996. Postmortemism for postmodernism. *Contemporary Sociology: A Journal of Reviews* 25: 25–7.

Denzin, Norman K. 1986. Postmodern social theory. *Sociological Theory* 4: 194–204.

——. 1994. Postmodernism and deconstructionism. In David R. Dickens and Andrea Fontana, eds, *Postmodernism and Social Inquiry*, 182–202. New York: Guilford.

——. 1996. Sociology at the end of the century. *The Sociological Quarterly* 37: 743–52.

——. 1997. Whose sociology is it?: Comment on Huber. *American Journal of Sociology* 102: 1416–23.

Dewey, John. [1929] 1988a. *The Quest for Certainty. John Dewey: The Later Works, 1925–1953*. Vol. 4, ed. Jo Ann Boydston. 17 vols, Carbondale and Edwardsville: Southern Illinois University Press.

——. [1929–30] 1988b. *Individualism, Old and New. John Dewey: The Later Works, 1925–1953*. Vol. 5, ed. Jo Ann Boydston. 17 vols, Carbondale and Edwardsville: Southern Illinois University Press, 41–123.

——. [1935] 1987. *Liberalism and Social Action. John Dewey: The Later Works, 1925–1953*. Vol. 11, ed. Jo Ann Boydston, 17 vols, Carbondale and Edwardsville: Southern Illinois University Press, 1–65.

Dews, Peter. 1987. *Logics of Disintegration: Post-Structuralist Thought and the Claims of Critical Theory*. London and New York: Verso.

Dickens, R. David. 1994. North American theories of postmodern culture. In Dickens and Andrea Fontana, eds, *Postmodernism and Social Inquiry*, 76–100. New York: Guilford.

Dubord, Guy. [1967] 1983. *Society of the Spectacle*. Detroit: Black and Red.

Durkheim, Émile. [1893] 1964. *The Division of Labor in Society*, trans. George Simpson. New York: Free Press.

Ebert, Teresa L. 1995. The knowable good: post-al politics, ethics, and red feminism. *Rethinking Marxism* 8 (2): 39–59.

Etzioni, Amitai, ed. 1995. *Rights and the Common Good: The Communitarian Perspective*. New York: St Martin's Press.

Farganis, Sondra. 1994a. Postmodernism and feminism. In David R. Dickens and Andrea Fontana, eds, *Postmodernism and Social Inquiry*, 101–26. New York: Guilford.

——. 1994b. *Situating Feminism: From Thought to Action*. Thousand Oaks, CA: Sage.

Ferry, Luc and Alain Renaut. 1990. *French Philosophy of the Sixties: An Essay on Antihumanism*, trans. Mary H. S. Cattani. Amherst: University of Massachusetts Press.

Fish, Stanley. 1996. Professor Sokal's bad joke. *New York Times* May 21: A23.

Foucault, Michel. 1979. *Discipline and Punish: The Birth of the Prison*, trans. Alan Sheridan. New York: Vintage Books.

——. 1980. *Power/Knowledge: Selected Interviews and Other Writings 1972–1977*, ed. Colin Gordon and trans. Gordon, Leo Marshall, John Mepham, and Kate Soper. New York: Pantheon Books.

Frank, Tom. 1996. Textual reckoning. *In These Times* May 27: 22–4.

Fraser, Nancy. 1989. *Unruly Practices: Power, Discourse, and Gender in Contemporary Social Theory*. Minneapolis: University of Minnesota Press.

——. 1992. The uses and abuses of French discourse theories for feminist politics. *Theory, Culture & Society* 9 (1): 51–71.

——. 1993. Clintonism, welfare, and the antisocial wage: the emergence of a neoliberal political imaginary. *Rethinking Marxism* 6 (1): 9–23.

——. 1995a. From redistribution to recognition, dilemmas of justice in a "post-socialist" age. *New Left Review* 212: 68–93.

——. 1995b. Politics, culture, and the public sphere: toward a postmodern conception. In Linda Nicholson and Steven Seidman, eds, *Social Postmodernism: Beyond Identity Politics*, 287–312. Cambridge and New York: Cambridge University Press.

——. 1996. Multiculturalism and gender equity: the US "difference" debates revisited. *Constellations* 3: 61–72.

Fraser, Nancy and Linda Nicholson. 1988. Social criticism without philosophy: an encounter between feminism and postmodernism. *Theory, Culture & Society* 5 (2–3): 373–94.

Fukuyama, Francis. 1989. The end of history? *The National Interest* 16 (Summer): 3–18.

——. 1992. *The End of History and the Last Man*. London and New York: Penguin Books.

——. 1996. *Trust: The Social Virtues and the Creation of Prosperity*. New York: Free Press.

Giddens, Anthony. 1990. *The Consequences of Modernity*. Stanford, CA: Stanford University Press.

——. 1991. *Modernity and Self Identity: Self and Society in the Late Modern Age*. Stanford, CA: Stanford University Press.

——. 1992. *The Transformation of Intimacy: Sexuality, Love and Eroticism in Modern Societies*. Stanford, CA: Stanford University Press.

——. 1994a. Living in a post-traditional society. In Ulrich Beck, Anthony Giddens, and Scott Lash, eds, *Reflexive Modernization: Politics, Tradition and Aesthetics in the Modern Social Order*, 56–109. Stanford, CA: Stanford University Press.

——. 1994b. *Beyond Left and Right: The Future of Radical Politics*. Stanford, CA: Stanford University Press.

Gitlin, Todd. 1995. *The Twilight of Common Dreams: Why America is Wracked by Culture Wars*. New York: Free Press.

Gordon, David M. 1996. *Fat and Mean: The Corporate Squeeze of Working Americans and the Myth of Managerial "Downsizing"*. New York: Free Press.

Gottdiener, Mark. 1993. Ideology, foundationalism, and sociological theory. *The Sociological Quarterly* 34: 653–71.

——. 1994. Semiotics and postmodernism. In David R. Dickens and Andrea Fontana, eds, *Postmodernism and Social Inquiry*, 155–81. New York: Guilford.

——. 1995. *Postmodern Semiotics: Material Culture and the Forms of Postmodern Life*. Oxford and Cambridge MA: Blackwell.

Gutmann, Amy, ed. 1994. *Multiculturalism: Examining the Politics of Recognition*. Princeton, NJ: Princeton University Press.

Habermas, Jürgen. 1981. Modernity versus postmodernity. *New German Critique* 22: 3–14.

Habermas, Jürgen and Adam Michnik. 1994. Overcoming the past (discussion ch. Adam Krzeminski). *New Left Review* 203: 3–16.

Hanson, F. Allan. 1993. *Testing: Social Consequences of the Examined Life*. Berkeley and Los Angeles: University of California Press.

Haraway, Donna. 1988. Situated knowledges: the science question in feminism and the privilege of partial perspective. *Feminist Studies* 14: 575–99.

Harding, Sandra. 1990. Feminism, science, and the anti-Enlightenment critiques. In Linda Nicholson, ed., *Feminism/Postmodernism*, 83–106. London and New York: Routledge.

Harrison, Bennett. 1994. *Lean and Mean: The Changing Landscape of Corporate Power in the Age of Flexibility*. New York: Basic Books.

Hartsock, Nancy C. M. 1984. *Money, Sex, and Power: Toward a Feminist Historical Materialism*. Boston, MA: Northeastern University Press.

——. 1987. The feminist standpoint: developing the ground for a specifically feminist historical materialism. In Sandra Harding, ed., *Feminism and Methodology*, 157–80. Bloomington and Indianapolis: Indiana University Press.

Harvey, David. 1989. *The Condition of Postmodernity: An Enquiry into the Origins of Cultural Change*. Oxford and Cambridge, MA: Blackwell.

Hassan, Ihab. 1985. The culture of postmodernism. *Theory, Culture & Society* 2 (3): 119–31.

Heelas, Paul. 1996. Introduction: detraditionalization and its rivals. In Paul Heelas, Scott Lash, and Paul Morris, eds, *Detraditionalization: Critical Reflections on Authority and Identity*, 1–20. Oxford and Cambridge, MA: Blackwell.

Hirsh, Arthur. 1981. *The French New Left: An Intellectual History From Sartre to Gorz*. Boston, MA: South End Press.

Hodgson, Godfrey, 1978. *America in Our Time*. New York. Vintage Books.
Hollinger, Robert. 1994. *Postmodernism and The Social Sciences: A Thematic Approach*. Thousand Oaks, CA: Sage.
Huber, Joan. 1995. Centennial essay: institutional perspectives on sociology. *American Journal of Sociology* 101: 194–216.
——. 1997. Of facts and fables: reply to Denzin. *American Journal of Sociology* 102: 1423–9.
Hughes, H. Stuart. 1977. *Consciousness and Society: The Reorientation of European Social Theory 1890–1930*. New York: Vintage Books.
Huyssen, Andreas. 1984. Mapping the postmodern. *New German Critique* 33: 5–52.
Jameson, Fredric. 1984a. Foreword. In Jean-François Lyotard, *The Postmodern Condition: A Report on Knowledge*, trans. Geoff Bennington and Brian Massumi, Minneapolis: University of Minnesota Press, vii–xxi.
——. 1984b. Postmodernism, or the cultural logic of late capitalism. *New Left Review* 146: 53–92.
——. 1984c. Periodizing the 60s. In Sohnya Sayres, Anders Stephanson, Stanley Aronowitz, and Fredric Jameson, eds, *The 60s Without Apology*, 178–209. Minneapolis: Univeristy of Minnesota Press.
——. 1988. Cognitive mapping. In Cary Nelson and Lawrence Grossberg, eds, *Marxism and the Interpretation of Culture*, 347–57. Urbana and Chicago, IL: University of Illinois Press.
——. 1991. *Postmodernism, or, The Cultural Logic of Late Capitalism*. Durham, NC: Duke University Press.
——. 1996. *Late Marxism: Adorno, or The Persistence of the Dialectic*. London and New York: Verso.
Kaufman, Cynthia and JoAnn Martin. 1994. The chasm of the political in postmodern theory. *Rethinking Marxism* 7 (4): 86–102.
Keller, Evelyn Fox. 1996. Comment in the section "The Sokal hoax: a forum." *Linguafranca* July/August: 58.
Kellner, Douglas. 1988. Postmodernism as social theory: some challenges and problems. *Theory, Culture & Society* 5 (2–3): 239–69.
Kloppenberg, James T. 1986. *Uncertain Victory: Social Democracy and Progressivism and American Thought, 1870–1920*. Oxford and New York: Oxford University Press.
Knorr-Cetina, Karin. 1981. *The Manufacture of Knowledge: An Essay on the Constructivist and Contextual Nature of Science*. Oxford: Pergamon.
Koelb, Clayton, ed. 1990. *Nietzsche as Postmodernist: Essays Pro and Contra*. Albany: State University of New York Press.
Kumar, Krishan. 1995. *From Post-Industrial to Post-modern Society: New Theories of the Contemporary World*. Oxford and Cambridge, MA: Blackwell.
Laclau, Ernesto and Chantal Mouffe. 1985. *Hegemony and Socialist Strategy: Towards a Radical Democratic Politics*. London and New York: Verso.
Lasch, Christopher. [1979] 1991. *The Culture of Narcissism: American Life in an Age of Diminishing Expectations*. New York and London: W. W. Norton.

——. 1995. *The Revolt of the Masses and The Betrayal of Democracy*. New York and London: W. W. Norton.

Lash, Scott. 1994. Expert-systems or situated interpretation? culture and institutions in disorganized capitalism. In Ulrich Beck, Anthony Giddens, and Scott Lash, eds, *Reflexive Modernization: Politics, Tradition and Aesthetics in the Modern Social Order*, 198–215. Stanford, CA: Stanford University Press.

Latour, Bruno. 1993. *We Have Never Been Modern*, trans. Catherine Porter. Cambridge, MA: Harvard University Press.

Latour, Bruno and Steve Woolgar. 1986. *Laboratory Life: The Construction of Scientific Facts*. Princeton, NJ: Princeton Univeristy Press.

Lefebvre, Henri. [1962] 1995. *Introduction to Modernity: Twelve Preludes September 1959-May 1961*, trans. John Moore. London and New York: Verso.

Leinberger, Paul and Bruce Tucker. 1991. *The New Individualists: The Generation After the Organization Man*: New York: HarperCollins.

Levine, George. 1996a. Comment in the section "The Sokal hoax: a forum." *Linguafranca* July–August: 64.

——. 1996b. Science and citizenship: Karl Pearson and the ethics of epistemology. *Modernism/Modernity* 3 (3): 137–43.

——. 1996c. Letter to the editor in section "Sokal's hoax: an exchange." *New York Review of Books* October 3: 54.

Lyotard, Jean-François. 1984. *The Postmodern Condition: A Report on Knowledge*, trans. Geoff Bennington and Brian Massumi. Minneapolis: University of Minnesota Press.

Mellucci, Alberto. 1989. *Nomads of the Present: Social Movements and Individual Needs in Contemporary Society*. Philadelphia, PA: Temple University Press.

——. 1996a. *Challenging Codes: Collective Action in the Information Age*. Cambridge and New York: Cambridge University Press.

——. 1996b. *The Playing Self: Person and Meaning in the Planetary Society*. Cambridge and New York: Cambridge University Press.

Myles, John. 1992. Is there a post-Fordist life-course? In Walter A. Heinz, ed, *Institutions and Gatekeeping in the Life Course*, 171–85. Weinheim: Deutscher Studies Verlag.

Nicholson, Linda, ed. 1990a. *Feminism/Postmodernism*. London and New York: Routledge.

——. 1990b. Introduction. In Nicholson, ed., *Feminism/Postmodernism*, 1–16. London and New York: Routledge.

Nicholson, Linda and Steven Seidman, eds. 1995a. *Social Postmodernism: Beyond Identity Politics*. Cambridge and New York: Cambridge University Press.

——. 1995b. Introduction. In Nicholson and Seidman, eds, *Social Postmodernism: Beyond Identity Politics*, 1–35. Cambridge and New York: Cambridge University Press.

Nietzsche, Friedrich. [1873–6] 1983. *Untimely Meditations,* trans. R. J. Hollingdale. Cambridge and New York: Cambridge University Press.

——. [1886] 1966. *Beyond Good and Evil: Prelude to a Philosophy of the Future,* trans. Walter Kauffmann. New York: Vintage Books.

——. [1883–8] 1968a. *The Will to Power,* trans. Walter Kauffmann and R. J. Hollingdale. New York: Vintage Books.

——. [1887] 1969. *On the Genealogy of Morals,* trans. Walter Kaufmann and R. J. Hollingdale, and [1888] *Ecce Homo,* trans. Walter Kaufmann. New York: Vintage Books.

——. [1888] 1968b. *Twilight of the Idols* and *The Anti-Christ,* trans. R. J. Hollingdale. London and New York: Penguin Books.

Offe, Claus. 1996. *Modernity and the State.* Cambridge, MA: MIT Press.

Parsons, Talcott. 1971. *The System of Modern Societies.* Englewood Cliffs, NJ: Prentice Hall.

Piccolomini, Michele. 1996. Sustainable development, collective action, and new social movements. *Research in Social Movements, Conflict and Change* 19: 183–208.

Piccone, Paul. 1988. Reinterpreting 1968: mythology on the make. *Telos* 77: 7–43.

——. 1995. Postmodern populism. *Telos* 103: 45–86.

Plant, Sadie. 1996. *The Most Radical Gesture: The Situationalist International in a Postmodern Age.* London and New York: Routledge.

Richardson, Laurel. 1991. Postmodern social theory: representational practices. *Sociological Theory* 9: 173–9.

——. 1996. The political unconscious of the university professor. *The Sociological Quarterly* 37: 735–42.

Robbins, Bruce and Andrew Ross. 1996. Mystery, science theater. *Linguafranca* July–August: 54–7.

Rorty, Richard. 1991. *Objectivity, Relativism, and Truth: Philosophical Papers.* Vol. 1. Cambridge and New York. Cambridge University Press.

Rosenau, Pauline Marie. 1992. *Post-Modernism and the Social Sciences: Insights, Inroads, and Intrusions.* Princeton, NJ: Princeton University Press.

Ross, Dorothy. 1991. *The Origins of American Social Science.* Cambridge and New York: Cambridge University Press.

Saatkamp, Herman J. Jr., ed. 1995. *Rorty and Pragmatism: The Philosopher Responds to His Critics.* Nashville and London: Vanderbilt University Press.

Sandel, Michael J. 1996. *Democracy's Discontent: America In Search of a Public Philosophy.* Cambridge MA and London: The Belknap Press of Harvard University Press.

Schrift, Alan D. 1990. *Nietzsche and the Question of Interpretation: Between Hermeneutics and Deconstruction.* London and New York: Routledge.

——. 1995. *Nietzsche's French Legacy: A Genealogy of Poststructuralism.* London and New York: Routledge.

Seidman, Steven. 1991a. The end of sociological theory: the postmodern hope. *Sociological Theory* 9: 131–46.

——. 1991b. Postmodern anxiety: the politics of epistemology. *Sociological Theory* 9: 180–90.

——. 1992. Word power: is rhetoric all there is? *Sociological Theory* 10: 255–8.

——. 1995. Deconstructing queer theory or the undertheorization of the social and ethical. In Linda Nicholson and Seidman, eds, *Social Postmodernism: Beyond Identity Politics* (Cambridge and New York: Cambridge University Press.

——. 1996a. The political unconscious of the human sciences. *Sociological Quarterly* 37: 699–719.

——. 1996b. Pragmatism & sociology: a response to Clough, Denzin and Richardson. *Sociological Quarterly* 37: 753–9.

Sennett, Richard. [1974] 1992. *The Fall of Public Man*. New York and London: W. W. Norton.

Smith, Dorothy, E. 1993. High noon in textland: a critique of Clough. *Sociological Quarterly* 34: 183–92.

Sokal, Alan, D. 1996a. Transgressing the boundaries: toward a transformative hermeneutics of quantum gravity. *Social Text* 46–7: 217–52.

——. 1996b. A physicist experiments with cultural studies. *Linguafranca* May–June: 62–4.

——. 1996c. Alan Sokal replies. . . . *Linguafranca* July–August: 57.

Stabile, Carol A. 1994. Feminism without guarantees: the misalliances and missed alliances of postmodernist social theory. *Rethinking Marxism* 7 (1): 48–61.

Staples, William G. 1997. *The Culture of Surveillance: Discipline and Social Control in the United States*. New York: St Martin's Press.

Touraine, Alain. 1992. Beyond social movements? *Theory, Culture & Society* 9 (1): 125–45.

——. 1995. *Critique of Modernity*, trans. David Macey. Oxford and Cambridge, MA: Blackwell.

Turner, Jonathan H. 1990. The misuse and use of metatheory. *Sociological Forum* 5: 37–53.

van den Berg, Axel. 1996. Liberalism without reason. *Contemporary Sociology: A Journal of Reviews* 25: 19–25.

Wallerstein, Immanuel. 1997. Social science and the quest for a just society. *American Journal of Sociology* 102: 1241–57.

Weber, Max. [1904–17] 1949. *The Methodology of the Social Sciences*, ed. and trans. Edward A. Shils and Henry A. Finch. New York: Free Press.

West, Cornel. 1989. *The American Evasion of Philosophy: A Genealogy of Pragmatism*. Madison: University of Wisconsin Press.

——. 1993. *Beyond Eurocentrism and Multiculturalism: Prophetic Thought in Postmodern Times*. Vol. 1. Monroe, ME: Common Courage Press.

——. 1994. A conversation with Cornel West, int. William Olson and Antonio Callari. *Rethinking Marxism* 7 (4): 8–27.

Wood, Ellen Meiksins. 1986. *The Retreat From Class: A New "True" Socialism*. London and New York: Verso.

——. 1995. *Democracy Against Capitalism: Renewing Historical Materialism.* Cambridge and New York: Cambridge University Press.

2 A Thesaurus of Experience: Maurice Natanson, Phenomenology, and Social Theory

Mary F. Rogers

Today social theory brings together such scholars as literary theorist Eve Kosofsky Sedgwick, philosophers Sandra Lee Bartky and Susan Bordo, and sociologists Patricia Hill Collins, Arthur W. Frank, R. W. Connell, and Dorothy E. Smith as well as disciplinary fugitives Judith Butler, bell hooks, Evelyn Fox Keller, and Patricia J. Williams. These theorists illustrate a "linguistic turn" in much social theorizing over the past thirty years. They also illustrate a more consequential shift, an *experiential turn* that focuses theoretical attention on the wherewithal and presuppositions of human experiencing. In the social sciences that shift shows up in renewed engagement with those qualitative methods where narrators' experiences command center stage (see Reinharz 1992; Riessman 1990; Chase 1995). The experiential turn also finds expression in feminist, queer, and Afrocentric theory where the experiences of historically excluded groups focus multiple theoretical spotlights. This turn is observable in critical as well as feminist pedagogy, too (see Friere 1970; hooks 1994).

Thirty years ago, Michel Foucault ([1966] 1973: 320–1) observed as well as furthered the experiential turn. He saw that social theory

has been unable to avoid . . . searching for the locus of a discourse that would be neither of the order of reduction nor of the order of promise: a discourse whose tension would keep separate the empirical and the transcendental, while being directed at both; a discourse that would make it possible to analyse [the human being] as a subject, that is, as a locus of knowledge which has been empirically acquired but referred back as closely as possible to what makes it possible.

Foucault goes on: "Such a complex, overdetermined, and necessary role has been performed in modern thought by the analysis of actual experience" using "a discourse of mixed nature." In that context Foucault takes note of the "network" linking positivist or eschatalogical thought and "reflections inspired by phenomenology" (p. 321). That network of meanings may help account for the experiential turn, but my interest is more modest: it lies with the phenomenological side of things, specifically Maurice Natanson's philosophical labors. Natanson's work offers philosophical grounding for that "discourse of mixed nature" Foucault mentions and, therefore, a fertile meeting ground for theorists insistent on honoring people's lived experiences. At root, Natanson's work lets us "excavate the ground [we stand] on" so as to see how we establish any "chance of being ordinary" (Barker 1993: 48, 185).

This small space leaves me feeling like a frustrated tour guide, but I reject that metaphor in favor of one from Natanson. Writing about Robert Burton's "Equivocations of Melancholy," he makes of Burton's project a thesaurus and of Burton "a rather cabalistic thesaurean" (Natanson 1989: 130). I turn the tables here, making of Natanson's work a dense thesaurus and of Natanson himself a towering thesaurean of human experiencing.

I begin with four terms I take to be phenomenology's bedrock, namely, consciousness, intentionality, constitution, and sedimentation. Then I quickly turn to five other terms – the mundane, expression, enclave, horizon, and madness – for more detailed exploration before finally looking at common sense. Together, these nine terms are capable of anchoring social theorizing about selfhood and social location, human dignity and social bonds, community and freedom. Terms alone, however, do not a thesaurus make. A thesaurus presupposes an authoritative voice like Natanson's, which resounds with modernist conviction and postmodernist relevance.

Phenomenology's Bedrock

Phenomenology is philosophy's commitment to consciousness. In human consciousness phenomenologists find the roots of reality, the possibility of society and selfhood, the makings of history and culture. Everything of phenomenological interest comes back to the noetic/noematic flow of consciousness whereby experiencing proceeds and worlds get made, including individuals' biographies and communities. The hallmark of consciousness is its intentionality, its insistent "consciousness-of."

Intentionality is constitutive. Consciousness makes realities; above all, it constitutes meanings. Ultimately, the "observer's experience . . . is taken as the object of phenomenological inspection" (Natanson 1956: 245). Yet no one's experience is absolutely idiosyncratic, despite its profound singularity. Meanings get sedimented as people make and share worlds together. Sedimentations of meaning into various "finite provinces" make for different worlds of experiencing built atop the world of everyday life. Thus, the world of theory or the world of drama presupposes the *lebenswelt* ("life-world"), where consciousness establishes a home while making its most recalcitrant meanings.

As I turn now to other entries in the thesaurus, I adopt an eidetic approach. Eidetics involves "the irrealization of the particular, start[ing] with something existent and then tak[ing] it as an example of a type" (Natanson 1973: 69). For each theorist mentioned earlier, I take some published iteration as illuminating their social theorizing. I thus typify their work by treating one or two formulations as exemplary. In turn, I show how those iterations gain further philosophical acuity in the dense context of Natanson's findings.

The Mundane and Human Expression

The mundane world is an accomplishment of the highest order. That consciousness constitutes what passes for "the world" is a finding at the heart of Natanson's work (as well as Berger and Luckmann's [1967] social constructionism). Natanson (1974: 101) says common sense "is at first approximation our natural habitat." What he calls "mundanity" comprises "taking-for-granted, naivete, unsophistication" among its "complex, rich modes." Time and again, Natanson (1973: 127) shows that the mundane, the ordinary, the familiar, the unremarkable enfold "an experiential density in everydayness which commands philsophical respect."

The mundane commonly commands respect among the theorists at hand. Bartky (1990: 119), for instance, looks at how heterosexual women "inscribe and reinscribe [their] subjection in the fabric of the ordinary." Like many feminist theorists, she links subordination not only to federal policies, popular culture, and gendered schools but also to such mundane activities as "the duties we are happy to perform and . . . what we thought were the innocent pleasures of everyday life." Much to her credit and expressive of her phenomenological bent, Bartky in no way denies the pleasure of soothing a husband's hurt in the wake of defeat. Rather, she theoretically complicates (heterosexual) women's mundane lives by probing the ins and outs of their "common sense." Bartky lays grounds for what Bordo (1993: 167) describes as "a disourse that will enable us to account for the subverison of potential rebellion." These philosophers imply what Natanson (1974: 101) articulates: common sense is less "a special faculty of the mind" than "a mark of sociality, an emblem of . . . involvement in the public world." It points to "the character of social order, its traditions, its formulas for handling problems, and its recipes for actions." More broadly, they illustrate Natanson's (1973: 17) finding that "the search for self-knowledge coincides with the illumination of mundanity."

Smith's work also resonates with Natanson's, which comes as no surprise in view of her phenomenological bent. Often Smith (1990: 4) focuses on "the practices of thinking and writing . . . that convert what people experience directly in their everyday/everynight world into forms of knowledge in which people as subjects disppear and in which their perspectives on their own experience are transposed and subdued by the magisterial forms of objectifying discourse." Smith discloses what Natanson (1973: 5; 1969: 91) sees as the "infinitely rich logic" built into common sense as well as the philosophy implicit "within mundane existence." Such disclosures affirm people's lived experiences in the world of everyday life while chastening theoretical claims to have superseded common sense. Put differently, phenomenology vindicates common sense by showing that the wind filling the sails of theorists comes up within and gains momentum from the life-world. As Smith (1990: 18) puts it, objectified knowledge presupposes the "suppression of the local and particular as a site of knowledge." Such knowledge takes shape uninformed by philosophy and wrested from lived realities.

In this broad context let me quote Natanson at length. Here he (1968: 504) first refers to "the promise of multiple descriptions, destined to knock against and upset each other." He then forswears "phenomenological method" as a universalizing tactic, one which announces absolute results, a tower of essences. . . . The conception of phenomenology which underlies my efforts must be understood on a different plane. The universalizing impulse of phenomenology commits no outrage on concrete presentations and their manifold contexts and distinctive differences. Quite to the contrary, phenomenology turns with great patience to the detailed and the minute and seeks to illuminate the specificity and the uniqueness of what gives us a world. The result is a liberation of detail, an epiphany of the familiar.

In that liberation and throughout that epiphany one finds human expression. There, too, one often finds language. As Natanson (1986: 47) observes, "in the dense hive of mundane chatter, in the argot of everyday banter and barter, language hurtles or traces its own laconic arc." That arc knows few practical limits. Natanson continues:

The elasticity of the idiom of daily discourse, the vernacular, the collo-quial, empowers conceptualization in common-sense thinking. Nor is the correct word always the empowering word. Here ordinary language shares something with poetry: the direct, effective word – the word which *works* – is not always chosen for use; the oblique or stray word may give to the casual scene, the offhand encounter, an auditory flush of sudden awareness.

"Nor," to repeat, "is the correct word always the empowering word." What is terminologically correct may be stingy or pomp-ous; it may unashamedly lie or hypocritically fib. Hooks (1989: 5, 9) recalls: "I was never taught absolute silence, I was taught that it was important to speak but to talk a talk that was in itself a si-lence." Her work involves "Moving from [such] silence into speech"; hers is "the expression of . . . movement from object to subject."

Such expression exceeds language, even interpretation (cf. Natanson 1968: 503). Indeed, expression eludes observation when the typificatory schemes orienting people in a sociohistorical life-world render it invisible. Consider what Collins (1994) says about some *types* of individuals: "On the most basic level survival is a form of resistance." Williams (1991: 195) makes a similar point: "The very existence of such a statistical category [black profes-sional women] is against all the odds." Like Collins, Williams sees survival in unexpected forms as expressing resistance to the life-world's typificatory structure. To survive means to have held at bay the forms of exclusion and oppression entailing a deflation of self or a leaking of self onto the uncharted territory of madness. To say the utter least, then, expression often lies beyond interpretive reach. Social silences hide some people's lived meanings.

Enclaves and Horizons

Enclaves also often hide individuals' lived meanings. Here I back into the meaning of "enclave" in Schutz's and Natanson's work using Frank's (1995: 9) observations about illness: "In modernist thought people are well *or* sick. Sickness and wellness shift definitively as to which is foreground and which is background at any given moment. In the remission society [of cancer survivors] the foreground and background of sickness and health constantly shade into each other." Membership in the remission society catapults the individual way beyond either/or: "In the beginning is an interruption. Disease interrupts a life, and illness then means living with perpetual interruption" (Frank 1995: 56). Living in the remission society entails the rupture of reliable familiarity, a seepage of taken-for-grantedness, and restricted access to the world of everyday life one once readily entered for long sweeps of time. Becoming a cancer survivor or a person with AIDS (PWA) means no less than that one's experiences again and again (repetition) involve enclaves where "and so forth and so on" (continuity) holds newly lived, painful sway. One final observation, implicit in Frank's work, concerns how easily we "forget" that hospitals are total institutions (Goffman 1961) – custodial, high-surveillance organizations where issues of dignity and personhood weigh heavily on inmates. Although hospitals, unlike prisons and monasteries, usually claim their inmates for relatively short periods, residence there *and the prospect of repeated stays* help establish the enclaves experienced among participants in the remission society.

Natanson (1986: 96) says Schutz saw that finite "provinces of meaning overlap, that meaning in the paramount reality [everyday life] may be infiltrated by meaning elements which are derivative from" other worlds. Natanson (1986: 95) describes such enclaves of experience as "othernesses . . . which impinge on placement in one 'world' or another." Here "otherness" means not that one's experience "could be otherwise." Rather, "Otherness is common sense stripped not only of the possibility of being 'otherwise,' but negated in what it is" (Natanson 1986: 107). Thus, "What lies within the enclave . . . includes an intensity of experience concerning several provinces of meaning, a remembered, anticipated, imagined, or phantasied state of affairs in which only the aspect of experience relevant to the enclave is attended to while the rest – an intense remainder – is not only set at distance but is apperceived as anonymous" (Natanson 1986: 111).

The enclave of *my* current experiencing, for instance, lies where the world of theory intersects the world of the remission society where my consociates Bruce, Cheryl, Don, Gen, and Yolanda join innumerable other contemporaries living one and-so-forth-and-so-on day at a time. I cannot think about enclaves and illness without remembering their experiences and phantasizing them *well* once and for all instead of again and again, one day at a time. Within this enclave, too, are memories of people gone because of or engaged in fierce combat with AIDS – Kathy, Mark, Phil, and countless others. So the "arrow of [my] intentionality" here and now cannot take "flight" toward a single destination; it cannot "be fitted into time's bow" (Natanson 1986: 50) except by stretching that bow into the past, while sensing how it continuously lurches forward into the next moment and the next and the next of the future ahead of us (hopefully).

"Enclave" offers grounds for talking about being "outsiders" who are "within" (Collins 1986). It provides for experiences like Williams's, where everyday life goes astray as one remembers humiliations and hurts from times past but not gone. Williams cannot, for example, leave behind the world of theory as she walks on city streets. With her she carries knowledge of the harsh demographics treating her as an "exception" while sanitizing the homelessness, despair, and dehumanization of other African Americans. Within parentheses, creating a kind of enclave in her own essay, Williams (1991: 195) writes, "(Yet, as a social statistic, sometimes I feel less like I'm single than socially widowed. Sometimes when I walk down the street and see some poor black man lying over a heating vent, I feel as if I'm looking into the face of my companion social statistic, my lost mate.)"

Broadly, "enclave" resonates with Simmel's and others' observations about marginality, "strangers," anonymity (as Natanson [1986] emphasizes), and the existential project of transcendence. "Enclave" surely resonates, as Natanson indicates, with Schutz's findings about multiple realities. Here, though, I touch upon how "enclave" resonates with "horizon," that is, how "punctured" experiences disclose the plentitude of possibilities inherent in our intending of any object. Doing so positions us to examine madness before finally visiting common sense.

The idealizations of repetition ("again and again") and continuity ("and so forth and so on") concern the temporal horizons of experiencing, the individual's prereflective sense of having experienced this (type of) thing before and of being able to experience it (or its type) again. More generally, "horizon" concerns the "stance or line of access in terms of which experience presents itself" (Natanson 1973: 37). The concept points to the fundamental incompleteness of any experience or, more positively, to possibilities integral to the experience of any object. As I once put it, "Individuals intend objects not as extractions from a wealth of experiences but as filaments of a stream of experience" (Rogers 1983: 26). Mixed metaphors aside, such filaments get tangled together in the enclaves of an individual's experiences. In some prospectively maddening sense enclaves emerge in an individual's experiences when horizons bump into or jar one another.

Broadly, horizons concern expectations built up and possibilities given shape as the individual's stream of experiencing goes on and on. As experience instantiates some possibilities, it also points toward other possibilities. Experience thus points beyond itself. Consider this experience here and now. Like you, I suppose, I am in the world of theory trying to instantiate the possibility of illuminating human experiencing. Like all instantiations, this one is radically modest. Its utter specificity can be meaningful only to the extent that its boundaries can in principle be burst, reconfigured, reinforced, or adjusted slightly in the wake of enacting other such possibilities. If I sensed that this one experience here and now struggling with Natanson's work (never mind hooks's, Bartky's, or the others') held no further possibilities, experiential dizziness would ensue. I *need* to sense that this experience opens onto possibilities beyond itself. In the natural attitude I take such possibilities for granted.

Yet sometimes my experiences in one world get tangled up with those from another world and, therefore, one set of possibilities impinges on another set so as to make of my here-and-now an enclave. Chasing my earlier example, I find that in the world of theory I expect to make order, shed light, gain insight, and pursue other important, satisfying possibilities. Theory's horizons promise all that and more. While I am trying to make order, I remember the emotional messiness and physical clutter of this or that person's hospital room where a caregiver has kept round-the-clock watch. Or while I am trying to shed light, I fear anew the dark senselessness of cells run amok and death come calling. To be sure, I can shift to another example. Instead of serious illness as a line of access to "enclave," I can choose something joyful like babies' first utterances and the other astonishing ways they leave their initial marks on the world and on their caregivers. Instead of loved ones with cancer or AIDS, then, I can think about Marie's or Jarrett's faltering seizures of language. What makes those occasions for joy, though, is that they create order, enlarge possibilities, and promote coherence. I begin to think, then, that enclaves typically involve experiences of pain or unsettling disruption. That thought implies a horizon, an array of possibilities for further instantiating the types of theoretical struggle I am experiencing here and now.

With that thought also comes an awareness of how Natanson's phenomenology makes theoretically accessible the kinds of experiences often reported by queer, feminist, Afrocentrist, and other "outsider" theorists. Sedgwick (1990: 68) observes, for instance, that "there can be few gay people, however courageous and forthright by habit, however fortunate in the support of their immediate communities, in whose lives the closet is not still a shaping presence." More concretely, Williams (1991: 205) describes a shopping trip with a friend "hunting for suitable costumes" for a samba party. Horizonally, such an experience typically includes here-and-now possibilities such as purchases besides the item sought, coffee and dessert in the department store's eatery, browsing at will, *and so forth and so on*. Additionally, the horizon includes future such trips to other department stores for other items, whether alone or with the same or other friends. On this trip, though, Williams comes across a fashion show where models "dressed up to fit a freedom (if not fighter) image" parade up and down the runway to the music of Brazilian liberation songs. Her experiencing becomes an enclave. She decides the fashion show is "A setup for lonely discontents like me, who don't know when to stop complaining, who fill in meaning where none was meant" (p. 206).

Where Williams had expected one set of possibilities instantiated, another set also gets instantiated – one set clamoring for her intentionality in competition with the other set. Unless she steps outside the role of shopper and thus tests the limits of normality and respectability, salespeople and other shoppers cannot grasp the character of Williams's experiences. She stands outside typicality, beyond consumerist typifications. Williams's description shows how "a problem that upsets the applecart of everyday experience may nevertheless linger in enclaves shared by the mundane and the strange" (Natanson 1986: 107). Put differently, "strangeness penetrates familiarity as the potential debilitation of the structure of the life-world" (Natanson 1973: 136). Where typifications falter and recipes for action momentarily fail, one meets up with "the obverse side of familiarity: estrangement and finitude" (Natanson

1970: 125). The horizons of one's here and now then include the lived possibility of madness.

Madness and Common Sense

In Natanson's work "madness" is a doublesided concept. On the one side, it is insistently nonclinical and has to do with individuality, improvisation, and the regeneration of the mundane. On the other side, it is generically (but not technically) clinical and has to do with disconnection, pathos, and the horizons of the mundane. This doublesided usage provides a wide passageway into the riches of common sense.

Natanson (1986: 2) points toward the first sort of madness when he says "academic philosophy may be the last stronghold of subsidized madness." Similarly, he (1967–8: 210) cites as a "reliable maxim" a "Galician proverb which says: A philosopher without madness in him is like a bone without marrow." A related clue about madness comes in Natanson's (1963b: 99) observation, "Philosophy thrives on embarrassment."

Indeed, "the gift of madness must be paid for at the price of embarrassment" (Natanson 1963b: 4). "By 'madness,'" Natanson (1963b: 2) says, "I mean something less horrific than insanity. . . ." He means something capable of infiltrating everyday life (and other worlds) through actions typically seen as "sane" yet "strange." Madness thus entails the strangeness expressive of the individual's "attunement . . . to what is possible for him [or her] alone" (1963b: 5–6). It entails a measure of "rebellion and refusal," a "radicality of spirit," a "foundational independence," and a "searching for interior freedom." The "sense of improvisation and spontaneity of spirit" fuel what we might call *transcendental madness*. Its "very mark" or "sign" is that the individual "*does* act" as he or she sees fit (Natanson 1963b: 6). Rooted in a struggle to act honestly, transcendental madness "may consist in nothing more than the commitment of the individual to his [or her] individuality" (Natanson 1963b: 6). It may often find expression in wearying, recurrent returns to the question, "What does it all mean?" That interrogation, Natanson (1992: 167) says, is "far from being a question of meditation"; it "is better understood as a cry of fury. The 'it' is sometimes the expression of exhausted patience."

Natanson sees philosophy as an invitation to such transcendental madness. In his own work he "rel[ies] on the debris of cities, on wanderers of the streets, loiterers and idlers, what are to [him] the lunatics of the mundane" (Natanson 1989: 137). Natanson (1986: 36) postulates "a tougher meaning of 'philosophy' which also belongs to common sense and of which no one need be ashamed. That meaning is philosophy as the hardness, the adversity of existence, the creaking of the life-world, its hernias and hemorrhages."

That "tougher meaning" finds expression in the logic of inquiry mapped out by feminist scholars such as Evelyn Fox Keller (1985: 125), whose point of departure is "actual science . . . described by the multiplicity of styles and approaches that constitute its practice than by its dominant rhetoric or ideology." Keller's methodology revolves around "dynamic objectivity" which is like empathy and unlike objectivism. Hers is a passionate methodology emphasizing engagement, closeness, and recognition of the "connections between our subjectivity and our science" (Keller 1985: 70–1). Like other anti-scientistic methodologies, Keller's tends to elicit criticisms not only about its lack of rigor but also about its whimsical, willy-nilly character. The practitioners of such "unscientific nonsense" are widely dismissed as virtual crackpots. Theirs is a methodology built out of transcendental madness driven by reflexive engagement with "such fundamental questions as 'What is it that I am doing?'" (Natanson in Webb 1992: 289).

The other variety of madness Natanson describes is no less important than the transcendental sort. This second type reeks of the irrational, the aberrant, the abnormal; it lies beyond "what most people in a society at a given time take to be rational, reasonable, acceptable behavior" (1986: 33–4). In mundane life we encounter this sort of madness "in the lunatics who loaf on the street corners of daily life or roar through its thoroughfares" (1986: 146). This might be called *existential madness*, a significant departure from established typifications and commonplace recipes that leaves the individual connected with only "*some* aspects of the life-world" (1986: 87).

In its seemingly less extreme but more socially consequential versions existential madness takes shape around "a pathology of sedimentation" whereby some "polythetic acts (and *their* sedimented meaning) may be condensed into an acceptable forgetfulness, so that the monothetic result varnishes over or conceals what formed the result" (1986: 58). Here madness shades into Sartrean bad faith; such madness involves "retarded negation" (Natanson 1970: 91) and promotes collective amnesia. Natanson (1986: 59) observes that "The sedimented memory of cruelty and shame may be transformed" so that even "the heroism of evil" emerges as such.

It strikes me that widely held beliefs about social inequality and systems of domination in American society reflect institutionalized madness of this existentialist sort. Collectively and institutionally, we transform our past of indifference, intolerance, and systematic deprivation into portraits of ill-motivated, undeserving individuals who recklessly insist on falling through the cracks or cutting holes in the safety net (small as it is). At its best social theory intervenes in such madness. Even though "Theory is not inherently healing, liberatory, or revolutionary," it can serve such ends "when we ask that it do so and direct our theorizing" along those lines (hooks 1994: 61). I count Connell among the theorists who ask precisely those things of theory and direct their theorizing accordingly. Concerned with schooling and social justice, for instance, Connell (1993: 19, 27, 39, 43) emphasizes that "Justice cannot be achieved by distributing the same amount of a standard good to children of all social classes"; that we need to theorize "an 'advantage cycle' as well as a 'poverty cycle'"; that usually "the position of those who carry the burdens of social inequality is a better starting-point for understanding the totality of the social world than is the position of those who enjoy its advantages"; and – following John Rawls – that the "standpoint of the least advantaged" must predominate in discussions of justice and injustice. In connection with existential madness and bad faith Connell (1993: 44) asserts, "Justice is not a question of ease and it is the opposite of anaesthesia."

To be sure, justice is *not* a "question of ease," but it *is* a question. Every such question has a horizon. As Natanson (1968: 502–3) puts it, "The horizon in which the question perches is the migration of persons in the mystery of sociality, a community of beings bounded by historical distance, social disruption, and cultural misgivings." The "horizon of questioning" is, I think, a set of possibilities for further instantiating common sense and its offsprings such as art, science, religion, and theory of all sorts. Like pathology, questions "offer no essential escape from the matrix of common sense. But if common sense has so few exits . . . its intersections are many; it is replete with enclaves" (1986: 109) where one often grasps pre-reflectively what is unavailable in any world's typifications. In the enclaves associated with closeted experiencing, for instance, one can acutely sense that "gay is to straight *not* as copy is to original, but, rather, as copy is to copy" (Butler 1990: 31).

The kinds of theorists likely to benefit from the phenomenological thesaurus I have begun to open here might thus be considered "enclave theorists." I prefer, though, to name them "theorists of common sense." Coming full circle, then, I see in today's ascendant social theories a renewed concern with common sense as well as with *a* common sense, even among those inclined toward postmodernist stances. Let me draw from Natanson's thoughts on common sense to support that viewpoint.

Natanson (1986: 105) sees in common sense "a hermeneutical lalapalooza." He of course knows "it *is* common, it is not a 'pearl of great price,' it is like a handkerchief into which a hundred noses have trumpeted their best." Yet common sense is "richly textured, well traveled, and thoroughly experienced in the business of being human" (1986: 107, 106).

Common sense presupposes the typifications of the life-world and its recipes for action, but it can neither be reduced to nor best approached through them. Common sense invites an egological approach centered on the embodied career of the individual making his or her own "microcosmic history" (1970: 94). As that individual "come[s] to know the social world more definitively," she or he comes to "recognize that the ingredients of [the] recipes for action must be modified or even changed" (1986: 56). One's own experiences give way to one's own common sense, then – that is, one's singular grasping of the resources of mundanity. Natanson (1970: 16) emphasizes that

Each of us can profit from advice, from the tips and warnings of those who have "been through it before," only within narrow limits. Although it may be true that there are overarching patterns of problems which confront almost all individuals in similar fashion, the career of the concrete person is embedded in a "once-given" reality which makes each choice an original event, a world-creating occurrence.

Natanson (1986: 102) notes that "If one can puzzle things out within the framework of an established scheme of reference, then common sense proves to be an activity which utilizes what our stock of knowledge provides in order to take a step beyond what has previously been taken for granted." He (1970: 66) finds, then, that "Improvisation, experiment, risk, and flexibility are features of mundanity." Common sense is thus how we get through and occasionally triumph over the "babble of violence, confusion, distortion, and suffering" in our everyday lives (1986: 113). It is how we keep finding our way back to and renewing our membership in one or another " 'We' whose meaning each of us is called to decipher" (1986: 142).

Spatial constraints preclude my saying anything more about common sense. I have said enough, I hope, to translate the experiential turn in social theory into a turn toward the profundity of common sense as people enact it in their everyday lives. Williams and Frank, hooks and Keller, Bordo and Connell, Collins and Butler are theorists of that kind of sense no less than Bartky and Smith are. They also strike me as theorists whose work renews the modernist hope of (re)constituting *a* common sense where often there seems only a shrunken, misshapen "We" vaguely implied, never mind deciphered. At the same time these theorists strike me as seeking the conditions whereby each of us might more readily find in the "Other" a *person* – that is, a prospectively close consociate – rather than a typification lacking pulse or spirit. These theorists know, as does Natanson (1970: 65), that most of the time "The Other, as imperatively a *person*, appears or is at least sought in the urgencies of mundane existence, in radical human need, in the terrors of exposure and sudden affliction, in the insurrections and aggrievements of the spirit."

These theorists thus engage in what Natanson (1968: 491) calls "a dialectic of uncovering or 'de-sedimentation.'" In that engagement lies great promise – promise likelier to be realized by using the thesaurus Natanson's own engagement has created. I end with his vision of such a resource: "a thesaurus is not a compilation of new words; what is new, I think, is the way in which words have traversed their boundaries, the way in which their meanings have overridden convention and enlarged experience" (Natanson 1989: 131).

References

Barker, Pat. 1993. *Regeneration*. New York: Penguin Books.

Bartky, Sandra Lee. 1990. *Femininity and Domination: Studies in the Phenomenology of Oppression*. New York: Routledge.

Berger, Peter L. and Thomas Luckmann. 1967. *The Social Construction of Reality: A Treatise in the Sociology of Knowledge*. New York: Anchor Books.

Bordo, Susan. 1993. *Unbearable Weight: Feminism, Western Culture, and the Body*. Berkeley: University of California Press.

Butler, Judith. 1990. *Gender Trouble: Feminism and the Subversion of Identity*. New York: Routledge.

Chase, Susan E. 1995. *Ambiguous Empowerment: The Work Narratives of Female School Superintendents*. Amherst: University of Massachusetts Press.

Collins, Patricia Hill. 1986. Learning from the Outsider Within: The Sociological Significance of Black Feminist Thought. *Social Problems* 33 (6): 14–32.

——. 1994. Keep Your Eye on the Prize. . . . *Women's Review of Books* 12 (3): 32.

Connell, R. W. 1993. *Schools and Social Justice*. Philadelphia: Temple University Press.

Foucault, Michel. [1966] 1973. *The Order of Things: An Archaeology of the Human Sciences*. Trans. not cited. New York: Vintage Books.

Frank, Arthur W. 1995. *The Wounded Storyteller: Body, Illness, and Ethics*. Chicago: University of Chicago Press.

Friere, Paul 1970. *Pedagogy of the Oppressed*. New York: Herder & Herder.

Goffman, Erving. 1961. *Asylums: Essays on the Social Situation of Mental Patients and Other Inmates*. Garden City, NY: Anchor Books.

hooks, bell. 1989. *Talking Back: Thinking Feminist, Thinking Black*. Boston, MA: South End Press.

——. 1994. *Teaching to Transgress: Education As the Practice of Freedom*. New York: Routledge.

Keller, Evelyn Fox. 1985. *Reflections on Gender and Science*. New Haven, CT: Yale University Press.

Natanson, Maurice. 1956. Phenomenology from the Natural Standpoint: A Reply to Van Meter Ames. *Philosophy & Phenomenological Research* 17: 241–5.

——. 1963a. Introduction to Part II. In Natanson, ed., *Philosophy of the Social Sciences: A Reader*, 97–100. New York: Random House.

——. 1963b. On Academic Madness. *Carolina Quarterly* 16 (1): n.p.

——. 1967–8. Disenchantment and Transcendence. *Journal of Value Inquiry* 1 (3–4): 210–22.

——. 1968. The Fabric of Expression. *Review of Metaphysics* 24 (3): 491–505.

——. 1969. Philosophy and Psychiatry. In Natanson, ed., *Psychiatry and Philosophy*, 85–110. New York: Springer-Verlag.

——. 1970. *The Journeying Self: A Study in Philosophy and Social Role*. Reading, MA: Addison-Wesley.

——. 1973. *Edmund Husserl: Philosopher of Infinite Tasks*. Evanston, IL: Northwestern University Press.

——. 1974. *Phenomenology, Role, and Reason: Essays on the Coherence and Deformation of Social Reality*. Springfield, IL: Charles C. Thomas.

——. 1986. *Anonymity: A Study in the Philosophy of Alfred Schutz*. Bloomington: Indiana University Press.

——. 1989. From Apprehension to Decay: Robert Burton's "Equivocations of Melancholy." *Gettysburg Review* 2 (1): 130–8.

——. 1992. The Iliac Passion. *Yale Journal of Biology and Medicine* 65: 165–71.

Reinharz, Shulamit. 1992. *Feminist Methods in Social Research*. New York: Oxford University Press.

Riessman, Catherine Kohler. 1990. *Divorce Talk: Women and Men Make Sense of Personal Relationships*. New Brunswick, NJ: Rutgers University Press.

Rogers, Mary F. 1983. *Sociology, Ethnomethodology, and Experience: A Phenomenological Critique*. ASA Rose Monograph Series. New York: Cambridge University Press.

Sedgwick, Eve Kosofsky. 1990. *Epistemology of the Closet*. Berkeley: University of California Press.

Smith, Dorothy E. 1990. *The Conceptual Practices of Power: A Feminist Sociology of Knowledge*. Boston, MA: Northeastern University Press.

Webb, Rodman B. 1992. The Life and Work of Alfred Schutz: A Conversation with Maurice Natanson. *Qualitative Studies in Education* 5 (4): 283–94.

Williams, Patricia J. 1991. *The Alchemy of Race and Rights*. Cambridge, MA: Harvard University Press.

3 From Content to Context: A Social Epistemology of the Structure–Agency Craze

Steve Fuller

In at least one important respect, sociology has yet to escape its philosophical roots. Sociological theory, which is now largely autonomous from the rest of the discipline, continues to be devoted to preserving, elaborating, and transmitting the *concepts* of the continental European polymaths – Marx, Weber, Durkheim, and increasingly Simmel – who are said to have founded the field about 100 years ago. Whatever innovation there has been in sociological theory since that time has largely consisted of ways of arranging these figures for classroom consumption so that they are seen as contributing to a common disciplinary project, since, truth be told, they had little to do with each other in their own lifetimes. The paradigm of this synthetic exercise is Parsons ([1937] 1968), though Anthony Giddens (1979, 1984) has proven how one can become a world-class sociologist simply by engaging in this exercise often

My thanks to Alan Sica for inviting me to participate in the theory session of the American Sociological Association meetings in New York (August 1996), where a prototype of this essay was first delivered, and for waiting patiently the arrival of the final draft of this essay.

enough until the latest generation of British students come to think that Giddens himself is responsible for originating the concept of modernity. The so-called *structure–agency* debate perhaps epitomizes this synthetic impulse in action. From the standpoint of my own research program, *social epistemology*, such a fixation on a trans-cultural, transhistorical problematic is a very unsociological way of theorizing – though it is certainly recognizable from the design of introductory philosophy courses.

In this essay, I shall argue that what is theoretically worth pre-serving from the history of sociology (as well as other disciplines) are the *contexts*, not necessarily the concepts, of our predecessors. In the first section, I explain this departure from the norm in sociolo-gical theory in terms of a much neglected arena where the implica-tions of tracking content vs. context have been amply explored, namely, *translation*. The second section begins with a history of the contexts in which making a choice like the one implied in the op-position of structure vs. agency has made a difference to ambient social concerns. Sacred and secular formulations of the problem of justice turn out to form the narrative of this history. I then ana-lyze three versions of the secular formulation, which are them-selves moments in the constitution of the modern nation-state. This is only fitting, given sociology's historic ties to the maintenance of the nation-state's integrity – and the discipline's subsequent loss of identity with that political unit's decline (Wallerstein 1996). In the conclusion, I reflect on the implicit visions of history that separate contemporary constructions of the structure–agency debate from the one suggested from my own social epistemological standpoint.

The History of Social Thought as Translation

Professional translators draw a distinction between providing the *formal* and *dynamic* equivalent of an original utterance. The former aims at reproducing the *content* of the original in a new context, whereas the latter aims at reproducing the *context* of the original even if that means providing substantially new content. Sometimes this distinction is drawn in terms of the translator focusing, re-spectively, on the "semantic" and "pragmatic" character of the text in question. Thus, a text of Shakespeare's *Romeo and Juliet* that includes notes explaining its archaic expressions provides a formal equivalent of the original, whereas the text of *West Side Story*, a mid-twentieth-century adaptation of Shakespeare's play, provides a dynamic equivalent. In our own day, most "proper" translations aim to provide at least a formal equivalent of the original, with the achievement of dynamic equivalence regarded as a supplementary virtue (Fuller 1988: 128–38, 1993a: 96–106). This assumes that the content of the original utterance is of sufficient cross-cultural import that it can be captured in the target language without appearing completely alien. In that case, students should still be able to grapple with Shakespeare's four-century-old English because what he was trying to say has contemporary relevance. This is a noble idea, to be sure, but it is betrayed by the fact that, even in those rare cases when students cut through Shakespeare's archaisms to grasp his "timeless truths," their achievement is likely to be seen as comparable to having plumbed the depths of some secular scripture, *not* to having enjoyed some popular entertainment, which is how his original audience responded to the performance of his plays. (Indeed, only after Romanticism radically transformed highbrow literary standards – over 150 years after Shakespeare's death – was The Bard accepted unequivocally into the Western canon.) In reality, then, there is more of a tradeoff between the pursuit of formally and dynamically equivalent translations than may be first realized. It follows that those interested in rendering past utterances in present-day settings must decide whether priority is given to reproducing the content or the context of those utterances.

The difference between a stilted but literally rendered *Romeo and Juliet* and an accessible but loosely rendered *West Side Story* casts the tradeoff in translation strategies in very bold relief. But how does it appear in works of philosophy and sociology? Although sociology is my ultimate target, philosophy provides a more illuminating point of departure from literature. For example, there are two basic ways of rendering Plato for contemporary philosophical audiences. Usually, formal equivalence is given precedence. Thus, the interpreter focuses on the ontology of Pure Forms that figures so prominently in Plato's writings. Plato's arguments are presented, explicated, supplemented, and/or refuted. As much as possible, the interpreter draws on Plato's actual utterances to make sense of his arguments. When this strategy fails, Plato is presumed to be saying something unusually subtle, which then calls forth alternative schools of Plato interpretation. The overall effect of this hermenutical activity is to suggest that Plato's text ought to be read with a care that is normally not extended to other texts written in one's own time. Thus, Plato is, so to speak, "performed" as a classic. Notice that by restricting the role that Plato's original context played in his thought, Plato is simultaneously made *both* more and less accessible to today's interpreter. He is more accessible in that relatively little knowledge of Plato's sociohistorical background is needed to make sense of what he says. (Indeed, texts written by Plato's contemporaries and precursors are more likely to be used in "intertextualizing" Plato.) But ultimately Plato is rendered less accessible, since his text appears *prima facie* quite alien, which explains the need for extended interpretation.

However, we may decide that Plato's greatness lies less in his specific utterances than in the exigences that gave rise to his utterances, specifically the fall of Athens to Sparta in the Peloponnesian Wars, which Plato witnessed during his youth. The exigences that provided the context from which Plato's distinctive philosophy emerged, especially as delineated in the *Republic*, was perhaps most clearly articulated in his day in the chronicles of that failed Athenian general, Thucydides. Basically, the Athenians were too clever for their own good. They deployed the dialectic indiscriminately in the public sphere, which enabled virtually anyone with a quick wit to steer the city-state in what invariably turned out to be a disastrous direction. Recognition of this Athenian trait motivated Plato's hatred of rhetoricians (who earned their living from teaching Athenians how to be persuasive in public forums), his fixation on the fate of Socrates as an object lesson in the dark side of the "open society," and his formation of a school that developed the arts of reasoning in a highly disciplined and cloistered setting that resembled more a monastery than a courtroom. Bearing Plato's context in mind, we can see his ideal realm as a form of indirect speech that, in other times and places, would be expressed rather differently. Corresponding to the Pure Forms that played such a central role in Plato's own ontology might be God or even a sense of Society whose existence transcends that of social facts and social relations (Milbank 1990). In that sense, those who want to follow the spirit of Plato should not follow him literally (or repeat him mindlessly, which amounts to the same thing), but try to translate his sociohistorical context into our own.

These first few paragraphs capture the methodological perspective of this essay, namely, that of *social epistemology*, a normative sociology of knowledge whose ideological orientations have been as diverse as Friedrich Nietzsche ([1872] 1956), Leo Strauss (1989), and Alvin Gouldner (1965) – to name just three social epistemologists who translated Plato's context into one of relevance to their contemporaries. To be sure, Nietzsche, Strauss, and Gouldner framed the Platonic context rather differently. According to Nietzsche, Plato grossly overreacted to the events of his day, which led him to suppress the heroic dynamism of Athenian society, which might be brought to fruition in the more auspicious political culture of a united Germany. Strauss wished to preserve the circumspection with which Plato came to terms with Athenian failure, specifically, his delicate textual balance between the conveyance of hard truths to the elite and noble lies to the masses, an art which was lost from political theory once Hobbes openly declared power to be the essence of government. For his part, Gouldner viewed Plato as an existentialist who realized that without the self-imposed discipline of the philosopher-king, Plato's own spirits would have been as capricious as those of his fellow doomed Athenians. In all three cases, the theorists are less concerned with remaining faithful to Plato's texts than with establishing the conditions to which those texts might be construed as a reasonable response. In Robin Collingwood's terms, Plato's philosophy is thereby cast as an implicit answer to certain questions that form the "absolute presuppositions" of his inquiry. The recovery of those questions simultaneously establishes Plato as a social agent relating to specific audiences and circumstances and offers guidance on the terms by which Plato's project may be evaluated and extended in our own time. In this way, the descriptive and normative sides of social epistemology are met at once.

To put the point in slightly crude but perfectly general terms, the social epistemologist is less interested in what we ought to think and do than in the conditions for deciding such things. In that respect, the social epistemologist is less *connoisseur* than *constitutionalist*. In these postmodern times, when "serious" academics recoil from issuing clear value judgments, it is not just pedagogically useful, but even intellectually impressive, to offer judgments about the past, present, and future of some aspect of social life. To be sure, then, connoisseurship is in short supply. However, to avoid the charge of being a disguised elitist or tyrant, the social epistemologist needs to create some conceptual distance between her personal judgments and the framework (or "constitution") within which she would have final judgments on these matters be delivered. To take a contemporary American example, a social epistemologist may believe (on what she regards as very good grounds) that Creationism should not be accorded the same status as evolutionary biology in science courses, while at the same time granting that the final decision should be taken by the local educational authorities, to whom the social epistemologist would argue her case as

	Content	Context
Normative	Classical epistemology	Social epistemology
Empirical	Scientific knowledge	Sociology of scientific knowledge

Figure 1. Locating social epistemology

vigorously as possible but ultimately accept whatever judgment they reach. Hopefully, under such a democratic regime, the social epistemologist would stipulate that any judgments reached by the local authorities should be in principle reversible at some later time, depending on their consequences.

The scope of social epistemology is laid out schematically in Figure 1. The implication of this diagram is that social epistemology's appeal to constitutionalism should be seen as a normative contextualism that defines the frame of mind within which to address pressing social and sociological problems. For example, from what standpoint(s) does the distinction between *agency* and *structure* appear to be a pressing problem for either society or social theory to resolve? While workaday social theorists may simply presume that there is an answer to this question, the social epistemologist's job is to figure out what that answer is. The rest of this essay is mainly devoted to this task. The task admittedly has few precedents. Perhaps closest to a fellow traveler is Rawls's (1970) *A Theory of Justice*, which stipulates an "original position" from which the principles of justice should be delivered. However, Rawls validates the original position in terms of the actual principles delivered, which he himself admits were the ones he was trying to derive all along, in order to provide philosophical underpinnings for the liberal welfare state. Social theorists who have emulated Rawls's procedure, especially Jürgen Habermas, have failed to register the obviously self-serving character of this exercise, perhaps because they themselves share similar substantive views about the normative structure of society. However, the social epistemologist, regardless of her agreement with the political orientation of a Rawls or a Habermas, would ideally like to distinguish judgments about the content of the just society from the context in which judgments are delivered.

The Structure–Agency Craze: A Case Study in Social Epistemology

Only in the last quarter-century have Anglophone sociologists discovered "the central problem" of their field, namely, the resolution of two incommensurable discourses: one centering on *structure* and the other on *agency* (Giddens 1979; Ritzer 1991: 223–31). Considering that sociologists routinely claim that their discipline had existed for at least an entire century before this revelation, one wonders how they managed to persevere so long in the absence of a clear understanding of their guiding "problematic." Those familiar with the history of philosophy will recognize social theory's structure –agency craze for what it is, namely, a replay of *the problem of free will* – and we know what Marx thought happens to history the second time around. The first time around, St Augustine had inferred that humans possess a faculty of "will," since he had no other way of explaining how we could resist our destiny of eternal damnation after having inherited Adam's Original Sin. However, the main conduit to Christendom's understanding of Aristotle, the Muslim philosopher Averroes, complicated matters by suggesting that if God is perfect, then whatever limitations we perceive in ourselves and nature must be the result of our deficient understanding of how the divine mind works, not some imperfection in Creation itself (Fuller 1997: 114–21). Faced with the conflicting testimonies of Augustine and Averroes, do we conclude that the apparent openness of everyday life reflects a genuine opportunity for redemption or our sheer ignorance of what will happen anyway: i.e., agency or structure?

A proper survey of answers to this question would begin with a study of the theological discipline of *theodicy*, which is concerned with God's sense of justice: why did the Creator grant the world its peculiar design, which includes natural disasters and moral atrocities? Theodicists naturally assumed that God was the principal source of agency in the world. However, by the late eighteenth century, this idea had been largely discredited for exceeding the limits of human credulity. Voltaire's satire of this being "the best of all possible worlds," *Candide*, signalled this sea change, after which theodicy underwent secularization. An early manifestation was the doctrine of unintended consequences so favored in Scottish Enlightenment philosophical histories of civil society. Here omniscient divine agency was dispersed into fallible human agents who fail to see the ultimate import of their actions. Nevertheless, the summative effects of these actions justify our faith in the implicit rationality of social life. Note the sublimation of justice into "justification," which by the end of the nineteenth century had become almost completely submerged as Darwin's "explanation" of natural order by the principle of natural selection. Here, so to speak, God has delegated His decision-making capacity to such an extent that the only way to discover the workings of the divine mind is by empirical observation of the everyday lives of *all* His creatures.

Theodicy had already started to lose its philosophical luster with the advent of modern rationalism in the seventeenth century. The rationalists made a deliberate effort to abstract the content of the question that divided Augustine and Averroes from the socioreligious contexts in which it had been embedded over the previous centuries. Descartes and Spinoza are the principal witnesses here. While it would be easy to suppose that these seminal thinkers had boldly sorted the wheat from the chaff for future generations, it is more likely that they were trying to avoid persecution, which had the inadvertent effect of making their thought more appropriable by those not caught up in their immediate religious struggles (Toulmin 1990). In this respect, intellectual history is probably unique in rewarding the cowardice and duplicity of its actors with assignments of subtlely and genius – though, to be fair, the two sets of traits probably enjoy the same level of "cognitive complexity" (some biopsychological backing for this snide aside may be found in Byrne and Whiten 1988).

The principal legacy of the rationalist disembedding of theodicy is that freedom and determinism, or agency and structure, are nowadays seen as alternative ways – or a "double aspect," to borrow a phrase common to Spinoza and Giddens – of talking about the same thing, which carries an appropriately equivocal name, such as "creation" or "structuration." One wonders, then, how so much blood could have been spilt on choosing sides over what would seem to be a purely semantic dispute. The answer, of course, is that each discourse had been linked to a set of specific social interests whose collective hand would be strengthened by widespread adoption of its manner of speaking. Abstracted from that agonistic setting, the problem of free will is all too easily "solved," namely, by what philosophers call "compatibilism," whereby the original social conflicts are somehow forgotten in the course of linguistic therapy. However, even the most therapeutically minded theorists have had to admit that such secular versions of freedom-talk and determinism-talk as mind-talk and body-talk (in psychology), or agency-talk and structure-talk (in sociology), employ radically different categories and only correspond at the level of specific utterances: e.g., that all thoughts about horses involve some set of neurons but not necessarily the same set in each case, that all decisions about where to go to college can be explained by a combination of social factors but not the same ones in each case (Davidson 1980 is the *locus classicus* for this argumentative strategy). Incommensurability at the level of semantic categories, then, is all that remains of the deep social differences that originally forced people to choose sides and often risk their lives. (See MacIntyre 1970 for a similar explanation of how secularization reduced the stakes of religious commitment to such an extent that, from today's standpoint, religious wars of the past appear irrational.) Consequently, philosophers and social theorists content themselves with reconciling recalcitrant texts whose authors are unavailable to recreate the social conflicts originally associated with their words.

While it is beyond the scope of this essay to suggest how social theorists may come to reconnect their words and deeds with the prospect of greater social effect (but see Fuller 1998 for clues), we can clear the path to such a reconnection by isolating a crucial distinction that we blur at our peril (*contra* Giddens 1984: 19ff): between *making (or breaking) a rule* and *following a rule*. This is the *Ur*-difference that grounds the freedom/determinism and agency/structure distinctions. Notice that I have drawn the distinction in terms of (logical) contexts rather than (propositional) contents. The distinction, which corresponds to the roles of legislator and judge in a legal system, was famously invested with substantial philosophical import by Kant and has since been made a cornerstone of the philosophies of law and language by John Rawls (1955) and John Searle (1969), respectively. In *Critique of Pure Reason*, Kant argued that our capacity to deal with reality is structured by a distinction that appears, in elementary form, as steps in the syllogism: namely, the difference between "All X is Y" and "This is an X." In logical terms, this is nothing more than the difference between the major and minor premise. However, Kant made much of the fact that these two statements are substantiated in rather different ways. In today's terms, the major premise is freely chosen and justified by the good that follows from its acceptance as a basis for thought and action. For Kant, such a premise is a "regulative principle," which means that it defines the limits on our sense of reality by specifying the world we presume ourselves to inhabit – that is, until further notice. For, if we are repeatedly disappointed while operating on the basis of this premise, then it is clearly time to adopt a new regulative principle.

Packed into "repeatedly" is the assumption that the premise had been applied consistently to a significant number of cases, regardless of the consequences in each individual case. Kant called this consistent application of a prior principle "constitutive." Constitutive principles give a rule-based system its fixed character, which has been described in a variety of ways that highlight the principles' rigidity and autonomy: "gamelike," "a priori," and "innate" are three words that come to mind here, all of which imply the prior existence of a human or divine legislator. Whereas legislators typically design rules with an eye toward the future, judges are mainly concerned with applying rules as they were applied in the past. The intuition behind this sharp distinction between regulative and constitutive principles is clear enough. It is difficult to know whether a rule does what is desired (the legislator's goal) unless it has been given a trial run under relevantly similar conditions (the judge's goal). Max Weber (1965) recognized this point as fundamental to the institutionalization of religion. Because the original prophetic vision does not issue in an instant "heaven on earth," the priesthood is necessary to sustain the flock's adherence to the faith until that fateful day occurs. In a more secular vein, Thomas Kuhn's ([1962] 1970) distinction between revolutionary and normal science captures the relationship between the "genius" involved in the initial proposal of a paradigm and the discipline required to bring it to fruition by working through its remaining problems. Without the institutionalization of these complementary roles, the natural sciences would be just as susceptible to the vicissitudes of fashion as the human sciences and other less epistemically esteemed elements of society.

In contemporary analytic philosophy, the difference between the maker and applier of laws tends to be seen in purely ethical terms: a steadfast judge places a systematic check on the legislator's utilitarian impulses, thereby enabling the emergence of a more edifying legal system, *rule-utilitarianism* (Johnson 1985). However, upon returning to Kant's Enlightenment context, the first clear realization of the legislator/judge distinction was the US Constitution of 1787, heralded in its day as the first instance of "philosophically designed" order. Since philosophy had not yet metastasized into the mutually incomprehending discourses of "ethics" and "epistemology," the Founding Fathers had no qualms about turning to Newton's popularization of the scientific method for a model of government (Cohen 1995). If scientific hypotheses or civil codes were revised each time the consequences of their application went against their framers' intentions, there would never be a sufficient track record to determine the exact source of error. The corrections would always seem *ad hoc* and erratic, and their import endlessly ambiguous. In this respect, a legal system that separates the powers of legislation from those of adjudication conceptualizes society as a laboratory in which legislators function as theorists who propose policies based on an hypothesized understanding of social action, whereas judges are the experimentalists who determine the environment in which those policies may be given a trial run. In their ideologically opposed ways, the most distinctive schools of jurisprudence of the last 100 years – legal formalism and legal realism – are simply alternative articulations of the hidden scientific roots of modern constitutionalism, the former stressing the consistency of the judge needed for a fair test of the laws and the latter the foresight of the legislator needed to propose laws that are likely to increase society's well-being.

As an *Ur*-difference, the distinction between making (or breaking) a rule and following a rule can be seen as grounding our ability to tolerate deferred gratification, which may be *the* evolutionarily crucial feature of human intelligence – at least so argues psychiatrist George Ainslie (1992), whose theories have provided the empirical basis for Jon Elster's (1983, 1984) fecund view that the institutionalized subversion of irrationality is the closest that people ever come to simulating collective rationality. Our animal nature prefers short-term to long-term rewards, even though our intellect places a higher value on the latter. According to Ainslie, this preference structure is designed for a Hobbesian state of nature, where it makes sense to live each day as if it were one's last. However, once a society is sufficiently stabilized that the future is no longer entirely up for grabs, "discounting" the future is no longer adaptive. Welfare economics, itself largely an attempt to render utilitarianism a principled ethical project, has recourse to a variety of mechanisms, from forced taxation to investment incentives, to ensure that immediate self-interest does not undermine the ultimate collective good. Ainslie holds that, even absent the machinations of the welfare state, human beings in complex social settings delay each other's attempts at gratification by imposing unwanted demands that unintentionally result in our thinking more deeply about exactly what it is that we need to have satisfied. Put in more explicitly market terms, the overall quality of the goods exchanged is increased by the presence of obstacles that inhibit producers from clearing their products as quickly as possible. These obstacles may range from state regulation to consumer awareness. Finally, in terms of the original Kantian setup, the judge functions as the

	Agency-like	Structure-like
Normative orientation	Prescription	Evaluation
Defining virtue	Efficacy	Consistency
Temporal Orientation	Forward-looking	Backward-looking
Type of activity	Making (breaking) a rule	Following a rule
Type of rule	Regulative ("All X is Y")	Constitutive ("This is an X")
Legal function (School of jurisprudence)	Legislation (Legal realism)	Adjudication (Legal formalism)
Ethical orientation	Utilitarianism	Deontology
Religious function	Prophecy	Priesthood
Scientific orientation	Revolutionary science	Normal science
Scientific function (in positivist terms)	Theory (Explanation)	Experiment (Confirmation)

Figure 2. The normative implications of the agency–structure distinction

unwanted party who impedes the legislator's speculativeness, which left unchecked could lead to policy changes at a rate that would have unbearable consequences for society at large.

My redefinition of the agency/structure distinction in terms of alternative normative orientations is represented in Figure 2. It captures the many versions of this distinction that have been discussed in the previous paragraphs. In the rest of this essay, I articulate three distinct contexts in which this distinction has made a difference. Here the reader should think about the following question: given a particular social action, how does one decide whether it is agency-like or structure-like? My own answer is that any social action can in principle be regarded either way, and that ultimately we come to think of something as having either perpetuated (cf. structure) or disrupted (cf. agency) the status quo in terms of its consequences, which are then read back into its past.

It took Talcott Parsons's first major work, *The Structure of Social Action* ([1937] 1968), to establish the premise that Weber and Durkheim somehow "complemented" each other in an emerging unified science of sociology. Weber was presented as having cultivated the agency side of social action at the expense of structure, and Durkheim vice versa. Marx was conspicuously absent from this synthesis. But even accepting Parsons's original project on its own terms, it was a mystery why he never seemed to keep straight the distinction between structure and agency in his later theoretical endeavors, as structural–functionalist action theory often seemed on the verge of blending into a symbolic interactionism like the one discussed in the previous section (Ritzer [1983] 1988: 447–50).

Given all of the supposedly abortive attempts at solving the structure–agency problem, one is tempted to conclude either that sociologists are not smart enough to solve the problem or that the problem itself is spurious. As my remarks so far have suggested, I am inclined toward the latter conclusion. Specifically, "structure–agency" is a metaphysically inspired abstraction from a variety of relatively distinct problems of social control that arise in the modern era. Moreover, the move to metaphysics is not merely the result of theorists looking for an underlying pattern to empirical diversity, but more significantly, it reflects the ambivalence that theorists have increasingly felt about deploying their knowledge as an instrument of social control, which is to say, a "structuring agency." I shall review three of the contexts in which such concerns have arisen. Taken *seriatim*, they constitute an archaeology of the structure–agency debate, each digging a bit deeper:

(a)   The context closest to the surface of the debate pertains to the use of social research to inhibit social change. Here the structure–agency dichotomy is suspect because it renders such agents of collective change as social movements "mixed types" that fail to conform to the ideal types of either "structure" or "agency." It is then a short intuitive leap from such theoretical hybridity to the conclusion that movements are not proper social formations.

(b)   Still deeper lies the question that animated Talcott Parsons's own project: does greater knowledge of social structure enhance or impede one's own sense of social agency? In 1937, the history of economics from Marshall to Keynes suggested a hopeful answer, which Parsons tried to use as a springboard for a theoretically unified social science that could address all levels of social policy. In one sense, the ultimate failure of Keynesianism, and *a fortiori* Parsons's attempted expansion of it, is commemorated by the irresolubility of the structure–agency debate.

(c)   Finally, at the deepest level comes the question of whether an entire society can be regarded as a purposeful agent, an "organism," so to speak, whose physiology is its legal system? At stake is the idea that there may be a "natural" rate of social change that, in turn, dictates the terms on which the sociologist can legitimately intervene in its workings. Here we find the alternative attitudes to structure and agency that characterize the hallowed *Gemein-/Gesellschaft* distinction.

Structure–agency and the exclusion of subversive social forms

Contemporary social theorists often trace the stalemate in the structure–agency debate to the inherited failure of the classical theorists to take the fluidity of social life sufficiently seriously. The missing quality is typically indexed by such adjectives as "constructive," "processual," "creative," and "temporal" (Joas 1996). Despite an historical tendency for sociologists to associate "structure" with the more "objective" (or less phenomenologically transparent) features of social life, and "agency" with the more "subjective" ones, both poles are prone to reification, as sociologists develop technical vocabularies that allow them to articulate aspects of agency that the agents themselves merely display in their activities. Traditionally, sociologists have tolerated this drift toward reification because they have presumed that the agents under study themselves engage in a less self-conscious version of the sociologist's reifications (what Alfred Schutz called "typifications"). However, the more that recent theorists have sought a place for fluidity in the metaphysical space "between" structure and agency, the more the reified vocabulary of professional sociology has seemed to throw up obstacles. After all, can the more creative aspects of social life be represented within a methodological framework so focussed on the idea that agents are "always already" structured and then impose still more structure on each other's actions?

Of course, this question may be addressed purely at the level of metaphysics. In that case, the reification of social life can be traced to sociology's captivity to a physicalist conception of time, one that treats the difference between one's experience of the closure of the past and the openness of the future as reflecting, not the process by which the future is ultimately realized as the past, but merely an asymmetry in one's present-day knowledge of the two temporal states: the future is not less real than the past; in the present, one simply knows less of the future than of the past (Horwich 1986).

Thus, such future-oriented feelings as novelty, uncertainty, risk – and indeed, hope – are, strictly speaking, reifications of ignorance, not opportunities for creation. However, a less metaphysical diagnosis of the situation may be gleaned from the origins of the first self-defined school of "microsociology," symbolic interactionism.

From the writings of symbolic interactionism's signature theorist, Herbert Blumer (1969), it was already clear in the mid-1930s that the reifying tendencies of sociological inquiry had to be checked if the field was to do more than serve as a means for "solving" (i.e., resisting) innovative social relationships that clients in government and business regarded as "problems" (cf. Turner and Turner 1990). The social formations that Blumer held to be especially threatened by the reifying tendencies of social inquiry were patterns of collective behavior whose goals significantly deviate from those of the institutions out of whose material and ideological resources they are constructed. Numbering among these patterns are social movements, industrial action in the workplace, and even team spirit in sports. But the case with which Blumer was probably most preoccupied over his career was the consolidation of racial identity in his own culture, as Americans have prided themselves throughout this century as a "melting pot" officially devoted to eliminating any forms of discrimination that stem from the origins of the people in question (Lyman and Vidich 1988).

Blumer objected equally to treating either racial minorities or their majority oppressors as pathological, the former in need of assimilation and the latter in need of therapy. Rather, he held racial attitudes to be symptomatic of the need to maintain a fixed hierarchy of social relations during a period of change. Thus, one should expect to see the "color line" shift historically, not disappear completely, unless a time came such that no group could gain advantage by stigmatizing another as a "race." Even the advance of industrialization would not erase the color line, but simply reconstitute it in other terms that were not explicitly racial, but which sanctioned roughly the same behavior as the old racism. Methodologically speaking, that is why one needs to observe behaviors, not simply expressed attitudes, even in a phenomenon like racism, which had been traditionally defined in attitudinal terms. Moreover, popular political agendas, however well-meaning, can often obscure sociological analysis in a way that turns to be politically counterproductive, as they give the impression that the mere passage of civil rights legislation in the 1960s ended racism in the US. In the hands of Blumer and his followers, fear of capture by the clientele has often, albeit ironically, engendered an excessively purist pursuit of social inquiry that provides perceptive criticism of sociology's positive knowledge claims, but offers little by way of improvement on the work criticized. Indeed, much of the microsociological literature conveys the impression that one of the best things sociologists can do is to impede appropriations of their work that would restrict the fluidity of the human condition. In this way, Blumer's self-contextualization marks a shift from the sociologist as *stranger* (Georg Simmel's model) to *spoiler*.

The analytic problem of any kind of collective behavior is that its emergence is often behaviorally indistinguishable from riots, mass hysteria, cults, and conspiracies – phenomena that require diagnosis and treatment as "social pathologies." Symbolic interactionists were among the first to make a methodological point out of the fact that the initial disposition of a group is not a reliable indicator of the ultimate value of its actions. Well-organized, normatively acceptable patterns of behavior can produce brutal results, whereas spontaneous, disorganized gatherings can issue in beneficial ones. Constructivist sociologists of science have grown accustomed to this point under the rubric of the *symmetry principle*, which enjoins the inquirer not to presume that the genius or error of a piece of research can be anticipated simply by knowing the research design, funding source, team style, or professional status of the scientists prior to their actually doing the work (cf. Bloor 1976; Knorr-Cetina 1981). However, in less symmetrical days, authoritative sources for the pathological conception of collective behavior included the Durkheimian image of the relationship between society's normative structure and the individual's moral disposition as being akin to the relationship between gravitational attraction and inertial motion. An implication of the analogy was that a collection of interacting "bodies" whose combined force breaks away from the society's centripetal force could only embark on a self-destructive course. A theorist who thinks in terms of this analogy would be prone to understand "structure" as a kind of superego that the agent internalizes through "socialization" in order to keep his or her biological instincts in check. From this example, it becomes clear that, contrary to its opponents' caricatures, "microsociology" is not committed to the agency pole of the structure–agency debate but rather to deconstructing *both* poles of the debate (cf. Scheff 1990: esp. ch. 2).

Structure–agency and the pursuit of social science for social policy

Given the credit that Talcott Parsons ([1937] 1968) regularly receives for having provided the conceptual basis for today's structure–agency debates, it is odd that the opening sentence of *The Structure of Social Action* is "Who now reads Spencer?," followed by detailed critique of the methodological assumptions of Alfred Marshall's political economy. Why this offbeat beginning? Though a mere 34 years in the grave, Herbert Spencer, the prophet of Social Darwinism and the most popular English-speaking philosopher of his day, was already consigned to the dustbin of history by the time Parsons's book came out. For Parsons, Spencer's rapid decline symbolized the bankruptcy of laissez faire as a principle of social order. Published in 1937, in the midst of the New Deal in the US and the Keynesian Revolution in Britain, Parsons was making a point, not merely about the conceptual inadequacy of methodological individualism, but also about the failure of unregulated markets to produce socially desirable outcomes. Marshall's career represents the first step in that realization. He was the person most responsible in Britain for converting political economy from a set of analytic tools for promoting liberal policies into "economics", a mathematical science fit for universities. But while Marshall famously defined the domain of economics as the entire "business of life," he was unwilling to reduce the variety of people's wants to a common unit of currency like "hedons" or "utiles," as his utilitarian forebears did, or their biological equivalents, as Spencer tried to do. In fact, Marshall limited the role of economics to studying the comparative efficiency of systems designed to satisfy a society's wants. In one sense, by raising the discipline's level of abstraction in this way, Marshall made it more closely resemble a "universal science" like classical mechanics. However, at the same time, his move amounted to an admission that people's wants are determined by the character of the society in which they live. Consequently, it would be difficult for an economist to offer policy advice without knowing and evaluating the substantive interests of the population (cf. Stehr 1992: 109).

Now let us translate this shift in the status of political economy to the terms of the structure–agency debate. Marshall formalized the economy as a system of exchanges tending toward equilibrium, the efficiency of which could be measured by the economist and administered by the economically informed policymaker. In that sense, Marshall identified a "structure," knowledge of which transcended the knowledge had by ordinary economic agents. It also justified the elevation of the economist from the status of just another interested agent in policy debates (e.g., David Ricardo and John Stuart Mill, both of whom had served in Parliament) to a university professor who presides over an esoteric body of knowledge that is taken to be the normative ground of what economic agents do. However, as Marshall himself realized, the idea of the economy having a structure independent of the agents who constitute it flew in the face of the "invisible hand" model of capitalism to which all political economists had paid lip service since Adam Smith, and which had been integral to Spencer's Social Darwinism. Indeed, the idea of an economic system suggested the very opposite of the invisible hand model: namely, that a system-ically undesirable state may result from the aggregation of short-sighted agents acting out of their own sense of self-interest. Thus, unemployment, inflation, overproduction of goods, and maldistribu-tion of wealth could no longer be presumed to be temporary tremors of the invisible hand, but rather, persistent normative violations that may require state intervention for their correction.

Nevertheless, while Marshall was clear in his academic writings that capitalism's *fin-de-siècle* move toward monopolies and colonial expansion was hardly the healthiest route for the British economy to take, he was reluctant to use his chair as a pulpit to pronounce on policy matters (Collini et al. 1983: ch. 10). The institutional de-tachment of "structure" from "agency" (a.k.a. the distance between Cambridge and "The City," London's financial center) made it difficult for Marshall to identify appropriate points of leverage for making agents change their behavior in a normatively desirable direction. Indeed, with its virtual monopoly on the use of force, the state was potentially in a position to do more harm than good for the economy by disrupting historically evolved patterns of ex-change. Thus, Marshall favored the creation of charities and other private associations that mediated the more inequitable aspects of capitalist relations without directly involving central government (Deane 1989: 140–1). The great promise of the Keynesian Revolu-tion, four decades later, was the claim that the relevant levers for productive state intervention into the economy had been identified in terms of the national bank's control of interest rates and money supply (Stehr 1992; cf. Fuller 1993b: 64–5).

It would seem that Marshall pioneered the now common social scientific gambit of complaining that the complexity of social life impedes practice – even though the most successful scientist-practitioners have, like John Maynard Keynes (1936), operated with rather simple theories. Indeed, an ironic testimony to this develop-ment is that social scientists nowadays tend to presume that social agents are themselves effective simplifiers who adapt well to chang-ing conditions. This would seem to imply that social scientists have refused themselves the benefit of the doubt that they grant the people they study! Faced with this paradox, it is worth remembering that, no less than the natural sciences, the social sciences aim at showing interrelations among a few variables, the generalizability of which is underwritten by the abstract conditions of the scientist's inquiry – be they a laboratory, a computer simulation, or an explanatory narrative. The two types of sciences are distinguished by the sociopolitical climate for realizing those conditions of inquiry. Because social actors can more easily see themselves as having a stake in the outcome of social science research, they are more likely to try to influence the conditions under which the research is done – and inquirers are also more susceptible to such influence. This is especially true when the researcher tries to contribute significantly to both theoretical and practical concerns, such that his or her theory offers the prospect of imposing a uniform policy across a variety of contexts.

For example, Keynes wanted to transform both economics and public policy, largely by making the former the scientific foundation of the latter. He first advanced policy statements specifically targeted to Liberal (and later Labor) Party policies on the Great Depression of 1929, and then erected a theoretical structure from which those statements could be deduced. Not surprisingly, Keynes reverted to the pre-Smithian, mercantilist assumption that the nation–state is the unit of economic analysis, even though that meant slighting the significance of international trade and global interdependence, factors that ought to have been crucial in any long-term solution to the Depression. Moreover, the economic statements advanced by Keynes referred to a few aggregate indicators – official statistics concerning income and employment – that were taken to epitomize the entire economy and presented as manipulable by altering the level of investment. Thus, the economy became an abstract entity whose empirical side could be observed directly by government statisticians, and whose experimental potential was in the hands of the state treasury and banks. The formal scientific character of Keynes's picture of the economy – with most of the actual people, products, and prices submerged in *ceteris paribus* clauses – offered a flexible rhetoric for changing economic circumstances: unfortunate turns in the few key indicators could be explained away as aberrations, if not simply redefined. Thus, while the general Keynesian framework has served to legitimate state intervention in economic activity, it has led neither to a consistent economic policy nor even to a consistent statement of the economy's actual conditions. At the time of *The Structure of Social Action*, Parsons had plainly accepted Keynes's assessment of Marshall's strengths and weaknesses (Parsons [1937] 1968: 130–1), and was drawn to E. C. Tolman's "purposive behaviorism" as the psychic substratum that enabled agents' goals to be shaped – as Keynes had managed to do – by altering their incentive structure (ibid.: viii). However, as with Keynes, the plausibility of Parsons's strategy for creating a theoretically unified, policy-relevant social science has evaporated over time.

Structure–agency and the spirit of the laws

The ultimate source of ambivalence for modern social theorists was the construction of rational legal systems for the rapidly modernizing nation–states of Europe in the nineteenth century. Within a 25-year period (1789–1814), the Constitution of the US and the Code Napoléon, in different ways, testified to the possibility of a "philosophically designed" social order based on an Enlightenment-inspired "science of human nature," one capable of deducing from first principles the means for avoiding the centuries of injustice institutionalized in other legal systems. Those who opposed converting the fantasy of the social contract into reality appealed to the "natural rationality" implicit in the accumulated wisdom of tradition, judicial precedent, and historical entitlement. This version of the structure–agency debate raged in both Britain and Germany, where it became known as the *Kodifikationstreit* (Kelley 1990: 243).

To be sure, there were considerable ideological differences among the people who championed the same sides of the argument in Britain and Germany. The British anti-codifiers were mostly jurists in the tradition of William Blackstone, paternalistic believers in natural rights who were sanguine that judicial discretion in applying the law would ultimately mitigate against any unjust pieces of legislation. However, "injustice" was not a systemic, or class, issue for Blackstone, but a matter of not attending to the disposition of the particular case. In contrast, the German anti-codifiers were mostly professional historians who followed the lead of Karl von Savigny in tracing the historical assimilation of Roman civil law into German common law. They were keen to show that the current distribution of property rights reflected the collective wisdom of judges adapting the best elements of the two legal traditions. This wisdom was essentially the empirical correlate of the *Volksgeist*. According to Savigny, only ignorance of past decisions would lead one to see German law as arbitrary, unwieldy, and chaotic, and not (as Savigny believed it to be) the subtlest instrument available for expressing the corporate will of the nation. However, both Blackstone's and Savigny's followers could agree that the interpretive flexibility of any legislative code was its saving grace, especially when it came to protecting the most vulnerable members of society (whose status was never expected to improve). Ultimately, faith in the cumulative consequences of judicial discretion depended on the social structure being founded on bonds of trust according to which every transaction presupposes a commitment to a common way of life that goes beyond the particular exchange of goods or services. Externally motivated violations of these bonds – as with the influx of French revolutionary ideas into Britain and British utilitarian ideas into Germany – were held to be the cause of various peasant and workers' revolts.

On the other side of the issue, the drive to rationalize the British legal system was promoted by Jeremy Bentham and the utilitarians, whereas in Germany it was advanced by the left-wing followers of Hegel (including the young Karl Marx). But the commonalities between the two camps were at least as significant as their obvious differences. In both countries, rationalization was associated with a "philosophical" approach to the law, one specifically concerned with discerning the consequences of the law for all the people subsumed under its rule, regardless of their social station. (Of course, Benthamites and Hegelians differed over whether these "consequences" were better rendered as the aggregated pleasures and pains of the members of society or as a transcendent social totality). It was thus generally understood that the codification of the law was the first step toward instituting a uniform legal procedure that would remove many traditional class privileges. Moreover, the British and German codifiers agreed that the social foundation of the law is the exchange, or "alienation," of property, which suggested a zero-sum mentality toward ascribing legal agency. Thus, all legislative attempts to empower the disempowered would somehow have to involve disempowering the empowered. Both Bentham and Hegel held the unconditional conception of "natural right" associated with the Lockean political tradition and enshrined in the American Declaration of Independence to be metaphysically suspect. In its place, they defined "right" in terms of "duty," the constraint imposed on oneself in order for another to act. But here Bentham and Hegel disagreed over whether this "definition" amounted to an outright rejection of the concept of right (Bentham), or rather, its sublimation (Hegel).

According to the first major American survey of the history of sociology, authored by Albion Small in 1924, the *Kodificationstreit* was the source of the dichotomy that would come to demarcate the problem-set of sociology from that of the other social sciences. In short, the opponents of codification stood for *Gemeinschaft*, while the codifiers stood for *Gesellschaft* (Kelley 1990: 270). In terms specific to our debate, the former saw the social structure as already infused with agency in the form of a purposeful application of the law, whereas the latter regarded agency as a quality of purposefulness that had to be introduced via legislative fiat, lest the social structure remain captive to an inherently purposeless tradition (225). In terms of modern theories of justice, *Gemeinschaft* was backward-looking and entitlement-based, while *Gesellschaft* was forward-looking and welfare-based (cf. Rawls 1955). The more "structure" and "agency" could be seen as opposed, the more artificial the social order appeared, and hence the greater the justification for political intervention.

Conclusion

Perhaps the most pernicious feature of social theory's current structure–agency craze is its reduction of decisions about alternative courses of action to alternative interpretations of the same course of action. Giddens's (1984) structuration theory is a prime offender in this respect. The strategy does scant justice to the original social contexts in which theorists have had to deal with matters that are naturally split along structure vs. agency lines. Because these contexts have been erased – or "detraditionalized," to use a term that Giddens and other leading lights favor these days – the structure–agency debate now seems better suited to the common room than the agora. To be sure, the philosophy of science suffers from an analogous problem. Much ink is spilt over whether science has been driven primarily by instrumentalist or realist concerns, but both sides agree on the episodes from the history of science that need to be explained by their accounts, and consequently neither realists nor instrumentalists have much to say about how the *future* of science should proceed, aside from providing a tacit endorsement of the status quo (Fuller 1994). Thus, nowadays you would never find a philosopher of science (the late Paul Feyerabend being the distinguished exception that proves the rule) claiming, say, that the Newtonian paradigm outlived its usefulness long before Einstein's revolution and that now we should redistribute science funding in order to get back on the right track.

However, this preemption of alternative historical perspectives may occur rather subtly, suggesting that perhaps structure and

Classicism	Romanticism
The past consists of resources that are available in the present for constructing the future	The past eventuates in the future unless disrupted in the present
The past is raw material: it delivers an unformed potential to the present	The past is an inheritance: it delivers the burden of tradition to the present
History has no natural direction	History has a natural direction
Decay is natural unless order is actively maintained, be it to continue or change the past	Development is natural unless impeded, to which radical disruption is an appropriate response
Need to impose global rules in order to structure the pattern of local decisions	Global rules simply articulate the order already emergent in local decisions
A theory is tested in the expectation that it will be replaced as it fails to deliver on its promises	A paradigm is developed in the expectation that it will thrive as it spreads its influence in the world

Figure 3.   Two alternative ways of translating the past into the future

agency are not two sides of the same process, but rather two poles locked in dialectical opposition. For example, Kuhn ([1962] 1970) argued that scientists are not rationally justified in switching paradigms until *both* the unsolved problems of the old paradigm become unbearable and the basis for a new paradigm is in clear view. Yet, from the standpoint of social epistemology, this is little more than letting the collective inertia of tradition do one's own thinking, hardly the hallmark of a self-proclaimed "rationalist" and "progressive" science or the society that houses it. Even if their image of structure–agency divide differs, it would seem that both sociological theorists and philosophers of science are content to let the anonymous hand of history prescribe the normative constraints within which they then evaluate particular scientific developments (Fuller 1999 deconstructs Kuhn's influence in this respect). The intellectual historian John Pocock (1973: ch. 8) has observed that much of the excitement surrounding Kuhn's distinction between normal and revolutionary science came from a "romantic" view of history which relied on heroic revolutionary agents disrupting the otherwise inexorable reproduction of the past.

For the founding fathers of modern social theory, the term "tradition" captured this sense of the encumbered and intertial past. Its conceptual kin included "legacy," "inheritance," and in a more logical vein, "presumption." However, the idea that the past weighs down the future, and hence genuine agency requires a break with long-standing structures, is at most 200 years old. More common has been what Pocock calls the "classical" view of history, which treats the past as raw material out of which the future is constructed. Accordingly, the openness of the future is defined by the variety of ways available to deploy the past. (The major differences between the romantic and classical views are presented in Figure 3.) Despite its ancient pedigree, Pocock's classical view of history provides a distinctly "third way" for understanding the true significance of the debates that have been collected under the structure vs. agency rubric. Whereas some social theorists may pronounce magisterially (à la Giddens) that partisans of structure and agency are like blind men groping on opposite sides of the same elephant, and others may urge more provocatively (à la Kuhn) that partisans of the two perspectives are locked in mortal combat, I would propose a standpoint along more classical lines. Specifically, in a given social context, the forces of "structure" (i.e., the so-called voice of order and the past) and "agency" (i.e., the so-called voice of change and the future) are determined less by the content of their views, which draw largely on the same cultural resources, than on the difference in their access to those resources as they compete to define a common future. In short, people become vehicles of change when they fail to see themselves in the most probable future because others have already appropriated what had been their common past.

References

Ainslie, G. 1992. *Picoeconomics: The Strategic Interaction of Successive Motivational States within the Person*. Cambridge: Cambridge University Press.

Bloor, D. 1976. *Knowledge and Social Imagery*. London: Routledge & Kegan Paul.

Blumer, H. 1969. *Symbolic Interactionism: Perspective and Method*. Englewood Cliffs: Prentice Hall.

Byrne, R. and Whiten, A., eds. 1988. *Machiavellian Intelligence*. Oxford: Oxford University Press.

Cohen, I. B. 1995. *Science and the Founding Fathers*. New York: W. W. Norton.

Collini, S., Winch, D., and Burrow, J. 1983. *That Noble Science of Politics*. Cambridge: Cambridge University Press.

Davidson, D. 1980. *Essays on Actions and Events*. Oxford: Oxford University Press.

Deane, P. 1989. *The State and the Economic System*. Oxford: Oxford University Press.

Dennett, D. 1995. *Darwin's Dangerous Idea*. Harmondsworth: Penguin.

Elster, J. 1983. *Ulysses and the Sirens*. Cambridge: Cambridge University Press.

———. 1984. *Sour Grapes*. Cambridge: Cambridge University Press.

Friedrichs, R. 1970. *A Sociology of Sociology*. New York: Harper & Row.

Fuller, S. 1988. *Social Epistemology*. Bloomington: Indiana University Press.

———. [1989] 1993a. *Philosophy of Science and Its Discontents*. 2nd ed. New York: Guilford.

———. 1993b. *Philosophy, Rhetoric, and the End of Knowledge*. Madison: University of Wisconsin Press.

———. 1994. Retrieving the Point of the Realism-Instrumentalism Debate: Mach vs. Planck on Science Education Policy. In *PSA 1994*, vol. 1., ed. D. Hull, M. Forbes, and R. Burian. East Lansing, MI: Philosophy of Science Association, pp. 200–7.

———. 1995a. Is There Life for Sociological Theory After the Sociology of Scientific Knowledge? *Sociology* 29: 159–66.

———. 1996. Recent Work in Social Epistemology. *American Philosophical Quarterly* 33: 149–66.

———. 1997. *Science*. Milton Keynes and Minneapolis: Open University Press and University of Minnesota Press.

———. 1998. A Social Epistemology of the Future of Social Theory: From Theology to Rhetoric. *European Journal of Social Theory* (forthcoming).

———. 1999. *Being There with Thomas Kuhn: A Philosophical History for our Times*. Chicago: University of Chicago Press.

Giddens, A. 1979. *The Central Problems of Social Theory*. London: Macmillan.

———. 1984. *The Constitution of Society*. Berkeley: University of California Press.

———. 1994. *Beyond Left and Right*. Cambridge: Polity.

Glaser, B. and Strauss, A. 1969. *The Discovery of Grounded Theory*. Chicago: Aldine.

Gouldner, A. 1965. *Enter Plato*. London: Routledge & Kegan Paul.

———. 1970. *The Coming Crisis in Western Sociology*. New York: Basic Books.

Horwich, P. 1986. *Asymmetries in Time*. Cambridge, MA: MIT Press.

Joas, H. 1996. *The Creativity of Action*. Cambridge: Polity Press.

Johnson, C. 1985. The Authority of the Moral Agent. *Journal of Philosophy* 82: 391–413.

Kelley, D. 1990. *The Human Measure: Social Thought in the Western Legal Tradition*. Cambridge, MA: Harvard University Press.

Keynes, J. M. 1936. *The General Theory of Employment, Interest and Money*. London: Macmillan.

Knorr-Cetina, K. 1981. *The Manufacture of Knowledge*. Oxford: Pergamon.

Kuhn, T. [1962] 1970. *The Structure of Scientific Revolutions*. 2nd ed. Chicago: University of Chicago Press.

Lyman, S. and Vidich, A. 1988. *Social Order and the Public Philosophy*. Fayetteville: University of Arkansas Press.

MacIntyre, A. 1970. Is Understanding Religion Compatible with Believing? In B. Wilson, ed., *Rationality*. Oxford: Blackwell.

Merton, R. [1949] 1967. *Social Theory and Social Structure*. 3rd ed. New York: Free Press.

Milbank, J. 1990. *Theology and Social Theory: Beyond Secular Reason*. Oxford: Blackwell.

Nietzsche, F. [1872] 1956. *The Birth of Tragedy in the Spirit of Music*. Garden City, NY: Doubleday.

Parsons, T. [1937] 1968. *The Structure of Social Action*. 3rd ed., 2 vols. New York: Free Press.

Pocock, J. G. A. 1973. *Politics, Language, and Time*. New York: Atheneum.

Rawls, J. 1995. Two Concepts of Rules. *Philosophical Review* 64: 3–32.

——. 1970. *A Theory of Justice*. Cambridge, MA: Harvard University Press.

Ritzer, G. [1983] 1988. *Sociological Theory*. 2nd edn. New York: Alfred Knopf.

——. 1991. *Metatheorizing in Sociology*. Lexington, MA: Lexington Books.

Scheff, T. 1990. *Microsociology*. Chicago: University of Chicago Press.

Searle, J. 1969. *Speech Acts*. Cambridge: Cambridge University Press.

Skinner, Q. 1969. Meaning and Understanding in the History of Ideas. *History and Theory* 8: 3–52.

Stehr, N. 1992. *Practical Knowledge: Applying the Social Sciences*. London: Sage.

Strauss, L. 1989. *The Rebirth of Classical Political Rationalism*. Chicago: University of Chicago Press.

Toulmin, S. 1990. *Cosmopolis: The Hidden Agenda of Modernity*. New York: Free Press.

Turner, S. 1994. *The Social Theory of Practices*. Chicago: University of Chicago Press.

Turner, S. and Turner, J. 1990. *The Impossible Science: An Institutional Analysis of American Sociology*. Newbury Park, CA: Sage.

Wallerstein, I. 1996. *Open the Social Sciences*. Palo Alto, CA: Stanford University Press.

Weber, M. 1965. *The Sociology of Religion*. Boston, MA: Beacon Press.

4 Making Normative Soup with Non-normative Bones

Stephen Turner

Robert Brandom's *Making It Explicit* (1994) has revived a problem with a long and fascinating history both in social theory and in the history of philosophy, especially in the philosophy of law. Brandom's discussion of the problem in chapter one of his book derives from more recent philosophical literature motivated largely by a problem in the interpretation of Wittgenstein ([1953] 1958: 186–201). The problem, put simply, is this: what is the ultimate basis of normative assertion? Brandom's answer is that explicit normative assertion must be based on implicit norms, hence implicit norms exist. In this essay I will treat Brandom's argument in his first chapters as a problem within social theory, and specifically within the familiar realm of problems of explanatory structure and form in social theory. What I will try to show is that Brandom's thesis is in part a thesis about how norms must be *explained*, and that he needs a plausible solution to the problem of the origins of normativity. In the course of the discussion I will show that his solution to this problem is less plausible than competing accounts. The problem is not merely an issue with Brandom, for Brandom's argument is closely related to similar claims in the history of social theory, notably Parsons's claim in *The Structure of Social Action* (1937: 74–82) that the "normative" is an ineliminable dimension of all action explanations, and to the claims of ethnomethodology. The reason for these similarities is quite simple. Both Brandom and Parsons borrow a notion of the normative from Kant, and both are faced with the consequences of the Kantian distinction between fact and value. Ethnomethodology shares the idea of the normative as well, and adds to it, as Brandom does, the claim that there are implicit norms, which are taken by ethnomethodology to be "resources" for "members" and to form the subject matter of ethnomethodology.

Brandom's Problem

Brandom asks what justifies explicit normative assertions, such as statements about the correctness or incorrectness of actions and claims, and says that the best explanation is this: ultimately justification rests on implicit norms or "practices," meaning, for him, regularities of action which are normative. This is a very simple social theory. It takes the following form: there are such things as implicit norms, or "practices," and they explain why the things that are taken to be normatively correct *are* taken to be correct. The meaning of "normative" is a complex issue that I will return to later, but it will suffice to say at this point that Brandom seems to be making a distinction within language – that is to say between normative and non-normative language – and between the expectations that are bases for the claims made within language, some of which are normative and some of which are not.[1] The expectation created by a promise, for example, is normative; some expectations, for example that the sun will rise on the morrow, are not. We may even have normative and non-normative expectations about the same thing. I may correctly expect, empirically, that my deadbeat brother-in-law will not pay his debts to me; but I will also be correct if I claim that by failing to pay his debts to me he has wronged me. The latter is a normative expectation, and, as Brandom says, it is an expectation about statuses, in this case the statuses of "in debt" and "out of debt."

Brandom identifies two constraints on answers to the question of what justifies explicit normative assertions like "my brother-in-law is in debt to me." The first is the "regress problem." The argument here is that norms, such as "debts are created by promises to

---

[1] The issue of what is normative and what is not is itself a puzzle, but clearly Brandom has in mind that some claims are normative and some are not. He quotes Frege, with approval, to the effect that Logic is a normative science (1994: 12), and goes on to make, as a central claim of the text, that inference is too – "that inferring should be understood in an impersonal context, as an aspect of an essentially *social* practice of communication" (1994: 158).

repay plus the giving of something," are not self-applying. The correct way to apply an explicit rule is a matter that is also "normative." Because there is a notion of mistake and correctness the implicit rules governing the correctness of the application of a rule are also normative in character. However, it would be absurd to suppose that implicit rules are governed in their application by other implicit rules, which are governed by other implicit rules, which are governed by other implicit rules on into an infinite regress of rules for applying rules. So the regress needs to stop. It cannot stop at the point of explicit rules, which are not self-applying and need to be applied in accordance with implicit rules, but it can stop at the point of implicit norms or practices. One might take the regress problem differently: to be simply a *reductio ad absurdum* of the notion of implicit rules. One might ask why they can be thought to be self-applying if explicit rules are not, or indeed whether it is sensible to talk about "rules" for whatever is not explicit. This possibility we may leave aside, for the moment.

The first constraint, the regress problem, has the following implication. Implicit norms must be a kind of stopping point for analysis rather than the sort of things that are themselves justified "normatively" by other rules (Brandom 1994: 26) or "explained" by deeper norms. Ordinarily in discussions of implicit norms there is some sort of appeal to the notion that implicit norms are in some sense connected to the facts of community life or membership in a community. This connection, which is often rather hazy, is understood not so much as a justification of the rules or an explanation of them as a kind of characterization of their location or fundamental character. Brandom has a good deal to say about this, particularly in criticizing Kripke (Brandom 1994: 38), who is the source of the other major constraint, which Brandom calls the "gerrymandering problem."

The gerrymandering problem is the problem made famous by Kripke in his book on the private language argument. Kripke took from Wittgenstein the point that any continuation of the mathematical series 2, 4, 6, 8, can be characterized as the following of *some* explicit mathematical rule (1982: 92). Thus although we "naturally" continue the series 2, 4, 6, 8 with the rest of the even numbers, there is , and can be, no mathematical reason for doing so, for there is potentially a very large set of mathematical formulae which fit any set of numbers that could be claimed to "continue" the series, and thus be representations of the "implicit rule" to which a person was appealing to when saying: "continued the series." This means that mathematics rests on something outside of mathematics.

Brandom takes this problem to have implications for the issue of normativity. It rules out, he claims, the possibility that "continue this series" can be construed non-normatively. Because such a large array of possible rules or possible sequences are theoretically consistent with the claim that they continue the series 2, 4, 6, 8, any account that attempts to treat this as a matter of a "regularity," meaning a purely causal phenomena, will fail, or in some way cheat by defining as inappropriate all of the series other than the "correct" series. The only way to pick out the correct sequence is to appeal to something normative rather than something merely causal.

The gerrymandering argument together with the regress argument establish that implicit norms are necessary to account for normative claims and that they are understandable only as norms, and not as regularities. Brandom's slogan for this is that these social practices are "normative all the way down" (1994: 44). Brandom quotes a saying of Dretskes's that one can't bake a normative cake out of non-normative ingredients: The point is that the ingredients of the cake must already be normative (1994: 41).

We can see what these two constraints together mean in terms of the practice of promising. By making a promise, we alter the normative relations between individuals, or what he calls their statuses. A practice like promising is "normative all the way down" in the sense that the end-point for an account of promising cannot be a causal fact or process of some kind that is "non-normative." The idea of expectation in and of itself is non-normative. We have various causal expectations about the world which may or may not be true and which we correct empirically. His point is that these expectations cannot suffice to explain how it is that making a promise amounts to a means by which something in the way of statuses is changed, because the change in status is a change in the *normative* expectation that we are permitted to have about someone who makes a promise rather than in any causal fact. Whether someone has made a real promise is not a matter of a predictive law that says if someone makes a promise they will fulfill it. Such a law would obviously be false, and my deadbeat brother in law would be its refutation. No refinement of this empirical law, it seems, would work either. The only true "law" that one might form about promising is a normative one that anyone who makes a promise is *bound* to fulfill it. This of course is also overly simple, because there are many conditions under which we could think that a person's promise was no longer binding. But Brandom's point is that all of these exceptions are also in the form of normative expectations or riders involving "statuses" such as being unable to fulfill the promise for some reason, and these statuses are themselves normative in character. Brandom's account is designed to resolve a complex dilemma. He does not, as I have suggested, wish to accept that the regress argument is a *reductio ad absurdum* of the idea of implicit norms, as this would still leave him with the problem of explaining how anyone could justifiable say "correct" or "incorrect" or how anyone could have normative as opposed to causal explanations. He also does not wish to say that the regularities that make up social practices are merely empirical and non-normative, but somehow become so because many people do the same thing. He quotes McDowell's point that "If regularities in the verbal behavior of an isolated individual, described in norm-free terms, do not add up to meaning, it is quite obscure how it could somehow make all the difference if there were several individuals with matching regularities" (quoted in Brandom 1994: 659 n. 46). So he is forced to accept implicit norms, or practices, i.e., normative regularities, as an explanation.

The term explanation may seem to be misplaced here, and with it the notion that Brandom is just another social theorist whose theory can be assessed in familiar social theoretical terms. But the idea that it is misplaced rests on a confusion about what Brandom is doing. Brandom is not *justifying* normative justification. He is *explaining* the phenomenon of normative justification. The problem which has the greatest similarities to this in the history of philosophy is the problem of explaining the phenomenon of legal validity, as Brandom himself notes. He quotes Samuel Pufendorf at length on this, and accepts something like Pufendorf's idea that

as the original way of producing physical entities is creation, the way in which moral entities are produced can scarcely be better expressed than by the word imposition. For they do not arise out of the intrinsic nature of the physical properties of things, but they are superadded, at the will of intelligent entities, to things already existent and physically complete, and to their natural effects, and, indeed, come into existence only by the determination of their authors. . . . Hence the active force which lies in them does not consist in their ability directly to produce any physical motion or change in any thing, but only in this, that it is made clear to men along what line they should govern their liberty of action. (quoted in Brandom 1994: 48)

Brandom points out that this does not commit Pufendorf to any thesis about the physical nature of the process of "imposing." As he puts it, it is possible to agree with Hamlet that "there is nothing either good or bad, but thinking makes it so" (Brandom 1994: 49), and also to reject the idea that there must ultimately be some sort of physical explanation of the thinking that makes it so. To put the point in a somewhat different way, Brandom's task is sociological rather than normative. It is not to do what philosophers of law sometimes have thought they could do, namely to account for legality itself, but rather to account for legitimacy, that is to say the phenomenon of taking an order as legally valid.

The Parallel Case of Legal Validity

As this comparison suggests, the same kinds of issues arise in connection with the law. What justifies a law? That it is legally enacted? And what justifies the law ordaining what counts as legal enactment? Eventually, as one questions the justifications, one must arrive at some sort of justification that must be outside the law proper, just as the justification for continuing 2, 4, 6, 8 with 10, 12, 14, 16 must be something outside mathematics. But with the law the problem is typically framed in the reverse of the notion of normativity all the way down. What is seen to be required is the distinctive fact that makes a body of regulations and predictable behavior genuinely "the law," something that is binding normatively upon us (cf. Olivecrona 1948). The special thing that makes a command or regulation legal, is however, elusive. One traditional answer was the will of the sovereign, understood as a kind of transformative element which takes mere rules and activities and makes them genuinely legal and binding. There is no law that says the will of the sovereign is binding – it just is. So the will of the sovereign is part of the definition of law, as well as, so to speak, its causal source.

Needless to say a huge body of legal thinking in the nineteenth century went into this problem, and the problem was ultimately finessed or abandoned by legal positivism, which simply rejected the problem and said that the law should be treated as a normative fact which required no further justification or basis. As Schmitt puts it, according to Kelsen

The state, meaning the legal order, is a system of ascriptions [Brandom-like norms!] to a last point of ascription and to a last basic norm. . . . For juristic consideration there are neither real nor fictitious persons [i.e., actual or theoretical sovereigns], only points of ascription. The state is the terminal point of ascription, the point at which the ascriptions, which constitute the essence of juristic consideration, "can stop." This "point" is simultaneously an "order that cannot be further derived." The decisive argument, the one that is repeated and advanced against every intellectual opponent, remains the same: The basis for the validity of a norm can only be a norm. (Schmitt [1922] 1985: 19)

So what positivism in the legal context does is to cut off a certain kind of regression problem. And it does so in order to avoid the bad end toward which the regression problem, in this case the problem of the legal justification of legal enactment, leads.

The bad end is a historical one. Once a legal system is in place, its transformations can be examined with respect to their legality, and this may be done "normatively," entirely within the system of law. But establishing a legal system seems to require something more – a transformation from something prelegal or non-legal to something legal, or at least to some moment of the origin of legal validity. Norms generally, one might think, also have to have origins, for they are diverse and mutable. So there ought to be some sort of solution to the problem of what gets norms going in the first place.

Brandom does not deny that the problem of origins is a legitimate explanatory concern. He says that "the issue of what it would be for norms to be implicit in practice ought to be kept distinct from the issue of how such practices might in fact plausibly arise" (1994: 658–9 n. 45). But even if the issues should be kept distinct, in the sense that different answers might be given to the latter issue without affecting the answers to the former, for Brandom's purposes there does need to be *some* plausible answer to the question. His arguments establish the explanatory necessity of "implicit norms" or practices. But "practices" is a theoretical term. Establishing the explanatory necessity of practices does not establish their possibility. If, however, one can establish the possibility of the existence of practices, the argument for their explanatory necessity turns possibility into necessity. Identifying a plausible explanation serves to establish possibility. But there are problems with the plausibility of the available explanations.

Kripke's explanation is that norms are based on "communal assessment," that is to say, as Wright puts it elsewhere, they rest on "the authority of securable community assent" (quoted in Brandom 1994: 38). Brandom objects to this line of argument on the quite solid ground that the notion of communal assent is a fiction and "that assenting endorsing, accepting, and regarding as right are in the first instance things done by individuals" (1994: 38). Accepting this fiction is like accepting a fictional origin of the law or a fictional sovereign. It is not an explanation at all, but merely a stand-in for an explanation. Is there a plausible explanation? Or can something like Kripke's notion of communal assessment be made into an explanation by removing its fictional quality? With these questions we move into the realm of actual explanation and the problem of plausibility itself, rather than the problem of possibility. And here some new constraints emerge.

The ideal account would answer at least three basic questions about normativity: a question about the historical anthropology of normativity or alternatively about the emergence of particular moral notions, a question about the genealogy of morals or particular morals, about socialization, and about the problem of the historical diversity of morals. One may think of these three issues differently, namely as constraints on a general account of morality that a minimally adequate theory must meet. In either case, it is useful to survey the actual history of theories of morality for an answer to the question of what the range of plausible solutions might be.

The Explanatory Problem I: Getting to the Source of Normativity

Brandom discusses, or alludes to, several social theories of normativity, including Pufendorf's theory of law, Hobbes, and Weber. Each of these thinkers supports, in some fashion, the idea, as Brandom puts it, that

our activity *institutes* norms, *imposes* normative significances on a natural world that is intrinsically without significance for the guidance or assessment of action. A normative significance is imposed on a nonnormative world, like a cloak thrown over its nakedness, by agents forming preferences, issuing orders, entering into agreements, praising and blaming, esteeming and assessing. (1994: 48)

It is difficult to see what it means, as a matter of social theory, to impose normative significance in this sense. What sort of action does this? But it is somewhat easier to see how one might do so in the case of law, and the case of law suggests some problem with these kinds of explanations.

A somewhat obscure figure, Rudolph von Ihering, provides a good place to start on the problem. His account is the account that the much more influential formulations of Nietzsche (1982, [1887]

1956), Durkheim ([1925] 1973), Tönnies (1961), and Weber ([1922] 1978) respond to. Ihering begins with the problem of the binding character of law ([1877] 1913: 105–10, 189–92, 239). The theory he proposes works, to the extent that it does work, for law. It operates as follows. Legal commands are initially simply imposed by force – here "imposing" is an intelligible phenomenon. Some person or faction makes commands backed by force which are initially accepted simply and only because they are backed by force. But in time people come to recognize the benefits of operating under these commands and this recognition is at once, Ihering suggests, a recognition of the normative character of the commands and of their collective basis or significance. The moment of recognition is one in which something non-normative, namely commands backed by force, transmutes into something normative, the law. Brandom accepts something like this account himself, when he comments that contractarian explanations of rights and obligations, as well as those that invoke positive law, "explain . . . these deontic statuses in terms of what agents are doing in instituting or constitutively recognizing such entitlements and commitments" (Turner and Factor 1994: 49). One may note that the diversity of legal orders falls out of this account quite naturally since different commands are imposed by different leaders at different times.

Ihering's explanation (Turner and Factor 1994: 105–10) of the "binding" or normative character of the law is nevertheless elusive. The account explains people's interest in obeying the law and in there being a legal order rather than the validity of commands made by the legal ruler. But does it explain their recognizing them as normatively binding? Wouldn't they need a normative notion of the law in order to recognize something as an example of the law and hence binding? Is recognizing the benefits of an order the same as recognizing the order as binding? A parallel problem arises in connection with socialization. To explain an aversion to stealing, John Austin cites the fact that as a child a person is punished for stealing and associates stealing with pain. Austin thought that this association accounts for belief in the wrongness of stealing (1954: 37, 50–2). Critics of these explanations noted that there is an illegitimate inference being made here from pain to the quite different kind of belief, a normative belief in the wrongness of stealing. The right inference would have been the painfulness of or the possible consequences of stealing, which would not be a "moral" response at all. "The burnt child shuns the fire" is an explanation of the child's expectations, but it is entirely within the causal world. Normativity somehow needs to get inserted into the process of learning (or recognition) at some moment at which the purely causal is replaced by or altered or transmuted into the normative.

These are amusing philosophical problems, but they ordinarily do not generate much philosophical interest. Somehow, people do come to regard stealing as wrong, and one can proceed to analyze the logic of normative claims about stealing and the conceptual problems the concept of stealing generates. Social theory cannot avoid the problem, but for the most part it has been ignored in recent discussions. The serious attempts to deal with it were in the late nineteenth century.

Tönnies provides a clever solution to the problem with Austin's explanation by identifying the voice of moral command with the voice of the parent. The child is in awe of the parent, responds to the commands of the parent, and habitualizes these commands. The commands of parents are themselves normative, so this solves the problem of the insertion of normativity in socialization by deriving it from the fact of parental command. The commands are then habitualized and more importantly habitualized as norms rather than merely as prudentially useful habits. Norms are thus acquired.

But on examination, Tönnies's account has the same problem as Austin's. When, later in life, we respond to the habitualized commands of our parents, we regard *some* of them as moral and binding upon other people, but others as merely the peculiarities of our parents. And we seem to make this distinction by reference to something other than commands of parents. So the difference between moral commands and commands has to arise from another source. Tönnies has a kind of a solution to this problem: norms derive from the commands of the will of society and are merely expressions of this will. When we listen to our conscience we are really listening to the will of society commanding us to behave in a particular way or to feel particular feelings. Of course this answer rather closely resembles answers to the question of the validity of law, which refer back to the will of the people or the will of the sovereign and suffer from the same problems.

Appealing to society in this way is perhaps not much better than appealing to a fiction. But Durkheim, who presents an even more radical solution to these problems, does seem to go one better. Durkheim's approach is similar to Tönnies's notion that within each of us there is a feeling of the social will in addition to our own individual will. For Durkheim there are actually two forms of consciousness within us, one collective, the other individual, and the phenomenology of our feelings is a product of the causal pushing and shoving of these forms of consciousness, each of which operates in a slightly different way. Durkheim's solution to the problem of normativity is to identify it, under the broader heading of constraint, with the causal pushing and shoving that arises out of the collective consciousness and experienced by us phenomenologically, like our conscience, as internal to us. Durkheim solved the socialization problem in a way that also parallels Tönnies. The problem of moral education, for Durkheim, is a problem of building up the collective consciousness in a way that distinguishes the collective constraints from the mere constraints that one individual might exercise over another. The solution to Tönnies's problem is that the collective is moral, and the moral can have no origin other than the collective. There is no problem of separating the parental will from the social will, because the source is the social will, to which some of the commands of the parents conform.

Durkheim focuses on the child's experience in the classroom and describes the need for the teacher to subordinate themselves to the rules and higher symbols of authority. Through observing the teacher subordinating him or herself to authority and having the teacher's authority exercised on behalf of this higher authority in accordance with it on the student, the student develops the collective heart of the consciousness and comes to see the binding character of the commands of society which are initially mediated through symbolic representations like the flag. Durkheim has the idea that, parallel to the special moment in Tönnies in which the child in awe of the parent internalizes commands, it is in the moments of high collective emotion in which the individual is especially susceptible to common feelings and common senses of subordination to something higher.

Durkheim's views are instructive in relation to Kripke's because they point to what a "normative all the way down" social theory would have to look like, if by all the way down we mean all the way down historically, and seek to explain the origins of communal assessments, their changes, and their diversity.[2] Durkheim provides an explanation of normativity by identifying it with collective constraint. But it is not clear that the idea of a collective consciousness is a plausible explanatory idea. And it raises the question of whether going all the way down historically in our quest for a plausible account of normativity makes sense. Durkheim

---

[2] For a more elaborate discussion of Durkheim's actual theory on these subjects, especially on the role of collective effervescence and the fusion of minds in the creation of morals, see Turner (1993).

and appeals to collective phenomena do not exhaust the possible forms of explanation of communal assessments, of course, and communal assessments may not need to be a part of the explanation of normativity. Brandom indeed, as we shall see, has a different suggestion, that does not appeal to any communal facts.

The Explanatory Problem II: Explaining Non-normativity

McLuhan says at one point that there is no such thing as a grammatical error in preliterate society, by which he means that the rules of grammar are the byproduct of practical exigencies of writing. Whether this view is correct or not I would not attempt to say. However, it points to an interesting form of argument. Rules of grammar do not need to be "normative all the way down" in the historical sense, if we accept McLuhan's argument as at least logically possible. Prior to writing, there is no correct or incorrect grammar, there are merely utterances that are understood and utterances that are not understood. It may be that we can have an activity, perhaps even an extremely complex activity, which is not characterized in normative language at all, much less in the language of binding rules or "norms" proper. But it may subsequently come to be characterized in normative language, and in so doing become normative.

Something like this reasoning, I take it, is essential to both Nietzsche's and Weber's genealogies of morals. Both Nietzsche and Weber begin their accounts of morality not with Ihering-like individuals who are, so to speak, already rational and faced only with the problem of whether to accept legal orders or norms as binding, but rather at a somewhat more primitive level of the herd, a group driven by primal, quasi-biological urges, of which one important urge is simply the urge to conform. There is a certain similarity between this primal stage and childhood in Tönnies and Durkheim, but for Nietzsche and Weber this stage is not properly speaking moral at all. The herd has no real consciousness, and certainly no moral consciousness. Nevertheless, there is a kind of collective reflex of such that if anyone in the herd does anything unusual the rest of the herd recoils in a kind of fearful horror. For Nietzsche and also for Weber early morality or the early development of society in the historical/anthropological sense has this character.

In Nietzsche's account, it is only at the very late stage at which an individual breaks out of this fearful conformity and makes their own morals that there is any real issue of morality at all. Once an individual steps out of the herd, the herd comes to define itself in moral terms in opposition to this individual. So, strictly speaking, the origins of morality are in the actions of the exceptional individual and the morals he makes for himself, without which the herd would simply remain a herd. Actual moralities in the form of moral doctrines are simply, so to speak, ideological articulations of the impulses and aims of this exceptional individual and, when it is stirred to respond, of the herd itself. The herd ideologizes its horror of exceptional individuals and forms morality through a process of resentment of these individuals, and the exceptional individual articulates justification or accounting of his own project which is characteristically also a project of commanding others, so it requires a kind of theory – though obviously this can be a pretty minimal affair, such as the "theory" that the gods will be angered – legitimating the command.

Weber handles these problems in a somewhat different way. He begins with the same biologically driven conformist herd and argues that the biological urge to conform continues to drive much of human action, along with the force of habit. Rational action or action approximating rational action is only a small portion of human life and actions themselves are characteristically mixed, being partly determined by rational considerations and partly by forces of emotion and habit. It is only at, so to speak, the highest levels of the articulation of moral theories that it makes sense to speak of morality, and "implicit norm," to the extent that they exist at all can only be habitualizations, perhaps married to emotion, of previously articulated moral theories of one kind or another. In a sense, this is the McLuhan argument applied to morality. Moral theories are not about preexisting implicit norms, but are rather the beginning of norms and normativity as such.

This of course applies to the historical/anthropological moment of the origins of norms rather than to the problem of socialization, but one may imagine socialization being given a parallel treatment. Children are not born making elaborate distinctions between the will of parents, that which is causally effective, that which is universally commanded or obligatory, and so forth. The distinctions are obviously the product of developed explicit ideas or, in a minimal sense of the word, "theories" of one sort or another, and most of the relevant theories or beliefs are magical or religious in character. Ideas about natural justice or natural morality, and obviously Kantian ideas about obligation are very late developments. We can identify two processes here. One is the process by which feelings and responses become theorized about in such a way as to make them "moral," that is to say, the McLuhan process. Another is the process by which moral distinctions degenerate from the level of conscious belief to a level of habit together with a moral vocabulary of approval and disapproval in which the original "theory" is forgotten. Once it is forgotten it can be reflected upon in new ways. There is, in connection with these processes, no need to appeal to the notion of implicit norms as some sort of distinct order of fact, or to think of moral reflection as the making explicit and theorizing about these supposed implicit norms. In fact, as I have noted elsewhere, Weber goes out of his way to categorize actions and repeated actions, as well as repeated actions governed by or understood in terms of theories about their validity, in such a way that no category of action corresponding to "action governed by implicit norms" actually arises (Turner and Factor 1990). In the case of Nietzsche the problem is less clear, but what is clear is that the stuff that is reflected upon and articulated by moral theories is not some sort of mass of implicit norms but rather a mass of common feelings of resentment, which are neither collective nor obligatory, but are merely common to the individuals who make up the herd and respond herd-like to one another.

Something similar to this form of argument, but far more clever, is to be found in the writings of the philosopher of law Axel Hägerström. Hägerström very effectively ridiculed theories of the law based on ideas of the will of the sovereign or the will of the people and thus paved the way for legal positivism, though in some respects legal positivism was quite alien to his understanding of the law. Rather than positing a *Grundnorm*, like Kelsen, which simply evades the question or blocks the question of causes and of legal validity, Hägerström constructs a kind of sociological history of the Roman law in which he makes the point, evident even in writers like Weber, that a great many of the legal formulae familiar to us from Roman legal practice are essentially magical in character (Olivecrona, in Hägerström 1953: xiv).

This approach may be usefully compared to the line of attack Brandom employs with respect to performative utterances. The classic performative utterance is the priest who says "I pronounce you man and wife," thus changing their statuses. Classifying this as a performative utterance is valuable for some philosophical purposes, no doubt, and one might construct a "philosophical theory" of performative utterances. But the obvious question raised by this particular performative utterance is why anyone takes it to have the magical effect of transforming the statuses of the relevant individuals and, more importantly, the effect of making them into a different kind of people bonded in a different kind of way. It is possible to speak of these changes purely in van Gennapian terms, as Brandom quite unconsciously does, and think of this as a ritual involving a changing of statuses (van Gennep 1960). The point Hägerström makes is that the issue is not so much the mere changing of statuses, and consequently of normative expectations, but rather the magical powers that are attributed to the priest that make him alone, or something with the same powers, capable of performing this magical transformation as well as the beliefs of the participants in the detailed specifics of the transformation they have gone through. Obviously this transformation is more than a mere change in statuses, in legal powers in relation to one another. But even the notion of "legal power" in relation to another has a kind of magical significance that is not accounted for in the bloodless notion of changing statuses, unless we understand status itself, as Weber would, to imply something essentially magical itself about the charisma and powers of the individuals in question.

My point in mentioning Hägerström is to show that something like the undifferentiated state that Nietzsche and Weber attribute to pre-moral society applies, or can be employed, in the case of the law. Reasoning like this obviously has its nineteenth-century roots in writers like Comte, who also begin with a kind of undifferentiated magical thinking in the case of science which gradually becomes differentiated first through theological reasoning and later through science but which retains, for example in the case of the concept of causality, the remnants of the age of magical thinking, for instance the notion of causal powers or the notion of law as in physics as something more than mere description. For Comte, when physics reached the positive stage all of these prepositive notions would evaporate, and that we would no longer feel the need for metaphysical notions such as "cause." Hägerström may be read as suggesting that in the law they never quite evaporate, or rather that they leave as a residue a "general social estimation" (which is something like a set of habitual expectations produced by the experience of living under law as a method of cooperation) which will persist "even if feelings originally produced by superstition should lose their power over men's minds" (Passmore 1961: 154). To put this point in terms of an example, consider promising. It is difficult to get an account of the origins of promising. But it is plausible to say that it arises from the kinds of institutions, and beliefs, that Marcel Mauss describes in *The Gift* ([1950] 1954). The idea that one must fulfill promises makes perfect sense if it is associated with a belief that in accepting something one accepts a spiritual attachment to the thing which must go home to its source through a return gift. That the ritual of promising survives the decline of the belief also is understandable, as the belief depends on other beliefs that are not about promising.

Wittgenstein

Wittgenstein may be taken, as indeed Brandom takes him, to have a "norms all the way down" account of the learning of rules, and consequently also to have a pervasive notion of the normativity of social life. One might also interpret Wittgenstein as claiming that norms in some sense inhere in or are rooted in or based upon facts about communities, and that expressions about what we do or say are expressions of a kind of community "we."[3] I think these are all bad interpretations. I nevertheless do not intend here to mount a full-scale assault on them. However, I would like to sketch out an alternative answer to both the problem of the two moments of normativity and to the problem of regression on the basis of some Wittgensteinian texts. What I have said about Weber and Nietzsche is especially relevant to this interpretation.

Let me begin with some material from the lectures of the early 1930s. Wittgenstein speaks of rules being based on "language habits" (Ambrose 1979). When he says this I take it that he means to distinguish between something that is not a matter of "rules" and something that is. This raises an appropriate question about the notion of norms going all the way down. All the way down in the sense of the actual causal basis of rule-following seems in these passages to mean all the way down to our language habits which are the psychological facts which are the causal basis of rules. We may ask the question "are the habits themselves normative?" Some things that Wittgenstein says in these lectures, something about training, suggests that these habits *are* already "normative." When we train someone in such a way that they acquire the language habits that are the basis of or conditions of rules we train them by saying things about whether something is right or wrong. Training, one might say, inherently involves rightness and wrongness and consequently normativity. So the moment of training is the moment of normativization in the socialization sense.

---

[3] A useful discussion of these issues is to be found in Schatzki 1996: 65–8 and *passim*.

But there are other places in which Wittgenstein seems to come closer to McLuhan in thinking that the distinctions between normative and practical do not apply universally or are not universally meaningful. In the second paragraph of the *Philosophical Investigations*, in discussing the builders, for example, he describes a language game in which there is no vocabulary for right and wrong. Moreover, certain familiar linguistic distinctions do not have any application to the example as he has described it. This raises an interesting possibility, namely that the child's experience of learning a rule or learning how to speak is not (in the same way that the language of builders is not) yet differentiated into the categories of normative and practical or causal. When one teaches a child to say "please" in order to have a request honored the child simply repeats the term and learns, so to speak empirically, what happens when the term is used. She or he learns that it increases the likelihood that requests will be honored, perhaps, and may also be corrected when the term is misapplied, if indeed the child misapplies it.

The idea that this is the "right" thing to do is somewhat problematically related to its causal effectiveness. One could imagine discussing with a more experienced user of the term, a child who noticed that it worked sometimes and not others, and explaining that saying "please" is a polite thing to do whether or not it works, or whether or not it works with a particular person. One wonders whether it is at this stage that one begins to differentiate between the causal practical sense of "please" and the normative sense, but one also notices that at this point one is giving explicit accounts – a "theory of politeness" so to speak, in which saying "please" is claimed to be "normative" – not something implicit.

The same question may be asked more generally about language. When we train a child in linguistic use, are we simply giving some sort of normative lesson (and perhaps do we think we are doing something normative because we know something historical/ anthropological about language, namely that the rules of language are normative), or are we simply conveying a practical skill which is no different than other practical skills, like tying a shoe, in which we teach a technique? One answer to these questions might be that in the initial formation of language habits, and many other things, these distinctions are not really applicable. Giving a child linguistic knowledge or forming a linguistic habit by ostensively training a response to "bird," for example, is more or less like saying "call this thing and things like it 'bird' and other people will understand what you are talking about." We can think of this knowledge as altogether causal, and indeed high functioning autistics and people with personality disorders of the sort that prevent them from acting morally or recognizing moral obligations also can learn to use this language to serve their purposes.

It is an interesting question as to whether a body of sociopaths, that is to say, users but not normative followers of moral rules, could create moral rules or develop moral vocabulary in the historical/anthropological sense. But what they would create, if they created any rules, would be causal prudential rules that would be indistinguishable from what we call moral rules. It is an interesting question as to whether one could have a community of high functioning autistics and sociopaths, but there is no question that such individuals exist and often nicely mimic both rule-following and moral behavior which, arguably, they apprehend in a non-moral fashion.

It might be objected at this point that a trick has been introduced into the argument. Language habits are not rules, for language habits as such do not involve the notion of mistake. As soon as the notion of mistake appears, one has normativity and one is in an entirely different domain. Notions like mistake are inherently normative, and don't in any obvious way derive from a theory that has been habitualized and forgotten leaving merely the residue of the moral vocabulary of right and wrong. So it is as though a condition for language use, namely language habits, has been substituted for the whole explanation of a norm which must include a "normative element" in addition to the habit. One might also reason, as Brandom does, that this normative element is the thing that solves the problem of gerrymandering because it picks out the one possible habit that is the correct one. In short, someplace, some sort of tacit normative element has been snuck into this discussion or else the moment of the emergence of the normative has been misdescribed in some way.

I think this objection has something to it, but not what it appears to have. Consider a mundane example. I am teaching my child to hammer a nail. I believe that there is a right and wrong way to do this, and I even have some criteria for distinguishing the two. I can say, for example, that some ways of hammering a nail leave hammer marks on the surface of the thing that the nail is being hammered into. If the nail is bent, the hammering job is incorrect. These are all external factual criteria that do not really dictate the "right way" to hammer a nail, which I believe to be in three successive strokes, one soft, one hard, and another soft. I train my child in my preferred method until the child can do it easily. A habit has been acquired, along with a vocabulary of right and wrong. It looks as though we can actually use the notion of gerrymandering here to distinguish between the causal and the normative part of this acquisition of a technique. The causal part is the part that pertains to the damage done to the surface or to the nail. But there are obviously many other ways to drive nails that fulfill these criteria than the particular method that I advocate and call correct. Now I, the trainer, am picking out one of the possible ways of doing this that I label correct. Unfortunately, in this case, I also have a theory about what is correct. I do not merely know the right way of pounding a nail when I see it, but can actually articulate some aspects of the process.

Suppose, however, that I am an inarticulate carpenter and I know both how to drive a nail and how to recognize that one is being driven correctly, so that I can say "that was a mistake" or "that was right" and I apply these notions not to the result – the driven nail, which might have gone in nicely as a result merely of a lucky blow – but to the technique. What would training consist of for the inarticulate carpenter? The trainee would merely get "correct" and "mistake," or "right" and "wrong," or a nod or shake of the head as responses to his attempts to drive the nail. So of all of the habits that he might at the beginning be forming, gradually one after another is extinguished as the responses of "mistake" or "wrong" narrows down the possible habits out of the total range of possible habits with which the trainee began. Now consider the following. Are nods and shakes of the head any different, from the point of view of the trainee, than the appearance of a mark or a bent nail as a result of a hammer swing? The difference is their source, obviously. But the effects are identical in the sense that each of them forces the habit into a smaller possible range. In the end, the training produces performances within some acceptable range, no less for the bending of nails and the making of hammer marks than for the "rights" and "wrongs" uttered by the trainer. At some stage the trainee may come to recognize that he was getting the hang of it and also to recognize other people doing it correctly. The trainee may even come to reflect on this even to the extent of developing a theory of his own about these habits.

The cutting-down of the scope, or the gerrymandering, is done as a matter of habit, and there is no essential difference from the point of view of psychological mechanisms, or for that matter of eliminating alternatives, that differs between somebody saying "right" and "wrong" and somebody looking at the marks made by the hammer or the bent nails. This is important because it suggests that normativity does not enter into language habits at some mystical point at which the term "mistake" first gets applied by someone, nor does any mystical transubstantiation occur, because in addition to the feedback one gets from the nail and the surface one gets "right" and "wrong" from a trainer. For indeed, to this point in the discussion, nothing mystical happens at all. In a sense it is only when we make some sort of distinction between two kinds of right and wrong, the one that derives solely from the trainer and the one that derives from the physical world, do we have a hint of something distinctly "normative." And the distinctive thing turns out to be nothing other than the input of the trainer. But even this input is not normative in the differentiated sense. The trainer may not even be aware that there is any other way to hammer a nail without bending it or making a mark, and think that his "right" and "wrong" are themselves solely in the domain of the causal or practical world, and he may even be right about this. It seems like a factual question whether there are other ways of producing results with the hammer. One way you might go about answering this factual question would be to survey other carpenters or other communities of carpenters and see whether they posses any such technique, and if they do, then it is clear that what has been added is in some sense normative and connected to particular communities, as this case may be. In this case one could be normative without knowing it. And perhaps this is the only case of implicit norms that can be made to pass muster. But what is implicit in this case is not the activity or the standards of right and wrong but their normative character, which is misrecognized as something else or not noticed at all.

Consider a third case. The carpenter is completely inarticulate. He hammers, and produces goods, but cannot train anyone by saying "that's right." Is it the case that no one can learn carpentry from this person? Is it the case that this person could not have learned carpentry from another person without that other person using normative language like "right"? Would there be any visible difference between carpentry done by a person who learned in this way and one who learned "normatively"? Wittgenstein clearly wishes to answer this question by saying that it is possible. He discusses the possibility of a person picking up chess by observing chess-players without learning the rules. The problem with this case is this: is the person's knowledge of chess normative knowledge? Does the fact that some people play by and know rules mean that everyone does so, only that some do so without realizing it?

The issue arises in connection with each of these examples. If the inarticulate carpenter says "yes" or "no," are these terms used normatively, or could they simply be expressions of preference and distaste, or comprehension and incomprehension, or satisfaction and fear? Learning to perform the activity is consistent with any of these. The only responses that are unambiguously normative as distinct from expressing something else are those in which terms explicitly classed as normative are explicitly given, and given an explicit justification in terms of something that is explicitly normative. And this means that whatever is implicit cannot be distinguished as normative.

Perhaps the largest source of support for the notion of implicit norms, once we get rid of the notion that only normativity solves the problem of gerrymandering, is the problem of what makes something normative, which we can now see as a kind of aspect of the regression problem. Justifying something as normative seems to require normative justification, which according to the regression problem eventually must be implicit. So the implicit thing must be normative. But if Weber, Nietzsche, and, as I have argued, Wittgenstein, are right, there is a great deal of undifferentiated causal and "normative" activity which goes on and even may be associated with various emotions, without being clearly normative in the sense that a normative–causal distinction clearly applies to it. This is important to recognize, because it is sometimes tempting to think that organized activity is not possible without normativity, and that normativity requires some sort of universally applicable and radically separated notion of normativity. If it does not, the real issue is not the activity or even its social character, but rather the question of the nature of justifications for the use of terms like "mistake" and "wrong." Here I think Nietzsche, Weber, and Hägerström are more plausible.

Brandom cites Weber's use of the term *Entzauberung* by way of explaining the notion that we impose normative significance on the world. He comments that "One of the defining characteristics of early science is its disenchantment of the world" (1994: 48). The process of disenchantment is one in which "The meanings and values that had previously been discerned in things are stripped off along with the supernatural and are understood as projections of human interests, concerns, and activities onto an essentially indifferent and insignificant matter" (1994: 48). But Weber's *historical* point is quite different from this sentence, and closer to what Brandom says about early science. For Weber, the fact that matter is essentially indifferent and insignificant is a late discovery. We did not impose the meanings and values and supernatural on these things – we never separated supernatural from natural until very late in our intellectual development. The world came to us, so to speak, enchanted: we disenchanted it through explicitly theorizing about it. We do the differentiating between normative and factual on our grounds, in the course of improving our expectations about the world. There is no process of imposing norms on the world, such as Brandom supposes. But there is a process of reading normativity back into phenomena, such as the grunts of the carpenter or the acquisition of the practice of carpentry, which are not unambiguously normative, and this is the process in which Brandom is engaged.

If we return to the original question of this essay, the question of whether one can make normative soup out of non-normative bones, we can now see a number of possible answers. One answer would be that normative and non-normative, causal and intentional, are distinctions that arise late both in the historical/anthropological development of social life and in the child's development. When they emerge, they emerge through the differentiating of something that is already there. In the case of historical/anthropological development, the initial thing is some sort of magical thinking which is neither normative nor causal but which is retained in some sense in the categories "normative" and "causal" that ultimately emerge. It is very difficult to eradicate from science quasi-magical notions such as a causal power or theological notions such as law, just as it is very difficult to eradicate charismatic elements from legal procedure and mystical theological elements from moral discourse. In each case the difficulty betrays the origins of the things that we have now elected to put into these categories. In this case the normative soup is not being made from non-normative bones so much as decomposed from something that is neither normative nor causal, such as magic, into something normative and something causal.

An alternative way of looking at this problem of making normative soup is a bit more reductionist. Consider the poets' saying that "stone walls do not a prison make." The cynics' response to this is "but throw in some guards and barbed wire and you have something there." Something similar may be said with respect to norms and normative practice. We call something normative not because we think there is a normative element but because, taken together, the activity amounts to something we call normative. Calling something normative is a factual rather than a normative enterprise, much less a matter of imposing or instituting. It requires having grounds for doing so, and the grounds may be highly varied, and justify quite different kinds of normativity claims. To say that one must do something, or that something is the right way to do it, because it the way the "best people" do it is to give a justification of this sort, and to assert a very specific kind of normativity, the normativity of etiquette books. These justifications or theories may not be very good theories, and in the end they may all rest on quasi-magical notions, such as a quasi-magical notion of the goodness of the "best people." But they are theories nevertheless.

Brandom's Account of Origins

Brandom's own suggestion of an answer to the problem of the origins of normativity is found in a footnote. His starting point is in the phenomenon of "acting correctly according to one's intentional states" (1994: 659 n. 49), and his problem is the question of how correctness in this sense, which requires "the distinction of perspective between producing performances and assessing them" (1994: 152), can arise in the first place. Brandom agrees with Davidson "in seeing intentional states and speech acts as fundamentally of coeval conceptual status, neither being explicable except in an account that includes the other" (1994: 152). Davidson's reasoning is that understanding speech acts requires the attribution of intentions to the actor, but only language users can attribute intentional states.[4] Put differently, assessing performances and having the perspective of assessment is a language-dependent phenomenon; but at the same time language use depends on attributing intentions. Normativity is thus coeval with language.

Brandom observes that what Davidson has given us is not so much an argument as the form of one, and Brandom seeks to remedy this (1994: 153). What I have done in this essay is also to deal

---

[4] A more complete quotation follows:

it is not evidently incoherent to imagine one organism shaping its own behavior by responding to its responses with positively and negatively reinforcing behavior. What makes such a suggestion odd is that one would think that the capacity to distinguish correct from incorrect performance that is exercised in the postulated responsive disposition to assess would also be available at the time the original performance is produced, so that no behavior-shaping ground is gained by the two-stage procedure. But this need not be the case; the assessment might be addressed toward the performance as characterized by its consequences, discernible more readily in the event than the advent . . . the behavior-shaping in question is not here . . . deliberate, a matter of explicitly expressible intentions. . . . If the intra-organism reinforcement story is coherent, then regularity versions of the sanctions approach to implicit norms need be social only in the sense that they essentially involve the distinction of perspective between producing performances and assessing them. (Brandom 1994: 658–9 n. 45) with the form of arguments about normativity rather than to provide actual explanations of norms. But even at this level some important things can be seen. One is that any account of rules behind the rules – implicit norms – has two major defects. The first is that making norms implicit does not make them self-applying. The second is that any account that demands some sort of radical alteration in kind between non-normative and normative requires an explanation that can account for a radical alteration in kind. As Brandom sees, it is unhelpful to appeal to the emergence of a perspective of assessment, or the emergence of speech acts, or of intentionality, because they all depend on one another, and because there is no equally radical prior alteration of similar magnitude that is independent of these things to which an explanation can appeal. So it is unlikely that there will be a plausible resolution of a problem constructed in this way. But *some* plausible argument must be constructed to give the necessity argument its explanatory force.

If an alterative account that avoids the problem of a radical alteration is possible, it is instantly better, if it is at all plausible. What I have tried to show here is that an account that is, to make a geological analogy, uniformitarian, that does not depend on supposing there to have been processes in the past that differ from those of the present, can handle the explanation of the taking of particular things as normative. The account is simply this: the fact that we can give explicit arguments, or mini-theories, in justification of claims that something falls into the family of thins that we call "normative" *is* the answer to the problem. The fact of something becoming normative is that these arguments are accepted (though they may later be forgotten). Ihering was half-right in his recognition theory of legal validity. It is not the recognition of good effects that makes the law binding, so much as the acceptance of *explicit* arguments to the effect that it is binding that makes it binding.

The arguments are not necessarily themselves normative, though they may appeal to "magical" or charismatic notions. One can say that these are "normative." But in the end, the classification of explicit theories, for example the concept of *mana*, into these categories is of little interest, for there is no mysterious fact of normativity, no normative ingredient, that the classification will enable us to filter out. "Normativity" is just our category for distinguishing theories of this sort from theories of another sort, factual ones. Brandom, of course, insists that explicit arguments, and theorizing about commitments of this sort always depends on implicit norms of argument. He is caught in the trap described by Schmitt in relation to the law. But if what I have said about the pragmatic character of the child's use of "please" is correct, the point may be extended to argument as well. To establish that there is a moment at which the whole business of human conduct, such as using language to persuade, becomes normative requires us to read back features of our account of normativity into the conduct.[5]

Parsons and ethnomethodology, as I have suggested, rest on a similarly "read back" notion of the normative. In the case of Parsons, the problem of normativity arose from the problem of the explanation of action. He reasoned that every action had to have, by definition, an end, and that ends were ultimately either means to other ends or ends in themselves, and that all means to other ends had to lead to ends in themselves. Such ends were, by definition, normative, and all action thus had, by definition, a normative dimension. So the fact that actions could not all be accounted for by reference to explicit norms, such as the law, meant that they had necessarily to be explained by implicit ones. But this necessity follows not from any fact, but from the theory of action and definitions of means and ends with which Parsons begins. Ethnomethodology employs a different notion of necessity. It claims, like Brandom, that various social activities are impossible without the existence of implicit rules, which it purports to discover. But it cannot rid itself of the suspicion that these activities can be accounted for by a combination of explicit considerations and habits, and thus that the rules it "discovers" to operate have themselves also been read back into what is not normative or even rule-governed.

[5] I should note that a great deal of Brandom's actual discussion, especially in his conclusion, is congenial to the approach I have taken here, as when he discusses the moment at which we, in effect, discover that we have had assumptions and can become explicit about how ours differ from those of others. "Having been all along implicitly normative beings, at this stage of expressive development we can become explicit to ourselves *as* normative begins – aware both of the sense in which we are creatures of the norms and of the sense in which they are creatures of ours" (Brandom 1994: 641–2). The difference between us is a difference over what we are doing when we reach this stage. I think we become aware that other people behave and reason differently (a process I discuss in Turner 1980) and construct theories about these differences, some of which help us to make sense of their behavior or reasoning. Brandom thinks that in doing this we are making something explicit – hence the title of his book. I think there is no "it" there to be made explicit. The "assumptions" we attribute to them are at most useful accessories to our ways of constructing and translating their actions into ours, not things in their head, or in the social ether. The only "it" that is not explicit is habits of mind (cf. Turner 1994).

References

Ambrose, Alice, ed. 1979. *Wittgenstein's Lectures Cambridge 1932–1935* from the notes of Alice Ambrose and Margaret Macdonald. Chicago: University of Chicago Press.

Austin, John. 1954. *The Province of Jurisprudence Determined*. New York and Cambridge: Cambridge University Press.

Brandom, Robert B. 1994. *Making It Explicit: Reasoning, Representing, and Discursive Commitment*. Cambridge, MA and London: Harvard University Press.

Durkheim, Emite. [1925] 1973. *Moral Education: A Study in the Theory and Application of the Sociology of Education*. New York: Free Press.

Gennep, Arnold van. 1960. *Ritets of Passage*, trans. Monika B. Vezidom and Gabrielle L. Caffe. Chicago: University of Chicago Press.

Hägerström, Axel. 1953. *Inquiries Into the Nature of Law and Morals*, ed. K. Olivecrona, trans. C. D. Broad. Uppsala: Almqvist & Wiksell.

Ihering, R. Von. [1877] 1913. *Law as Means to an End*, vol. I, 4th ed., trans. I. Husik. New York: Macmillan.

Kovesi, Julius. 1971. *Moral Notions*. London and New York: Routledge & Kegan Paul.

Kripke, Saul A. 1982. *Wittgenstein on Rules and Private Language: An Elementary Exposition*. Cambridge, MA: Harvard University Press.

McDowell, John H. 1984. Wittgenstein on following a rule. *Synthese* 58: 325–63.

Mauss, Marcel. [1950] 1954. *The Gift: Forms and Functions of Exchange in Archaic Societies*, trans. Ian Cunnison. Glencoe, IL: Free Press.

Nietzsche, Friedrich. [1887] 1956. *The Birth of Tragedy & the Genealogy of Morals*, trans. Francis Golffing. New York: Doubleday.

——. 1982. *Daybreak: Thoughts on the Prejudices of Morality*, trans. R. J. Hollingdale. Cambridge and New York: Cambridge University Press.

Olivecrona, Karl. [1939] 1971. *Law as Fact*. 2nd ed. London: Stevens.

——. 1948. Is a sociological explanation of law possible? *Theoria* 14: 167–207.

Parsons, Talcott. 1937. *The Structure of Social Action. A Study in Social Theory with Special Reference to a Group of Recent European Writers*. New York and London: McGraw Hill.

Passmore, John. 1961. Hägerström's philosophy of law. *Philosophy* 36: 143–60.

Schatzki, Theodore R. 1996. *Social Practices: A Wittgensteinian Approach to Human Activity and the Social*. Cambridge and New York: Cambridge University Press.

Schmitt, Carl. [1922] 1985. *Political Theology: Four Chapters on the Concept of Sovereignty*, trans. George Schwab. Cambridge, MA and London: MIT Press.

Tönnies, Ferdinand. 1961. *Custom: An Essay on Social Codes*, trans. A. Farrell. Borenstein. Glencoe, IL: Free Press.

Turner, Stephen P. 1980. *Sociological Explanation as Translation*, Cambridge and New York: Cambridge University Press.

Turner, Stephen P., ed. 1993. London and New York: Routledge.

———. 1994. *The Social Theory of Practices: Tradition, Tacit Knowledge and Presuppositions*, Chicago: University of Chicago Press.

Turner, Stephen P. and Regis A. Factor. 1990. Weber and the end of tradition. In *Midwest Studies in Philosophy XV*. Notre Dame, IN: University of Notre Dame Press.

———. 1994. *Max Weber: The Lawyer as Social Thinker*. London and New York: Routledge.

Wearne, Bruce C. 1989. *The Theory and Scholarship of Talcott Parsons to 1951: A Critical Commentary*. New York: Cambridge University Press.

Weber, Max. [1922] 1978. *Economy and Society: An Outline of Interpretive Sociology*, trans. E. Fischoff et al., ed. G. Roth and C. Wittich. Berkeley: University of California Press.

Wittgenstein, Ludwig. [1953] 1958. *Philosophical Investigations*. 3rd ed., trans. G. E. M. Anscombe. New York: Macmillan.

Wright, Crispin. 1980. *Wittgenstein on the Foundations of Mathematics*. Cambridge, MA: Harvard University Press.

5 Criteria for a Theory of Knowledge

Jennifer L. Croissant

Introduction

This essay is framed in the context of a "dialogue of sociology and philosophy."[1] The first step toward adequate examination of this dialogue is to expand the conversation to include science and technology studies (STS) as a product of specific intersections of sociology and philosophy. The second step is to include feminist theories, and the third to focus the dialogue on sociological theories of knowledge and the transformations of epistemologies as complex and contentious convergences of philosophical and sociological discourse. The project is to find the criteria for social theories of knowledge as framed by postmodern philosophical discourses, the insights of postpositivist sociological theory, and the normative considerations of feminist and other progressive social change agendas.

The goal of this essay is to articulate some propositions and criteria for evaluating theories of knowledge as knowledge claims.[2] I begin with a brief analysis of criteria for theories of knowledge, beginning first with an examination of the possibilities and perils

[1] This essay is based in part on a selection from my dissertation (Croissant 1994), and a presentation at the American Sociological Association Annual Meeting (New York), August 16–20, 1996, in the Theory Section Session, "Sociology and Philosophy: The Dialogue to Date." I wish to thank Professor Alan Sica, organizer of the panel, the other panelists, and the audience members for valuable discussions.
[2] As has been noted in studies of technological innovation, inventions often suffer in comparison to traditional devices and activities, since the criteria by which innovations are judged have been based on the previous "paradigm." Constant (1973) implies that innovators should be prepared to suggest the criteria by which their innovations be judged.

of theory in general, and then moving to theories of knowledge more specifically. This will facilitate a transformation of the apparent stagnation of feminist epistemological programs as well as dilemmas apparent in science and technology studies as a broadly defined theoretical and political field. In addition, examination of possible criteria of knowledge is essential to the further development of programs in the sociology of objectivity, validity, and knowledge. Science studies, in its sociological manifestations, needs the insights of feminist theory. The corollary holds as well: there is a marked necessity for sociologizing feminist accounts and the general project of critical theories of science. What is at stake are notions of theory, variously critical, feminist, and sociological. I will discuss theories of knowledge in relation to questions about what a theory of knowledge must "do" or account for, in relation to itself as knowledge, in relation to social theory generally, and in relation to the (often conflicting) interests and political agendas of feminism and professionalized inquiry.

While postmodernist interrogations of knowledge are essential to the ongoing debates about the intersections of sociological and philosophical epistemologies, a detailed discussion of the relations of postmodernism, its negations of explanatory enterprises and dismissals of humanism, are beyond this essay. I have instead focussed on feminist critiques informed by postmodernism and the dilemma which they generate. Teresa de Lauretis (1987: 146) situates this as a problem in women's studies of cinematic representations: "most of the terms by which we speak of the construction of the female social subject bear in their visual form the prefix *de* to signal the deconstruction or destructuring, if not destruction, of the very thing to be represented." Similarly, feminist engagements with science, or inquiry more generally, have the critique down pat. But we have little yet to help us select among alternatives or to endorse projects. The solution to this problem is to use critical approaches as a necessary step in generating new theories and cultural productions, and to turn the critique into criteria for positive work. As cultural productions feminist critiques of science are in themselves generative, but the positive problem- or hypothesis-generating possibilities of feminist analyses of science are generally latent rather than manifest.[3]

It is simply unimportant whether philosophers decide we can or cannot generate theories understood to be "universal" in some

---

[3] That is, feminist projects explanatory *of* and *within* the social and natural sciences are few and far between.

sense. And, unlike Hartsock (1987a, 1983) for whom "right" explanations are necessary for social action, I am arguing for thinking of social explanations as necessary but not sufficient for informing progressive agendas.[4] This aligns this project with other emergent postpositivist sociological theories move beyond monocausal, deterministic models and into more flexible and strategic accountings in constructing explanations for facets of social life, including technoscientific production.

While Nye (1995) argues for productive critical re-engagements with canonical works and figures, continuation of the tradition of conventional sociological theory understood to be focussing on the canon (Marx, Weber, and Durkheim) generally reduces social theory to literary theory, and while much fun, is a disservice to the profession and to progressive social change agendas. Similarly, much meaningful work remains to be done re(re)discovering lost sociological sisters (such as the recurrent rediscovery of Gilman or Martineau) or examining the gendered assumptions or treatments of gender and sexual difference in sociological and philosophical scholarship.[5] These approaches generally reinscribe conventional criteria for sociological theory and practice. Instead I want to more generally reopen "theory" to a multiplicity of discourses and empirical engagements.

When someone says they are interested in "theory" or "doing theory," what is required is an interrogation of the *prepositions*. Theory has had much success in scrutinizing its subjects and objects, and smaller and yet significant successes in looking at its practices and causal models (the verbs of sociological sentences). Instead, what is contemporary social theory *about*? Or *of*? Who is it *for*? If it is about only itself, of canonical figures, for a self-perpetuating professoriate, then it has wandered into the territory of scholasticism that C. W. Mills (1961) so cogently described, of grand theories abstracted from intelligible discourse, verifiable propositions, and the possibility of ameliorating social problems.[6] The strategy for the remainder of this essay takes on the question of the relationship between prepositions and propositions, and I do this by looking for pronouncements about what theory is in pedagogical and other didactic or synthetic texts, engaging briefly the problematics of what counts as theory and explanation.

[4] Hartsock's formulations border on Hume's naturalistic fallacy, positing a sufficient connection between *is* and *ought*.
[5] See, for example, Kandal (1988), Bologh (1990), and Fraser (1989).
[6] Loughlin (1992) describes the missing feminist revolution in science studies in similar terms.

In the following section, I describe theory as a dangerous and yet productive enterprise. Far from fully redeeming theoretical enterprises, I sustain the possibility of the impossibility or inherent undesirability of theory, at least as conventionally practiced, while I uphold the necessity of a refashioned social theory. Theories of knowledge are particularly tricky in this regard, primarily with respect to the notion of reflexivity. I discuss some formulations of what theory is said to be, and to do, as I meander through debates about theory from feminist perspectives, including the relations of theory and knowledge to experience, and feminism to sociology. The next section is a discussion of *knowledge* and formulations of knowledge in theoretical projects. Finally, I present a set of concerns about gender, power, and culture, and close with a discussion of social legitimation and emancipatory agendas for inquiry.

Doing Theory and Theory Undone

Social theory is a *normative* project, although that agenda has been hidden in various quests for legitimacy and objectivity by the field. I will here begin briefly with "what is a theory," or better, "what counts as theory."[7] Theories are expected to *explain*, particularly to explain why, not merely how (cf. Wilson 1981: 2). To explain [according to the *Oxford English Dictionary (OED)*] is to interpret, or to make plain, intelligible, or to clear of obscurity. Theories must also be testable, and preferably predictive. Further, "any worthwhile theory should [thus] perform the double function of explaining facts already known as well as opening up new vistas which can lead us to new facts" (Kaplan and Manners 1972: 11). These kinds of criteria, which might be organized loosely under the rubric of positivism, are easily targeted for criticism, not only because of outmoded assumptions about knowledge but also on political grounds. For example, Baym (1984: 45) comments that "Theory is, by nature, legalistic; infractions – the wrong theory, theoretical errors, or insouciant disregard for theoretical applications – are crimes; theory is a form of policing."

It is also worthwhile to note in this light an obsolete usage of the word "explain" from the *OED*, in which to explain is to smooth out or remove the roughness from something. Theories, then, as explanatory projects, are said to smooth over, or perhaps just ride roughshod over details and individual experiences. It also serves

---

[7] Calhoun (1996) recently inquired as to what should be the content of the journal *Sociological Theory*. Note immediately that this is a *normative* as well as an *analytic* or intellectual question.

well to note that theory is "a dubious project, when feminists build their theory using the master's tools" (Lorde 1981: 98).

Sociology was intended by its founding fathers to become a "male profession."[8] General textbooks occasionally note sociology's origins as a science of morality, and "moral statistics". It has been described as a field which proffers a degree which amounts to "three years of middle class men's class analysis."[9] Feminist theory in sociology is seen as feminist, rather than as a contribution to *sociological* theory generally (Smith 1990b: 21). The failure of much social theory to notice, address, explain or empower women's lives, if not adding to their oppression, is enough of a problem.[10]

To theorize is to contemplate, survey, suppose or assume. It is a looking at or viewing, or the contemplation or speculation of a sight or spectacle. Theory has its roots in ancient Greek as contemplation, especially as the perception of beauty, or the viewing of athletic contests. And it is understood to be a moral faculty. Theory, to continue with the *OED*, is understood to be a systematic statement of rules or principles; a statement of facts on which art or technology's subjects depend; or methods distinct from practice. Theory is also defined as a statement of general principles or laws, or only mere hypothesis or speculation. In engaging feminist theory, the field of discourse is diversified even further. As Kramarae and Treichler (1985: 447–8) note, there are significant differences in the use of the concept "theory" in feminist discourse, and significant resistance to it. Theory is primarily opposed to "experience" on one hand, and the overarching problem of interrelationships between the "specific" and the "general." The relationships between experience, knowledge, and theory provide the next turn toward the development of criteria for theories of knowledge.

Experience, Knowledge, and Theory

Knowledge, like theory, is often opposed to experience. I will be using the following orientation to this problem. Experience, which is always structured, can be understood, interpreted, perhaps reflected upon, articulated and made communicable, and can be acted upon. In becoming understood or meaningful, experience as the actuality of lived existence, the messy data of everyday life, is subject to reinterpretation and reevaluation. In that sense, I am using

[8] See Kramarae and Treichler (1985: 426); Kandal (1988); and Oakley, in Stanley and Wise (1983: 13).

[9] Monster, in Kramarae and Treichler (1985: 426).

[10] See especially Spender (1982), Smith (1987, 1990a, 1990b, 1992), and Patricia Hill Collins (1990), as well as Abbott and Wallace (1990).

"experience" and "understanding" much like Gerda Lerner (1986: 11) uses history with a lower-case "h" to identify "what happened in the past" and History, capital "H" for the institutionalized narrations and explanations of The Past. When "understanding" and "explanation" are institutionally legitimated, formal knowledge is the outcome. Science and technology can be understood as specific historical manifestations (or, more accurately, an institutionalization) of these general processes.

Part of the feminist reluctance to generalizing from experience is warranted, as I mentioned above, because the process of generalizing smooths over the rough details of everyday life. However, an additional discomfort comes from the idea that explanation is a form of domination and invalidates experience. Take, for instance, de Beauvoir's observation:

In the midst of an abstract discussion it is vexing to hear a man say: "You think thus and so because you are a woman"; but I know that my only defense is to reply: "I think thus and so because it is true," thereby removing my subjective self from the argument. It would be out of the question to reply: "And you think the contrary because you are a man," for it is understood that the fact of being a man is no peculiarity. (1952: xv)

Only if a complex "sociology of errors" is in force does the explanation of a belief, in this case "because you are a woman," result in its invalidation.[11] Unfortunately, explanation very frequently is experienced as a form of domination and negation of authority or the ability to author one's own subject position. Further, if the belief about explanations for beliefs as invalidating were not so popular, I would not be having as much trouble as I have with having "feminist" in the titles of my papers, or doing a sociology of knowledge at all. In the meantime, however, feminist hesitations about constructivist sociologies of knowledge are related to the postmodern problem that Haraway, Harding, Hartsock, and others have noticed: scholars pronounce the death of the subject and of authoritative knowledge just at the point where women, minorities, the oppressed and the previously unspoken and unauthored begin to theorize and speak authoritatively and *knowledgeably*, from experience and in various communities, about their silence and oppression. These issues require that sociologies of subjectivity be reconfigured to place voices in communities, and take the empowerment of collectivities, and through them individuals.

[11] Haraway (1991: 135) has more recently made note of this phenomenon: "For Westerners, it is a central consequence of gender difference that a person may be turned by another person into an object and robbed of his or her status of subject."

Consider, then, the criterion that theories be grounded in experience, which corrupts traditional distinctions between empiricist and rationalist epistemologies. A theoretical enterprise that considers and accounts for the "subjective" as *necessary*, but not sufficient for the production of "knowledge," will appear to be more productive or robust. Although it need not be explicitly phenomenological, theory which is based on adequate assumptions about the constitution of subjects will work more coherently. Social theories should address experience by showing where it comes from and how it relates to material social practices and the power relations which structure them, and as feminist theory, be attuned to women's experiences. Social theories of knowledge accounting for material and discursive structures and processes as sources of change and for resistance and differences in subjectivities and institutional forms will prove useful.

Although problematic for feminists, theory is nonetheless a vital necessity: . . . rather than turning our back on theory and taking refuge in experience alone, we should think in terms of transforming both the social relations of knowledge production and the type of knowledge produced. To do so requires that we tackle the fundamental questions of how and where knowledge is produced and by whom, and of what counts as knowledge. It also requires a transformation of the structures which determine how knowledge is disseminated or otherwise produced. (Weedon 1987: 7)

Theory, like inquiry generally, is a redeemable project if the relations of its production are transformed. This requires, however, a profound transformation of the notion of experience which is generally posited as pre- or non-discursive and not subject to revision or debate. Instead, as Haraway (1991: 109, 113) notes:[12]

Experience is a crucial product and means of the women's movement; we must struggle over the terms of its articulation. Women do not find "experience" ready to hand anymore than they/we find "nature" or the "body" preformed, always innocent, and waiting outside the violations of language and culture. Just as nature is one of culture's most startling and

---

[12] Haraway's position is somewhat in conflict with Grant's (1987) critique of experience-based epistemologies, although they have much in common. Grant provides a critical assessment of essentialist experienced-based theories of knowledge, which presuppose a social or biological nature which all women share. Grant (1987: 13) argues that "if experience is to be used as the basis for feminist epistemology it must be redefined," but she remarks that "experience simply exists." This is to presuppose, and mystify, the relationship between lived existence and "experience," and makes it difficult to analyze the ways in which the very basics of lived existence are structured by individuals and larger institutions.

non-innocent products, so is experience one of the least innocent, least self-evident aspects of historical embodied movement. . . . What counts as experience is never prior to the particular social occasions, the discourses, and other practices through which experience becomes articulated in and able to be articulated with other accounts, enabling the construction of collective experiences, a potent and often mystified operation.

To Harding and Hintikka (1983: x), "what counts as knowledge must be grounded in experience." One might take that to be a critique of rationalist epistemologies or idealist ontologies. But Harding and Hintikka are instead arguing for basing the legitimacy of knowledge claims in the experiences of those studied, preventing them from becoming objects of inquiry. Finally, the criterion that theory be based on "experience" is nearly redundant: all theories *are* based on experience – it is a matter of *whose* experiences, and the levels of abstraction and generalization drawn from such experiences.

Addressing experience in feminist theory is also associated with the criterion of "thinking from women's lives" (Harding 1991). This is a tightrope on one side of which lies a problem of appropriation and on the other, a radical hyphenization of identity and the presumption of incommensurable experiences. The length of the fall to either side might be measured by the methodological limitations of starting with women only and continuing to assume the stability of "men." When male theorists Culler and Derrida can put forward arguments about writing or reading as women, not merely as feminists, a whole set of problems surface, primarily ones of authenticity and the appropriation of "otherness" in conjunction with its dismissal. The usual move against this is either essentialist epistemology or the assumption of an otherwise intrinsic stability of experience and identity. Harding's argument that we can "think" our way into other experiences, other sexualities, or racial and ethnic heritages other than our own, reopens the classical "rationalism" to which science already attaches itself: it doesn't much matter exactly who you are, because if you work at it, you can think *like* or *for*, anybody else. The "actual lives" of the multiple "subjects" of social and natural inquiries are then still profoundly disengaged from "actual" and active participation in research.[13] This is colonization and appropriation. It is better, perhaps, rather than

[13] The notion of "actual lives" and a fundamental authority of lived experience is similar to Smith's formulations (1987, 1990b). She begins from a position of negotiating what people "really want" in their interactions with institutions and each other, problematic if those wants and interactions are essentialized or considered non-discursively produced. This neither eliminates the problems of "false consciousness" nor the indexical and bounded character of rationalities.

to *assume* either incommensurability or an easy "walk in someone else's shoes," to explore the conditions where either might be possible, and legitimate. The incommensurability of the knowledge of "subjects" of research in relation to formal "objective" knowledge can only be addressed through profound institutional and cultural transformations.

The relations of knowledge and "experience" are also puzzling in their relationship to "common sense." In a recent critique of constructivism in science and technology studies, Sismondo (1993: 536) argues that its formulations "violate current notions of causality." He relies on "common sense" and a colloquial intuitionism to reject conjectures about the social construction of knowledge: "And even though common sense should not be the touchstone of sociology or philosophy of science, large violations of it should require justification" (Sismondo 1993: 536). Ziman (1984) similarly objects to sociological epistemologies that offend the common sense of scientists. Non-obviousness or counter-intuitiveness of course could easily be applied to contemporary physics and other sciences. Since when is Newtonian physics "intuitive" and "common sense" unless one is fully encultured to it? Caught up in that is also an assumption about causality, which, among other things, is under negotiation.[14] Finally, embedded within this "common sense" -based critique is just a twinge of anti-intellectualism, a sometimes appropriate but nevertheless frustrating (from an intellectual's point of view) suspicion (again) of generalizations about social life. This, when coupled with the "parsimonious" explanation requirement, becomes a real impediment to meaningful social theory. If life is complicated, why shouldn't our theories reflect that complexity?

Knowing Knowledge: What Counts in Science and Technology Studies

"Knowledge is a way of ordering the world; as such it is not prior to social organization, it is inseparable from social organization" (Scott 1988: 2).

If one continues perambulating through the *OED* one can discover that to know is, among other things, to admit to, confess or own; perceive with senses; be acquainted or have familiarity with; be intimate with; memorize; admit a claim or authority; recognize and distinguish; approve; disclose; or to be skilled in something.

[14] For a discussion of contingencies and ideas about causality in physics, see Forman 1971.

Knowledge is also conceived as relational, as Scott remarked above, a form of organization, and requiring (at least) knowers and knowns.

The primary demarcation between knowledge and experience has generally rested upon the concepts of legitimacy, or formal processes of validation to be found within an institution, and of abstraction or formalism, that is, the degree to which an experience is generalized and generalizable in relation to a community of knowers and provided with "articulations." Conceptualizations of knowledge in terms of legitimation models are problems the sociology of scientific knowledge has presented for feminists. Because science and technology studies is generally the study of knowledge within the formal organizing and legitimating framework of science, it consistently devalues other ways of knowing, and sets the terms of evaluation. In other words, if the sociology of knowledge continues to define knowledge in comparison to science and by way of its legitimacy, non-legitimized experience and "other ways of knowing" continue to be unstudied and undervalued.[15]

In the sociological formulations of science and technology studies, knowledge is understood to be something other than a purely "contemplative" product. Barnes (1977: 1) explicitly eschews the description of knowledge as a contemplative product of disinterested observers, but rather takes knowledge to consist in accepted belief, and publicly available, shared representations. Scientific knowledge is asserted to be and assessed in relation to "institutionalized technical procedures of its specialization and is entirely typical of knowledge in general" (Barnes 1977: 4). Latour (1987, 1990) and Latour and Woolgar (1986) formulate knowledge as codified experience, which has properties such as "mobility" and "immutability."

Knorr-Cetina (1981) describes knowledge as a product of scientists' interactions, particularly but not exclusively their textual realities and statements. Bloor ([1976] 1991: 3) places knowledge at the same level as beliefs generally, that is, if we can study primitive [sic] cosmologies, then sociologists can at least offer some analysis of the content and nature of "our own" scientific knowledge.

---

[15] Gieryn and Figert urge researchers and scientists in STS not to adopt a priori definitions of "science" and scientist and to let the actors in a particular scenario or discourse provide the definitions in practice and "on the fly" (Gieryn and Figert 1990: 69). This is the source of two problems: (1) it generally recapitulates existing notions of what science is and scientists do; and (2) it stumbles on the problem of the adequacy of explanations by the "natives" for their own behavior. The former is a problem of "ideology," the second of "imputation" and a project far from solved in postcolonial anthropology and less settled in the study of the relative "elites" of science.

To H. M. Collins, knowledge has a certain element of "thingness," that is, although it may be tacit, it "flows" between individuals. Knorr-Cetina (1981; Knorr-Cetina and Mulkay 1981) to some extent, remove the "thing-like" quality of knowledge by making it not simply a product or outcome of rituals and social interactions, but making rituals and social interactions constitutive of knowledge.

Because "knowledge" is represented as legitimated, and at least conditionally "correct" and "objective," it is worth here reiterating Bloor's criteria for a theory of objectivity.

A theory about objectivity must primarily address the object-like stability of the things we believe in, and the external, compelling character of the standards, rules, and procedures that we use. A good theory should be able to illuminate the objectivity of specific beliefs, say beliefs in the existence of atoms, gods or tables, as well as the objectivity of mathematics and of moral principles. (Bloor 1984: 229)

The relationship of science to knowledge is fairly flexible within sociological and philosophical scholarship. Rather than discuss science as an essentially methodological issue, the parlance of philosophers, a sociological approach requires no a priori assumptions on the part of the researcher: "An effective theory of science in society must attend first to the interpretive flexibility of science. . . . [Then] it must attend to those who close boundaries down . . . those who tell us that *this* is what science is all about as they use such boundary work to get what they need" (Gieryn and Figert 1990: 91).

This definitional problem has arisen in feminist critiques of science, in part based on the "gynocentric" visions of validating women's works and knowledge as "science." Code (1991: 12) describes knowledge as "acknowledged cognitive products." She makes a very powerful argument for the reassessment of women's more "traditional" understandings as epistemologically valid knowledge. Much of women's traditional "lore" passes formalistic tests of testability, objectivity, and generalizability.[16] She argues that the devaluation of women's understandings is related to the power and differential authority rhetorically encoded in "purity" demanded of "real" objectivity, that is, the justification of "a system that enshrines male subjectivity in the name of objectivity" (Code 1991: 68–9).

Feminist work, particularly Longino's (1990: 69), on the social nature of knowledge defines knowledge rather loosely, although

---

[16] This argument could be extended to a fully ethnographic project.

it generally refers to the explanations and facts accepted by a community of scientists. It is also important to note that legitimate, credentialed community membership is a prerequisite for being knowledgeable. Harding (1991: 26) also differentiates between knowledge and science, but is more critical of the distinction between what is understood and what counts as knowledge.

Thus, defining "science" and "knowledge" is not only a methodological and theoretical issue, but also an ethical–political problem. What counts as science is recognized to be supported and defined by the material, historical contexts in which it emerges and develops. Just as important, scientific activity is understood to have consequences for the constitution and transformation of the natural and social worlds. For this reason, efforts to construct and evaluate knowledge in relation to a pure epistemological, timeless conception of scientific method are seen to be no less morally bankrupt than they are illusory. In contrast, a praxis orientation takes as its central problematic and concern the inevitable and dialectical embroilment of science, however conceptualized, in the production of everyday life and self-consciously embraces a *commitment* to fostering, within the conduct of research, an awareness of, and concern for, the practical consequences as well as the conditions of scientific activity. (Jackson and Willmott 1987: 371)

Smith's (1990a, 1990b, 1987) sociology of knowledge also brings this "embroilment" of science and knowledge into relations of ruling and everyday/everynight life. Like Knorr-Cetina, Smith (1990b) works from ethnomethodological insights of Garfinkel and Schutz to achieve her understanding of knowledge and the "conceptual practices of power." From her sociology of knowledge one gets some indication of the "structural" possibilities of understanding knowledge, the orderings of experiences which knowledge provides. It is here that we find steps toward Mills's (1961: 6) methodological connections between biography and history, between personal troubles and public issues, and a framework capable of satisfying more recent requirements for the sociology of knowledge as a critical, structural endeavor (Restivo 1988).

Discourse in general, and scientific discourse in particular, is so complex a reality that we not only can, but should approach it at different levels and with different methods. . . . It seems to me that the historical analysis of scientific discourse should, in the last resort, be subject, not to a theory of the knowing subject, but rather to a theory of discursive practice. (Foucault 1973: iv)

From these concerns, it is apparent that adequate theories of knowledge connect intellectual change to *practice* and to *culture*. And both are conceived to be *structural* in a Millsian sense, that is, to be matters of material and relational attributes, of which "discourse" is a part.

Since a theory of knowledge is itself knowledge, symmetry continues to be one of the more problematic concepts in science studies. It starts as an amelioration of the unfortunate asymmetry of the "sociology of errors," but is what led Hetherington to conclude that "no epistemology can rationally be about itself."[17] It has also led to charges of relativism, of idealist ontologies, of pure subjectivism, and is generally the most misconstrued facet of the sociology of knowledge and current science and technology studies.[18] Without some form of symmetry or a first step of methodological agnosticism about knowledge statements, the sociology of knowledge irreparably undermines itself.[19] The symmetrical frameworks which do not purport to adjudicate the "correctness" of claims to scientific knowledge or do not a priori define knowledge in general, are methodologically more sustainable for two primary reasons. The first is that researchers have more freedom to study whatever it is that people say that they know, although that agenda has not been adopted particularly widely in science studies. Associated with this is the studied neglect one can adopt toward a priori definitions of science, especially as broadcast by philosophers. Second, however, science studies researchers have had a problem with the temporality of explanations, whether knowledge claims at first stabilized and refuted, or vice versa, and a consistently sociological and symmetrical approach is then necessary to avoid tautologies and other problems of fallacious, primarily *post-facto* and anachronistic, reasonings.

Taken together, these considerations of theory and experience, and of how best to conceptualize and operationalize "knowledge"

---

[17] Hetherington 1992: 13 n. 5. Two other assumptions are at work in Hetherington's analysis of "epistemology's paradox." The first is that knowing subjects are irremediably other to each other, the second that knowledge is a cognitive product which inheres in individuals. If knowledge is instead postulated to be constituted in communities, and epistemological reflexivity a necessary (but not sufficient) condition for enhancing, rather than undermining, knowledge claims, then "epistemology's paradox" becomes the sociology of knowledge.

[18] See, for example, Barnes (1994).

[19] See Hollis and Lukes (1982) for variations on this good old "et tu" argument. More recently, however, the arguments have been fine-grained debates about what *kinds* of symmetry (and relationships to sorts of *neutrality*) are effective. See *Social Studies of Science* 26(2) (May 1996), "The Politics of SSK."

at the level of comparative meta-analysis (perhaps even as a program in "comparative ontologies"?) necessitates development of critical theories of legitimation. Social theories of knowledge which are methodologically agnostic, reflexively coherent and capable of using the same terms and levels of analysis as justifications for their own knowledge claims, and are structural and adequately account for subjectivity, are likely to be robust, and to be able to make the eventual adjudications of legitimacy and veracity of knowledge systems. These are reasonably necessary (but certainly not sufficient) criteria for a theory of knowledge, but a number of other considerations warrant our attention before these are considered the last words.

Power, Gender, and Time

While it would be difficult to disprove that power is productive of knowledges, meanings, and values, it seems obvious enough that we have to make distinctions between the positive effects and the oppressive effects of such productions. And that is not an issue for political practice alone, but, as Wittig forcefully reminds us, it is especially a question to be asked of theory. (de Lauretis 1987: 18)[20]

Knowledge and power frequently are mentioned in the same breath, although not always in that order. The knowledge/power nexus has been of vital interest to feminists, and theories of knowledge which do not account for the practices of power are likely to be inadequate for either explanatory or emancipatory projects. In this section I will briefly review some of the concerns and criteria that have emerged from considering power, gender, and very briefly, time, in social theory and science studies.

Politics are frequently mentioned as a correlate to power: "politics is the process by which plays of power and knowledge constitute identity and experience" (Scott 1988: 5). To return to etymological foraging through the *OED*, power is the ability to get things done, to command resources, perform effectively, and also to exercise control, or military might, or to have influence *over* others. There are important distinctions to be made between the power to and the power over, coercive rather than coactive power (Harding 1983). The distinction is apparent when examining manifestations of power in assertion and aggression rather than, for

[20] De Lauretis is citing Wittig's "The Straight Mind," *Feminist Issues* 1 (1980): 106–7.

instance, nurturance. Hartsock recommends thinking of power as capacity, rather than thing (1983). Conceptualizing power as process or politics brings a wide variety of problems and resources into reach for theorizing:

The mention of politics inevitably raises the question of causality: In whose interest is it to control or contest meaning? What is the nature of that interest, what is its origin? There are [at least] two ways to answer those questions. One, in terms of an objectively determined, absolute, and universal interest (economics or sexual domination, for example); the other in terms of a discursively produced, relative, and contextual concept of interest. The second is not the reverse of the first, rather, it refuses the opposition between objective determination and its subjective effects. In both cases we grant the effects of "interest" in creating social groups (classes or genders, for example). But in the first case there is a separation assumed between material conditions and the human thoughts and actions they are said to generate. In the second case, no such separation is possible, since "interest" does not inhere in actors or the structural positions but is discursively produced. (Scott 1988: 5)

Scott provides an interesting refinement of the "interests" thesis by Barnes (1977) and a start to a sociology of subjectivity. It certainly provides some redress to Harding's critiques of Bloor ([1976] 1991) and negates Longino's (1990: 73) equation of "interests" with "subjective preferences" and biases in background assumptions, since subjectivity is not inherent in individuals but, like objectivity, discursively produced.

This formulation of the convergence of politics and knowledge of course borrows heavily from Foucault. Although most of his formal writings focus on the coercive nature of institutions, his lectures and interviews provide a more subtle perspective on the relations of power and truth: "What makes power hold good, what makes it acceptable, is simply the fact that it doesn't only weigh on us as a force that says no, but that it traverses and produces things, it induces pleasure, forms knowledge, produces discourse" (Foucault 1984: 61). Latour provides (1988; Latour and Woolgar 1986) a particular application of Foucault's thesis, especially in his description of the lines of force which scientists like Pasteur follow in and out of the laboratory. Power is conceived as operative in a conflictful ground, and invokes agency in the participants as distinctly "humanist" qualities.

While theories of knowledge have relied on conflict-oriented perspectives to different degrees, the scholarship has generally been associated with "radical" orientations to social life (Wilson 1981; Collins 1989), and certainly provides a redress for the conservatism of functionalism. The critical approaches are not exclusive of "reactionary" tendencies. For example, Latour, like Foucault, revels too much in the combat and the potency and valor implied by his subjects.[21] Similarly, central to Randall Collins's general conflict-based sociological theory is an assumption that cooperation is not an effective strategy for distributing scarce resources, and cannot lead to change. This is acutely the case in his theory of intellectual change (Collins 1989).

Hartsock (1983: 3) is particularly critical of the overly agonistic theories of power and social order, because "theories of power are implicitly theories of community." This can be used to critique a number of formulations in science studies. Take, for example, Latour's (1988) "lines of force" which scientists follow out of the laboratory, and which account for the deployment of new techniques and ideas across society. But Latour's formulation does not, and cannot, provide an analysis of the work of the many men and women that enabled the rails from the laboratory to be laid on a stable foundation.

With a bit of mental gymnastics, one can also imagine Latour's lines of force as paths of least resistance. To use a "hydraulic" metaphor, water, in this case some aggregate of scientists trying to establish new knowledge, seeks its own level, that is, the intra- and extra-mural audience with the most fundamental common assumptions. Further, the scientists follow a path of minimum energy and least resistance to begin a journey "out" into the countryside. I could keep going with this, into meandering streams, river formation, catastrophic floods, dams, sandbagging, Grand Canyons, Niagara Falls, marshes, quicksand, and eutrophying lakes. The point is that the "railroad tracks" out of laboratories are too linear and rely too much on volition, rather than contingency, to explain the accumulating and dissipating power of scientists and technoscience, and the flows *into* the laboratory. Latour's project is in effect a rationalist reconstruction of Pasteur's actions. Of course much of technoscience's hegemony is established by bulldozing, backfilling, and otherwise coercing the existing landscape, much like the builders of the railroads traversing the American continents did. However, perhaps social theorists should hesitate, as Lorde warned, when they find the masters' tools so readily at hand.

---

[21] See especially Latour's (1990) review of Serres, Shapin, and Schaffer, and Traweek, and Hess's (1993, 1992) reconstructions of this review.

Renegotiations of concepts of force are particularly important for renegotiating agency as situated in optimizing, rational actors. Barnes (1983) addresses this as a problem of stability with a premise of conventionality and what amounts to a mental form of inertia by means of inductive reasoning, as a measure of closure. This is related to Remmling's (1967: 4–6) notion of mental entropy. Knorr-Cetina (Knorr-Cetina and Mulkay 1983: 6) also recognizes the volitional problem, noting that satisficing behaviors, rather than optimizing, are the marks of most scientific work. Hartsock (1983: 6) criticizes "rational economic man" as ethnocentric and as a mono-maniacal maximizer. "Homo economicus presents perplexing problems for an aspiring feminist theorist, not the least of which are the apparent contradictions and the dissolution of unitary identies into fragmented ones of post-Enlightenment discourse."

Agents in social theory, not excluding science studies, thus figure as masculine, separated from social life, physically and psychologically autonomous. Theory, and/as knowledge, is very frequently presented as inherently visual, and as law-oriented and requiring a measured distance between viewer and viewed. In a very particular sense contemporary notions about theorizing *produce* "the feminine" in that what is taken to be adequate theory rests on the production of an object designated as viewed, which does not share in the coauthoring of the resulting explanatory project as a "subject." Haraway noted the sadistic element of modern humanism, which is based on sadism as the creation of a perfectly controlled mirror of self. Modern inquiry is thus, from this perspective, an elaborate "erotic visual discipline for self-objectification": "Sadism is about the structure of scientific vision, in which the body becomes a rhetoric, a persuasive language linked to social practice. The final cause, or telos, of that practice is the production of the unmarked, abstract universal man" (Haraway 1989: 233).

Any knowledge, including a theory of knowledge, which does not address social oppression and configurations of power substantively and reflexively aids and abets it. Of course, Marx made note of the distinction between studying the world and changing it, as did Foucault (1984: 74–5):

The essential political problem for the intellectual is not to criticize ideological contents supposedly linked to science, but that of ascertaining the possibility of constituting a new politics of truth. The problem is not changing people's consciousness – or what's in their heads – but the political, economic, institutional regime of the production of truth. It's not a matter of emancipating truth from every system of power (which would be a chimera, for truth is already power), but of detaching the power of truth from the forms of hegemony, social, economic, and cultural, within which it operates at the present time.

With this in mind, it is very easy to critique the "scientism" of many projects in the sociology of science and scientific knowledge. Harding critiques the tradition of which Bloor is a part for being "stalwartly androcentric" (Harding 1986: 34), the Strong Programme for being scientistic. Specifically, Harding claims that the Strong Programme supports the value neutrality of "true" scientific products. The scientistic turn also implies that a scientific sociology of knowledge would be predictive. H. M. Collins (1983: 99–100) also makes a scientistic maneuver for the Epistemological Program of Relativism, or EPOR, (cf. Collins 1983), ostensibly to strengthen the authority of the scientific institution and thus his own authority. The quantity of reflexive turns in Sociology of Scientific Knowledge (SSK) notwithstanding, little of the ink is spent on discussing institutional commitments, both material and symbolic, and gendered, that underpin the authoring of SSK projects in themselves.

The scientistic maneuver also opens up a can of worms on the supposedly self-refuting nature of the sociology of knowledge project, especially the relativistic problem where SSK programs cannot go beyond how "appeals to rationality function as resources" (Harding 1983: 318). This is the source of Harding's criterion where a theory/critique of knowledge must explain why "things work," developed in the context of critiques of Bloor ([1976] 1991) and Restivo (1988). A number of feminists express a similar disappointment with and rejection of feminist epistemological scholarship, because "whatever alternatives feminism offers to research and understanding must account for the achievements of traditional research and patriarchal science" (Miller with Treitel 1991: 4). These problems of alleged self-refutation and the use of the instrumental successes of conventional science as judging the relative merits of both alternative sciences and social and cultural studies of science and technology illustrate why the project of redefining the criteria by which to evaluate knowledge claims is of more than intellectual interest. Latour and Foucault of course provide several answers to this which might be useful to feminists. Similarly Vandana Shiva (1987) notes that whenever someone (primarily from the West) mentions "discovery," one should perhaps substitute "invasion." That is, it is not so much that scientists have provided "Truths," but that they are capable of marshaling the resources, suppressing dissent, or fabricating consent so that lives are rearranged to make "truths" work. Rather than continuing to defer to "truth," and "nature" as ahistorical adjudicators of knowledge claims (serious scholars rarely defer to "god" on matters of explanation in studies of morality, so why should those interested in studying knowledge defer to nature?) truth and objectivity should be reconceptualized as an *achievement*, fully explicable in sociological terms.[22]

There are scientistic tendencies in feminist research, although the general weight of the argument is away from rigid formulations of science, method, truth, and objectivity. Mostly, scientism is a matter of wanting to hitch one's wagon to the existing trains of authority. Feminist research is generally understood to "necessarily be interpretive and critical of the logocentrism of positivism and the natural science model of investigations" (Denzin 1984: 126). That is, most of it questions whether that particular train is worth riding on. I make no pretense to "scientific" knowledge in the formal, conventional sense, unless one is considering a potentially radical representation of the "natural" sciences as interpretive, for example, for which Gadamer (somewhat ambiguously) argues (1989).

Latour mentions the conditions of *failure* for a theory of knowledge, noting that a theory should explain knowledge without "bypassing technical content," or without refusing the help the social sciences might like to offer. Further, failure should be noted in a reduction to "social conditions" which exempts technical contents from scrutiny, and if the theory has recourse to the notions and terms belonging to the folklore of the people studied, such as efficiency, proof, efficacy, demonstration, or even "revolution" (Latour 1988: 9). That is, relying on the notion that science "works" and adopting that as an explanatory criteria already marks a project for the (feminist) sociology of knowledge for failure.

Underpinning the feminist critiques of power has been the emergence of concepts of gender. While gender is important to important theories of science, technology, and knowledge, I will here discuss gender and social theory more generally. Do gender and feminist theory matter to the adequacy of social theories? Adam (1989), as well as Waithe (1989) and Harding and Hintikka (1983) doubt that women can simply be enfolded into current social theory.

---

[22] Two points are relevant here. Latour (1993) rather anthropomorphizes the world in his otherwise cogent critique of the nature–culture dichotomy. Further, much of the preceding analysis is rather old news to science studies scholars, but it still ruffles feathers of sociologists, especially those with science envy, and of many but not all who work in the natural sciences.

My point here is that gender is clearly and unambiguously a construct, and for the most part those who use it are reflexively aware of its radically contingent nature. And yet relative to the communities to which it has referential significance, it sustains its meaning and provides explanatory resources. For example:

Gender is not a point to start from in the sense of being a given thing but is, instead, a posit or construct, formalizable in a nonarbitrary way through a matrix of habits, practices, and discourses. (Alcoff 1988: 431)

gender is the social organization of sexual difference. But this does not mean that gender reflects or implements fixed and natural physical differences between women and men; rather gender is the knowledge that establishes meanings for bodily differences. (Scott 1988: 2)

Conceptualizing "woman" . . . is a metaphysical problem. (Alcoff 1988: 429)

Although an analysis is beyond the scope of this essay, the invention of gender is an example of the development of the objectivity of a concept or "thing" as a product of contingencies, indices, and community processes. Gender constitutes knowledge about sexual difference in two parts. The first is in signifying the relationships of power by way of symbols and subjective identity and politics by way of social institutions. The second is in the deployment of normative interpretive frames for codifying and enforcing symbols. Gender is the organization of re/productive experience and the knowledge about sexual differences discursively constituted in that organization. It provides an integration, to avoid the dual-systems debates, of class and individual reproductive issues (Sacks 1989: 536) and recognizes domestic and unwaged, and often unrecognized labor which sustains social life. Gender is manifest in the emotional work (Hochschild 1983) and material work of sustaining the world in interpersonal relations.

Finally, social theory and feminist theory need time (Adam 1989, 1990). First, "needing time" means that social theorists need to recognize themselves and their theories as historically contingent. This necessitates new formulations of reflexivity, and probably greater humility. Unfortunately, the formulation of reflexivity currently floating around the sociology of scientific knowledge community verges mainly on the narcissistic. Second, "needing time" means taking care in negotiating the notions of causality and constitutive natural/social order invoked in explanatory frameworks

(Adam 1990). This can be expanded to include C. Wright Mills's remark: "The general problem of a theory of history cannot be separated from the general problem of a theory of social structure" (Mills 1961: 47). Finally, it also entails taking note of "textual time," that is the narrative or other temporal reasoning structure that provides the framework for establishing veracity in texts (Smith 1990a) as an analytic and reflexive issue.

Gender can inform theory in several ways, as Millman and Kanter note specifically for sociology. Gender, as an analytical possibility redresses the neglect of women, or the treatment of "women as footnote" in studies of political action. It also grounds critiques of prior theory and practice by the development of the compensatory or "add women and stir" perspectives, although this focusses on women as special cases and neglects the facts that men have gender, and that gender is a central analytic question (Walby 1988). Regarding the dimensions of political theory and gender issues, the feminist agenda focuses on goals for or against women's interests, rather than on women per se. Feminist agendas also question the extent and nature of gender politics existing in the definition of politics. The same argument has also been extended to the relations of scholarship on science and technology from historical perspectives. Featuring gender in social theory destabilizes prior social theories (Waithe 1989: 132; Adam 1989: 464).

Feminism itself exemplifies the criterion that its historical and political limits are what confer legitimacy. From this, then, it is clear that authority and legitimacy are the most problematic issues for imagining new knowledges and their concomitant social forms. Clearly, gender matters to social theory. As a criterion for theories of knowledge, gender should be evaluated as a relevant analytic category. Further, treating gender as historically specific but nonetheless powerful index of structures of social life might provide a model for theory building and the emergence of legitimacy in knowledge claims.

(A) Social Theory of Knowledge

"'Method' has to do first of all, with how to ask and answer questions with some assurance that the answers are more or less durable. 'Theory' has to do, above all, with paying close attention to the words one is using, especially their degree of generality and their logical relations" (Mills 1961: 120). In this section I want to outline briefly the limits of the minefield of sociological imperatives present in science studies and which have (quite unfortunately) set many of the terms of discourse for theories of knowledge. Then I will discuss briefly the requirements and criteria for new social legitimations for knowledge.

Microsociological formulations of laboratory practice and scientific discourse as interaction and textual production have been extremely useful in fully developing the social construction conjectures in science studies. One becomes, however, easily embroiled in debates about the relationships of these microsociological formations in relation to larger-scale institutional structures (meso-theories if you must), and macrosociological formations. Or one becomes submerged in overwhelming details of conversation analysis and the gratuitous use of punctuation.

Ethnomethodological purists insist on the primacy of interaction: things like "structure" are epiphenomenal accretions of individual interactions. Of course macro-sociologists of various stripes invert the relationship. Without a more engaged, critical ethnography, conversation analysis and ethnomethodology rely on a suspect voluntarism.[23] Meso-theories of intellectual change and varieties of institutional studies are based on competitive models, and are not useful for understanding the content of knowledge claims.[24] They do very well, however, in explaining the variations within a given frame. That is, they are not sufficient for explaining cultural change on the broadest scale. Various theories of the macrosociological order and theories of culture then come into play. But they tend to be interaction-insensitive and have had, to date, teleological tendencies. Further, they are the most politically problematic. For example, conventional (Parsonian) functionalist theories, as well as the "cyberneticized" holistic and systems projects of postwar social science are problematic for feminists, primarily because of the assumption that sex-stratified social roles are functional.[25]

Sociological theories of knowledge must clearly make adequate assumptions about microsociological interactions, and should make "no a priori assumptions about the unidirectionality of social motion and causal influence." Feminist considerations demand that social theory " 'foregrounds' the problems of dominance and

---

[23] Becker and McCall (1990).

[24] For an example of how mid-ranger theories can explain variation within an intellectual milieu, see R. Collins (1989).

[25] See Heims (1993) for an analysis of the assumptions of postwar sociology as influenced by cybernetics. Adam (1989: 459) discusses the feminist hesitations about functionalism, as does Carroll (1990).

subordination" (Fraser 1989: 138).[26] Theories of knowledge need to be adequate theories of culture, assuming neither inherent stability nor instability, and not succumbing to surface illusions of homogeneity or hegemony. And finally, social theories of knowledge need concern themselves with materialism. This requires, however, moving into a more profound consideration of the relations of re/production, including the interrelationships between ecological/economic, symbolic, libidinal, and status or political systems. While social theory has been inconsistent in reflecting on its normative assumptions and agendas, feminist theory is just beginning to move to the scale and scope of inquiry necessary for facilitating fundamental changes in inquiry and social life.

I want to return briefly to the prospect of abandoning sociology and social theory from two directions. Latour has of course made this move, and I discussed earlier many of the feminist hesitations about theoretical work. Latour (1988, 1993) argues for an "a-sociology," that is, the study of associations, and of the "nonhumans" of the world which have an as yet sociologically undertheorized role in knowledge production, although philosophers have presumed to say much about it.[27] If, as I noted earlier, the "real world" underdetermines or is otherwise not a *sufficient* condition for establishing objective and reliable knowledge, it is of course necessary. Then the challenge is to articulate a sociology of knowledge which is adequate to this expanded task.

The first step in this is nevertheless a strong justification for the critical studies of the social legitimation of knowledge claims. It is inauspicious to so quickly move back to what amounts to a "naturalist" explanation for correct knowledge when the "social construction" theses and conjectures have only tentatively begun to make a difference. I suggest, after Wright (1992), that the way around constructivist ontological "relativism" is to be found at a processual, political level, with the co-constitutive establishment of authority, social order and knowledge. "Problems" of relativism indicate tensions in those political processes. *Accounts* of reality are logically equal; *actions* have efficacies to be judged and evaluated. The negotiation of multiple descriptions of the natural world will provide not a way "around" relativism to some apolitical Truth,

---

[26] All in all, I prefer what might be considered "realist" social theory, that is, things are "real" if they bring about change, even if not observable in a formal, perceptual sense (Wilson 1981: 167). But I resist the positivism that Wilson's or similar social theory generally entails.

[27] See also Addelson (1990).

but through relativism as establishing the grounds for political process into situated, relational, contingent – relativistic, if you will, or relational, as Mannheim described it – knowledge. In any given era, the perceived "nature" of relationships of human beings to the natural world is best characterized as constituted by political agendas and interactions.[28] And what is generally seen by critics as a "lapse" to relativism by programs in the social construction of knowledge is, rather, the effective placement of the evaluation of knowledge claims at an appropriate level, one of politics, power relations, and human agency.

Kenneth Gergen (1988) has similarly remarked that because knowledge claims are constitutive of social life they should properly be opened to evaluation by the full range of discursive communities. Longino makes some nods as well in this direction, although her reliance on intra-scientific diversity is much less effective as an emancipatory or merely reformist agenda than one might otherwise hope. Smith's feminist sociology is of course premised on a sociology for women providing not only the political legitimation, but the cognitive or "objective" status of the work. An adequate theory of knowledge recognizes that experience, understanding, and knowledge are produced in many ways. Theory needs to address specific, political processes and gender ideologies that enforce distinctions between legitimated or formal knowledge, technoscience, and other understandings. It also needs to describe and explain the relative political and social empowerment arising from the legitimation processes. It will need to answer questions about when, how, and why information and arguments are seen as "scientific" or more legitimate than those produced from other grounds and organizations of inquiry. Theory must be honest about what is at stake in its production.

Enfolding gender into social theory does not provide "better knowledge" in any conventional sense, such as theoretical expansiveness, accounting for "data," or enhanced (empiricist criteria for) validity. Thinking about gender requires us to think about the lives we live and the people we depend on. Feminist scholarship cannot rely on conventional notions of objectivity and "evidence": they are notoriously fickle. It requires a substantive break from any form of scientism, and especially "successor science" programs. Feminist

---

[28] If one needs a human nature (and most postmodernists have dispensed with that construct) humans are natural animals, whose nature apparently includes complex sociality. Anything more specific generally appears unstable when viewed cross-culturally or historically.

perspectives on adequate theories of knowledge usually require that they be grounded in the realities of women's lives, that they adequately theorize gender, and that they be reflexively sensitive to the relations of their own production. Fricker (1994: 96), arguing for the integration of ethics and epistemology, notes: "There are two specifications for any adequate epistemology. . . . First that it must posit norms for belief; and second, that it must distinguish between a first and second order perspective on belief in a way which sustains the capacity for self criticism."

Still, most of us are distinctly uncomfortable with an epistemological justification for knowledge that often misinterpreted to imply "well, they mean well, so they must be right." The distinction between the social and natural is fundamental to our definitions of inquiry, and to the arbitration of truth claims. Haraway argues that we need to be able to adjudicate between illegitimate and legitimate social agendas, and Hartsock asks for "real knowledge" so that we might have confidence and justification for pressing for social change. The challenge – and the depth of this challenge should not be underestimated – is to produce theory and explanation, about the social and the natural worlds (if the distinction still holds for you), and demand its legitimation without reference to external (and thus non-accountable) authority – neither God nor Nature (human or otherwise), nor the state, nor "Society" as a reified entity. Haraway (1989: 13) remarks that:

It makes sense to ask what stakes, methods, and kinds of authority are involved in natural scientific accounts, how they differ, for example, from religion or ethnography. It does not make sense to ask for a form of authority that escapes the web of the highly productive cultural fields that make the accounts possible in the first place.

Similarly, Mary Hawkesworth (1989: 547) notes that to decide among knowledge claims, one cannot appeal to "the authority of the body, intuition, or a universal woman's experience," nor can such conflict be decided by "reference to neutral scientific or philosophical methods."

"All knowledge which does not recognize, which does not take social oppression as its premise, denies it, and as a consequence objectively serves it" (Delphy 1981: 73).

Theory should be an emancipatory enterprise. As long as the social role of "researcher" stands in conflict with that of "subjects," theorists will be in conflict with activists, and both will need to negotiate the potential orthogonality of the interests held by a researcher in relation to those interests held by various interlocutors (formerly known as "research subjects").

A politically adequate "successor epistemology" would have to give pride of place to questions such as "Whose knowledge are we talking about?" Is it the knowledge that interchangeable observers have of cups, pens, and books on tables, or is it knowledge that committed Marxists have about capitalism? that committed supporters of apartheid have about blacks? Is it the knowledge of privileged intellectuals with the leisure to analyze the nature of freedom and oppression, or is it the knowledge that women who desperately need work must have so that they can weight the dangers of radiation in a factory job against the humiliation of unemployment and welfare? The diversity of situations and circumstances in which people need to be in a position to know makes it difficult to see how a theory of knowledge, *an* epistemology could respond to their questions. (Code 1991: 315)

To produce a social theory of knowledge means weaving one's way between the Scylla of predetermined explanatory necessities from disciplinary perspectives (how many of you will turn to my references and grumble about which traditional theorist I did not cite?), and the Charybdis of assumptions and relevant topics for inquiry which frame those requirements (who in their right mind, besides feminists, talks about love nowadays?). One enters a minefield of political and ethical commitments for emancipatory politics and epistemological and sociological requirements for justifiable knowledge. One faces a Sisyphean task of providing an explanation for a dynamic and politically contentious world, in a professional structure suited best for accretion and "hardening of the categories." And one is beset by the Harpies and Furies of interdisciplinary politics, scholarly "one-upmanship," and symbolic violence prevalent in a competitive and status-crazy academic field.

I have argued with colleagues that the real goal of any profession should be to make itself obsolete. What will physicians do if everyone is healthy? What will engineers build after the global infrastructure is filled in? A number of scientists are worried about how to keep themselves busy since all of the good and important questions (the Big Bang and the Genome) have been answered. Who will anthropologists study when there is no "other"? Little in their methods and discourse is theoretically capable of studying "us." And I suppose every social scientist will have to become an historian, once the problems of social life, governance, and the distribution of goods and services are solved. Isn't that what we are after? Is there some finalization and unification, as that European philosophy of science would have it? Does that notion rely on a view of social stability solidified by functionalism? Social theory as sustained professionalized inquiry is impossible, social theories of knowledge more so, in that they both are constituted and legitimated by the various systems and institutions that they purport to study.

These institutionalizations of inquiry have led to powerful and attractive stratospheric abstractions, powerful criteria for evaluating the merit of arguments and individuals, and to a rarefied atmosphere toxic to those not yet disembodied by sociological discourse. And yet, perhaps "theory" is also absolutely necessary, in the way that conceptual art is necessary, to impel the imagination and challenge the status quo. The "literary" studies mode so prevalent in social thought may be justifiable, but not in the terms that it have traditionally legitimated that activity. In any case, what theory needs is to be radically reinstitutionalized. It is certainly not changing at the rate that our university homes or the world at large are changing. Teresa de Lauretis notes: "the tension of feminism's condition in contrary directions – the critical negativity of its theory, and the affirmative positivity of its politics – is both the historical condition of existence of feminism and its theoretical conditions of possibility" (de Lauretis 1987: 26).

With all of these contradictions, one might be tempted to just give it up and/or go crazy. The preferred technique in feminist and social theory has been to use an ironic stance to keep going in face of contradictions. This entails managing a tension between longing for and being wary of a secure epistemological home. It produces, among other things, a "humility" concerning theory and an ability to sustain wanting what cannot fully be had (Ferguson 1993: 35). However, irony is a response from a position of relative powerlessness. Elaine Scarry (1985) pointed out in her reading of Sartre's *The Wall* that the ironic circumstances surrounding Pablo's inadvertent betrayal of his friend, which ensured his own freedom and his friend's death, are too profound to be fully captured under the textual rubric of irony. One begins to see, then, the book/anti-book writings of Dostoevsky and the "deasthetics" (de Lauretis 1987: 146) of feminist cinematic theory as essential models for the theory/anti-theory necessary for really innovative explanatory projects.[29]

---

[29] Cohn (1987) uses Harding's discussion with Hintikka (1983) of the simultaneous deconstructive and constructive agendas for feminist theory. Neither, however, fully develops the explanatory possibilities that their critical agendas imply, nor the structural challenges that follow from their techniques.

This essay is an outline of criteria and considerations which must inform the development of theories of knowledge. The end results will be variations on social, feminist theories of knowledge and new processes for question-generation by researchers and their interlocutors. In this regard, Dorothy Smith's work is exemplary (1990a, 1990b). I discussed the complex interrelations of experience, knowledge, and theory which frame critiques in feminist and other social theories. Associated with this is the problem of deciding about what one is responsible for studying, and to whom, when one sets out to study knowledge. I also very briefly discussed notions of power and politics relevant for social theories of knowledge, and argued that gender matters to social theory. I also discussed the impossibility of theory because it is institutionalized in such a way that necessary statements are mortgaged to institutional and community imperatives (whether these be disciplinary, gender, class, or otherwise). But social theory is also necessary, when envisioned, or I should say, embodied, as an imaginative enterprise for social change. The questions of postmodernity have opened up the concepts of "truth," "objectivity," and the standards by which we judge scholarship. The criteria for theory presented here can be only temporary. Because the criteria for evaluating scholarship are no longer self-evident, transparent, or can be stated as non-arbitrary, establishing criteria for theory, in this case theories of knowledge, is essential to opening up social theory to new voices and institutional engagements.

References

Abbott, Pamela and Claire Wallace. 1990. *An Introduction to Sociology: Feminist Perspectives*. London: Routledge.

Adam, Barbara. 1989. Feminist Social Theory Needs Time. *Sociological Review* 37 (3): 458–73.

———. 1990. *Time and Social Theory*. Philadelphia, PA: Temple University Press.

Addelson, Kathryn Pyne. 1990. Why Philosophers Should Become Sociologists (and Vice Versa). In Howard S. Becker and Michael M. McCall, eds, *Symbolic Interaction and Cultural Studies*. Chicago, University of Chicago Press.

Alcoff, Linda. 1988. Cultural Feminism versus Post-Structuralism: The Identity Crisis in Feminist Theory. *Signs* 13 (3): 405–36.

Barnes, Barry. 1977. *Interests and the Growth of Knowledge*. London: Routledge & Kegan Paul.

——. 1983. On the Conventional Character of Knowledge and Cognition. In Karin D. Knorr-Cetina and Michael Mulkay, eds, *Science Observed: Perspectives on the Social Study of Science*, 19–51. London: Sage.

——. 1994. How Not to Do the Sociology of Knowledge. In Allan Megill, ed., *Rethinking Objectivity*, 21–37. Durham, NC: Duke University Press.

Baym, Nina. 1984. The Madwoman and Her Languages: Why I Don't Do Feminist Theory. *Tulsa Studies in Women's Literature* 1 (2): 45–9.

Becker, Howard S. and Michael M. McCall. 1990. *Symbolic Interaction and Cultural Studies*. Chicago: University of Chicago Press.

Bloor, David. [1976] 1991. *Knowledge and Social Imagery*. Chicago and London: University of Chicago Press and Routledge & Kegan Paul.

——. 1984. A Sociological Theory of Objectivity. In S. C. Brown, ed., *Objectivity and Cultural Divergence*, 229–45. Cambridge: Cambridge University Press.

Bologh, Roslyn W. 1990. *Love or Greatness: Max Weber and Masculine Thinking – A Feminist Inquiry*. London: Unwin Hyman.

Calhoun, Craig. 1996. Editor's Comment: What Passes for Theory in Sociology. *Sociological Theory* 14 (1): 1–2.

Carroll, Berenice A. 1990. The Politics of "Originality": Women and the Class System of the Intellect. *Journal of Women's History* 2 (2): 136–65.

Code, Lorraine. 1991. *What Can She Know? Feminist Theory and the Construction of Knowledge*. Ithaca, NY: Cornell University Press.

Cohn, Carol. 1987. Sex and Death in the Rational World of Defense Intellectuals. *Signs* 12 (4): 687–718.

Collins, H. M. 1983. An Empirical Relativist Programme in the Sociology of Scientific Knowledge. In Karin D. Knorr-Cetina and Michael Mulkay, eds, *Science Observed: Perspectives on the Social Study of Science*, 85–114. London: Sage.

Collins, Patricia Hill. 1990. *Black Feminist Thought*. London: HarperCollins/ Unwin Hyman.

Collins, Randall. 1989. Toward a Theory of Intellectual Change: The Social Causes of Philosophies. *Science, Technology & Human Values* 14 (2): 107–40.

Constant, Edward W., III. 1973. A Model for Technological Change Applied to the Turbojet Revolution. *Technology and Culture* 14 (4): 553–72.

Croissant, Jennifer L. 1994. Bodies, Movements, Representations: Elements Toward a Feminist Theory of Knowledge. Unpublished dissertation, Department of Science and Technology Studies, Rensselaer Polytechnic Institute, Troy, NY.

de Beauvoir, Simone. [1952] 1974. *The Second Sex*. New York: Random House.

de Lauretis, Teresa. 1987. *Technologies of Gender: Essays on Theory, Film, and Fiction*. Bloomington: Indiana University Press.

Delphy, Christine. 1981. For a Materialist Feminism. *Feminist Issues* 1 (2): 69–76.

Denzin, Norman. 1984. Review Essay: Towards an Interpretation of Recent Feminist Theory. *Sociology and Social Research* 69 (1): 122–6.

Ferguson, Kathy E. 1993. *The Man Question: Visions of Subjectivity in Feminist Theory*. Berkeley: University of California Press.

Forman, Paul. 1971. Weimar Culture, Causality, and Quantum Theory 1918–1927: Adaptation by German Physicists and Mathematicians to a Hostile Intellectual Environment. *Historical Studies in the Physical Sciences* 3: 1–115.

Foucault, Michel. 1973. *The Order of Things: An Archaeology of the Human Sciences*. New York: Vintage/Random House.

——. 1984. *The Foucault Reader*, ed. Paul Rabinow. New York: Pantheon.

Fraser, Nancy. 1989. *Unruly Practices: Power, Discourse, and Gender in Contemporary Social Theory*. Minneapolis: University of Minnesota Press.

Fricker, Miranda. 1994. Knowledge as Construct: Theorizing the Role of Gender in Knowledge. In Kathleen Lennon and Margaret Whitford, eds, *Knowing the Difference: Feminist Perspectives in Epistemology*, 95–109. London: Routledge.

Gadamer, Hans-Georg. 1989. *Truth and Method*. 2nd rev. trans., Joel Weinsheimer and Donald G. Marshall. New York: Continuum.

Gergen, Kenneth. 1988. Feminist Critique of Science and the Challenge of Social Epistemology. In M. Gergen, ed., *Feminist Thought and the Structure of Knowledge*, 27–48. New York: New York University Press.

Gieryn, Thomas, and Anne Figert. 1990. Ingredients for a Theory of Science in Society. In S. E. Cozzens and Gieryn, eds, *Theories of Science in Society*, 67–97. Bloomington: Indiana University Press.

Grant, Judith. 1987. I Feel Therefore I Am: A Critique of Female Experience as the Basis for a Feminist Epistemology. *Women and Politics* 7 (3): 99–114.

Haraway, Donna. 1989. *Primate Visions: Gender, Race, and Nature in the World of Modern Science*. New York: Routledge.

——. 1991. *Simians, Cyborgs, and Women: The Reinvention of Nature*. New York: Routledge.

Harding, Sandra. 1983. Why has the Sex/Gender System Become Visible Only Now? In Harding and M. Hintikka, eds, *Discovering Reality: Feminist Perspectives on Epistemology, Metaphysics, Methodology, and Philosophy of Science*, 331–24. Dordrecht: Reidel.

——. 1986. *The Science Question in Feminism*. Ithaca, NY: Cornell University Press.

——. 1991. *Whose Science? Whose Knowledge? Thinking from Women's Lives*. Ithaca, NY: Cornell University Press.

Hartsock, Nancy M. 1983. *Money, Sex, and Power: Toward a Feminist Historical Materialism*. Boston, MA: Northeastern University Press.

——. 1987a. Rethinking Modernism: Minority vs. Majority Theories. *Cultural Critique* 7: 187–206.

Hawkesworth, Mary E. 1989. Knowers, Knowing, Known: Feminist Theory and Claims of Truth. *Signs* 14 (3): 533–57.

Heims, Steven Joshua. 1993. *The Cybernetics Group: Constructing a Social Science for Postwar America*. Cambridge, MA: MIT Press.

Hess, David. 1992. Introduction: The New Ethnography and the Anthropology of Science and Technology. *Knowledge and Society* 9: 1–26.

———. 1993. Anthropology, Inter/Disciplinarity, and STS Politics. Presented at the Society for Anthropology of Religion, October.

Hetherington, Stephen. 1992. *Epistemology's Paradox: Is a Theory of Knowledge Possible?* Savage, MD: Rowman & Littlefield.

Hochschild, Arlie Russell. 1983. *The Managed Heart: The Commercialization of Human Feeling*. Berkeley: University of California Press.

Hollis, Martin, and Steven Lukes, eds. 1982. *Rationality and Relativism*. Cambridge, MA: MIT Press.

Jackson, Norman, and Hugh Willmott. 1987. Beyond Epistemology and Reflective Conversation: Toward Human Relations. *Human Relations* 40 (6): 361–80.

Kandal, Terry R. 1988. *The Woman Question in Classical Sociological Theory*. Miami: Florida International University Press.

Kaplan, David, and Robert A. Manners. 1972. *Culture Theory*. Englewood Cliffs, NJ: Prentice Hall.

Knorr-Cetina, Karin D. 1981. *The Manufacture of Knowledge*. New York: Pergamon Press.

Knorr-Cetina, Karin D. and Michael Mulkay, eds. 1983. *Science Observed: Perspectives on the Social Study of Science*. London: Sage.

Kramarae, Cheris and Paula A. Treichler. 1985. *A Feminist Dictionary*. London: Pandora.

Latour, Bruno. 1987. *Science in Action: How to Follow Scientists and Engineers Through Society*. Cambridge, MA: Harvard University Press.

———. 1988. *The Pasteurization of France*. Trans. Alan Sheridan and John Law. Cambridge, MA: Harvard University Press.

———. 1990. Postmodern? No, Simply Modern! Steps Towards an Anthropology of Science. *Studies in History and Philosophy of Science* 21 (1): 145–71.

———. 1993. *We Have Never Been Modern*, trans. Catherine Porter. Cambridge, MA: Harvard University Press.

Latour, Bruno and Steve Woolgar. 1986. *Laboratory Life: The (Social) Construction of Scientific Facts*. Princeton, NJ: Princeton University Press.

Lerner, Gerda. 1986. *The Creation of Patriarchy*. New York: Oxford University Press.

Longino, Helen. 1990. *Science as Social Knowledge: Values and Objectivity in Scientific Inquiry*. Princeton, NJ: Princeton University Press.

Lorde, Audre. 1981. The Master's Tools will Never Dismantle the Master's House. In Cherie Moraga and Gloria Anzaldua, eds, *This Bridge Called My Back: Writings by Radical Women of Color*, 98–101. Watertown, MA: Persephone Press.

Loughlin, J. 1992. The Feminist Challenge to Social Studies of Science. In T. Brante et al., eds, *Controversial Science*, 12–38. Albany, NY: State University of New York Press.

Miller, Connie with Corinna Treitel. 1991. *Feminist Research Methods: An Annotated Bibliography*. New York: Greenwood Press.

Mills, C. Wright. 1961. *The Sociological Imagination*. New York: Grove Press.

Nye, Andrea. 1995. *Philosophy and Feminism: At the Border*. New York: Twayne/Simon & Schuster Macmillan.

Remmling, Gunter W. 1967. *The Road to Suspicion: A Study of Modern Mentality and the Sociology of Knowledge*. New York: Appleton-Century-Crofts.

Restivo, Sal. 1988. Modern Science as a Social Problem. *Social Problems* 35 (3): 206–25.

Sacks, Karen Brodkin. 1989. Toward a Unified Theory of Class, Race, and Gender. *American Ethnologist* 16 (3): 534–50.

Scarry, Elaine. 1985. *The Body in Pain: The Making and Unmaking of the World*. New York: Oxford University Press.

Scott, Joan Wallace. 1988. *Gender and the Politics of History*. New York: Columbia University Press.

Shiva, Vandana. 1987. The Violence of Reductionist Science. *Alternatives* 12 (2): 243–61.

Sismondo, Sergio. 1993. Some Social Constructions. *Social Studies of Science* 23 (3): 515–54. With reply by K. Knorr-Cetina, pp. 555–62, and response by Sismondo, pp. 563–8.

Smith, Dorothy E. 1987. *The Everyday World as Problematic: A Feminist Sociology*. Boston, MA: Northeastern University Press.

——. 1990a. *Texts, Facts, and Femininity: Exploring the Relations of Ruling*. London: Routledge.

——. 1990b. *The Conceptual Practices of Power: A Feminist Sociology of Knowledge*. Boston, MA: Northeastern University Press.

——. 1992. Sociology from Women's Experience: A Reaffirmation. *Sociological Theory* 10 (1): 88–98.

Spender, Dale. 1982. *Women of Ideas and What Men Have Done to Them*. London: Routledge & Kegan Paul.

Stanley, Liz and Sue Wise. 1983. *Breaking Out: Feminist Consciousness and Feminist Research*. London: Routledge & Kegan Paul.

Waithe, Mary Ellen. 1989. On Not Teaching the History of Philosophy. *Hypatia* 4 (1): 132–8.

Walby, Sylvia. 1988. Gender Politics and Social Theory. *Sociology* 22 (2): 215–32.

Weedon, Chris. 1987. *Feminist Practice and Poststructuralist Theory*. Oxford: Basil Blackwell.

Wilson, John. 1981. *Social Theory*. Englewood Cliffs, NJ: Prentice Hall.

Wright, Will. 1992. *Wild Knowledge: Science, Language, and Social Life in a Fragile Environment*. Minneapolis: University of Minnesota Press.

Young, Iris Marion. 1990. *Throwing Like a Girl and Other Essays in Feminist Philosophy and Social Theory*. Bloomington: Indiana University Press.

Ziman, John. 1984. *An Introduction to Science Studies*. Cambridge: Cambridge University Press.

6 Examples, Submerged Statements, and the Neglected Application of Philosophy to Social Theory

Stanley Lieberson

How can a theory be true and the facts contradict it? On the other hand, how can a theory be in error and the facts support it? Until we recognize how easily these conditions can and do occur, it is impossible for us to think about theories in a reasonable way, let alone evaluate them appropriately. These problems exist because of the fallacies involved in the reasoning we use to evaluate the evidence that overtly appears to support or contradict a given theory. Moreover, our theories are often formed in ways that encourage such errors. Until these fallacies are recognized and avoided, there are limits on what we can hope to accomplish in theoretical work.

Methodology is a well-developed enterprise; ranging from concerns about fieldwork, interviews, questionnaire construction, to statistical inferences. Ironically, relatively little attention is paid towards the question of evaluating the *relevance* of the information for a given theory. As Amassari (1992) observes: "Epistemological

This is a revised version of a paper presented at the American Sociological Association Annual Meeting, New York, 1996, Session on "Philosophy and Social Theory: The Dialogue to Date."

awareness among sociologists is very recent, and epistemological themes and problems are either subsumed under the methodological quest or dealt with very unsystematically. Therefore, since methodological questions are usually resolved by technical procedures, epistemological validity is often reduced to technical validity" (p. 550).

Curiously, we tend to neglect areas of the philosophical enterprise that are very much concerned with just such questions, and can help us greatly to reason clearly and understand the nature of our evidential processes. I have in mind concerns with logic, the nature of scientific thinking, and philosophers' analysis of language. Accordingly, philosophy is of potentially great importance insofar as it helps us improve our reasoning as we go about building and advancing social theories. Since theory attempts to incorporate what is already empirically known, my comments here about the influence of philosophy on theory is at least implicitly a comment on the potential influence of philosophy for research. Indeed, for those who operate as if an impenetrable wall exists between theory and research, the first important lesson from philosophers is to understand that most definitions of theory imply a constant absorption by theorists of empirical work and, in turn, theoretical modifications which then inform researchers. See the discussion of theory by the logicians, Woods and Walton (1982), as well as the comments on contemporary practices in Lieberson (1992). In any case, I will view philosophy as a potential *tool* which can help us think clearly about our social theories and their evaluation, rather than as an *end* in itself, as it should be for philosophers.

A word of caution is in order. On the one hand, since it is very difficult to either evaluate or enhance our theories, rules are needed to help us evaluate and enhance our theories when we confront a morass of information that can be gathered, but are usually less than ideal. It will be clear that philosophy can help us develop the distinctive set of principles that must guide analyses based on the obstacles that arise because our complex problems are mainly not readily resolved through experimentation or statistical simulations of experimentation (see Lieberson 1985). On the other hand, the goal of the social scientist is not philosophy – although who can object to any incidental contributions to philosophy that may occur? Rather, our end is the advancement of social science knowledge – and there is far from an identity between the two. This distinction comes into play whenever either the goals or forms of evaluation do not overlap. There is nothing to be gained from our doing second-rate philosophy. This means that philosophy *per se* is no more the object of social science than is, say, statistics *per se*. It is only when either helps us reach our social science goals that we are interested. Philosophical efforts to answer normative questions – whether it be personal morality or social and political philosophy – are relevant to us as individuals and citizens, but not when we seek to meet the goals of social science. Likewise, philosophical debates, for which we have no unique tools *qua* social scientists to help resolve or evaluate, are also not part of our enterprise. There is a certain irony here because the areas of philosophy that are of potentially greatest help to us in advancing social science seem to have less appeal to social theorists than these other areas which are not really capable of helping us build a scientifically grounded social theory.

Obviously, the objective of developing a set of principles for evaluating social theories is a large task – one that can hardly be resolved in this essay. And obviously, it requires more than merely adaptation of philosophical ideas, whether they be in logic, the philosophy of science, or other lines of philosophical work. However, I will discuss several specific problems to illustrate the kinds of principles, partially derived from philosophy and partially from good social science, that will help us reach this goal. Each are valuable in themselves because they help clarify what is now muddled thinking. Additionally, each illustrates major directions of future work on reasoning that must be pursued, and which can benefit greatly through the clarification available from those areas of philosophy addressing issues of sound reasoning. Ironically, developments in the philosophy of social science are far less obtuse and far more grounded in its concern with the development of a scientific study than the philosophical treatises that seem to attract the attention of many social theorists (see, for example, the recent collection by Martin and McIntyre, 1994).

In any case, the applications that I discuss below are, in my estimation, of value in themselves. Rather than simply developing platitudes about the potential value of this merger entailing a social science application of philosophical knowledge, I analyze several specific contemporary fallacies which are themselves of deep importance and which should help theorists and others to reason effectively about social processes.

Examples[1]

Examples are monsters. On the one hand, it is hard for us to avoid using examples as we think through an idea. (Indeed, they are

---

[1] In some instances, the term "cases" could be used interchangeably with "example" (see arguments developed in Ragin and Becker 1992).

such a central part of our reasoning process that I cannot avoid using examples in this discussion of the dangers of examples.) On the other hand, unless we are very careful, examples can easily lead us to totally incorrect conclusions. It is not hard, in an abstract way, to recognize the pitfalls that they present. Everyone knows – or should know – that examples are shaky sources of evidence such that you cannot argue by example. After all, an example means simply that the specified event can and does happen. Yet, one constantly encounters an example being used as if it is powerful evidence either in support of a theory or evidence against it. Indeed, if one observes the actual way ideas are discussed, whether they are theories – about which we are specially concerned here – or an inductive analysis of virtually any topic, one finds an almost constant flow of reasoning by example such that they are used to strongly support or strongly undermine a conclusion. Even contradictory examples lend themselves to fallacious evaluations. Often, contradictory examples are used to show that the initial thesis – at the very least – is inadequate, because here is an example that runs in the face of it. The next challenge for the supporter of the thesis is to show why and how the contradictory example is really not quite the same thing as the supporting example and, hence, the original thesis is indeed correct. And, on and on.

The following proposition about the weight given to examples is probably a tautology: *the weaker the body of evidence gathered to evaluate a theory or a speculation, the stronger the importance attached to the question of whether an example appears to support or contradict the theory.* Hence, the reader should observe the importance usually attached to examples in spontaneous social discussions. However, our concern here is: what is the logic behind the use of examples in evaluating a theory?

Let us start with the extreme, namely under what conditions does an example or two provide powerful support or powerful disproof of a theory, or in the evaluation of one theory vs. another? First, let us consider a *deterministic* theory, that is, a theory which generates a conclusion that condition X will always cause condition Y to occur. Also, let us assume that the theory is viewed as so powerful that, under any and all possible conditions, it will correctly account for the events that are observed or predicted on the basis of the theory. In other words, the theory is so powerful that the outcome of Y cannot be swamped by forces working towards an outcome in the opposite direction. This second precondition is specially important in a non-experimental social science, where all sorts of conditions could normally be expected to at least

sometimes overcome the influence of the theory under consideration. If there is one case (example) where condition Y does not
occur in the presence of X, *under these assumptions*, it means that
the example is powerful evidence that something is wrong with
the theory. The theory, as stated, does not work since a prediction
derived from the theory fails to hold.

Note, however, that an example or two where condition Y *does*
occur in the presence of X is not particularly strong evidence that
the theory is correct. It is certainly favorable evidence, to be sure,
and in that sense gives us a tad more confidence in the theory than
we started with, but not a lot more. Although we now know of a
few examples which are harmonious with the theory, this is hardly
a strong test. Hence, these examples, under these conditions, provide an asymmetrical form of evidence, giving us more confidence
in rejecting the theory if an example runs counter to the theory
than when they are in harmony with the theory.[2]

Probabilistic theories, by contrast with deterministic ones, imply
a very different view of the damaging role of negative examples.
By "probabilistic" I mean a theory which leads to propositions in
the form that condition X will increase (or decrease) the occurrence
of Y and therefore that the non-X condition will decrease (increase)
the probability of Y occurring. Here, the importance of examples
declines radically – a counter-example to the theory does not disprove it. Indeed, under these circumstances, a counter-example
literally does not at all contradict a probabilistic theory. The influence of cigarette smoking on cancer illustrates this difference. Virtually all would agree that cigarette smoking causes cancer. Suppose
I cite a heavy smoker who lives a long life and does not die of
cancer. Does this example mean anything? Obviously not. The proposition is really meant to be a probabilistic one, such that cigarette smoking increases the likelihood (or chances) of death from
cancer. This cigarette example is of interest because it clearly shows
that probabilistic theories are less demanding and more tolerant
of counter-examples: they do not fall with a negative example.
Also of interest is the fact that many verbal statements are made in
a deterministic manner (cigarette smoking causes cancer) when
they really meant to be probabilistic (cigarette smoking increases
the chances of cancer).

The other strong assumption discussed earlier, that the theory
will operate under all possible conditions such that it will overcome any conditions that by themselves would generate an outcome

---

[2] This is, of course, reminiscent of the use of tests of significance in statistics.

different from it, also means that the theory collapses with a negative example. Here too we find that relaxing the notion of inevitability under all possible conditions will keep a theory from being contradicted simply by a negative example. Under this more relaxed assumption, the empirical outcome derived from the theory need not always occur under all possible conditions. With many cases, there is at least a chance of overcoming this difficulty through multivariate analysis, in which the operation of the expected influence can be statistically seen even if the net outcome under a multitude of different forces operating may be a net outcome in the opposite direction from what the theory predicts. Obviously, an example or two will not allow for this kind of analysis – which is not always successful even when there is a large data set. Hence, the assumption that a correct theory will generate a specific outcome, under all conditions, is a very strong assumption which allows a counter-example to lead to the rejection of the theory. Here we see that relaxing this assumption is more realistic and means that a theory is not so easily rejected.

Often theorists evaluate "competing" theories by considering situations where each theory has different expectations. Hence, the argument runs, a crucial test is available. If theory A, which leads to the prediction of Y under condition X, is compared with theory B where non-Y is expected under condition X, then a single example (read case study) will tell us which theory is correct (or at least between the two alternatives). If an example is to provide much meaning, the same two assumptions are required as before: (1) both theories have to be deterministic; and (2) both theories have to assume the predicted outcome will occur regardless of the presence of any other conditions which might lead to a different outcome. Under these circumstances, if Y occurs in the example, then we could conclude that theory B is wrong, or vice versa. However, if neither Y nor non-Y occurs (assuming it is not just a dichotomy), then one would have every right to conclude that the example shows both theories are wrong. However, for psychological reasons that I will develop later, we can be reasonably confident that it will be rare for neither Y nor non-Y to occur.

Note there is a standoff if only one of the two theories makes these assumptions. If the other theory is either probabilistic or does not assume the outcomes will occur under all conditions, then the evaluation of competing theories is more complicated. Let us suppose the first theory, A (which predicts the outcome to be Y) is based on these strong assumptions and the second theory, B (which predicts the outcome to be non-Y), has weaker assumptions. If the outcome is Y, then the results are harmonious with theory A but are not totally damaging to theory B. This is because the latter can encompass such an example – since either a probabilistic theory or a theory which is not expected to overpower the influence of all other possible conditions cannot be rejected if non-Y fails to occur in a given example. On the other hand, theory A crashes if the predicted Y fails to occur in the example. One theory is more demanding than the other, such that actual conditions can undermine the demanding theory but not the other.

Let us sum up the logical implications of this so-called "critical test" of one theory vs. another. If neither theory is based on these demanding assumptions, then no single example, or two, or three can allow us to discard one theory over another. At the other extreme, if both theories incorporate these demanding assumptions, then the outcome of a single example will indeed eliminate one or the other theory (depending on whether Y or non-Y occurs) or could eliminate both cases if the predictions from the two theories do not cover all conditions (suppose one theory would predict Y, another theory predicts W, and the actual outcome is Z). If several examples are considered and the outcome is inconsistent, then these strong assumptions would require us to reject both theories, since each has failed one of the critical tests and its assumptions cannot tolerate this. If one theory makes these demanding assumptions and the other makes neither or only one of the assumptions, then the test is lopsided. The examples can only eliminate theory A but cannot eliminate theory B.

Notice, in all cases, that confidence in a theory is only modestly enhanced if the example is harmonious with the outcome predicted. For the *example* is nothing more than an *example*. Examples serve to illustrate that a given state of affairs does exist, not always a trivial matter, and it may also serve to illustrate what the theory is about, and also that a given theory is harmonious with the outcome in some specific instance or two. But not much more. Elsewhere (Lieberson 1991), I argue that conclusions based on a small number of occurrences are obliged to make these strong assumptions, because otherwise the evidence would have relatively little meaning since a small number of cases (read here examples) would not allow us to draw a conclusion based on a probabilistic or non-universal set of assumptions.[3] In other words, the available evidence – or

---

[3] The absence of interaction effects is really the same as assuming a given outcome under all conditions, and hence no other variable(s) can overcome the outcome predicted by the theory.

at least the evidence used – forces such assumptions if one wants to make much of the limited evidence. In the discussion here, one can also look at the matter from the opposite direction: a theory making the two strong assumptions can only tolerate a small number of examples. One deviant example, in a large set of cases, would mean that the theory would have to be rejected. Since it is hard to believe that there are many social theories that are so powerful that the predicted outcomes will occur regardless of any other conditions which operate in themselves to generate a different outcome, a large set of cases makes it very difficult to have a theory which is deterministic and drives the outcome regardless of all other conditions.

All of this might appear to be an argument in favor of using large data sets to evaluate a theory. Although certain problems are diminished, some of the very issues discussed above do not disappear. No matter how many cases are included in a quantitative study, from another perspective the implications of the research for evaluating a theory operates as nothing more than one example. How can this be? First, we have to think about what statistical analysis can and cannot do for us. It allows us to study our data set with full appreciation of the role of random influences, to see whether a given model (read theory) holds even if not every single case behaves as the theory predicts. In other words, it allows us to work with our data in a probabilistic way. And statistics enable us to attempt to take the influence of a variety of other factors into account when evaluating a given theory.[4]

However, it is a separate matter to decide how much weight we can attach to a given study with respect to its linkage to a theory. And this decision is not merely decided by how closely the model fits the data, the size of the "N," or the variance explained. This evaluation entails a separate matter which cannot be helped by statistics. Namely, any given study can be viewed as itself being an *example*. Consider a study of a very large school system. Suppose we have a theory about how teaching style influences classroom performance. Further, suppose that every classroom in the entire system is studied, and – for the sake of the argument – suppose that elegant research methods are used such that everything is learned as well as a limited ethnographic study would generate. Clearly, this will generate greater confidence in the conclusions

---

[4] Note that I use the term *attempt* since in point of fact it is questionable at times how well a complex multivariate statistical analysis of a given data set can accomplish this goal (see Lieberson 1985).

drawn than what is possible on the basis of a few examples drawn from the same school. If the theory about teacher influence on classroom performance is very narrow – indeed narrow enough to make us wonder if it deserves to be called a "theory" – then we have strong evidence. But if there is a much broader theory – say about the impact of leadership behavior on a group, then the results gathered from a study of thousands of students is nothing more than an example. We have confidence that we have a valid picture of what is going on in that school system (just as we can have confidence that we have a valid picture of the state of affairs in the three specific classrooms that were studied very closely in a qualitative research effort.) However, from the perspective of this broader theory, neither effort provides much more than an example. In other words, even if we may have more confidence in the quantitative study's description of the situation in the school system, either way it is merely one example. Therefore, all of the rules developed earlier about the linkage between an example and a theory also apply here. As before, our evaluation of the theory in terms of the evidence is again affected by the way the theory is stated. If we think of all of the possible contexts in which the leadership theory would have implications, then clearly this is very weak evidence in support of the theory. Again, results counter to the theory are of minimal consequence for the probabilistic and modifiable form of a theory, but are totally damaging to a theory that is both deterministic and operates under universal conditions. Under circumstances where one can have confidence in the quality of the information that can be gathered, big-N studies of a given setting based on statistical analysis of a large data set are superior to a few examples drawn from the setting. However, once we link the theory with the data, the reasoning rules for examples apply equally. This holds for the different consequences of using a probabilistic or a deterministic theory, as well as the assumption that the predictions generated by the theory will operate in all conditions. Also, the earlier analysis of comparisons between two theories also holds.

The selection of examples is not a trivial issue and, to my knowledge, is not normally addressed. Ideally, examples should be drawn from a random set of possible examples. Or, if a small number of examples exist, all should be considered. I doubt if either occurs very often. Here we have the problem of whether the choice of examples involves a selectivity problem such that examples harmonious with a theory are selected by its proponents and, on the other hand, examples that contradict a theory are selected by its opponents. This is not an issue that I can address here, but some sort of formal rules are needed that will deal as much with psychological processes as anything else.

Finally, it is literally impossible to avoid thinking of any and all data as anything but a set of examples, albeit varying greatly in the rigor of their determination and the use of data which permit the example to run counter to the theory. However, as wide a variation in the data sets will increase our confidence in the theory. For example, if there is a theory about leadership, adding studies of ten more school systems will increase our confidence far less than will ten more studies of leadership in widely different times, places, and conditions.

Submerged Statements

All statements are embedded with submerged statements that are, hopefully, understood by the reader or listener. By *submerged statements* I mean there is a set of conditions, limitations, definitions, contexts, and other modifications of what is literally being said that are – if the communication is to work – understood by the receiver. "It is a nice day" is a good example of the embedded nature of a statement. In the Northeastern part of the United States, or any other area where there is considerable variation in weather through the year, what would be defined as a "nice day" in the middle of the winter would be different from what would meet that definition in the spring or fall, let alone in the summer. A sunny day at 45°F would certainly be a nice day in January, but would hardly be described as such in the middle of the summer. Beyond that, not everyone would agree on what they would define as a nice day in the same part of the year. Some like sunny days; others may prefer a slightly overcast day, or even one with a certain amount of fog and drizzle. Likewise, a snowy day might make a skier happy in the winter, but would not necessarily be appreciated by the same person if a long drive was scheduled. Indeed, a snowy day might be indeed a nice day if it occurs on Christmas morning, but not if it occurs a few days later.[5] The point is clear, and is widely understood in different parts of the sociological world: survey researchers, ethnomethodologists who study the meaning of a sentence or two of text, and theorists who are concerned with understanding the various meanings that can be attached to a text.

[5] Even this straightforward discussion involves submerged statements, for example, there will be many meanings to the phrase "a long drive."

There is, in that sense, nothing novel here. However, let us consider the implication for theories. If there are innumerable hidden assumptions, or what I call *submerged statements*, embedded in such a simple statement about the weather, it is not hard to imagine how many *submerged statements* occur in a social theory. In turn, we can begin to think about how such statements might impact on theories and their evaluation – particularly if we want to avoid throwing up our hands in despair and decide not much can be done to develop theories that can be communicated in a way such that the recipient gets the message intended by the sender.

There is a paradox here. On the one hand, no matter how detailed and precise a theory is, it entails a massive number of submerged statements. In my estimation, it is virtually impossible for any theory (whether it is a complex one or a simple one; mathematical or verbal; formal or casual) to actually state all of the submerged conditions that it is predicated on. Often this is of no great concern, since it entails commonly shared hidden assumptions that are so much part of the fabric of the discipline, that we are unaware of them unless it is pointed out to us. This is no different than the cultural assumptions that we usually do not see until a foreigner or an especially acute observer points it out to us. For a long time, sociological theories were almost uniform in their assumption that the biology of humans had nothing to do with the social organization or culture that occurs in societies. Then a group of sociobiologists appeared and began to raise a debate about the submerged assumption that, say, cooperation or conflict, occurs not because of some hard-wired genetic factor, but because of social conditions. If we examine gender differences in income and changes over time, we operate with many hidden assumptions, say that changes in diet are driving (or restricting) changes in the income gap. I do not believe this, but simply use it as an example to show that such hidden assumptions exist.

This, however, is not a problem for us. It is easy for someone to bring the assumption to surface, challenge it, and provide relevant information supporting the proposition that the assumption is hiding an influential factor.[6] Hidden assumptions, if commonly shared by the discipline, cause us no great problem in terms of intellectual clarity. If unearthed, challenged, and proven invalid, there is an important step forward in knowledge since that which was assumed to be true (in a passive sense because it was ignored) is now found

---

[6] This is not to say that questioning a hidden assumption will not be resisted vigorously – particularly at the outset.

to be not true and hence opens up all sorts of empirical questions and, in turn, theoretical issues. We end up greatly admiring the person who in effect revises our basic understanding of society.

The notion of submerged statements involves more than hidden assumptions shared by the entire discipline – or at least that part of the discipline for whom the theory is relevant. Not all of the conditional assumptions in a theory can be fully specified. And this absence – which is inevitable, I claim – of a full specification of every element to the theory, causes enormous difficulties. It certainly means that every theory can be shown to be false. Since every theory has a variety of submerged statements (read unstated), then there is no difficulty displaying that it is false. For example, most theories are *written* as if they are deterministic and hold in all situations. All we need do is find an exception and we can say the theory is false. It would be as if we examined bureaucracy in one corner of the old Ottoman Empire in one decade and found the bureaucracy did not act as Weber said bureaucracy behaved. We can simply conclude Weber's theory is *wrong* because of this one case! I suspect that most of us would reject this conclusion, because implicitly we would recognize that Weber's theory has to be a probabilistic one and hence although literally wrong, is not wrong because we understand the submerged statements that underwrote the theory.

Weber, bureaucracy, and one corner of the Ottoman Empire in one particular decade provide an easy example. A more difficult problem stems from the fact that these submerged statements include an unspecified set of *ceteris paribus* conditions that are implicitly part of the theory. Consider, for example, how many factors we *assume* are constant when we consider the influence of, say, the economy on race relations in the United States. And when I say "assume" I do not mean conditions that we are obliged to assume are constant because we cannot measure them – I mean conditions that we assume are constant because we do not readily imagine them being anything but the way they are.

This means that sooner or later all theories will be wrong – or at least incomplete – not only because it is easy for us to make any theory wrong by ignoring the statements submerged in it. Rather, they will at least need major modification when they are applied to very different situations where the *ceteris paribus* assumption fails or, even if applied to the same set of societies, there will eventually be new and unforeseen conditions that are not part of the *ceteris paribus* assumption. There is not much one can do in advance. We must expect theories to have bounds, and finding them and understanding them is not the same as saying a theory is wrong. It is wrong in the sense that it does not have unlimited application: in other words, it is incomplete.

There is an interesting dilemma here. Earlier we observed that the failure of a theory to handle every single example does not mean the theory is in error, at least if it is not a deterministic theory. Accordingly, one has to be cautious and avoid the tendency to rewrite and revise a theory once a case fails to fit it. This is typical for those who see a whole new development when a minor blip turns out to be operating. As a matter of fact, there is a school of thought called "analytic induction" which immediately attempts to rewrite its theory to take into account every deviation from the existing one (Znaniecki 1934; Robinson 1951; Turner 1953). However, this can be shown to be based on a deterministic model (see Lieberson 1991).

I have no solution for when it is reasonable to conclude that the theory is either wrong or in need of reexamination of the *ceteris paribus* conditions. However, I am reasonably confident that efforts to call theories erroneous because an example does not fit it, or because the submerged statements are not considered thereby making the theory literally wrong, is overdone. And I think it leads to a kind of internal and non-productive game among theorists who – being bright and imaginative – can create flaws in a theory by ignoring what are the submerged statements. This leads to the appearance of constantly changing (and presumably progressing) theoretical developments, when the new theory is just as easily shot down in short order as the theory it claims to supersede. In other words, if we choose to ignore the submerged statements because of course they are not literally made, then we can reach conclusions that are outrageous. Suppose I pull a trick on you. Suppose I say that I have a drug that prevents all forms of cancer from occurring. That sounds good. Now suppose it is a poison, say arsenic. It is literally true that if you take this drug you will not die of cancer. You will die immediately, however. Now when someone says the drug will prevent all forms of cancer from occurring, there is a submerged statement (unless we are an advertising agency) that it will not accomplish this end by immediately ending our life. There are lots of variations on this. I could have said: "if you are a smoker, this drug will prevent you from getting lung cancer", or "it will prevent AIDS," etc.

Part of the answer to dealing with this massive set of submerged statements that we work in occurs if we can recognize what is critical to describe or define in a very precise way and what is reasonable to write about without such precision. In this way, the "meat" of the theory needs to be stated in as precise a way as is appropriate ("precise" does not mean narrow, because that is the opposite of what is intended in a theory). However, the theory should be as clear as possible as to what it is about, thereby making it as clear as possible to draw conclusions from it and determine how closely it does absorb existing evidence. On the other hand, we have to recognize that a theory *has* to use many concepts in a fairly imprecise way simply because there are too many of them, and the task will fall under the weight of dealing with them all. In evaluating a theory of race and ethnic relations, the term "bureaucracy" might be used, say, but it will probably be vague. And, if bureaucracy later proves to be a central issue in using the theory, then it makes no sense to hold the theory to whatever vague way it was used.

Finally, one of the big problems here is the language itself, and our use of it. Philosophers look at the interplay between the nature of language, semantics, and logic. The language structure and the form of a statement is something that merits great care. What is interesting here is that we are victims of the restrictions of our language such that, in common speech, we may make statements that are not literally what we intended but which – on the other hand – nevertheless do convey what we meant anyway (see Ryle 1951). The philosophical examination of language may aid us greatly in dealing with our theories, particularly in thinking about interpreting them and then figuring out how to evaluate them.

Concluding Comment

Theories should not exist in a vacuum. They respond to evidence of all sorts, and in turn they generate propositions which have to be investigated. In this essay, I have set out two important issues in the current use of evidence to evaluate theories. These are our use of *examples* and our use of *submerged statements*. I show how our evaluation of social theories involves commonplace steps that are erroneous. Indeed, I show how current procedures lead us to accept theories that are wrong and reject theories that are correct.

This discussion illustrates how philosophical contribution in three areas can contribute to an improved evaluation of theories. These are: logic; analysis of the nature of social science; and studies of the nature of language as a form of communication. It is unfortunate that many theorists seem to ignore these facets of philosophy – because they are likely to be the areas most helpful to the formation of theories and their incorporation of empirical evidence. Moreover, this is not simply a matter of taking philosophical propositions and immediately applying them to social science problems. In point of fact, the application must be done within the context of the distinctive issues facing the social sciences.

References

Ammassari, Paulo. 1992. Epistemology. In Edgar F. Borgatta and Marie L. Borgatta, eds, *Encyclopedia of Sociology*, vol. 2. New York: Macmillan, 550–4.

Lieberson, Stanley. 1985. *Making It Count: The Improvement of Social Research and Theory*. Berkeley: University of California Press.

——. 1991. Small N's and Big Conclusions: An Examination of the Reasoning in Comparative Studies Based on A Small Number of Cases. *Social Forces* 70: 307–20.

——. 1992. Einstein, Renoir, and Greeley: Some Thoughts About Evidence in Sociology. *American Sociological Review* 57: 1–15.

Martin, Michael and McIntyre, Lee C., eds. 1994. *Readings in the Philosophy of Social Science*. Cambridge, MA: MIT Press.

Ragin, Charles C. and Becker, Howard S., eds. 1992. *What is a Case?: Exploring the Foundations of Social Inquiry*. Cambridge: Cambridge University Press.

Robinson, W. S. 1951. The Logical Structure of Analytic Induction. *American Sociological Review* 16: 812–18.

Ryle, Gilbert. 1951. Systematically Misleading Expressions. In Anthony Flew, ed., *Essays on Logic and Language*, 11–36. Oxford: Basil Blackwell.

Turner, Ralph H. 1953. The Quest for Universals in Sociological Research. *American Sociological Review* 18: 604–11.

Woods, John and Walton, Douglas. 1982. *Argument: The Logic of the Fallacies*. New York: McGraw-Hill Ryerson.

Znaniecki, Florian. 1934. *The Method of Sociology*. New York: Holt, Rinehart & Winston.

7 Loosening the Chains of Philosophical Reductionism

Steven Rytina

I begin with a bold thesis or, more properly, a statement of prior judgment, i.e., prejudice. Philosophical reflection is the antagonist of fruitful sociological theorizing. The reason, put philosophically, illustrates the point. And helps to soften the arrogance of it.

Philosophy, as I would have it here, consists in asking the most fundamental questions, about the nature of knowledge, of being, and of social life itself. Said questions are deeply intoxicating. No one of any curiosity can resist being drawn in. Yet no philosophical system or school has yet succeeded in redeeming itself. For none can escape coming somewhere to rest on premises that are, however dressed up, merely premises.

That the preceding is banal, even sophomoric, serves my point. What can be stipulated is a negative: all deep questions resist ultimate closure. This defines the challenge. One cannot deny the force of such questions. But with answers nowhere on offer, the only fruitful path must be to somehow tame them.

The point then, is hardly to ignore the value, much less the intoxicating charm, of philosophical argument. However, what is required is to wax the ears against philosophy's siren-song of closure. The remedy, quite simply, is to ensure that philosophical questions are held open. Even the best philosophical answers are tentative; such tentative answers should not be taken as blinders, as proof that some lines of inquiry are unworthy for the adequately sophisticated.

To develop these concerns, and some tentative remedies, I shall present various images of systems of ideas. These images are, in origin, geometric and spatial, but they shall be rendered verbally. The first of these is of vast hierarchies, of questions, answered by distinctions or predicates, linked to still further questions, ascending into the heights of abstraction. Then, with the general point established that these are open constructions, with inevitable gaps that resist closure, the focus will narrow to finer images of the textures that are revealed by problem-defining predicates. Only some concepts reveal textures that are what I will call granular, both rich enough to pose a challenge, yet not so exquisitely subdivided as to defy overall intellectual grasp. In the penultimate section, I will illustrate how the compulsion to ascend to high abstraction may sometimes be tamed by substituting issues of degree for categorical oppositions. Where these are granular, they can provide the helpful "friction" of accessible yet challenging puzzles. Such friction can provide resistance against the temptation to ascend to excessive, albeit intoxicating, abstraction.

The overall aim is one of establishing perspective. In the nature of the case, I do not aim for logical closure,[1] but for illustration that I hope will prove useful, and even persuasive. Instead of directly grappling with substantive detail, I shall try to provide maps of intellectual journeys. In traditional sociological fashion, these maps aim to compactly summarize past empirical outcomes with the hope of anticipating the most likely future possibilities. To undertake such a journey, one must choose a path. Perhaps such maps will be an aid in picking a fruitful one.

The Ambitions of Philosophizing

One heritage of the Enlightenment is the prestige attached to the philosophical attitude (Im Hof 1994). "Philosophy" summarized the aim of the autonomous intellect. To undertake a topic

---

[1] I could dress this up as follows. The following is built from the broad assumption that knowledge is incomplete. Furthermore, its future extension is humanly creative and hence cannot be anticipated intensively, e.g., in predictive detail. Only coarse, open, and incomplete anticipation of future theorizing is feasible. A useful basis is attempting to derive generalizations from past experience. This is imperfect in principle (some creativity is in some degree novel) and yet more fallible in application (the generalizations may be inapt or even false), but no better alternative is at hand.

philosophically meant to do so in terms that were fully general, i.e., in terms of predicates of unqualified universality. A philosophical writer aimed to persuade without reference to particularities of history, or geography, or of custom. Such argument, by design, would hold force over the diversities of traditional usages. (It also afforded some protective cover against sanctions by defenders of the local institutions implicitly criticized.) The abstract universalism of philosophizing provided the higher ground from which to hold forth in the pure tones of Reason and thus lay a claim to universal assent.

The similarity of this to sociology's program is no accident since our field arose out of writers who saw themselves as philosophers in these Enlightenment terms. The grand objective is to grasp in fully general terms the social, or society, or the laws of societal reproduction and development. This ambition survives intact when introductory textbooks proclaim that sociology is the science of society. Unfortunately, this is inevitably followed by some gloss over an awkward gap: the absence of any positive, much less consensual, restriction of the term "society" to anything in particular.

There is an obvious remedy: analyze the term and achieve an adequate definition. And here we might call in a social theorist-cum-philosopher. And, to render a complex matter in simple, even simplistic terms, she would probably begin to spin conceptual distinctions. These often take the forms of questions that ask "why?" and answers where "because" introduces a new term or predicate. We try to answer "why"? by spelling out or specifying: "because" the object of interrogation is a this and not a that, an X and not a Y.

Although this hardly exhausts the possibilities, it points to a key one. When one tries to analyze a concept, a central move is to break it down. The hope is that it can be made to follow from some order of prior or more fundamental concerns. Many definitions are like this, particularly those of essentially primitive (fundamental) terms like "society." The aspiration of the definer is to distinguish "society" from not-"society" in such a way that, along with some auxiliaries like common sense and common usage, interesting subsequent arguments about "society" are valid.

The example of defining "society" rings false because, as noted, there is no accepted definition. One could as well say that over a century of effort has failed to produce any broadly accepted analysis of the notion. But intellectual nature abhors such a vacuum. And this vacuum has called forth attempts that fit a common schema. Instead of a positive definition, various analysts have attempted to lay out dichotomous contrasts, such as social/

biological, structure/culture, or material/ideal. One shared attribute is that such contrasts are universal and exhaustive; every object or facet is on one side of the either/or, at least in principle.

Said contrasts are hardly sufficient by themselves. What is further called for is a still deeper account, reasoning backward to yet further contrasts in hopes of illuminating where their logical descendants come from. Thus the contrasts or dichotomous oppositions become chains ascending into the heights of abstraction. The premise, or one might say promise, of such a program, is one of purification. Lower-level empirical statements, or those grounded in everyday usage, or statements in the modest abstraction of middle-range theory, need to be purged by reference to a sound foundation.

This image of a logic-knitted pyramid of foundations is a commonplace article of faith. For example, one finds it in Chapter 1 of Stinchcombe's (1968) *Constructing Social Theories* which describes a pyramid of logical dependency with a base of facts extending to an apex of general ideas about causality. It appears at the outset of Alexander's (1982) survey of grand theory.[2] An essential element of this faith is that the philosopher is king of this hill.

Subscribing to this image, as probably most of us do, brings a burden of commitments. The said pyramid of logically rigorous foundations exists purely in principle; no one can spell out in consensual substance what it actually contains. It is an open form. Closure exists only as a promise in principle. And we have bought into hierarchy. Our low-level observations, summaries taken to be facts, and even middle-range theories, are open to decisive questions. We are obliged to accept that properly posed deep questions trump "mere" observations or "incomplete" attempts at theorizing.

Because this image does not refer to agreed chains of reasoning, it is a game with a wide-open invitation. And graduate students, and others, learn to imitate, or more rarely, devise quick trumps. For example, nearly all social behavior is encoded in language, rule-governed and hence subject to the linguistic coding of rules, or is just plain speech. A key step here, quite impeccable in its logic, is the invocation of a universal predicate such as the ultimately linguistic character of much of what we deal with.

From there it gets easy. "Language" or "linguistic" are readily expanded into other equally universal predicates. For example,

---

[2] The diagram on p. 3 is horizontal, but the asymmetric primacy of the more abstract is a central theme in the following text.

language is negotiated, individually created, or full of gaps closed only by improvisation. It follows that, in the final analysis, one cannot understand social behavior except in such terms. It is then hopeless, without value, or disrespectful of deeper, higher views to advance explanations in less rich terms, such as by strictly limited reference to material interests. Again, this argument sketch, to say nothing of more sophisticated variants, strikes me as logically compelling. What is less than compelling are the judgments of value. These rest on the normative presupposition that all claims must be held vulnerable to movement up the logical hierarchy of deeper abstractions.[3]

A great part of the prestige of this image is due to the lasting influence of one of its most famous proponents, Immanuel Kant, and of his masterwork, *The Critique of Pure Reason* ([1787] 1965). Kant responded to Hume's skeptical empiricism with his backdrop of categories that were a priori, that is, that had to be presupposed if lower-level sense data were to be ordered into knowledge. The necessity that attached to the highest levels was that of grounding the tools of logic (and logic's daughter, mathematics); these had to somehow precede experience. But the sense of precedence had nothing to do with time. By analogy with such exemplars *par excellence* as axiomatic geometry and the mechanics of Newton, "precede" meant occupying a higher level in a chain of deduction.

In this context, "necessity" takes on two distinct meanings that can be usefully contrasted. First, it refers to a goal or desideratum. If Kant's program (or one like it) is to succeed, it is a necessity to uncover, through analysis, the terms and propositions from which follow derivative principles, like logic and her daughter mathematics, thence down to truths, like those of geometry, or empirical

---

[3] The notion of questions that trump less abstract considerations extends to writers whose principal point is some variant on the impossibility or arbitrariness of any final grounding. In a manner of speaking, I tend to agree that the greatest claims of Reason remain, to date, unredeemed, and one may doubt they ever will be. I part company with indiscriminate claims that all kinds of knowledge are, say, texts equally subject to interpretation. I see no point in denying the difference between physics and fairy tales, even allowing that this is difficult to define in absolute terms, much less to ground it in any complete, fully satisfactory theory of knowledge, for none is available. It seems to me contradictory, or at least self-defeating, to mobilize the tools of rational argument against the possibility of rational argument. In any event, there seems little point in attempting a rational appeal to those persuaded by such, beyond noting that my argument about questions without closure is directly applicable.

laws ordering sense data, like those of physics.[4] But this aspiration or dream contains no guarantee, that is, there might be no way to ground all that Kant sought to ground, or Kant might have failed to uncover it. This must be distinguished from the second sense of necessity, that insofar as Kant has invented the correct terms and propositions, and insofar as he has made the links downward according to the correct rules of thought, or logic, then his argument is binding on all.

Two caveats follow. Kant's dream of a great reduction back to one ultimate set of fundamentals may have been a chase of the will-o'-the-wisp. I think most would now allow something of this order at the very least with regard to his search for a universal and binding morality or ethics. Second, notwithstanding the first caveat, Kant's pyramid is best regarded as inverted, and at the bottom lies an abyss. Sooner or later, you come to the end, or some set of ultimate, most fundamental, assumptions. And these rest, as Nietzsche tirelessly pointed out, e.g., in *Beyond Good and Evil* ([1885] 1966) on no more, or less than Kant's judgmental assertions. After all, even the most comprehensive deductive reconstruction must somewhere come to ultimate premises and these, for better and for worse, stand on nothing.

Yet the Kantian aspiration lingers on, not least in social theory. Münch (1987) quotes Parsons on the centrality to his development of his study of Kant at Heidelberg in 1926 under Karl Jaspers. Münch's judgment was that *"Parson's sociology cannot possibly be understood apart from an understanding of Kant's critical project"* (p. 8, emphasis in original). Just as Kant deemed transcendental universals as prerequisites of ordering sense data into knowledge, Parsons held that selection over ends must be structured by exterior and universal constraints. He identified these with tracking out along means–ends chains until the ultimate principles governing choice came into view.

For present purposes, I wish to underscore the conditional on which this rests, which many find compelling. Just as Kant desired a rational foundation for knowledge, Parsons wished to delimit

---

[4] Kant was hardly reticent about the superiority of his contribution: "the transcendental ideas thus serve only for *ascending* . . . to principles." The rest of us could make do with the tools he provided, since "as regards to the *descending* to the conditioned, reason does, indeed, make a very extensive logical employment of the laws of understanding, but no kind of transcendental employment" (p. 325). The apex of this ascent is described in a footnote to the same page as "and thence to the knowledge of *God*" (emphasis in the original). To put it mildly, this expresses a hierarchy of prestige among concepts.

society as an object amenable to rational-cum-scientific investigation. He identified this with the requirement that it have a texture amenable to deductive reduction.[5] The *analytic necessity* of this scheme is contingent; some such dissection, not necessarily that of Parsons, is required to provide a deductive–logical foundation for the claim that societies as wholes qualify as topics for science. To satisfy this aspiration, Parsons had to invent a pyramid of distinctions establishing a deductive path back to first principles.

It is not surprising that many find this project compelling. The prize is in the aspiration. This groundwork, if successful, is the prerequisite for scientific insight into the fate of whole societies. Absent some such scheme, *society* may not have enough logical coherence to have a fate in any acceptable sense. In this case, no amount of accurate theory of local detail could possibly sum to knowledge binding over the entire ensemble. But aspiration to such grandeur has a price. Here, the price is the huge apparatus. To assume, after the style of Parsons, that society does have a texture subject to deductive dissection from top to bottom, seemingly commits one to a very baroque outlook.

And there is a principal rub. It is deeply attractive to imagine that the task of sociology is to grasp society as a totality. But it is hardly necessary. Hardly anyone would disagree that there are all sorts of challenging and unsolved puzzles that stop well short of directly bearing on the question of how it all fits together, if indeed it does.

A brief aside to another science may help give some substance to this possibility. Geology might be crudely summarized as addressing how to interpret local sequences of rocks, or strata. A central assumption is that processes like sedimentation, erosion and chemical weathering proceed by unalterable physical principles operating over long periods. Sediment layers may be dated, e.g., by fossils ordered by the assumption of an evolutionary sequence. Yet huge gaps, called nonconformities, occur. These are, at best, explained away, for example, by hypothetical episodes during which some stratum was folded away from the surface and not subject to sedimentation or erosion. Such folding is laid to past plate movements, at least in principle, but this is somewhat wishful, as the puzzle resembles reconstructing how a bedsheet became tangled solely from what is apparent in the morning. Insofar as dynamics such as rates of erosion crucially depend on the history of angles of inclination,

---

[5] More exactly, by direct analogy with Kant, one had to invent, by analysis, terms such that the structure followed by deduction.

interpretations are within wide, and not very calculable, ranges. In sum, even when one assumes that the details are strictly emergent from natural processes, there is no real possibility of a global or comprehensive reconstruction.

It is perhaps not so hard for geologists to live with this permanent open end to their world-view. The nitty-gritty detail of sequences of layers is usually strongly similar in adjacent terrains while abrupt discontinuities are less common. This imposes a comparative outlook and sharply limits the appeal of seeking the entire world in each and every grain of sand.

In contrast, the search for a logically complete totality of *the social* brings a double burden. First, as noted above, the project of totalization would bring society as a whole within the range of science. It is impossible not to have sympathy with this, although such sympathy might be tempered with doubt as to the ultimate feasibility of the totalizing project.

Second, however, the assumption that this is necessary, desirable, and possible leads some to assume that all analysis of every element of society must equally be cast in these terms. Thus the terms that pave the path to transcendence must enjoy hegemony, over concept formation, epistemology, and even ontology. This mistake overlooks the conditional, incomplete condition of the totalizing project. If one had such a complete edifice securely in hand, then it might well provide reference marks for securing validity. It hardly follows that such status should accrue to incomplete, contested attempts. One might compare it with the scientific aridity that early modern cosmologists saw in strict theological conformity.

My intent is to invoke a somewhat delicate balance. I mean to affirm that the questions that take one down the path toward possible analytic underpinnings are deeply compelling. But some perspective is called for. Answers to such questions would necessarily command widespread attention. But complete answers are not on offer. What available more often great contrasts, or key distinctions. These are never final and sufficient, i.e., are never complete and closed logico-deductive reductions back to an absolute foundation. Tracking them back, when it does not produce exhaustion or awe, will invariably reveal a base of supposition in brilliant (or obscure) rhetoric. One need not devalue this enterprise, in its own right, to keep squarely in mind that it is incomplete, and contested. In the final meta-analysis, this material is in no condition to justify dictating norms.

This does not mean we cannot learn from such writings, but one must be wary of an open term like "learn." What is to be learned are most often analytic distinctions in which profound open questions may be stated. We do not "learn" how to resolve such questions or to achieve closure. Some of the clearest examples concern the hoary old contrast of ideal/material. Simply put, the outside world can only influence choice or action through mediation by mental constructs. But "mental constructs" is a class or object with very little inner texture or specific content. We have no very good dissection or analysis to guide us. What is one to say of the transformation by which disks of yellow metal become money, other than it is obviously very important?

Such famous distinctions as Giddens (1984) "rules and resources" or Habermas's (1987) "life world and system" are variations on this contrast. And what do we learn? My present thesis is that the larger message admits of a schematic paraphrase: to understand social life back to its ultimate foundations, one would have to understand both sides of each author's central dichotomy. That strikes me as a valid summary of what one would find by exploring broad swaths of intellectual work on foundations. But note that neither author then provides much guidance as to how to carry out the assigned task. That vacuum should raise doubt. What is a good question in some (tentative) final analysis may not be a very good first or high priority.

Here we might turn back to the course of philosophy for some guidance. One of the most brilliant latter-day explorations of the Kantian pyramid was Wittgenstein's *Tractatus Logico-Philosophicus* ([1922] 1981). The aspiration might be summarized as unveiling the set-theoretic foundations of scientific truths securely grounded in sense data. But Wittgenstein then abandoned confidence in this variant of logical positivism. In what might be called the "intractatus" (more formally known as the *Philosophical Investigations*, [1953] 1983), he argued that language could not be grounded in a logico-deductive reconstruction or foundation.

One of my favorite passages is his claim that totality of all language games have no defining character(s) in common ([1922] 1981: 31–4). The upshot would seem to be that no concatenation of predicates could exhaust or bound the class; therefore no operation over such logical sentences could define or delimit how games may end. It then follows that meaning cannot be closed within purely formal or logical limits.[6] The Kantian pyramid is demolished as a futile aspiration.

---

[6] Of course, such an argument cannot *follow* from logical considerations. Wittgenstein's demonstration is semi-circular and rests on prior acceptance of his bold assertion that "game" is the proper analogue for securing closure of meaning.

Some implications of this were spelled out by Winch (1958). A key premise, amply sustained by quotations from founding texts, was that *the social* could not be understood without reference to meaning. As a corollary, explanation of social action intrinsically required reference to meaningful reasons.

And if we admit the force of categorical distinctions, Winch's argument seems valid. There can be no doubt that much of what makes action social is somehow intertwined with considerations of language, of symbol, and of meaning. And there can be no doubt that every one of these is deeply problematic in available philosophical treatments. It follows that to make essential reference to such concerns dictates engagement with philosophy. Winch scoffs at such stalwarts as Theodore Newcombe by extracting passages where Newcombe does an awkward skate around the consequent difficulties. Winch is quite right in pointing out that Newcombe provided no answers to the puzzles that rightly baffle philosophers.

Winch is, in my view, further correct in pointing out that key texts by founders in social science make essential reference to unresolved philosophical puzzles. (One might be tempted to attribute "unresolvable" on the basis of Winch's apparent reading of Wittgenstein.) In a similar way, a latter-day graduate student can be trained to uncover passages where any attempt at explanation or analysis makes some order of reference to what may be analyzed into moral order, meaning, language, or similar such puzzles. But Winch has already drawn the ultimate conclusion. It is pointless to call for more work; surely no amount of empirical investigation will crack philosophical puzzles. Nor is it likely that our philosophically challenged colleagues will any day soon produce success at the puzzles that eluded the likes of Wittgenstein and Russell.

Some unfortunately draw the opposite conclusion. For example, Wolfe (1991) thoroughly documented the failure of computer research into linguistics, psychology, or artificial intelligence to produce any computer program that mastered any sort of meaning. His conclusion was that students of sociology, which he took as centrally concerned with meaning, had little to learn from such programs. Certainly he is correct in reporting the failure to make any real headway on the problem of meaning. But why would sociologists succeed where so many others have failed? I think the better conclusion is that insistence, like Wolfe's, that meaning comes first, would condemn sociology to permanent futility.

One might similarly applaud the logic but question the strategic advice of Emirbayer's and Goodwin's (1994) thoughtful critique of network analysis from the standpoint of recent wrinkles in social

theory. As these critics conclude: "Network analysis gains its pur-
chase upon social structure only at the considerable cost of losing its
conceptual grasp on culture, agency, and process" (pp. 1446–7). Yet
it is only from the standpoint of a totalizing project that the "costs"
they invoke are some sort of unqualified loss. To oversimplify
considerably, network analysts have privileged the metaphor of
persons as points and relations as binary, present, or absent lines.
This restricted image, or deliberate reification if one prefers, is a
strategic commitment. Some kinds of variety are deliberately re-
pressed for the sake of focussing on the issues of pattern, and these
remaining issues are dauntingly challenging. The proffered advice
might be likened to conceptual acid, powerful but destructive. One
can raise, but hardly close, issues of what a relation, tie, or social
bond might mean, and in that conceptual state of self-induced
uncertainty, there remains no pattern of relations to study.

Thus the image of knowledge inspired by Kant has two mess-
ages, one trivial and the other cautionary. Both can be derived from
a single, summary aphorism: predicates that govern the social in
general open up deep, unresolved puzzles. The caution is the lack
of resolution, the trivia is that such predicates apply to essentially
all writing on social topics. Any text, conceptual scheme, or theory
that aspires to any degree of generality is vulnerable to unanswered,
deep questions. Such critique can be dressed up as learning by
forming questions out of universal predicates sanctified by one
or another great authority. This may seem all the more profound
when it applies to a passage where some author was at pains to
work around such puzzles. The game is not at all hard to play.
Practically all attempts at sociology, either in setting the stage or in
attempting closure, make reference to material that is, in the final
analysis, subjectively meaningful, morally binding, or otherwise
subject to transcendent concerns.

Deep puzzles merit our fascination. But they are almost infinitely easier to identify than to resolve. Familiarity with the literature on them does not bring access to solutions. We need not confuse
laudable erudition with capacity to recommend anything of much
practical use. Pointing out that traces of such puzzles are nearly
always to be found does not really give much guidance to where
progress may best be made.

Logic and Granularity

The image of the Kantian pyramid invokes an aspiration: almost
indefinitely long chains of reason that bind thought into strict

coherence. Because this involves the central faith, redemption through Reason, it is probably too much taken for granted. What would follow is that any predicate that poses a good question is a guide to good solutions.

This goes awry in a conflict of two background notions. First, it tends to be assumed that one can somehow rely on logic to bind. After all, the whole attraction of going up the pyramid is the assumption that something like deduction will guide, and bind, the path back down. The second, and conflicting, notion is that what makes a predicate appealing is that it harkens back to the largest, overarching issues. And it is precisely these that defy attempts at closure.

The asymmetry poses a challenge. Looking upward, we cannot, or should not, deny the attraction of predicates that promise to (someday perhaps) allow Reason to penetrate back to the very nature of things. Yet we can bring a critical faculty to bear on the presumption that the downward journey of scientific puzzle-solving is always or uniformly amenable to reason and logic. Like any predicates, those designed to connect back to the deep issues mark off conceptual fields or domains. Our real work is to creatively come to grips with the puzzles these pose. And this suggests that as a counterbalance to the pull of upward attraction, we might use critical concepts to help identify the kinds of textures that make reasoned puzzle-solving a promising endeavor. One such notion that I think distinguishes promising problems is granularity.

Granularity is slang among computer programmers which I first saw recorded as current at Microsoft. It gives a name to a ubiquitous experience in writing programs, especially large ones. In usage such as "getting down to the granularity of," say, up-dating the File Attribute Table,[7] it refers to gaining mental access to the full complexity of what something involves.

Now a crucial quality is that granularity is no one-shot epiphanal flash, e.g., like grasping that the history of all society is the history of class struggle. In pursuit of a single problem, it can happen again and again and again. It often takes the form of an unfolding as the (usually) finite but often lengthy list of relevant details come into consciousness. And it is commonly nested. What began as an element of a list (or metaphoric grain) proves, in turn, to itself

---

[7] Most of us wouldn't recognize a File Attribute Table or FAT if we saw one, but it is where the operating system keeps track of how locations spread over a hard disk are chained into what we, as users, see as files. When the FAT's contents become jumbled, one's hard disk becomes an expensive paperweight.

consist of many distinct elements. Each requires attention. And, one learns to one's continual surprise, elements that were not at all apparent three levels earlier often require elaborate and painstaking treatment. (In 1867, Marx wrote a letter to Engels anticipating that he would finish what would be Das Kapital in ten weeks. Ten years, one polished and two rough draft volumes later, Marx died. Probably not just of the granularity.)

Thus one might begin with an goal of making programs run in square windows on a monitor screen. But one detail would be writing code such that any program could write what it had to say into such a box. Writing to the screen requires a character set. This sub-problem then expands into a list of possibilities, drawing on different typefaces and different approaches to making letters of variable size. Once such a list is finalized, the program might access any one of these specific definitions at an address in some master-file. Accessing an address in a master-file requires loading the value of the address, bit-masked as needed, into an appropriate register, and issuing an interrupt call to initiate a disk read. Eventually, one is down to coming to grips with the nuance of CPU and bus design, close to the ultimate layer of incredibly lengthy yet deeply regular strings of 1s and 0s that are the ultimate "content" of a computer doing it's thing. Each of these nested layers may be as easily named as saying a simple phrase or word. But the puzzles of each level expand into a whole, absorbing world of complex, demanding detail. The "simple" goal of a screen window for programs masks an expansion that becomes inevitable months of programmers burning midnight oil by the gallon.

Those who have not known the joys of writing code may be more familiar with the mirror-image experience which awaits the user. Many modern programs come with simple-looking menu-bars at the top. The user selects some specific element in hope of doing something useful. More often than not, this gives rise to another menu and the necessity of making a further choice. And so forth. Not uncommonly, what seemed straightforward requires address of novel options, and choices within choices, deciding issues that many users do not comprehend and would just as soon not have to face. Some of this is bad design, but much of it, properly understood, is necessary to allow persons with sufficient skill to achieve precisely what they want with the same program. What seems a simple goal when first conceived often turns out to require significant mastery of intricate, granular complexity. And yet, once the details become familiar, the whole process can come to seem simple and logical after all.

The nesting of problems, or in reverse, aggregation, is an identifying trait of granularity. One might think of a jigsaw puzzle. But each piece, in turn, forms a whole other puzzle, whose dividing lines are, at first view, invisible. One passes through the trapdoor by shrinking one's perspective and allowing one's perceptual field to fill with the pieces that form the puzzle within the piece. Typically, each of these pieces, in turn, is trapdoor, so that another magnification reveals still another puzzle with its own shapes and complexities. As one addresses one of these independent puzzles, it can seem as if the problem in view is a whole unto itself. But freedom is limited. When one assembles all the tiny pieces into what is itself but a piece, you have to make sure that it all somehow fits into the available larger shape.

In programs, the fit is not, of course, geometric but functional. If the program is to work, the constituents must work together. This means that solutions must avoid resting on invalid assumptions about what may come from other elements. This vulnerability to the logic (or illogic) of other elements accounts for much of the abrasive quality of granularity. Some of the harshest abrasion comes from the supposed beneficiary, i.e., the puzzled end-user, blindly hitting keys in hope that something might work. Programs often fail because programmers unconsciously assumed away (or found unimaginable) some of the hopelessly stupid things that users sooner or later attempt. Programs fail even more often because programmers have written code that does unanticipated stupid things all by itself, especially when the results of one segment are fed to another.

A central feature of the experience of granularity is coming to grips with an exhaustive comprehension of the range of possibilities, of inputs, of states of the system. The shift, psychedelic swoop, or consciousness expansion of granularity is often in this transition. One opens a seemingly innocuous trapdoor and descends into a world of new detail that can prove quite challenging. Much of the challenge only emerges when thought moves beyond the easy, soft examples that are readily grasped and handily dealt with. Granularity dictates an attempt to rigorously grasp the entire range that the code must accommodate. Resolving granularity requires, in an older metaphor, "getting down to the nitty-gritty." This requires creativity, not mechanical thought, and possibilities inadvertently overlooked during early conception sometimes cripple otherwise nifty solutions. (That programs work at all shows that possibilities can be addressed with an approach to exhaustiveness. That nearly all sometimes fail is proof that it is very challenging.)

What appears to be, and for all practical purposes is, a separate puzzle must fit within very rigid boundaries, not exactly of space, but of the range of what is logically consistent with other levels. This, in turn, is in the terms or conceptual range implicit in the definitions that implement other levels.

Granularity is the source of an increasingly widespread social problem; the inability to plan information technology. Programmers and other knowledgeable insiders almost invariably err on the side of optimism in predicting feasibility, costs, time to completion, and effectiveness.

Mis-estimates of hundreds to one are not uncommon; nor are "carefully planned" projects that are ultimately abandoned as hopeless after running through vast sums. Even the most brilliant and technically adept make such mistakes. A famous example was inadvertently provided by the estimable Herbert Simon. In 1958 he published a list of goals or functions that he thought would be successfully computerized or programmed within the following decade. Among these was superiority to humans in chess and machine translation among natural languages. Nearly four decades later, the state of the art is just over the threshold of chess superiority. The goal of fluent machine translation of natural language remains elusive; it almost seems to recede with technological advance.

It is extremely common within organizations to embark on projects that assume that records or other information can be made manageable by computers. Advocacy is by no means limited to ignoramuses; scientists and engineers are often in the forefront. But success is elusive. Some writers now argue that the craze for information technology is a significant factor in the fall-off in productivity gains for the last generation. It would appear that humans are somehow basically ill-equipped to anticipate the full range of granularity. Goals or projects that appear readily doable to highly realistic persons often turn out to be utterly out of reach.

What accounts for this? The typical trapdoor is a goal or end, often stated in few words. For example, one might imagine, as some do at my university, that a student's academic record might be provided to an advisor's desktop. Beneath the trapdoor, "student's academic record," are the rich, yet specific details that grades are kept by course with each student identified by a unique number. But different faculties, or schools, such as Education, do not do this in the same manner. And one might further imagine that one could compile the student's progress toward completion of a program. But it turns out there are, by one count, 7,000 different degree programs in Humanities and Social Sciences, which only enrolls 6,000 students at any one time. Most programs are defined in a page or so of text, and many of these challenge human comprehension. Since students have been graduating for years, it all must somehow work. Evidently, when an advisor and a student agree to focus on one such page of text, they somehow settle what must be done to satisfy the requirements. (Apparently a magic talisman known as the "advisor's signature" is used to ward off logical difficulties.) But to embed all such possibilities in a computer program might well require more person-years than supplying one-to-one oral advice for all students for, say, a decade or more. In short, when one opens some seemingly innocuous trapdoors, one can confront a degree of complexity that beggars imagination.

Yet we must be careful to draw a distinction. Seven thousand different degree programs may seem a Herculean chore, but it is a finite and definite number. Some of those program definitions are horribly ill-written, but nearly all could be translated into algorithmic code. (This is, by the way, a statement of faith and might be misplaced.) The number of courses is finite, as is the number attempted by any student.

Compare this with the trapdoor of designing a program that will query the student of his/her life goals and then recommend an academic program. Only a fool (but see Herbert Simon above) would imagine that one could make a finite list of the elements implicit in 'life-goals.' Nor can one imagine any general operator that would take combinations of elements into anything coherent, such as program recommendations.

Open questions, including those implicit in universal predicates, are often trapdoors. In effect, they serve as injunctions to analysts and empirical workers: grasp the granular complexity herein and report back to us. Yet we must be wary that even well-posed questions, for all they identify valid goals, do not invariably signal feasible projects.

And one clear category to be avoided is trapdoors that signal language games. One might be lulled by the apparent fact that in any natural language the number of sentences (of finite length) is arguably finite. But the number of terminating sequences may not be. And Wittgenstein may be right that there can exist no overarching rule that governs termination. At best, no one can yet specify what conditions, logical or otherwise, have been satisfied when two parties to communication agree that they have arrived at closure. And Winch may be right, and I think he clearly is, that it would be woefully premature to attempt to resolve such matters by empiricism.[8]

This applies, with some degree of granularity, to what lies behind such trapdoors. For example, it is surely of great interest to know of the symbols that move members of some population. Yet suppose one aimed at the further question: how do these determine, shape, or condition action or behavior by members of the said group? By what rules or logic could one hope to say that such occurred? I, for one, cannot easily imagine that symbols do not play a major role in action. But it is a deep and unanswered question how that might occur.

However, I will share a strong suspicion. I seriously doubt that particular symbols, or meaningful sentences, or whatever the elements here might properly be, could be very sharply constraining. I doubt there is any kind of strong logic of implications that binds these together. Thus, if you or I entertain one or the other, we may smoothly pass or even leap to quite a diverse range of consequent motives or actions. As a personal example, it so happens that I experience the American flag as emotionally quite moving. I get a catch in my throat at baseball games which I imagine is a result of indoctrination into flag worship in my primary schooling. Yet having entered adult political awareness around 1968, my patriotism doesn't share much with, say, members of the National Rifle Association. There may be some sort of grammar that somehow governs this. But it seems very unlikely that it is such as to bring about much uniformity or regularity across diverse individuals.

This is not contradicted by repeating from the catechism that "meaning is shared." At most this requires that I find occasional partners for the relevant language games; it hardly requires me to find them at NRA conventions. Meaning is shared in interaction, electronics aids aside, in face-to-face encounters. I don't make a practice of interacting with whole populations, e.g., putative nations.

A metaphor for the granularity one finds beneath a trapdoor to a language game is that it is infinite, with grain so fine as to be like talc, or even mush. There are plenty of options in sight, but far too many to list, or to otherwise order. There are choices, but no way to make any sense of how anyone selects among them. There are sometimes apparent leading choices, but any degree of self-reflection, or of empiricism on how others reflect and choose, will soon

---

[8] I hardly mean to suggest that such matters are unworthy of investigation. However, it seems unwise in the extreme to put other matters on hold pending satisfactory resolution of such issues.

enough dissolve such peaks into ever finer-grained texture without terminus or bright paths. There is no way to single out particular sequences of elements, or symbols, and assign some compulsive attribute, such as validity.

One way to partly capture when granularity is manageable is when one can hope to apply logic. Logic would mean that the elements may be grouped, ordered, placed into definite sequences, or somehow reduced to a model. By model here I mean a symbolic construction whose manipulation simulates order in some more real world. A deductive theory that allows one to predict end-states from initial states is such a model. So also is any sort of calculus, such as one that derives overall states from micro-details or, more rarely, vice versa.

One major source of failed perspective is our woefully excessive claim to the use of logic in our arguments or theories. As I understand logic proper, it is a branch of set theory. Within this context, one can, at least in principle, settle issues of proof. Should someone put forward a string of symbols and allege that they show that proposition A entails proposition B, there is a mechanical procedure that will settle whether the claim of entailment is valid (There is, however, no mechanical procedure that can be guaranteed to produce such a proof whenever it exists. One variant of this is the famous theorem of Kurt Gödel that there can exist statements in arithmetic that could not be shown to be either true or false. Such undecidable propositions could not exist if there were a mechanical procedure for generating all valid proofs.)

Even in mathematics, almost nothing of real interest is actually done with this degree of rigor. From the latter part of the nineteenth century on, variants on this recognition caused assorted crises in mathematics. But as Kline (1980) made much of, the practical impact of this was almost nil. Long-used results, notably including the rules for transforming functions taught to undergraduates as "the calculus," survived intact, albeit with far more carefully formulated premises. To date, there remains lively doubt that the foundations are really adequate. From the standpoint of extreme rigor, there exist many widely accepted mathematical arguments that apparently could stand some sprucing-up. Yet the relation of premises to conclusions is, in practice, extremely rigid.

A distinctive feature of argument by formal logic is very long chains without any slippage. In a mathematical text, there is near-perfect consistency across tens and even hundreds of pages. Subsequent developments mesh perfectly with earlier ones. There is a strong conservation principle in force. For example, if some consequential classification is true of all matrices, it equally applies to, say, the transposed matrices of left eigenvectors of positive definite matrices. By that very token, any reader may construct examples that must obey the argument simply by close attention to definitions. One need not assume that the best, or safest, or only reliable illustrations are those specifically advanced in the text by the author.

Little argument in social theory obeys logic in anything like this strict sense. One source is the frequent use of typologies, such as Etzioni's (1961) coercive, remunerative, and normative incentives to comply with organizational demands. (This trichotomy, though not attributed, is nearly identical to a proposal by the philosopher Russell in his *Power* (1939). Thus the pedigree is impressive.) Yet it illustrates a common flimsiness when thought of as an operation on sets which, in turn, makes for very weak links in any attempt at a chain of reasoning.

First, such a typology sets off a category, "incentives," from everything else, or "not-incentives." Core illustrations are ready at hand, such as candy, money, and public praise. But there is no bright line or clear boundary. For example, to an eccentric collector of chewing-gum wrappers, what to most is trash could be an incentive.

Second, the typology invokes a sub-classification. Once again, for each sub-class one could readily conjure up core illustrations, that you and I know that Etzioni would almost surely accept as squarely within his intent. Yet there is a substantial part of the domain that would be borderline, problematic, and ambiguous. A telling illustration is that there does not seem to be any clear content to trying to imagine what is 50:50 between, say, remunerative and normative. There is no grain, no finer detail, no substance to graded differences, and the typology has no counterpart topology over anything very apparent.

The stage is then set for ambiguity to accumulate. For example, a subsequent statement about the remunerative sub-class should ideally apply to all members, but borderline or marginal instances will tend to slip out of mind. And, in this case, there is an overwhelmingly prominent core-element, cash money. Most readers would probably think it logical, i.e., persuasive, to draw on properties most strikingly true of money. Thus were one to say that "remunerative incentives can most readily be applied to problems outside the arena where they are won," it might not register that marginal illustrations like chewing-gum wrappers were now clearly excluded.

One might summarize this species of rhetorical logic as "true by virtue of core illustrations." Such arguments may not be true of bizarre or borderline illustrations. This reader, at least, often has a sense of some degree of robustness in this regard. An important dimension of critical reading is the ease of arriving at counter-examples. Accordingly, one assigns little value to a claimed derivation when exceptions come to mind which are everyday, prominent, well-known, or occur on some wide scale. Another red-flag violation is evident ignorance of received usage, e.g., equating "class" with income, absent some nod to the Marxian heresy involved. Thus illustrations can be made more core or made more salient by reference to widely studied texts.

What is commonly called "logic" in sociological argument is usually no more than rhetoric that persuades. ("Rhetoric" acquired perjorative connotations in the Modern era, but the quality of rhetoric that persuades seasoned scholars is not to be sneered at.) What makes such so-called logic somewhat more fragile than its formal counterpart is that it depends on judgment, in this illustration, judgment about the centrality or coreness of illustrations. At a fairly short remove, after not very many steps, there is nothing to guarantee equi-finality. Different practitioners will be trailing off down divergent pathways. Thus if we all began with the class "resources," you might track off with the "know-how" of "skills as means to attain ends," someone else might include the "know-who" of "connections as the key to success," and I might insist on "tangible, fungible, material means." Any of these are defensible, but they are surely not the same.

It should be stressed that what we presently tend to indiscriminately group under "logical" includes stronger as well as weaker illustrations. When Tilly (1990) refers to states, the referent is a list of illustrations that may number less than 1,000 and these are within fairly definite qualifications as to historical period. There is some room for dispute about what is, and is not, covered, but not very much. Or when Blau (1977) speaks of categorical contrasts that are salient for social relations, the list of illustrations trails off from highly salient core illustrations to marginal, less relevant, possibilities. And as Skvoretz (elsewhere in this volume) shows, the concept of salience can be equated with an index that takes on numerical values which, in turn, renders some of the steps in Blau's argument formally rigid in the sense of numerically rigorous. What is "more persuasive" about these rhetorics is that there is less room from slippage in (a) interpreting what the theorist intended and (b) pursuing ultimate agreement about whether the claims are empirically apt. That said, it remains prudent to allow that much useful sociology falls short of such high standards.

It is not my intent here to denounce any such "persuasion by virtue of core illustration." I don't believe such arguments are dispensable. After all, my argument about typologies is, itself, dependent on my supposed "logic of core illustrations." I can only hope that the illustrative typologies that this might call up in your mind appeal, in a parallel manner, to a core of illustrations shading off into an indistinct penumbra of less appropriate possibilities.

Tactics for Maintaining Granularity

There is no alternative to living with varied, sometimes loose, means of raising questions and knitting answers. I am hardly suggesting that we abandon or abolish classes of questions such as those that take us off into such depths as ontology. But I am suggesting different evaluations over answers.

I do not think that typologies or contrasts that do no better than the logic of core illustrations can be dispensed with. However, their weakness should be acknowledged. The concept of granularity helps clarify it.

Granularity refers to coming to grips with complexity in full, rigorous detail. Terms evocative only of core illustrations tend to fail us. Faced with such a term, one cannot list, analytically bound, or mentally grasp the full range of instances. Absent such guidance, an illustration that I place on one side of the border, you might place on the other, and neither of us might have achieved an accurate reflection of author's intent. (One could as well remark that such text does not record or contain author's intent; variety in readings is inherent in the initial expression.) When such distinctions are compounded, piled one upon another, there is rapidly diminishing of any real consistency – the hope that long chains have a coherence that is logical is a chimera. (The proof of the pudding should be in the eating: do varied readers attain independent consistency in illustration of the deeply compounded notions? Or must interpreters refer back to the exact illustrations of the author?) In particular, if one sends out a student equipped with such concepts, there is little chance that their independent operations will bear on the range of the concept. How could they, when the range or extent of the concept is intrinsically governed by variety in interpretation?

As noted above, the grand oppositions that launch the imagination up the Kantian pyramid tend to fail such tests. This is not to deny the appeal, or potential import, of exploration of the Kantian pyramid, but to urge that such products be decoupled. The start of the ascent is questions that certainly are unanswered, and unaddressed, by most analysis. But it does not follow that they should be addressed, or rather, that immediate gains would rapidly appear if only they were addressed. What too often will happen is that directing attention to distinctions motivated by the Kantian ascent will sacrifice granularity for a promise of closure that will never be kept.

The problem, then, is not that there are somehow bad questions, but quite the opposite. The questions are very good indeed. And the proffered answers, while incomplete, are provocative linkages. The remedy is not to deny the questions and, furthermore, to seek to appropriate at least some of the insightful distinctions that result. But we need some brakes, as it were, to resist getting drawn beyond granularity. To put it the other way around, a useful expedient can be to embrace the intent of a distinction while retaining access to an orderly range of illustrations.

One tactic (I doubt there could be a general strategy) is to appeal to probability or proportion. It is sometimes possible to take the sense of a distinction or dichotomy and enrich it by mentally imposing a matter of degree. In place of either/or, and the consequent drawing of focus toward core illustrations, one undertakes the mental exercise of reformulation in terms of a full spectrum of intermediate types. A variation on the same theme is to render any universal predicate as a matter of degree or proportion.

Note that were one able to do this in a manner amenable to inter-subjectivity, one would attain a high measure of granularity. If you or I sent out a student to work on such a problem, their solutions would tend to have a recognizable place in *our* mental frameworks. We would lower their risk that their illustration, or proposed puzzle solutions, would seem accidental, or non-illustrative, or even a tendentious distortion, of what we really meant or intended. And even when the exercise is purely a private one, the puzzle of attempting to impose an order on a collection of illustrations can be highly useful. (Lenski [1966] 1984 should be noted as an earlier advocate of turning contrasts into continua as a useful enrichment of theoretical analysis.)

It may be informative to start with a negative instance. Among the most resistant to such treatment, for me at least, are assorted grand dualisms, e.g., structure vs. culture. One source of the problem is that I can find no way to capture the range of usage of either in anything like a definition. To explicate them, for example to students, I find it most effective to typify such terms as placeholders that, at most, serve somewhat of a common function in diverse contexts. (Rytina 1992). In any event, I cannot imagine any content into specifics like "70 percent culture and 30 percent structure," if indeed they are mutually exclusive in such a manner. Nor can I then make headway at trying to ponder ordered fields of settings, arenas, or what-have-you. Much less can I arrange such settings into a pattern, however fallible, that anticipates the degree to which one polar alternative should prevail over the other. If nothing else, this establishes that I am unable to see any standards or rules by which research might bear on the contrast.[9]

A positive illustration can be made of brief consideration of a central result that Parsons developed at length in *The Structure of Social Action* (1937) and more succinctly presented as the Fundamental Theorem in *The Social System* (1951). Briefly put, Parsons premises were that (a) society is possible and (b) utilities were random. It follows that if Ego is to meet Alter's expectations, and vice versa, an exterior constraint on ends is necessary. Since Parsons's formulation rests on an unqualified universal, the famous result is of a consensus that overarches all. The same result, transformed into a probability statement, is more modest: "successful social interaction is probable for a given Ego-Alter pair insofar as their utilities are constrained toward cooperative choices."

This reformulation eliminates the universal in favor of a matter of degree. Successful conformity is no longer a given or universal but a puzzle. In one concrete variant, Ego now must take care to try to confine interaction to cooperatively inclined alters and to avoid those otherwise inclined. Anyone who has lived in, or visited, Manhattan understands the practical problem all too well.

Now one might still wish to undertake a journey into high abstraction to divine how any particular ego–alter pair (no longer capitalized) came by coordinated ends, but the problem has a richer texture. Any given ego only interacts with a tiny fraction of possible alters. There is a past record of accumulated frequency of interaction and a fairly similar probability profile over future possibilities. But the vast majority of alters, say in a national society, are

---

[9] The fine print is that such a continuous distinction could not be constructed without breaking faith with a great deal of usage. This is not to gainsay that I have a strong personal bias of the prevalence of structure over culture; however, it requires that the terms be defined as I would have them.

out of the question. (Dichotomizing relative frequency of interaction into present/absent produces the standard points and lines of a social network.) The problem is no longer what somehow enfolds all egos and alters jointly. The issue is narrowed to maintenance of cohesion in the tiny fraction of realized pairings whose recurring interactions are necessary to keep the whole ensemble a going concern.[10]

A further possibility is readily raised into view. Insofar as people persist in relationships where interaction "succeeds" and desist where it fails, the ties that bind the greater ensemble are subject to a strong evolutionary or selectionist pressure toward "coordinated utilities." A high rate of "meshing preferences" is potentially derivable as a contingent empirical regularity, and one that admits of exceptions. Any Utopian overtones of universal reciprocity are quickly stripped away by allowing that equality is hardly the context for all pairings. If some somehow control unequal amounts of scarce and critical resources, they could capture or deflect "cooperative" use of time toward their own ends. (Against simple Hobbes one would note that coercers must band or bond to sustain most kinds of advantages in "resources"; only groups can hold others in slavery.) And such imagery reveals other textures, for example, how the amount of effort captured by hierarchical vs. reciprocal forms varies over time and circumstance, as when McDonalds et al. strip-mines the family sector.

Evolutionary or selectionist imagery is a very powerful tool for taming categories. Do these refer to distinguishable entities, like organizations, modes of experience construed as blocks of time, commitments of scarce, hence usually countable, assets? Are there durations, births, deaths, even extinctions? Can one make a sensible problematic of the focused moment of selection where the one gives way to another?

However that might be, Parsons's grand premise of the analytic necessity of coordinated ends has been given a texture. One can

[10] Some other issues of scope and definition can be quickly and briefly tamed. For example, the otherwise questionable presumption that national societies form independent wholes is reformulated as the relative frequency and importance of cross-national links. Insofar opportunity for affiliation turns on physical proximity, persistence over time, in differentiated locales, is commonplace. Gradual renewal is continual. The persistence of the ensemble or web is consistent with some sprinkling or rate of ruptures and replacements. Disintegration of a pre-existing whole would be an acceleration of ruptures without a compensating increase in replacement of bonds. In short, many difficulties attendant upon reified holism give way to considerations of textures and tempos.

fruitfully ask: when are ends more and less successfully coordinated? The core issues remain intact. These can still be pursued, and
obviously the lines I have indicated hardly exhaust the possibilities. Furthermore, nothing forbids one from continuing with
Parsons up the analytic hierarchy, yet one can equally find cause
to pause. I hope what the illustration brings out is that the pause
forces one to consider coming to grips with examples, with the
potential questions that arise from allowing a range of variation. It
puts on brakes, helps leave open what simple predication seeks to
close, and not infrequently clarifies the heroic leap of faith required
to continue ascent up the hierarchy of deeper distinctions.

This tactic of imposing degree is quite widely applicable. For
example, in place of "what accounts for shared meaning?," one
might examine "what accounts for the degree of shared meaning?"
In place of "what accounts for moral order?," one might examine,
"what accounts for the degree of moral order?" Here again, issues
of degree will call attention to duration and to history. Does shared
meaning expand, for example, in proportion to time devoted to
overlapping reading lists? Or does it depend on the quantity of
face-to-face interaction accomplished by a pair? Moral order, in a
similar vein, is more tractable, and perhaps more interesting, as a
local property differentiating relationships and clusters, governed
by somewhat parallel concerns for durations and ruptures. One
can even envision a liberal or left variant, where moral order is
enhanced by reciprocity enforced by symmetric options for exit,
and undermined by unilateral dependence.

Commentators such as Peter Winch might, quite properly, reply
that I cannot coherently conceive of the sharing of meaning as a
matter of degree pending completion of philosophical analysis
establishing what such a notion might mean in the first place. As I
have repeatedly suggested, that is a cogent criticism, albeit only one
that is contingently cogent. If someone is willing to risk pinning
down "shard meaning" closely enough to characterize an array
of instances, I'll accept the risk that our apparent agreement on
that ordering reflected nothing ultimately defensible, the risk that
our agreement will be unveiled as wishful nonsense should the
long-awaited "final analysis" ever appear. There are plenty of reas-
suring examples in the history of sciences of conjectures, concepts,
and logical leaps that appeared philosophically dubious at first
proposal. The irreducible probability of the quantum theory that
Einstein denounced, but could not supplant, is a good illustration.
Once such monsters proved viable in bringing order to a range of
phenomena, discomfort with foundations faded away.

Conclusions

One way to try to tame our penchant for universal predicates, ripe with false promise of answers to the really big questions, is to pose the challenge I've labeled granularity. Such concepts are trapdoors: what lies beneath them? Can one conceive of an ordered array, or a finite list of alternatives, or a range of illustrations from the least degree to the greatest? Does it open to a field of alternatives to which logic might apply? Or does one confront an unmapped domain, where no more than typologies dependent on core illustrations are possible, such that long chains of rigorous logic are but a dream? Or does the trapdoor open to a language game, where no one yet has supplied a governing logic, and there are substantial grounds to doubt that they ever will?

One cannot reject a question for being intractable; it remains important. But one can and should temper judgments of intellectual priority. Failure to answer or address the big questions put forth by social theorists dreaming philosophical dreams of the final analysis is not a very interesting failing. It is universal. The largest questions are only askable, not answerable. The tactical issue that needs to be addressed is whether attention to such questions is the best way to make some headway.

We need to take seriously what philosophers have shown repeatedly (sometimes without intending to) certain questions resist closure. There is no known way to track back to the nature of things, to ground the *social* in satisfactory foundations. To insist on conformity with some, or another, ultimately incomplete attempt is not helpful. It is better by far to subject the operative predicates to an intellectual test. Those that delimit domains without order, boundaries, textures, or limits are traps. Beneath the bright arrow pointing the way toward transcendence a warning should be added: no one who enters here has yet found the way back.

References

Alexander, Jeffrey. 1982. *Theoretical Logic in Sociology. Volume 1. Positivism, Presuppositions, and Current Controversies*. Berkeley: University of California Press.

Blau, Peter M. 1977. *Inequality and Heterogeneity*. New York: Academic Press.

Emirbayer, Mustafa and Jeff Goodwin. 1994. Network analysis, culture, and the problem of agency. *American Journal of Sociology* 99 (4): 1411–54.

Etzioni, Amitai. 1961. *A Comparative Analysis of Complex Organizations: On Power, Involvement, and Their Correlates.* New York: Free Press.

Giddens, Anthony. 1984. *The Constitution of Society: Outline of the Theory of Structuration.* Cambridge: Polity Press.

Habermas, Jürgen. 1987. *The Theory of Communicative Action. Volume 2. Life World and System: A Critique of Functionalist Reason.* Boston, MA: Beacon Press.

Im Hof, Ulrich. 1994. *The Enlightenment.* Cambridge, MA: Basil Blackwell.

Kant, Immanuel. [1787] 1965. *The Critique of Pure Reason.* New York: St Martin's Press.

Kline, Morris. 1980. *Mathematics, the Loss of Certainty.* New York: Oxford University Press.

Lenski, Gerhard. [1966] 1984. *Power and Privilege.* Chapel Hill: University of North Carolina Press.

Münch, Richard. 1987. *Theory of Action.* New York: Routledge & Kegan Paul.

Nietzsche, Friedrich. [1885] 1966. *Beyond Good and Evil; Prelude to a Philosophy of the Future.* New York: Vintage Books.

Parsons, Talcott. 1937. *The Structure of Social Action: a Study in Social Theory with Special Reference to a Group of Recent European Writers.* New York: Free Press.

——. 1951. *The Social System.* New York: Free Press.

Russell, Bertrand. 1939. *Power: A New Social Analysis.* London: George Allen & Unwin.

Rytina, Steven. 1992. Social Structure. In Edgar F. Borgatta, ed., *The Encyclopedia of Sociology*, 1970–6. New York: Macmillan.

Stinchcombe, Arthur. 1968. *Constructing Social Theories.* Chicago: University of Chicago Press.

Tilly, Charles. 1990. *Coercion, Capital, and European States, AD 990–1990.* Cambridge, MA: Basil Blackwell.

Winch, Peter. 1958. *The Idea of a Social Science and its Relation to Philosophy.* London: Routledge & Kegan Paul.

Wittgenstein, Ludwig. [1953] 1983. *Philosophical Investigations.* New York: Macmillan.

——. [1922] 1981. *Tractatus Logico-Philosophicus.* London: Routledge & Kegan Paul.

Wolfe, Alan. 1991. Mind, self, society, and computer: artificial intelligence and the sociology of mind. *American Journal of Sociology* 96 (5): 1073–96.

8 Social Order and Emergent Rationality

Michael W. Macy

Nature seems to have played a cruel trick on our species. We lack the physical ability to thrive as self-reliant sovereigns in a state of nature, hence we must depend on cooperation with one another for our evolutionary edge. Yet unlike social insects, we are not genetically hardwired for cooperative behavior. Our dependence on cooperation is thus no guarantee that it will obtain. How, then, is social order possible?[1]

Sociobiologists suggest that humans may have genetic predispositions for reciprocity and kin altruism, as well as aggression and competition (Ruse and Wilson 1986; Alexander 1987). This implies only a capacity for cooperation, not its necessity (Dawkins 1989), a point also emphasized by Cooley (1964: 19). Cooley thus rejects "the notion that [human] collective behavior is to be attributed to an 'instinct of the herd'" (28n.). Such ontological beliefs, he suggests, are themselves social constructs – myths that affirm deeply ingrained patterns of social interaction.

If nature has endowed us with highly supple instinctual programming at the genetic level, then sociality is not inherited but must be acquired (and reacquired) through our capacity for phenotypic adaptation. This plasticity makes the paradox of social order especially compelling: in the absence of innate cooperative

This research was supported by the National Science Foundation #SBR 95-11461. I wish to thank James Kitts, Mary Godwyn, and Victor Nee for their comments and suggestions.

[1] One answer is that social order is imposed by the state. This only pushes the problem back a step: how are institutions possible? Institutions that can effectively enforce cooperation presume social order; they do not explain how it arises in the first place.

propensities, can social order arise entirely through our capacity for adaptation?

Adaptation is driven by the consequences of properties that change over time. Consequentialist explanations of adaptive behavior pose a teleological problem: how can the future influence the past? When the feedback loop passes through individual cognition, the ability for outcomes to generate their own causes becomes a problem in the theory of knowledge. This essay will explore two solutions to this teleological problem in theories of social and cultural adaptation, one grounded in a rationalist epistemology, the other in pragmatism.

Rationalists contend that knowledge need not be based on direct sensory perception but can be derived through a distinctively human capacity for higher-order reasoning. Hence, adaptation is not limited to *a posteriori* adjustments to experience but can be effected *a priori*. By grasping the logical or mathematical structure of a well-defined problem, the likely consequences of alternative courses of action can be known before the fact. Lave and March (1975: 248) have characterized this forward-looking behavior as "calculated rationality" in which "the individual uses information about the situation facing him to calculate, according to some rational process, the proper decision." "Calculated rationality" applies only to the intended consequences of action and assumes the capacity to gather and process large amounts of information. The calculated consequences instruct actions that entail actual consequences. If the calculations are accurate, then the temporal paradox in consequentialist logic disappears.

Pragmatists, in contrast, favor an "evolutionary epistemology" (Schull 1996). For James (1981), behavioral responses evolve through a process of competitive selection that parallels the Darwinian model. Alternative "possibilities" compete for "attention" through "the phenomena of consciousness" (1981: 142). If the chosen response has a favorable outcome, the neural pathways that triggered the behavior are strengthened, which "loads the dice ... in favor of those of its performances which make for the most permanent interests of the brain's owner" (1981: 143). Adaptation then proceeds through tests of alternative solutions to recurrent problems. Repetition, not calculation, brings the future to bear on the present, by recycling the lessons of the past. Through repeated exposure to a problem, the consequences of alternative courses of action can be iteratively explored, by the individual actor or by a population.

With repetition comes unthinking habit and convention. Language is a prominent example. We sometimes "choose our words carefully" for a desired effect, yet words are rarely invented for their utility. Symbolic representations of meaning in communicative acts evolve through the repetitive use of signs, as interdependent actors try to coordinate effective interaction (Peirce 1955). Moral habits and social norms evolve in much the same way. As Heise (1996: 1) summarizes the interactionist elaboration of pragmatism, "The majestic order of society emerges from repetitive application of evolved cultural resources to frame and solve recurrent problems." The solutions then become part of the cultural repertoire and are taken for granted by individuals.

The "taken-for-grantedness" of an evolved cultural repertoire does not preclude deliberate and conscious anticipation of the consequences of action before the fact. However, anticipated outcomes are but the consciously projected distillations of prior exposure to a recurring problem. Backward-looking problem-solvers may act with deliberate and purposeful intention, but they "look ahead by holding a mirror to the past" (Macy 1993).

Although behavioral economists contend that pragmatic, rule-based behavior is mandated by cognitive limitations and the costs of information (Simon 1992), social psychologists point to a much broader and more basic requirement: the possibility of social life (Berger 1966; for a similar view from economics, see Hayek 1973). Among social species, we are unique in our plasticity. Unlike social insects, our genes leave us free to leave the swarm and chart our own individual course. Were we not creatures of habit, routine, and heuristic devices, effective coordination might be impossible – a cacophony of inappropriate responses to unexpected reactions from others. Behavioral rules (including social norms and conventions) make social interaction predictable, so that interdependent individuals can influence one another in response to the influence they receive, thereby carving out locally stable patterns of interaction. In short, rules are not simply analytic shortcuts that lower the cognitive costs of decision-making. They are the grammar that structures social life.

Of course, our species is also unique in its analytical capabilities; hence, an obvious objection to the rule-based behavioral model is the portrayal of intelligent thinkers as robotic simpletons. Clearly, rule-based behavior would be hopelessly inefficient were it not for the fact that responses can improve (and become more sophisticated) over time. The key behavioral assumption is that the consequences of an action, which may or may not have been consciously anticipated, modify the probability that the action will be repeated the next time the same input conditions are met.

Human intelligence is not the issue. Our cognitive capacity for language does not obviate the evolution of words and signs, or our need to learn their meaning through practice. The same pragmatist epistemology also applies to problem-solving behavior and implies that rationality is grounded in action, not calculation. From a pragmatist perspective, rationality springs not just from the heads of the actors but also from their hands and feet – from problem-solving, trial and error, and other processes of gradient search.

Analytical and Evolutionary Game Theory

Rationalism and pragmatism inform alternative ways of formalizing the consequentialist logic of strategic interdependence: analytical and evolutionary game theory. Both techniques have been applied to the problem of explaining social order, and have led to important discoveries. Two of the most compelling are the analytical Nash equilibrium (Nash 1951) and the evolutionary stable strategy (Maynard-Smith 1979). However, the teleological mechanisms are very different. Analytical game theory, based on a rationalist epistemology, posits full comprehension of the logical structure of a well-defined problem and cognitive representation of the causal link between outcomes and the actions that produce them (Axelrod 1997: 47).[2] The models typically assume perfect information and may also require the "common knowledge" assumption, namely, that "I know x, I know that you know x, and I know that you know that I know x," etc. Game contestants may also need to know how to work back from the endgame to anticipate one another's rational choices.[3] Simply put, analytical game theorists study games played by people like themselves.

---

[2] Sociological applications include both cooperative and noncooperative games. Variable-sum noncooperative games have been widely used to study collective action in social dilemmas (Heckathorn 1996). Cooperative games have received much less attention by sociologists, but important exceptions include Willer and Skvoretz (1997) and Bienenstock and Bonacich (1993, 1997), who have used analytical game theory to model power inequalities in exchange networks.

[3] Analytical game theory can be applied to games with incomplete information, but this does not always reduce the cognitive demands. Players may need to know how much information to collect and how to use Bayes's rule to update their probability distributions for choice under uncertainty (Simon 1992: 35). The "endgame effect" arises when players reason backwards from the expected final move in the game to determine the optimal choice on the first (and every succeeding) move, a process called "backward induction."

In contrast, most games in everyday life are played by lay contestants. In everyday conversation, we do not usually "choose our words carefully," we just talk. Similarly, the "Hobbesian problem of order" (Parsons 1937) is not only about the formation of formal sanctioning institutions, it is also about the emergence of unthinking habits of cooperation that make social life possible without the need to post police officers at every corner. Informal cooperation and coordination are based on folk strategies – heuristics, habits, conventions, customs, norms, and the like – that evolve through repeated interaction.

Lave and March (1975: 248) call this "adaptive rationality," which they distinguish from "calculated rationality" in that the actors "learn in a regular manner from trial and error." I prefer the term "emergent rationality." Adaptation can be proactive or reactive, based on calculated as well as experiential consequences of action. "Emergent rationality" captures the pragmatist idea that solutions to recurrent problems unfold over time and across actors. It also captures the notion in complexity theory that very simple interaction patterns can generate highly complex, and often surprising, solutions.

Emergent rationality can be modeled using evolutionary game theory, a method that identifies stable distributions of competing strategies. Applied to multi-agent dynamical systems, the evolutionary approach can also identify "basins of attraction" on an ecological landscape (Epstein and Axtell 1996). "An evolutionary approach," according to Axelrod (1997: 47), "is based on the principle that what works well for a player is more likely to be used again, whereas what turns out poorly is more likely to be discarded." In short, in evolutionary game theory,

people are rational because they learn in the rough and ready sense that they adjust their strategies in the light of experience so as to move towards the strategy which shows the greatest pay-off in the repeated play of this game. Of course, such rationality need not reflect conscious learning; in the biological case it is ordinarily thought to arise because those who are fittest reproduce faster. The parallel here is that those who receive lower pay-offs in the long run tend to emulate those who receive high pay-offs. (Hargreaves Heap and Varoufakis 1995: 199)

This backward-looking definition of rationality greatly expands the scope conditions for game-theoretic models. Players need not be fully informed or capable of grasping the logic of interdependent strategies; indeed, they need not even be human. All that is required is an environment that is stable relative to the rate of change in the adaptive process. Evolutionary game theory is therefore applicable to the problem of social order in everyday life – the habits of association that generate unthinking compliance with social norms. These habits of association emerge not from the "shadow of the future" (Axelrod 1984) but from the *lessons of the past* (Macy 1998).

However, the nonlinear and stochastic properties of many dynamical systems make evolutionary game theory much less amenable to analytical modeling. Research on emergent social order in self-organizing multi-agent systems provides a promising application for recent advances in the simulation of artificial life (Simon 1992: 45; Axelrod 1997: 48).[4]

Rational Action and Rational Choice

Analytical and evolutionary game theory can be used to formalize alternative approaches to utilitarian decision-making: "rational choice" and "rational action." The distinction centers on the locus of rationality: is it the decision *process* that is rational, or is it the *outcome*?

Rational choice theory (RCT), like analytical game theory, assumes forward-looking actors with cognitive representations of causal relationships that are sufficiently accurate for optimal outcomes to attract the choices that generate them. The ideal type is "the neoclassical economic model in which rational agents operating under powerful assumptions about the availability of information and the capability of optimizing can achieve an efficient reallocation of resources among themselves through costless trading" (Axelrod 1997: 4).

As in analytical game theory, only the intended consequences of action can motivate choices. Outcomes that arise behind the backs of the actors, such as the unintended collective benefits of the "Invisible Hand," cannot attract the choices that produce them, a point that Smith underscored (1937: 14). Unintended outcomes may constrain future choices and even influence future preferences, but they have no explanatory power as incentives for present action. Since the consequences of expressive behaviors are generally unintended, these fall outside the theoretical scope of rational choice (Etzioni 1988; see also Hedstrom forthcoming: 10).

---

[4] For an overview of recent sociological applications, including genetic algorithms, neural nets, and cellular automata, see Bainbridge et al. 1994.

The actors must also have the information, cognitive capacity, and temperament to calculate the effects of alternative strategies, including the effects on the choices of others. These conditions are sometimes observed in the behavior of skilled entrepreneurs, legislators, or military strategists.[5] However, it seems clear that these conditions are less than universal. Indeed, "many sociologists find rational choice plausible in only a very small fraction of human interactions" (Hannan 1992: 134). In short, RCT seems most applicable to highly skilled decision-makers, such as might sometimes be found at the helm of formal social institutions. The usefulness of RCT in understanding informal social order is less obvious.

These limitations can be circumvented in rational action theory (RAT). RAT ignores the psychology of individual decision-making and focusses instead on the outcomes of action. Following Weber (1908), Friedman (1953) has argued that utility-maximizing behavior describes the end result of market exchange but not the actual decision process by which it obtains. The effort to explain the latter is misguided. Within each individual, utility maximization is complicated by a "mass of complex and detailed circumstances surrounding the phenomena to be explained" (Friedman 1953). A good theory aims not to capture the richness of this complexity but to "abstract the common and crucial elements" from the residuals, which, in the aggregate, can be dismissed as so much noise (Friedman 1953). The noise gets removed at the macro level as the errors cancel out, leaving a central tendency that conforms closely to the aggregate behavior predicted for fully rational actors (Hedstrom forthcoming: 19; see also Stinchcomb 1968). What matters, then, is not whether the actors are rational but whether they act, in the end, *as if* they are. They are like veteran outfielders who catch fly balls as if they had calculated the trajectory.

Becker (1991) has taken a similar position. Rational action is not a theory about choice but about the efficient allocation of scarce resources. Hence, this approach "is a powerful tool not only in understanding human behavior but also in understanding the behavior of other species" (Becker 1991: 307). Moreover, models of rational action are not limited to the intended consequences of instrumental choice but apply equally well to the unintended

---

[5] Simon (1992) has warned that the necessary conditions may not even be present where calculated rationality seems most plausible. "The study of actual decision processes (for example, the strategies used by corporations to make their investments) reveals massive and unavoidable departures" from the model (1992: 36).

consequences of emotional and expressive behavior. This "analytical continuity" is possible because Becker assumes that "nonhumans and even most humans do not consciously maximize" (1991: 321; see also Becker 1976: 7).

Instead, Becker argues that even randomly impulsive actors will find that they have no choice but to be rational under conditions of competition for scarce resources (1976: 164–6). Otherwise, they will exhaust their assets. Alchian (1950) and Boulding (1981) have extended economic theory as an analog of natural selection by positing the existence of competitive selection pressures that weed out maladaptive routines. Markets thus serve as tournaments to select optimal solutions. Suboptimal routines are improved or replaced by learning and imitation, or removed from the population by bankruptcy and takeover. The evolutionary process shapes and selects optimal strategies that make their hosts look much smarter than they actually need to be. So long as proactive and reactive processes converge at equilibrium, we can indulge the theoretical convenience of equating emergent and analytical rationality.

Still, the logical structures of rational choice and rational action entail fundamental differences about human agency. Applied to the outcomes of action, "rational" refers not to the capacity for analytical calculation of optimal solutions but to the efficiency of the solutions that can be expected to emerge from a competitive process constrained by finite resources. Rational choice is a theory about how individuals make decisions. Rational action is a theory about the decisions that attract individuals to them over time and in the aggregate. Rational choice is a theory of intentional behavior and human agency; rational action is a theory of efficient resource allocation. The rational action paradigm does not require human agency for two reasons. First, it does not assume agency, it assumes efficiency. Second, it assumes efficiency by any resource allocator constrained by competition and scarcity – from chess masters plotting sacrificial ploys, to birds confronted with the social dilemma whether to warn their neighbors about the presence of a predator, at some personal risk of exposure. Like chess players, the birds who get it wrong (or merely take too much time before moving) are eliminated from the tournament.

The assumption that agents merely act "as if" they are analytically rational appears to make RAT more broadly applicable than RCT, but this may be deceptive. The two approaches differ in their assumptions about how rational actors know what to do, but make identical predictions about the eventual outcome. Like RCT, the methodology of rational action theory remains analytical, not evolutionary. The theory uses analytical tools to identify the decisions actors ought to make if they want to flourish, and then simply assumes that an unspecified evolutionary or learning process, acting through the market or its functional equivalent, will eventually select for optimal decisions that converge with analytic shortcuts.

This convergence is less plausible than it might seem. Kiser and Hechter (1991; see also Elster 1989) contend that gradient climbing is highly vulnerable to becoming trapped in local optima (like the "false peaks" that can fool naïve mountain climbers). Hence, the scope of RAT may be limited by convergence postulates that are no more robust than the cognitive assumptions that limit the scope of RCT.

Rational Action: Emergent or Convergent?

The problem with the convergence postulate goes deeper than vulnerability to local optima. The assumption that competition for scarce resources necessarily selects for optimally self-interested strategies is a misreading of evolutionary logic. Contrary to the imagery in market analogies and popular discourse, evolutionary selection is not about survival, it is about reproduction. The individuals that thrive are those that learn how best to reproduce, a task that is not always reducible to individual self-interest. This suggests that cultural evolution differs fundamentally from ecological competition over limited resources. If survival and influence do not always coincide, then we cannot assume that competitive selection mechanisms will systematically target analytically derived self-interested strategies.

Recent contributions to evolutionary game theory have replaced the RAT convergence postulate with a "bottom-up" alternative (Epstein and Axtell 1996; Axelrod 1997). These models are meliorizing, not maximizing; there is no assumption that optimal strategies will evolve. Hence, the evolutionary mechanisms, which are implied axiomatically in RAT, must be fully and explicitly specified in "bottom-up" multi-agent models.

These evolutionary mechanisms generally involve two types of experiential feedback, *reproduction*, which alters the frequency distribution of strategies within a population of related individuals, and *reinforcement*, which alters the probability distribution of rules within the repertoire of each individual. Melioration is highly path-dependent and not very good at backing out of cul-de-sacs on the evolutionary landscape. Both reinforcement and reproduction are biased toward *better* strategies, but they carry no guarantee of finding the optimal solution. Hill-climbing thus violates the optimality assumption in rational choice theory. Actors cannot be assumed to attain the highest peak, however relentless the search. Even so, the highest achievements of natural selection far surpass anything created by the calculations of an engineer.

In biological evolution, rules are genetically encoded. However, reproduction need not be biological or genetic. In cultural evolution, reproduction occurs through role modeling, imitation, and reinforcement, the primary elements of what Bandura (1977) calls "social learning." The social equivalent of the gene is a cultural rule, encoded in a heuristic, norm, routine, convention, custom, protocol, or ritual. Dawkins (1989) refers to these cultural analogs of the gene as "memes," which he defines as "ideas" that can jump from one brain to another via imitation. Runciman (1989) calls them "practices." Following Hayek (1967) and Vanberg (1994), I prefer the term "rule" (or "norm" in cases that entail an expectation of rule-enforcement). Memes and practices invite confusion between genotype and phenotype, that is, between the underlying rule and its behavioral or physical manifestation. By "rule," I mean the smallest possible unit of instruction. Rules are patterned behavioral responses to stimuli, carved out through repetition, stored in neural pathways, and continually tested in local interaction. A set of inter-related rules forms an institution (Nee and Ingram 1998). Rules can be formalized as input–output functions, where the input is a set of conditions of varying complexity and the output is an action. The consequences of the action, which may or may not have been consciously anticipated, then modify (1) the probability that the action will be repeated the next time the input conditions are met, and (2) the probability that the associated rule will be replicated and diffused.

This iterative search function relaxes the assumption that course-correction and ecological selection pressures will necessarily steer gradient-climbers to act as if they were analytically rational. Convergence between calculated and emergent rationality can then be regarded as empirically variable rather than axiomatic.

Evolutionary models also allow for the possibility that rationality can emerge from behind the backs of the actors and can target both the intended and unintended consequences of action. If the link to the future is repetition, not calculation, then unintended outcomes can attract actions by altering the associated behavioral propensity. For example, unintended consequences may account for the persistence of expressive and righteous behavior that lacks any instrumental (or ulterior) motive. Frank's (1988) evolutionary model of trust and commitment formalizes the emergent rationality of emotions like vengeance and sympathy. An angry or frightened actor may not be capable of deliberate pursuit of self-interest, yet the response to the stimulus has consequences for the individual, and these in turn can modify the probability that the behavior will be repeated, through reinforcement, imitation, or some combination of learning and reproduction.

Still, the rationality of emotion is not the most radical departure from the conventional portrayal of self-interested optimizing. Not only may actors be unaware that their actions are self-serving, but these evolutionary models need not assume any benefit whatsoever to the individual. Hence, emergent rationality is applicable not only to expressive behavior but also to behavior that is genuinely altruistic.

Altruism entails more than a prudent detour in the pursuit of self-interest (e.g., a well-publicized charitable donation). By definition, altruistic behavior requires sacrifice – not just an investment that pays back with a compensating benefit, but a net loss – an outcome that is inferior to an available alternative. How can this be rational, and how can it evolve?

Emergent Altruism

RCT cannot account for altruistic behavior without the troublesome epicycle that altruists are simply egoists with other-regarding preferences, in which case, all behavior becomes rational by definition and analytical interest shifts to the origins of preferences, a problem outside the theoretical domain of rational choice.

While genuine altruism cannot be explained using the individual as the unit of analysis, it is readily amenable to functionalist explanations that import the sociobiological principle of group-selection, in which the deme, not the individual, is the starting point (Wynne-Edwards 1962). In group selection, demes that lack altruistic mores may be more prone to extinction than are competing groups whose members are more willing to sacrifice for the greater good (Boorman and Levitt 1980: 5). This makes altruism trivially easy to explain. Nevertheless, the group-selectionist account has fallen out of favor among sociobiologists for reasons that may apply to social and cultural applications as well. The problem is the need for "nearly complete isolation as between demes. Otherwise, demes rapidly lose their diversity as genetic units, and group selection through differential extinction fails to find continuing genetic variance on which to act" (Boorman and Levitt 1980: 7). Moreover, differential extinction searches much less efficiently than reproduction. Extinction "is inherently a negative force, acting only to eliminate demes having a relatively less adaptive genetic composition. In particular, it cannot in the first instance, *create* populations having a highly adaptive genetic makeup, but (if opposed by individual selection) must rely on relatively inefficient random effects such as drift to create such favored demes" (Boorman and Levitt 1980: 8). If individual selection favors egoism and is more efficient than group selection, then altruism can be expected to lose the evolutionary foot race.[6]

If altruism cannot be explained using either the individual or group as the unit of analysis, what is left? The evolutionary game theorist Maynard-Smith (1979) has proposed a provocative answer: the underlying strategy or rule (whether a genetic or heuristic instruction). The theory that *rules*, not groups or individuals, are the units of adaptation, not only provides a more rigorous explanation of altruism but also yields empirically plausible predictions as to the identity of the beneficiaries.

From a "rule's-eye" view of the problem, the altruist serves the interests – not of the beneficiary – but of the "selfish gene" that controls its behavior (Dawkins 1989). The "self-interest" of a gene refers to its evolutionary stake in the outcomes of the phenotypes that it instructs, insofar as these outcomes influence the odds that the gene will flourish in the face of competitive selection pressures. This rule-centered approach can be applied to an explanation of "kin altruism" in nature, the strategy to sacrifice for the benefit of close genetic relatives (Ruse and Wilson 1986; Alexander 1987; Hamilton 1964). A gene for kin altruism can improve its viability by directing a transfer of vital resources from its agent to another organism that carries the same gene.

Allison (1992) has extended the kin altruism model to benevolence based on cultural relatedness, such as geographical proximity or a shared cultural marker (for example, dress or language). However, as illustrated with kin altruism, a "self-interested rule" need not imply a program that instructs egoistic behavior by its agent. Suppose a rule could propagate faster by ordering its carrier to

[6] Boyd and Richerson (1990) have discovered a process of quasi-Lamarckian cultural evolution, characterized by individual learning and conformist cultural transmission, that appears to preserve group boundaries sufficiently to allow altruistic selection pressures to operate at the level of the group.

export life-chances to those who follow the same rule. Then the rule could be said to have a "self-interest" in the altruistic behavior of its carrier.[7]

The logic of kin altruism might explain why cultural evolution seems to favor a tendency to associate with those who are similar, to differentiate from "outsiders," and to defend the in-group against social trespass with the emotional ferocity of parents defending their offspring. Solidary expressions of identity can thus be reduced to rational self-interest, but it is the evolutionary interest of the rule, not the interest of its agent, that is the effective cause.

In-group altruism may in turn come to be imitated through the logic of "sexual selection." Sexual selection refers to the evolutionary advantage of traits that increase the probability of mating. For example, sexual selection explains the generous and colorful plumage of the male peacock. The cumbersome tail increases mortality but provides a net gain in fertility by making the males more sexually attractive, thus increasing their overall reproductive chances (Dawkins 1989). Much the same thing may happen in the selection of role models or mentors. Conspicuous prosocial behavior may increase vulnerability to predators, but also make it easier to attract a protégé – someone who can then be influenced to disseminate the emergent norm.

This points to a decisive difference between emergent and calculated rationality. Calculated rationality applies to the individual as the unit of analysis, and therefore entails the axiom of self-interested behavior. Emergent rationality applies to rules (or strategies) as the units of analysis, as well as to the individuals who act on these rules. This means that the behavior the rules instruct need not necessarily advance the interests of the individual agent. Individually self-interested behavior can then be modeled as empirically variable, not axiomatic.

It must be stressed, however, that the self-interested individual is clearly not precluded by emergent rationality. On the contrary, a rule-centered approach also applies to "reciprocal altruism," such as the trading of favors. Reciprocal altruism is fully compatible

---

[7] Care must be taken not to read purpose or intent into this characterization. By definition, rules instruct actions by individuals (and organizations) that have adopted the rule, and these actions have consequences that may alter the viability of the rule. Hence, like organizations, rules have interests, even though they are not purposive and do not pursue interests in the way that a purposive individual might. A rule-centered approach is thus incompatible with assumptions of purposive action and is strictly limited to applications where iteration, not intention, is the link between outcome and action.

with individual self-interest, and not a form of genuine altruism. Rather, it is "a straightforward illustration of prudent behavior," Frank notes, "enlightened prudence, to be sure, but self-interested behavior all the same" (1988: 34–5). An enlightened egoist may transfer resources to another, expecting that this behavior will trigger sufficient compensation.

Although reciprocal altruism can be modeled using the individual as the unit of analysis, it may nevertheless be instructive to consider a rule-selectionist formulation. Again taking a "rule's-eye" view of the problem, the manifestations of self-interested rules can be altruistic, so long as the outcomes ultimately promote the propagation of the rule. When these benefits to the rule obtain immediately from the behavior, we classify the behavior as self-interested. When the programmatic benefits are separated from the behavior in time and space, we classify the behavior as altruistic. With reciprocal altruism, the benefit is *temporally* removed in that the rule has learned how to export life-chances as a way to trigger a later return on the investment.[8] With kin altruism, the benefit is *spatially* removed, in that the rule has learned how to export life-chances from one of its agents to another, such that the "inclusive fitness" (Hamilton 1964) of all its carriers is greater than before. Given that space and time are alternative measures of distance, it seems reasonable to classify both reciprocity and kin-benevolence as altruistic behaviors (or phenotypes) that provide indirect benefits to the self-interested rules (or genotypes) in which these behaviors are encoded. The only difference is whether the benefits must leap over time or space to make their way back to the rules that generated them.

Note that the two dimensions can be combined, as in "generalized reciprocity" (Ekeh 1974), the rule to help one's in-group in the expectation that others in the group will return the favor later on. Hence, reciprocal altruism requires ongoing relations, as might be found in instrumentally motivated interest groups. Kin altruism requires densely clustered social ties among tightly knit "in-groups" and explains the importance of group boundaries around close

---

[8] Some readers may be bothered by the claim that rules can learn how to spread more effectively, as if they were intelligent viral entities that infect and manipulate humans for their own nefarious purposes. That might make interesting science fiction, but the point here is only to introduce a "rule's-eye" view of social life, so that our attention is directed to the evolutionary consequences of behavior, not for the agent, but for the rule that instructs the agent. Evolutionary game theorists often write about the fortunes of competing "strategies" using similar animating language.

cultural relatives, as well as the need for cultural markers that signify membership.

Summary and Conclusion

Sociologists characteristically avoid reliance on human nature as an explanation for social life. The evolution of cooperation is clearly much more challenging if all that is innate is our plasticity. Rationalism and pragmatism inform two different explanatory strategies. Rational choice theory (RCT) posits a calculated, analytical rationality: cognitive representation of causal structure and the use of higher-order reasoning to identify an optimal strategy. Analytical game theory formalizes the application of RCT to the problems of coordination and cooperation among interdependent actors. In contrast, pragmatism informs an experiential alternative to a rationalist specification of the link between action and outcome: workable heuristics evolve through repeated and collective exposure to a recurrent problem.

Rational action theory (RAT) broadens the scope of RCT by assuming evolutionary rather than analytical optimizing. Competitive selection and course correction steer adaptive individuals to optimal solutions, making simple gradient-climbers look much smarter than they need to be for the theory to hold. RAT also applies to expressive and obligatory responses to stimuli, as well as purposive behavior based on evolving folk strategies.

While RCT is limited by rationalist cognitive assumptions, RAT is limited by a convergence postulate that may be just as restrictive. Recent contributions using "bottom-up" evolutionary models have relaxed the convergence postulate and the assumption of individual self-interest. Evolution is an iterative and stochastic process that alters the probability distribution of rules in an ecology characterized by finite resources that constrain propagation. The survival chances of individual agents are secondary to the reproductive chances of the underlying rules that guide behavior. Individual fitness is relevant only as a determinant of biological reproduction or social influence.

A rule-centered influence function implies that individual self-interest is empirically variable, depending on the rule that governs the host's behavior. Altruistic rules are those that have learned how to replicate by transferring influence (or reproductive chances) from the present to the future and from one host to another. Reciprocal altruism typifies collective action in an ongoing social exchange, while kin altruism and "mentor-selection" (as an analog of sexual selection) may account for the importance of cultural markers and collective identity in successful social movements.

Social movement theorists debate the relative explanatory power of the consequences and meaning of participation in collective action. Consequences include the costs of contribution, value of the public goods, and access to selective incentives. The meaning of participation refers to the symbolic affirmation of shared social classifications and normative protocols that regulate interaction and structure social life. Yet expressive, symbolic behavior entails consequences, whether or not they are intended. By replacing the "as if" postulate with explicitly specified evolutionary microfoundations, a theory of emergent rationality can restore the explanatory power of the unintended consequences of symbolic collective action, in which egoism is a variable instead of a constant (Smelser 1992; Macy 1997). A dynamical theory of microsocial interaction, grounded in a pragmatist epistemology and formalized using artificial agents, appears to be a viable and promising new direction for theoretical research on interest-driven collective action, as well as social movements mobilized around emergent norms and identities.

References

Alchian, A. 1950. Uncertainty, evolution and economic theory. *Journal of Political Economy* 58.

Alexander, R. 1987. *The Biology of Moral Systems*. New York: Aldine de Gruyter.

Allison, P. 1992. The cultural evolution of beneficent norms. *Social Forces* 71 (2): 279–301.

Axelrod, R. 1984. *The Evolution of Cooperation*. New York: Basic Books.

——. 1997. *The Complexity of Cooperation*. Princeton, NJ: Princeton University Press.

Bainbridge, W., E. Brent, K. Carley, D. Heise, M. Macy, B. Markovsky, and J. Skvoretz. 1994. Artificial social intelligence. *Annual Review of Sociology* 20: 407–36.

Bandura, A. 1977. *Social Learning Theory*. Englewood Cliffs, NJ: Prentice Hall.

Becker, G. 1976. *The Economic Approach to Human Behavior*. Chicago: University of Chicago Press.

——. 1991. *A Treatise on the Family*. Cambridge, MA: Harvard University Press.

Berger, P. 1966. *The Sacred Canopy*. New York: Anchor.

Bienenstock, E. and P. Bonacich. 1993. Game theory models for social exchange networks: experimental results. *Sociological Perspectives* 36: 117–36.

——. 1997. The network exchange condition as a cooperative game. *Rationality and Society*.

Boorman, S. and P. Levitt. 1980. *The Genetics of Altruism*. New York: Academic Press.

Boulding, K. 1981. *Evolutionary Economics*. Beverly Hills, CA: Sage Publications.

Boyd, R. and P. Richerson. 1990. Culture and cooperation. In J. Mansbridge, ed., *Beyond Self-Interest*, 111–32. Chicago: University of Chicago Press.

Cooley, C. 1964. *Human Nature and the Social Order*. New York: Schocken.

Dawkins, R. 1989. *The Selfish Gene*. Oxford: Oxford University Press.

Ekeh, P. 1974. *Social Exchange Tehory: The Two Traditions*. Cambridge: Harvard University Press.

Elster, J. 1989. *The Cement of Society*. Cambridge: Cambridge University Press.

Epstein, J. and R. Axtell. 1996. *Growing Artificial Societies: Social Science from the Bottom Up*. Cambridge, MA: MIT Press.

Etzioni, A. 1988. Normative-affective factors: toward a new decision-making model. *Journal of Economic-Psychology* 9: 125–50.

Frank, R. 1988. *Passions Within Reason: The Strategic Role of the Emotions*. New York: Norton.

Friedman, M. 1953. The methodology of positive economics. In Friedman, *Essays on Positive Economics*, 3–43. Chicago: University of Chicago Press.

Gleick, J. 1987. *Chaos: Making a New Science*. New York: Viking.

Hamilton, W. 1964. The genetical evolution of social behaviour. *Journal of Theoretical Biology* 7: 1–52.

Hannan, M. 1992. Rationality and robustness in multilevel systems. In J. Coleman and T. Fararo, eds, *Rational Choice Theory: Advocacy and Critique*, pp. 120–36. Newbury Park, CA: Sage Publications.

Hargreaves Heap, S. and Y. Varoufakis. 1995. *Game Theory: A Critical Introduction*. New York: Routledge.

Hayek, F. 1967. *Studies in Philosophy, Politics and Economics*. Chicago: University of Chicago Press.

——. 1973. *Law, Legislation and Liberty, Volume I: Rules and Order*. Chicago: University of Chicago Press.

Hechter M. 1987. *Principles of Group Solidarity*. Berkeley: University of Clifornia Press.

Heckathorn, D. 1996. The dynamics and dilemmas of collective action. *American Sociological Review* 61: 250–77.

Hedstrom, P. Forthcoming. Rational choice and social structure: on rational-choice theorizing in sociology. In B. Wittrock, ed., *Social Theory and Human Agency*. London: Sage.

Heise, D. 1996. Social order through macroactions: an interactionist approach. Panel on micromacro processes and social order, Ninth Annual Group Processes Conference, August 21, 1996, New York.

James, W. 1981. *Principles of Psychology*. Cambridge: Harvard University Press.

Kiser, E. and M. Hechter. 1991. The role of general theory in comparative-historical sociology. *American Journal of Sociology* 97: 1–31.

Lave, C. and J. March. 1975. *An Introduction to Models in the Social Sciences*. New York: Harper & Row.

Macy, M. 1993. Social learning and the structure of collective action. In Ed Lawler et al., eds, *Advances in Group Processes*, 10: 1–36. Greenwich, CT: JAI Press.

——. 1997. Identity, interest and emergent rationality: an evolutionary synthesis. *Rationality and Society* 9: 427–38.

——. 1998. Social order in artificial worlds. *Journal of Artificial Societies and Social Simulation* 1: n. p.

Maynard-Smith, J. 1979. Game theory and the evolution of behaviour. *Proceedings of the Royal Society of London* 205: 475–88.

Mead, G. H. 1934. *Mind, Self, and Society*. Chicago: University of Chicago Press.

Nash, J. 1951. Non-Cooperative Games. *Annals of Mathematics* 54: 286–95.

Nee, V. and P. Ingram. 1998. Embeddedness and Beyond: Institutions, Exchange, and Social Structure. In M. Brinton and V. Nee, eds, *The New Institutionalism in Sociology*. New York: Russell Sage.

Parsons, Talcott. 1937. *The Structure of Social Action*. New York: McGraw-Hill.

Peirce, C. 1955. In J. Buchler, ed., *The Philosophical Writings of Peirce*. New York: Dover Press.

Runciman, W. 1989. *A Treatise on Social Theory*. Vol. 2. Cambridge: Cambridge University Press.

Ruse, M. and E. O. Wilson. 1986. Moral philosophy as applied science. *Philosophy* 61: 173–92.

Schull, J. 1996. William James and the broader implications of a multilevel selectionism. In R. Belew and M. Mitchell, eds, *Adaptive Individuals in Evolving Populations*, pp. 243–56. Reading, MA: Addison-Wesley.

Simon, H. 1992. Decision-making and problem-solving. In M. Zey, ed., *Decision Making: Alternatives to Rational Choice Models*, pp. 32–53. Newbury Park: Sage Publications.

Smelser, N. 1992. The rational choice perspective: a theoretical assessment. *Rationality and Society* 4: 381–410.

Smith, A. 1937. *An Inquiry into the Nature and Causes of the Wealth of Nations*. New York: Modern Library.

Stinchcomb, A. 1968. *Constructing Social Tehories*. New York: Harcourt, Brace, and World.

Vanberg, V. 1994. *Rules and Choice in Economics*. London: Routledge, 1994.

Weber, M. 1908. Marginal utility theory and "the fundamental law of psychophysics." Reprinted in *Social Science Quarterly* 56 (1975): 21–36.

Willer, D. and J. Skvoretz. 1997. Games and structures. *Rationality and Society* 9: 5–35.

Wynne-Edwards, V. 1962. *Animal dispersion in Relation to Social Behaviour*. Edinburgh: Oliver Boyd.

9 Theoretical Models: Sociology's Missing Links

John Skvoretz

Introduction

Theories must be coordinated with data in scientific inquiry. Models are the devices by which such coordination is achieved. Through models, a theory's claims can be evaluated against relevant data. Models perform a bridging function between a discipline's theories and its database of findings and observations. In sociology, typically, the objects that perform this function are derived from general methodological procedures that have wide applicability – they can be used to model data on crop yields as well as data on friendship choices. They may be termed *methodological models* to emphasize their origins. Theoretical models constitute an alternative way of forging the link between theory and data. We create these models by applying general mathematical modeling techniques to specify a theory's logic.

I address several points in this essay. The first point illustrates what difference it makes if one uses a theoretical rather than methodological model to coordinate a theory with relevant data. My example is Peter Blau's theory of intergroup relations as set out in his 1977 book *Inequality and Heterogeneity: A Primitive Theory of Social Structure*. I then discuss the advantages and disadvantages of using theoretical models rather than methodological models to build the bridge between sociological theory and sociology's database. Since I want to argue that many areas in sociology could benefit from a focus on theoretical as opposed to methodological models, I want to indicate in this section other examples. Finally, I locate my emphasis on the importance of theoretical models with respect to various philosophical approaches to explanation, in particular, positivism and realism. In this discussion, I rely on Fararo's (1989) analysis of these approaches.

The Gulf Between Theory and Data

It is apparent to anyone who does scientific research that the gulf between theory and data is wide and deep. Theories cannot be tested by simply "reading off" the results directly from the facts. In practice, what constitutes a "fact" can itself be subject to theoretical dispute. How easy it is to bridge the gulf depends greatly on the precision of a theory. If the theory's fundamental concepts are stated in vague and ambiguous terms, much room is left for their coordination with empirical observations. I must assume that a theory is sufficiently precise that researchers agree on what constitutes relevant data. That is, if a theory is about intergroup relations, then researchers must agree that census data collected in such and such a way constitute a proper database for examining the theory. Or if the theory is about job matching between employers and workers, then researchers must agree that the Government Statistical Service data on workers' jobs constitute an appropriate basis on which to test the theory (Logan 1996). In such cases, the gulf is "bridgeable." In other cases, we do not even know in which direction to start the bridge's construction.

To evaluate a theory, we must systematically coordinate predictions of a theory to regularities in relevant data. The entity through which coordination is achieved may be termed a model. One of its most important accomplishments is to rigorously represent regularities in the data. To build such a model, we may begin from either of two directions: theory via its predictions towards regularities in data or data via its regularities towards the predictions of a theory.

The latter path is more familiar to sociologists. We use general techniques for the analysis and summary of quantitative information, such as multiple regression, analysis of variance, or log-linear contingency table analysis, to uncover and to express regularities in the data. Such models express regularities in terms of various "effect" parameters. In regression analysis, these parameters are the regression coefficients; in log-linear models, these parameters are row, column, and cell effects. The idea then is to "interpret"

these parameters in terms of the theory's concepts and propositions. Testing the theory amounts to judging whether the effect
parameters behave as expected. These models are "methodological
models" because we use general methodological techniques for
data analysis to express regularities in the relevant data.

The first path begins with the theory and its predictions. From
the assumptions of the theory, we derive explicitly the relation
between key variables measured in the data set or derive the explicit
probabilities of various observable events encoded by the data. In
this path, the form of the regularities found in the data is derived
by theoretical analysis. Testing the theory means estimating the
theoretically derived form of the data regularities and judging
whether the fit between theory and observation is sufficiently close
to warrant acceptance of the theory. Sociologists are less familiar
with this path, in part because it requires that the theory be precise
enough that it is possible to derive the form that regularities may
be expected to take. Without formal statement, it is unlikely that a
theory can be this precise and few sociological theories are formally stated. Therefore, in many cases to build theoretical models,
we use general mathematical modeling techniques to specify a
theory's logic. The resulting models are called "theoretical models"
because the aim of these models is to capture the mechanisms
proposed by a theory with sufficient precision to express the form
that regularities in data may take on. In this sense, these models
are "theory-driven" in a way that does not characterize the methodological models. Figure 4 diagrams these points.

I should point out that this contrast between methodological and
theoretical models creates some problems. First, it makes it seem
like a methodological model is agnostic with respect to theory, that
is, that it does not embody any particular theoretical claims or
assumptions about the processes and phenomena of interest. But
even though such models are not derived from specific theoretical
assumptions, this does not mean that they cannot be derived from
some set of explicit assumptions. The problem is that we do not
know which assumptions. So methodological models undoubtedly
have theoretical parents, but we do not know who they are. Another way of expressing this point is that the application of a general methodology for data analysis brings with it a set of "default"
theoretical assumptions. The problem is whether these defaults faith-
fully express a particular theory's claims about the world.

This point echoes the discussion of Collins (1988) on statistics in
theory and method. He argues that statistics is typically viewed as
"concerned with empirical research problems involved in measuring

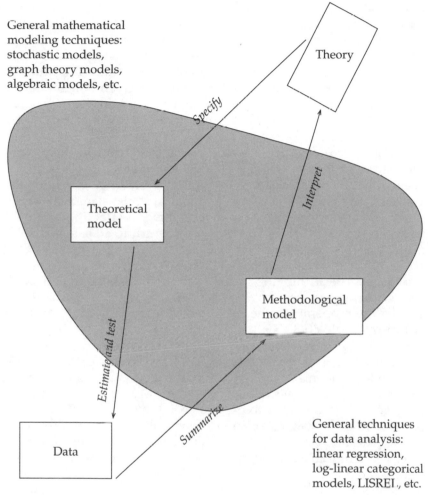

General mathematical
modeling techniques:
stochastic models,
graph theory models,
algebraic models, etc.

Theory

Specify

Theoretical
model

Interpret

Methodological
model

Estimate and test

Summarise

Data

General techniques
for data analysis:
linear regression,
log-linear categorical
models, LISREL, etc.

Figure 4.

and drawing inferences from data" (1988: 494). In this view,
statistics has no connection with theory: "it is a way of describing
relationships and testing theories, not of formulating them" (1988:
496). But for Collins statistical analysis carries with it a substantive
theory of the world, namely, one in which the operative causal
mechanism produces "random" distributions.

Second, the distinction makes it seem that theoretical models
are customized products without general significance for data
analysis. This impression too is misleading, particularly when the
theoretical models are probabilistic. These models use general

mathematical tools to formalize a theory, so it should not be surprising that such models may be transferred to other domains or be used to analyze data other than those originally intended. The appropriateness of such a transfer may be suggested by the similarity between domains in theoretical mechanisms postulated by researchers in each. Nevertheless, within a given domain, these models are distinguishable from those whose origins lie in general data-analysis techniques. They are marked by their focus on the formal expression of a theory's assumptive base.

Collins (1988) also provides an example relevant to this point. He notes that Poisson models as a general method for describing regularities in data began with Poisson's investigation into the propagation of heat. Then, "methodological statisticians with other interests transformed this from a substantive model into a purely procedural one" (1988: 505). He urges a return to statistics as substantive theory, asserting that *"the greatest value of statistics is as a theory rather than as a method"* (1988: 499, emphasis in original). That is, statistical thinking in the form of probabilistic models of social phenomena can provide theoretical models of mechanisms which "often operate in the social world, especially at the macro-structural level" (1988: 499).

Finally, the contrast is not intended to create or exacerbate antagonisms between theoreticians and methodologists. Theoretical models and methodological models serve the same purpose – to span the gulf between theory and data. My emphasis on theoretical models is intended to expand sociology's range of bridging options. In some cases, explicitly derived theoretical models may not be possible, yet we wish to evaluate a theory's claims. In that case, a carefully constructed methodological model may be our only recourse. But in the long run, sociology's scientific advance depends on formulating and testing theoretical models whose assumptions are explicitly stated and open to inspection.

Bridging the Gulf: An Illustration from the Theory of Intergroup Relations

To illustrate these remarks, I consider an example from the study of intergroup relations. Sociologists have long been interested in social ties that cross important social boundaries. From the societal level, their prevalence tells us about the extent to which different ethnic, racial, religious, or status groups are integrated with one another. For example, Kalmijn (1993) explores recent evidence that increases in black–white intermarriage have their basis in a declining significance of race for marital choice. On the other hand, the absence of intergroup ties reveals the extent to which the subgroups are solidary. For instance, Hechter (1978) uses intragroup marriage as a key indicator of a group's solidarity in his study of how the unity of a status group is affected by its positioning in a "cultural division of labor."

The most prominent theory of intergroup relations is that set out by Peter Blau in his 1977 book *Inequality and Heterogeneity: A Primitive Theory of Social Structure*. Blau's theory focusses on the social structural determinants of intergroup relations. Social structure is conceptualized as "population distributions among social positions along various lines – positions that reflect and affect people's role relations with one another" (1977: 3). The theory deduces how population heterogeneity and inequality – measures of a population's distribution into horizontal and vertical positions defined by nominal and graduated dimensions of differentiation – and the correlation between and among these positions affects the rate of dyadic association, e.g., marriage or friendship, between persons from different social positions.

The logic of the theory is that social structure conditions the opportunity for ties to form and thereby affects the rate of all types of intergroup association. Heterogeneity, inequality, and correlation or consolidation/intersection are fundamental measures of a population's opportunity structure with respect to the formation of social ties. The theory describes how the opportunity structure impacts the rate of intergroup association even in the face of ubiquitous preferences or "tastes" for ingroup associates. In fact, the theory fascinates precisely because it shows that preferences for ingroup associates are simply not sufficient to determine rates of intergroup association. Rather variation in rates over populations derives from variation in their opportunity structures. Blau emphasizes the structural nature of his theory in the following passage:

The theory . . . explains patterns of social relations in terms of properties of social structure. . . . The nature of the logical formulations employed makes the explanations structural. In a typical formulation, the major premise stipulates variations in structural properties, and the minor premise stipulates tendencies of people that are assumed to be invariant. . . . For example, the major premise refers to variations in the extent to which structural parameters intersect, and the minor premise refers to the tendency of people to prefer ingroup to outgroup relations, which is assumed to be given and variations in which are not considered. (1977: 246)

Blau casts his theory in terms of explicit assumptions and theorems. This format makes it easy to see how separate propositions are related. The statements, however, are not mathematical in form. At best, the theorems are derivable from assumptions or previous theorems by propositional logic. The absence of a fully formal model leads to an occasional misstep, most notably, the mistaken derivation that increasing inequality reduces the likelihood of status-distant association. Just the opposite follows from the assumptions, as Blau later recognized in the theory's revised formulation (Blau and Schwartz 1984).

Much research done to test this theory has examined various types of intermarriages: ethnic, regional, racial, educational, and occupation (Blau, Blum, and Schwartz 1982; Blau and Schwartz 1984; Blau, Beeker, and Fitzpatrick 1984; Rytina 1988). These tests use methodological models to coordinate predictions of the theory with the intermarriage data. At the same time, developments in the mathematical thoery of networks known as "biased net theory" have proposed probabilistic models for network formation, that is, models that portray how and where ties form between individuals (Fararo 1981; Skvoretz 1983; Fararo and Skvoretz 1984; Skvoretz and Fararo 1986). These models take into account subgroup memberships of actors. Biased net theory thus provides a source for theoretical models to link Blau's theory of intergroup relations with relevant data (Skvoretz 1990, 1991).

I depict these alternatives more vividly in Figure 5, a version of Figure 4. The imagery indicates that the point of departure for methodological models, in this case a linear regression model, is data while the point of departure for theoretical models, in this case a biased net model, is theory. The linear regression model summarizes the data on intermarriages in the form of coefficients. These coefficients are then interpreted in terms of the theory's claims and constructs. The biased net model, on the other hand, first specifies in formal detail the processes theorized about in the theory of intergroup relations, converting ideas like opportunity and ingroup preferences into exact formal constructs. The model is then estimated and tested using data on intermarriages. Both constructions bridge the gulf between Blau's theory of intergroup relations and the data from SMSAs on intermarriage. One might expect that they would yield the same results, but they do not. I first review findings from the research using the methodological model and then review findings from the estimation and testing of the theoretical model.

The data on intermarriages and population structure are constructed for the 125 largest SMSAs in the 1970 US Census. For each

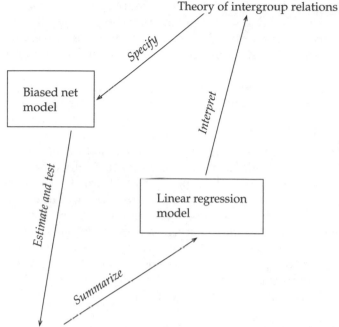

Figure 5.

SMSA, data from the one percent public-use sample are used to construct various measures of heterogeneity, inequality, and correlation between dimensions. The dependent variables either measure the proportion of recently married couples in the SMSA who are intermarried along one of the relevant nominal dimensions, or the average status difference between such couples along one of the relevant graduated dimensions. These dependent variables may then be "corrected" if gender is correlated with the dimension of interest (say, occupation), and thereby forces more dissimilarity in marriage partners than expected in the absence of correlation.

Early tests of the theory used weighted least squares (WLS) regression over these 125 cases to identify the hypothesized effects of heterogeneity, inequality, and correlation of parameters. WLS is the method of choice because the number of cases that contribute to the dependent variable indices vary from 30 in the smallest of the SMSAs to over 1,000 in the largest of the SMSAs. Both simple and multiple regression models are estimated to evaluate hypotheses. For instance, if heterogeneity is postulated to increase intergroup association, then SMSA racial heterogeneity is entered as a predictor (X) of racial intermarriage (Y, a proportion), and similarly for other independent variables, such as the consolidation between dimensions measured by various correlation coefficients. From these tests of the theory using methodological models, we learn:

- As expected, SMSA heterogeneity is significantly and positively associated with the rate of intermarriage, *except* for the most salient dimension in American society – race (Blau, Blum, and Schwartz 1982).
- Theoretically, ingroup preferences affect any rate of intergroup association, *but* no explicit measure of the strength of ingroup preferences with respect to intermarriage is provided.
- In 50 separate analyses, consolidation/intersection of social dimensions has no consistent effect on intermarriage rates, *contrary to a major theoretical prediction* (Blau and Schwartz 1984).
- The theory must be revised to state that "multiple intersection of independent dimensions of social differentiation promotes intergroup relations," a substantial complication of the thoery (Blau and Schwartz 1984: 90).

These findings (as well as some new ones based on an alternative model) are reprised in Blau (1994).

The theoretical model formalizes the logic that social ties within and between groups are a joint function of "tastes" for ingroup association and of the opportunities to form associations with similar or dissimilar others. The model does not address how ties are created, but only where they will be located once they form. The location of a tie, that is, whether or not it crosses a group boundary, is determined by a probabilistic process with both biased and random components. The biased components are events whose probability of occurrence depends on the strength of the (usually) ingroup preferences in a population. If these events related to the "tastes" for association fail to occur, the random component determines where the tie will be located, that is, ties fall within a group, as compared to between two groups, in direct proportion to the number of pairs of each type in the population. Thus the model uses simple probability theory to formalize the basic constructs of Blau's theory of intergroup relations.

From the biased net model's application to exactly the same data on intermarriage (Skvoretz 1990), we learn that:

- Heterogeneity is significantly and positively associated with the rate of intermarriage for all dimensions, *including* race.

- Estimates of specific parameters in the model are direct measures of the strength of ingroup marriage preferences:

$$_\tau\text{RACE} = 0.978$$
$$_\tau\text{NATL ORIGIN} = 0.680$$
$$_\tau\text{BIRTH REGION} = 0.463$$
$$_\tau\text{OCCUPATION} = 0.261$$
$$_\tau\text{INDUSTRY} = 0.215$$

The tau parameters measure the strength of ingroup tastes for association along each dimension of differentiation.
- In 26 of 39 analyses, consolidation/intersection has a statistically significant, negative effect, *just as the theory predicts*.

Thus the analysis of the intermarriage data based on the theoretical models reveals much broader and deeper support for the basic ideas of Blau's theory of intergroup relations than does the analysis based on the regression models. Based on the theoretical models, no significant revision of the theory is required.

Why do the data fit Blau's theory better under the theoretical model? There are several reasons. First, the two models use a different baseline against which to assess hypothesized effects. The regression model's baseline assumes the probability of an intergroup marriage is the same in all SMSA populations. The biased net model's baseline assumes intergroup marriages form independently of group background in all SMSAs. Skvoretz (1990) shows that the regression model's baseline assumes that "tastes" for ingroup association must co-vary with the heterogeneity of the SMSA in order for the intermarriage rate to be constant in SMSAs that vary in heterogeneity. On the other hand, the biased net baseline incorporates the assumption, made explicitly in the statement of the theory – see the above quotation – that ingroup preferences are to be assumed to be invariant.

Second, the two models differently specify how intersection affects intergroup relations. In the regression models, the intersection/consolidation of dimensions is measured by correlation coefficients appropriate to the scale type of the dimensions. In the models, these coefficients are entered as any other variable would be, namely, as a main effect additive to heterogeneity's impact, "since intersection and heterogeneity both predict a positive effect on intermarriage, both are included in all regressions to discern their independent effects" (Blau 1994: 71). The biased net models, however, imply an unusual specification, namely, that intersection/consolidation cannot affect intergroup relations independently of heterogeneity, rather it must be entered into the analysis only in interaction with heterogeneity. That is, the positive impact of one dimension's intersection with another on intermarriage in the first dimension depends on the level of heterogeneity of the first dimension – a given level of intersection will have a greater or lesser impact depending on how heterogenous the population is. Furthermore, intersection/consolidation will have any impact at all only to the extent that the second dimension is also one along which "tastes" for ingroup associates exist.

Here we have a clear example of how two different approaches to spanning the gulf between theory and data yield quite different conclusions regarding the acceptability of the theory. The choice between the two is not easy. It comes as no surprise that I judge the theoretical model to be the sounder approach of the two. The main idea of this essay is that theoretical models are too often missing as options to link theory and data. The development and cumulation of theoretical insight would benefit from the use of theoretical models. If the present example is any guide, theoretical models have a number of advantages as links between theory and data because they more clearly state and more accurately represent a theory's claims. First, methodological models summarize data by general-effect parameters which have no specific referent to theoretical constructs. On the other hand, estimates of parameters in theoretical models have direct interpretation in terms of key theoretical constructs – for instance, the tastes for ingroup association in Blau's theory. Second, methodological models may misrepresent the logic of the theory, produce apparent disconfirmations, and lead to unnecessary revisions. On the other hand, formal theoretical models permit more precise tests of a theory's claims and so ensure only necessary revisions are made.

I should note that Blau and his research group have been responsive to the points raised by the theoretical model. His work in 1994 offers a reformulated analysis of SMSA intermarriage rates, but the reanalysis does not support, in particular, the theoretical model's predictions that there will an interaction between heterogeneity and consolidation/intersection. The new procedures involve logging all variables before testing a linear relationship between them, thereby asserting that the relationships in the original metrics are multiplicative. This means that the interaction between heterogeneity and consolidation/intersection in the logged version would be a power relationship in the original metric. But this is not the specification derived from the theoretical model. Rather the specification is a multiplicative relationship *in the original metric*. In fact, it can be shown that if the theoretical model's specification is treated as fully multiplicative, then logging all variables produces an equation (linear in the logs) in which no interaction term between heterogeneity and consolidation/intersection is stipulated. Consequently, contrary to the impression Blau receives, the findings from the reanalysis support rather than contradict the predictions of the theoretical model.

The points I have made in favor of theoretical models have been noted by others, although they do not use this essay's contrast between model types. The work of Logan (1996) on employment outcomes as a joint function of employer-provided opportunity and worker-determined choice is a comprehensive and recent example. He proposes a theoretical model called a "random matching" model in which employers evaluate individuals and decide to make or not to make offers based on the individual's profile on attributes the employer values. Individuals evaluate the offers they receive based on the offer's profile on attributes they value, and then accept the offer that has the greatest value. The resulting model for data analysis is called a two-sided logit (TSL) model.

Of special interest in the present context is Logan's contrast of this theoretically derived model with other, methodological models of employment outcomes, in particular, linear regression of outcomes on individual characteristics and log-linear models of occupational mobility. While he recognizes that these other models have their uses and advantages, he notes that their parameter estimates have no "direct, behavioral interpretation as the preferences of employers and workers and, consequently, direct relationship to sociological ideas of structure" (Logan 1996: 145). Estimates from Logan's TSL model, since they refer directly to relevant theoretical constructs of preferences, do not have this liability. Logan's (1996: 146) diagnosis of the deficiency in log-linear models is worth quoting at length:

log-linear models have no mathematical relationship to any behavioral model of actors. This makes it hard to determine what the mechanisms of the various structural effects proposed in the models might be. Is a "barrier" in a log-linear model to be associated with the actions (or inactions) of persons or employers blocking the individual's mobility? If so, it is not clear how the parameters are related to these actions.

For Logan, therefore, the principal advantage of a theoretically derived model for data lies in its ability to relate parameter estimates to behavioral assumptions about actors. It is important to tie the results of data analysis to behavioral models of actors in order to understand and "determine" the mechanisms by which social processes produce regularities we sociologists seek to explain. Methodological models have many advantages, not the least of which is their technical sophistication and ease of use via standard statistical packages. However, because they typically have no theoretical derivation from assumptions about behavior of actors or groups, their effect estimates do not allow us to probe further, to uncover the underlying mechanism producing the regularities in question.

Conclusion: Philosophical Commitments

The choice between theoretical and methodological models as bridges between theory and data involves a philosophical choice about the nature of scientific explanation. Fararo's (1989) analysis of this problem discusses two families of philosophical models relevant to theoretical sociology, the logical positivist model and the realist model. In the logical positivist tradition (for instance, Braithwaite 1953 and Hempel 1965), explanation is the deduction of statements about events or particular occurrences from more general statements termed principles or laws. Realist explanation (as found in the writings of Harre and Secord 1973; Hacking 1983 or Leplin 1984) requires a model of a generative mechanism by which the regularities to be explained are produced. As Fararo (1989: 37) puts it, "positivism proposes covering laws and realism proposes generative rules or mechanisms."

The positivist explanatory format in sociology often takes the form of an informal system of sentences related by simple deduction using proposition logic. Blau's 1977 statement of his theory is a good example. Axioms and theorems are numbered and chains of deduction are indicated for each of the various theorems. However, as Fararo and Skvoretz (1993: 422) point out, these "well-intended but mostly unproductive attempts" overlook the crucial role of theoretical models in justifying the logical connections between statements. The real trick in scientific problem-solving is the creation of models with interesting properties. The "sentences" emphasized in positivist accounts of explanation summarize what our studies of models reveal. Without the underpinnings of a theoretical model, the explanation of regularities by subsumption under more general statements appears to be merely verbal sleight-of-hand.

If we use methodological models to bridge the theory–data gulf, we draw attention away from the need to construct theoretical models to properly understand how regularities are produced. Instead of focussing on the mechanisms producing such regularities, we engage in a variable–centric analysis. Such analysis looks for relations between variables that can be coded in the statements of the covering law explanations. Theory becomes a matter of informal guesswork about which variables affect which others and in what directions. We fail to build models from which the connections between variables measuring important constructs can be explicitly derived.

If we use theoretical models to bridge the gulf, we focus attention on "generative mechanisms" – underlying principles of action that account for observed regularities among variables. Research based on these models is more likely to lead to the accumulation of knowledge about general principles and the contexts under which the mechanisms reliably produce systemic connections among variables. Finally, if we build theoretical models, we address key points of the realist account of scientific explanation (Fararo 1989):

- Regularities to be accounted for are generated by an underlying structure or "mechanism."
- The mechanism produces the phenomena whenever it is triggered into action.
- Regularities are the consequence of the structure and the flow of triggering events.

Thus if we adopt these ideas of realist philosophers of scientific explanation, we must conclude that theoretical models are essential to scientific inquiry. In sociology, we must encourage the construction of these missing links. We must encourage a view in which theory is coordinated with relevant data through formally expressed models designed to lay bare the "socio" logic of our theoretical schemes.

References

Blau, Peter M. 1977. *Inequality and Heterogeneity: A Primitive Theory of Social Structure*. New York: Free Press.

———. 1994. *Structural Contexts of Opportunities*. Chicago: University of Chicago Press.

Blau, Peter M., Carolyn Beeker, and Kevin M. Fitzpatrick. 1984. Intersecting social affiliations and intermarriage. *Social Forces* 62: 585–606.

Blau, Peter M., Terry Blum, and Joseph E. Schwartz. 1982. Heterogeneity and intermarriage. *American Sociological Review* 47: 45–62.

Blau, Peter M. and Joseph E. Schwartz. 1984. *Crosscutting Social Circles*. New York: Academic Press.

Braithwaite, R. 1953. *Scientific Explanation*. Cambridge: Cambridge University Press.

Collins, Randall. 1988. *Theoretical sociology*. New York: Harcourt Brace Jovanovich.

Fararo, Thomas J. 1981. Biased networks and social structure theorems: part I. *Social Networks* 3: 137–59.

——. 1989. *The Meaning of General Sociological Theory*. ASA Rose Monograph Series. New York: Cambridge University Press.

Fararo, T. J. and J. Skvoretz. 1984. Biased networks and social structure theorems: part II. *Social Networks* 6: 223–58.

——. 1993. Methods and Problems of Theoretical Integration and the Principle of Adaptively Rational Action. In J. Berger and M. Zelditch, Jr., eds, *Theoretical Research Programs: Studies in the Growth of Theory*, pp. 416–50. Stanford, CA: Stanford University Press.

Hacking, I. 1983. *Representing and Intervening*. New York: Cambridge University Press.

Harre, Rom and Paul Secord. 1973. *The Explanation of Social Behavior*. Totowa, NJ: Littlefield.

Hechter, Michael. 1978. Group formation and the cultural division of labor. *American Journal of Sociology* 84: 293–318.

Hempel, Carl G. 1965. *Aspects of Scientific Explanation and Other Essays in the Philosophy of Science*. New York: Free Press.

Kalmijn, Matthijs. 1993. Trends in black/white intermarriage. *Social Forces* 72: 119–46.

Leplin, J., ed. 1984. *Scientific Realism*. Berkeley: University of California Press.

Logan, John Allan. 1996. Opportunity and choice in socially structured labor markets. *American Journal of Sociology* 102: 114–60.

Rytina, Steven, Peter M. Blau, Terry Blum, and Joseph Schwartz. 1988. Inequality and intermarriage. *Social Forces* 66: 645–75.

Skvoretz, J. 1983. Salience, heterogeneity and consolidation of parameters: civilizing Blau's primitive theory. *American Sociological Review* 48: 360–75.

——. 1990. Social structure and intermarriage: a reanalysis. In C. Calhoun, M. W. Meyer and W. R. Scott, eds, *Structures of Power and Constraint: Papers in Honor of Peter M. Blau*, 375–96. Cambridge: Cambridge University Press.

——. 1991. Theoretical and methodological models of networks and relations. *Social Networks* 13: 275–300.

Skvoretz, J. and T. J. Fararo. 1986. Inequality and association: a biased net theory. *Current Perspectives in Social Theory* 7: 29–50.

10 Sociological Models

Paul Humphreys

I shall present here a general scheme for modeling that is, I believe, applicable across a wide spectrum of theories in sociology, as well as in other disciplines. Models must conform to subject matter, as must methods, and since there is no universal subject matter in science (or in sociology, for that matter), there is unlikely to be a universal account of models. Of course by means of abstraction one can lessen the particularities of subject matter, and the trick is to capture the appropriate level of abstraction at which reasonably general features are represented, yet the flavor of the subject matter is retained.[1] I shall concentrate here upon formal models,[2]

---

[1] For the record, philosophers of science have very often resorted to logic to gain universality. In so doing, they lost contact with subject matter, often completely (for examples of this see, e.g., Carnap 1950; Putnam 1980) because logic is itself subject-independent – in the technical jargon, logical models are identifiable only up to isomorphism. At best, these approaches capture *structure*, which does indeed often differ between domains of inquiry. The structure of brains, whether natural or neural nets, differs from the structure of vitamin A, whether natural or synthetic, for example.

[2] By a "formal model" I mean a model that lends itself to an explicit mathematical treatment, even if only of an elementary kind. This includes ordinal (qualitative) models as well as quantitative models. Whether or not this treatment is actually carried out in practice is irrelevant here. I realize that a (perhaps significant) segment of the sociological community is opposed to, or dubious about the value of, formal models, and I acknowledge that formal methods can be abused (and have criticized such abuse in, e.g., Humphreys and Freedman 1996), but in my limited reading of the literature opposing formal models, an astonishing degree of ignorance about formal methods is on display. In Collins (1984), for example, it is claimed that "Godel demonstrated that any formal system is formally incomplete" (p. 352). This is nonsense; consider the theory of densely ordered sets without

simply because they lend themselves to a certain precision of treatment. We can start with a standard dichotomy, that between theory and (social) phenomena, and with the issue of how to get from one to the other (in either direction). Many suggestions have been made within the methodological community regarding that issue, and I do not intend to provide a grand tour of the history here. There is, however, a well-known division between so-called "theory-driven" (or "top-down") approaches, within which abstract theory plays the primary role, and so-called "data-driven" (or "bottom-up") approaches, within which analysis of the data is the starting place. My own preference is for the former, but the main theme I want to emphasize here is that taking these two approaches as opposed to one another is misguided,[3] for when construed properly, and when conditions are right, they both play a crucial role in helping us understand social systems. One well-known example of the theory-driven approach is the venerable hypothetico-deductive approach, favored by such philosophers as Carl Hempel and Karl Popper. Within that approach, laws play a crucial role in theoretical derivations, and specific conditions are represented by spatiotemporally definite propositions.[4] At least within the community of philosophers of science, however, the hypothetico-deductive method has lost ground in favor of more detailed (i.e., realistic) approaches focussing on models.[5] In particular, the simple division between theory, construed as a set of assumptions and their logical consequences, and social phenomena, construed as a collection of social units (individuals, social classes, institutions, etc.) and their social properties and relations, is replaced by a more complex hierarchy having models acting as the intermediaries between theory and data.

endpoints, the theory of real closed fields, Presburger arithmetic, the theory of elementary geometry – all formal systems and all complete. In fact, since Godel had in 1929 already demonstrated the completeness of yet another formal system, that of first-order logic, he would hardly have been in the business of contradicting himself in September 1930 when he presented his first incompleteness theorem at the same conference at which he discussed his earlier completeness result.

[3] Blau 1977: 13–14 takes pains to state that both approaches are legitimate.

[4] *Very* roughly, this corresponds within the physical sciences to the distinction between differential equations and their initial or (specific) boundary conditions.

[5] Some of what I have to say here was motivated by Patrick Suppes's prescient paper "Models of Data" (Suppes 1963). A second paper in this tradition is Laymon 1982. For those initiated into the jargon of contemporary philosophy, "models" does not refer here to set-theoretical structures, but to the idealized representations of phenomena that serve as the interface between high-level theory and empirical applications. The use of models is also emphasized in Skvoretz 1991, although the conception used there, of "a rigorous representation of patterns in the relevant data" (p. 276), is rather different than that used here.

We need first to define terms. As with any widely used terminology, we cannot possibly capture all the variant uses to which the terms "theory," "model" and "data" have been put. The best we can do is to note that our use here conforms to one common set of usages, and that these choices clarify a number of methodological issues.

Definition   A *formal theory* is a collection of basic sentences in some precisely specified language, together with the set of all deductive consequences of those sentences.

The basic sentences constitute the fundamental assumptions of the theory. In addition, the primitive concepts of the theory should be spelled out and, where possible, the other concepts used defined in terms of those primitives.

Definition   A *model* is an idealized representation of a specific system or type of system or of data incorporating specifically stated idealizations and approximations. It serves as an intermediary between a formal theory and the system.

Definition   *Data* are any raw measurements from a system.

Definition   A *system* consists of the generating conditions for data.

You will note that I have taken (social) systems as the lowest level in the hierarchy rather than data. This represents a realist attitude toward social systems, i.e., one is committed to the existence of social systems in addition to the data they generate, but I want to stress that this kind of realist attitude is consistent with the models of the system having significant empirical content.

There are two primary uses of models. The first is that they play a role in bringing abstract theory into contact with (processed) data. Theory, when well done, is too general to be directly applicable to specific systems, and some intermediary is needed for the job. More important is the fact that idealizations and approximations play a significant role in moving between theory and data, and these are a key feature of the modelling process.

The second use is in giving us some understanding of the system that generates the data. Regarding this second use, the idea that it is *unifying theories* that provide understanding has recently gained some popularity in philosophical circles.[6] That is, more or less grand

[6] See, e.g., Kitcher 1989. The modern originator of this view is Friedman (1974).

unifying schemes such as natural selection, general relativity, rational choice theory, interchange theory, and so on are said to give us understanding by showing that phenomena previously thought to be unrelated are in fact subsumable under a common theoretical framework. General theories certainly do that for us, but unification is not all there is to understanding. For we also want to understand particular examples of social phenomena, and that is where *models of the generating conditions* (of the data) enter, at least in helping us to understand why this particular system is an example of the theory and why the phenomena deviate from what is to be expected on the basis of general theory.

We thus have two distinct kinds of models in use – one to bring down abstract theory to a level where it can represent a specific kind of system, the other to model the specific (causal) influences on the actual system under investigation. The first kind is roughly a top-down use of models, the second, again roughly, a bottom-up use. I note here that of course the specific system under investigation is always a system of some specific type too, but that there is often a special set of circumstances that apply to the particular application. These special circumstances are not (just) values of parameters, but kinds of causal influence, the combination of which is often unique, and this incorporation of social influences is one of the most important places where specific, subject-dependent knowledge enters.

An aside on method: Much activity in science (including sociology) focusses on the top two levels of theory and theoretical models, in part because of the view that science must concern itself with general system types, at the very least to ensure reproducibility of outcomes, Yet science has to concern itself with specific applications too, at the very least to ensure testability. It is a great pity that philosophy of science has tended to place less emphasis on this latter, particularistic activity, perhaps mistakenly thinking that it is part of (here social) engineering, rather than science proper. The system can include experimental, non-experimental, or quasi-experimental contexts, although the degree to which specific causal knowledge enters into models of the generating conditions will differ between these kinds of contexts.

How do we construct models, and how do they link theory and data? (It needs to be emphasized here that models are *constructed*, even so-called "off-the-shelf" statistical models, the familiarity of which tends to mask their origins.) Now, in my experience, it is best to lay out a position initially using examples that are, from the audience's point of view, ideologically neutral, to avoid raising territorial hackles. So we'll begin with a well-known example from physics, and then work our way closer to home.

Consider Newton's Second Law, which I assume is familiar to you all. This is called a law, but that's not what is important about it. Its main interest is as a *computational template*. Let me tell you what I mean by that. Newton's Second Law can be stated in a variety of ways, but one standard characterization is that of a second-order, ordinary differential equation:

$$F = md^2y/dt^2 \qquad (1)$$

The first thing to note about Newton's Second "Law" is that it is only a schema. It describes an enormously general constraint on the relationship between any force, mass, and acceleration, but to use it in a particular case we need to specify a definite force function. We can call a mathematical representation a computational template when at least one of the variables and parameters of the representation is a (first-order) abstract property.[7] (Note: Ordinal models are included under this definition.) Then we have that a *theoretical model* is an application of a computational template to a specific (class of) application(s) wherein the highly abstract properties in the template are identified with a less abstract property that can be independently measured, i.e., measured in a way that is independent of the computational template.

It is in the process of this application that the model building begins. Choosing something like

$$F = GMm/R^2$$

will give us a model for a body of mass m falling under the action of a now specific, gravitational force near the surface of a spherical body (M is the mass of the body, R its radius). Then the equation characterizing the theoretical model:

$$GMm/R^2 = md^2y/dt^2 \qquad (2)$$

is easily solved. But the idealizations that underlie this simple theoretical model make it quite unrealistic. The model assumes,

---

[7] *Technical aside*: in Newton's Second Law, F is a first-order predicate, rather than a first-order variable, because force is itself a genuine property, but at a higher level of abstraction than specific kinds of influences such as electromagnetic or gravitational attractions. A variable would range over these lower-level properties, whereas a predicate names a specific, albeit here a highly abstract, property. (A first-order property is one that has instances that are individuals, in contrast to second-order properties that take [first-order] properties as instances.)

amongst other things, that (a) the gravitational force on the body does not vary with its distance from the spherical body's surface; and (b) that there is no air resistance on the falling body. These are the kinds of idealizations that make this stage a theoretical model. But now we want the model to be applied to the Earth, which has a radius of modest size compared to the height from which some bodies fall, and which also has an atmosphere. So we need to include a *data-generating model* by making the theoretical model a little more realistic. We do this by representing the gravitational force as $GMm/(R + y)^2$, where y is the distance of the body from the Earth's surface, and by introducing a velocity-dependent drag force due to air resistance. We obtain

$$GMm/(R + y)^2 - c\rho s \, (dy/dt)^2/2 = md^2y/dt^2 \qquad (3)$$

where ρ is the coefficient of resistance.[8]

We could, of course, add further terms to gain increased realism, but this is enough to illustrate the point.

Some morals to draw from this model include:

(a)   Each term in the theoretical and the data-generating model and the model as a whole is already justified on the basis of specific, subject-dependent background theory, using clearly articulated idealizations and approximations.

(b)   Thus, when either model fails to fit the data (and it will), specific components of the model will generally be known to have failed, because one or more of the idealizations used for that component were already known to be unrealistic, or too crude. Pure bottom-up models, i.e., those that are merely data-fitting devices such as multiple regression, quite aside from their notorious flexibility in accommodating data, fail to give us such guidance. Moreover, it was pointed out many years ago by the economists Marschak and Hurwicz[9] that one of the major advantages of theory-driven models was this: when the underlying structure of a system changes, or one moves from population to population, the underlying theory gives you a

---

[8]   As it happens, this equation is analytically unsolvable. Suppose we want to make a prediction of the position of this body at a specific time, given zero initial velocity, and initial position $y = y_0$. Then (3) has no known analytic solution – the move from (2) to (3) has converted a second-order, linear, homogeneous, ordinary differential equation into one that is second-order, homogeneous, and non-linear, and the move from linearity to non-linearity turns simple mathematics into intractable mathematics. This is the point at which numerical simulations become important.

[9]   See, e.g., Hurwicz [1950].

basis upon which to adapt the model to the new situation. This is not possible with empirically generated models.

(c) Specific, subject-dependent knowledge is required to construct and modify these models, especially at the data-generating end. As such, there is no "logic" of model building and modification, yet the construction is a transparent process that can be explicitly justified rather than relegated to the mysterious domain of psychological inspiration-generating hypotheses.

Now Newton's Second Law is, in its degree of generality, highly unusual as a computational template. Most such templates are much more similar to (3) than to (1) in that, fundamental as they may be to a field, they are themselves constructions from more basic, often non-quantitative, assumptions. It is thus instructive to look at a second kind of template, that of statistical models, such as binomial "models," hypergeometric "models," and so on. We can use one elementary case here, that of binomial models, to provide a somewhat more detailed, albeit still simplified, account of how models are used. I want to stress here that I am starting with an excessively simple model in order to reduce the clutter that inevitably accumulates as we get more realistic.

Binomial Models

The components in such models, with the application to coin-tossing in mind, are these:

(1) A general theoretical model for coin-tossing, including explicit physical reasons for stationarity and independence assumptions, together with a general theoretical physical basis for the parameter value (this may be a symmetry argument or a theory of mass distribution in coins).

(2) A mathematical model that is constructed on the basis of (1) above. This has the well-known form

$$P \text{ (}m \text{ successes in } n \text{ trials)} = n!/m! \ (n-m)! \ p^m \ (1-p)^{n-m}$$

(3) An idealized theory of measurement for the parameter. Usually, this will consist in a (limiting) relative frequency approach. This theory of measurement should be sharply separated from:

(4) Statistical analysis of data that allows parametric estimation This also includes issues such as sampling techniques, sample size, and so on.

(5)   Either
(i) (a) a general theory of coin types to generate the specific parameter value P, together with
(b) a theory of the experimental set-up, including a justification for physical independence, constancy of generating conditions.
or
(ii) an algorithm and program-specific simulation. (Here satisfaction of (a) and (b) above are guaranteed, assuming no logic errors, to be satisfied by the properties of the random number generator and the form of the algorithm.)

I note that even with something as elementary as binomial models for coin-tossing (or the equally simple case of die-throwing) a model of the specific system can be surprisingly informative. For example, in Iverson et al. (1971), an analysis is given of 4.38 million tosses of various dice by hand. In Appendix B, a model is given for a cheap dime-store brand of die and a linear correction for the effects of drilled holes for the pips is included. This results in a measurable bias in those dice, in contrast to professional quality Las Vegas dice for which, as I recall from a casino display some years ago, such a correction is not needed because the material used to fill the holes is chosen to have the same density as the body of the die itself.[10]

Having seen how this works in a simple statistical case, we can now construct a general scheme for relating theory to data, using sociological theories as an example. I am not suggesting that all sociological models will contain all components, but that the more there are, the more complete the theoretical treatment will be.

Warning: Additional levels could (obviously) be added to this schema, but the levels included are at least those needed for a moderately realistic account of modelling.

(1)   General theory of social structure
This includes (i) the fundamental assumptions of the theory (these may or may not include "laws" and/or social mechanisms);

---

[10] There is a considerable literature on such issues, and even for such simple systems as coins and dice a detailed model of the generating conditions can be given, for example Keller (1986), Diaconis and Keller (1989), Ornstein (1989), and at a much more abstract level, Chatterjee et al. [1995].

(ii) an explicit list of social units (these may be individuals, groups, institutions, and so on), parameters, independent, intervening and dependent variables, and constants[11]

(iii) idealizations, e.g., that individuals act from pure self-interest, or that interaction in small groups takes place between individuals in a pairwise fashion.

The important thing here is that the theory is couched in very general terms, with an abstract approach to what counts under (ii) and (iii). Nevertheless, the theory comes with an intended interpretation, even at this stage. It is a caricature of formal methods to suggest that abstract theories are couched in uninterpreted symbolic languages.[12]

(2) (1) is then used to derive, perhaps via further idealizations, formal models of stable features of social phenomena.

At this stage, the model will be general in form, the level of generality depending upon the level of abstraction at which (1) (ii) and (1) (iii) are stated.

(3) A theory of measurement for the dependent variables and the parameters, which will often be population-dependent.

(4) Statistical analysis of the data, which will include relations between the type of measurement scale used in (3) and the appropriate statistical treatment. Parameter estimation will often be primary here.

(5) (i) (a) A theory of specific social units, properties, and relations is then used to link (2) with (3) below. This will, amongst other things, construe the variables as binary, multivalued discrete, or continuous. In fact, the objects of this specific theory may be fictitious[13] (as opposed to idealized), or intuitive ideas of some of these objects may be used.

(b) A theory of the experimental or non-experimental setting within which the objects of the specific theory are located and which generates the data.

---

[11] To fix usage: by "parameters" I mean constants of the model that are population-dependent or context-dependent; variables represent properties or relations possessed by, or holding between, social units, the values of which can vary between different units; constants have fixed values across populations. Populations here are collections of social units.

[12] This has been widely recognized even within mathematics. For example, Tarski notes (1956) that it is incoherent to provide a semantics for a mathematical theory unless you already know what the intended interpretation of the theory is supposed to be, whether it is a theory of rings, lattices, probability measures, or whatever.

[13] Fictitious status characteristics are widely used in experimental tests of the theory of Berger et al. (1977), for example.

or

(ii) an algorithm and a program-specific simulation that replaces (a) and (b) above.

Comments: (a) There is no requirement that the theory in (1) has to contain sociological laws. It no doubt helps in forming such theories when general laws are available, but there is no sense that the theory is deficient because it is localized. The concepts involved must be abstract in the sense that they allow multiple, different applications of the theory. Here there is always the question of what is the appropriate level of abstraction at which to describe the social units and properties. For example, should we group individuals as clerical, professional, manual, etc., or as unionized versus non-unionized? This is the *horizontal issue* of how to group the social units. There is also the *vertical issue*: what level of abstraction is most appropriate to use? That is, do we use the classification of doctors, lawyers, bankers, etc., or just one of professionals? The point here is that it is social *properties* and not units directly that should be the primary focus of attention, and the answer to the vertical issue can only be given on causal grounds – which properties are causally effective. This is not a pragmatic but an empirical issue (this is more easily seen in the social sciences than in the natural sciences because it is *perceived* groupings that matter).

(b) Regression analysis, causal models, factor analysis, Bayesian causal inference (e.g., Pearl 1995), and so on do not count as any of the components of (1) through (5) above.

(c) The primary use of (1) is to allow theory refinement (i.e., relaxing of the severe idealizations involved in the initial formulations) and theory extension (i.e., generalization of the apparatus to cover situations falling outside of the scope of the initial formulations.

I want to call particular attention to components (5) (a) and (5) (b). Regarding (5) (b), what is missing in regression analysis and related general approaches (such as structural equation models) is that there is no specific model about the conditions that are generating the data, other than bare-bones statistical assumptions about normally distributed independent errors and the like. Component (5) (b) gives us a model of many of the factors that have been deliberately omitted from the abstract model in (2) (because (1) must keep its concepts general), facilitating theory extension and refinement. This is where the "data-driven" or empirical terminology is misleading. What is needed is not necessarily a *theory* of the generating system, but specific causal knowledge of what kinds of factors can influence a given system. (This is related to Polyani's concept of tacit knowledge.) So what is missing in pure data-driven approaches is a model of the generating conditions.

In fact, (5) (a) is optional, for there may be core examples of a theoretical entity, such as prestige, that can be used to motivate applications to similar cases. Moreover, although the theory is usually formulated in abstract terms, it comes with an *intended interpretation* to at least those core cases. (Of course it may be wrong in what it says about those core cases.)

Conclusion

I shall leave you with a question that arose in passing, and to which at present I have no answer. It strikes me as increasingly fundamental in all areas of science. It is: what is the appropriate level of abstraction at which to deal with a given (social) phenomenon? I have suggested here a multilayered approach to modeling, but this leaves almost completely open the answer to my question. Perhaps there is no general answer to it and the choice is simply made as part of the craft of theorizing. Yet the question is, of course, intimately connected with the issue of levels of social reality, and as an antireductionist and a realist about social phenomena, I like to think that there is a more interesting answer than that.

References

Berger, J., M. Fisek, R. Norman, and M. Zelditch. 1977. *Status Characteristics and Social Interaction*. New York: Elsevier.

Blau, P. 1977. *Inequality and Heterogeneity*. New York: Free Press.

Carnap, R. 1950. Empiricism, Semantics, and Ontology. *Revue internationale de philosophie*. 11: 208–28. Reprinted in R. Carnap, *Meaning and Necessity*. 2nd ed. Chicago: University of Chicago Press, 1956.

Chatterjee, R. et al. 1995. Coin Tossing as a Billiard Problem. *Physical Review E* V0052 N4 PA: 3608–13.

Collins, R. 1984. Statistics versus Words. In R. Collins, ed., *Sociological Theory 1984*, 329–62. San Francisco: Jossey-Bass.

Diaconis, P. and Keller, J. 1989. Fair Dice. *American Mathematical Monthly* 96: 337–9.

Friedman, M. 1974. Explanation and Scientific Understanding. *Journal of Philosophy* 71: 5–19.

Humphreys, P. and Freedman, D. 1996. The Grand Leap. *British Journal for the Philosophy of Science* 47: 113–23.

Hurwicz, L. 1950. Prediction and Least Squares. In T. Koopmans, ed., *Statistical Inference in Dynamic Economic Models*, 266–300. New York: John Wiley.

Iverson, G. et al. 1971. Bias and Runs in Dice Throwing and Recording: A Few Million Throws, *Psychometrika* 36: 1–19.

Keller, J. 1986. The Probability of Heads. *American Math. Monthly* 93: 191–7.

Kitcher, P. 1989. Explanatory Unification and the Causal Structure of the World. In P. Kitcher and W. Salmon, eds, *Scientific Explanation, Minnesota Studies in the Philosophy of Science, Volume XIII*, 410–505. Minneapolis: University of Minnesota Press.

Laymon, R. 1982. Scientific Realism and the Hierarchical Counterfactual Path from Data to Theory. In P. Asquith and T. Nickles, eds, *PSA 1982, Volume 1: Proceedings of the 1982 Biennial Meeting of the Philosophy of Science Association*, 107–21. East Lansing: Philosophy of Science Association.

Ornstein, D. S. 1989. Ergodic Theory, Randomness, and "Chaos." *Science* 243: 182–7.

Pearl, J. 1995. Causal Diagrams for Empirical Research. *Biometrika* 82: 669–710.

Putnam, H. 1980. Models and Reality. *Journal of Symbolic Logic* 45: 464–82.

Skvoretz, J. 1991. Theoretical and Methodological Models of Networks and Relations. *Social Networks* 13: 275–300.

Suppes, P. 1963. Models of Data. In E. Nagel et al., *Logic, Methodology, and Philosophy of Science: Proceedings of the 1960 International Congress*, 252–61. Stanford, CA: Stanford University Press.

Tarski, A. 1956. The Concept of Truth in Formalized Languages. In A. Tarski, *Logic, Semantics, Metamathematics*, pp. 152–278. New York: Oxford University Press.

11 Culture and Social Structure

Peter M. Blau

In this concluding essay, I distinguish between the cultural and the structural approach in sociological theorizing, concluding by presenting a précis of a macrostructural theory. To introduce the discussion, I briefly contrast the cultural and the structural perspectives.

The cultural conception of social life embodies Weber's *Verstehen* (meaningful understanding). It centers attention on common values and norms as fundamental orientations in terms of which social life should be interpreted. The structural form of analysis embodies Durkheim's concern with the external constraints of social facts. It focusses on the effects of these objective structural conditions on social life.

The historical roots of the distinction between the cultural and the structural approach can be traced back centuries to the difference between idealistic and materialistic philosophy. This juxtaposition found expression in the nineteenth century in the *Methodenstreit*, the conflict over methods in which Rickert and Dilthey attacked protagonists of Auguste Comte's positivism.

The German philosopher Windelband tried to resolve this controversy by drawing an analytical distinction between two kinds of knowledge: idiographic, which deals with unique human events, as history does, and nomothetic, which generalizes about nature, as the natural sciences do. This dichotomy, in turn, found systematic expression in the nineteenth century in the contrasting formulations of Hegel's idealistic and Marx's materialistic dialectical interpretations of historical development.

Culture

The classic symbol of the cultural (idealistic) approach in the disciple is Max Weber, who considered sociology as "a science concerning itself with the interpretation of action in terms of its subjective meaning and thereby with a causal explanation of its course and consequences" ([1922] 1978: 4). He also used Windelband's dichotomy, but only to deny the adequacy of the distinction between generalizing *natural* sciences and studies of human history. He was as much at home in economics and history as in sociology, but Weber considered sociology his own discipline and did not want to deny it the designation of social *science*. Although its data refer to particular events, so do the empirical data of the natural sciences, and he argued that its aim, just like theirs, is to derive generalizations about their respective subject matter.

The tool Weber developed for sociology's task – generalizing about human history – is the *ideal type*. This term refers to an unrealistically abstract core concept, exemplified by economic theory, which "always asks what course of action would take place if it were purely rational and oriented to economic ends alone" ([1922] 1978: 21). It is a pure concept, but not a perfect one in the sense of being very desirable. In other words, it is a prototype of either the best or the worst characteristics, which can refer to a saint or a villain. Weber formulated the terms to distinguish sociology from history: in contrast to history's concern with unique events and trends, sociology seeks to generalize about the common elements of social occurrences.

Weber's classic is *The Protestant Ethic and the Spirit of Capitalism* ([1904–5] 1930). His aim in this succinct analysis was to show that Marx's discussion about the material influences on the development of capitalism must be complemented by showing the role played in its development by Protestant asceticism, notably in Benjamin Franklin's (1748) secularized version.

At the very beginning of this century, a prominent, possibly the most prominent, author in the social sciences was Sumner. His major book, *Folkways* (1934), distinguished conventional practices, "folkways," from "mores," rules backed by moral authority, such as the Ten Commandments. But this century's dominant cultural sociologist was Talcott Parsons, whose first major work was *The Structure of Social Action* (1937). In it he argued that the task of sociology is the study of value orientations; he also claimed that this conclusion is implicit in Marshall's, Weber's, Pareto's, and

Durkheim's writings. (This classification of Durkheim in this cultural tradition is questionable, as I argue below.)

Parsons was often criticized for the inaccessibility of his writing and the high level of abstraction of his ideas (for example, see Mills 1961). But he was very prolific, writing about a dozen books, and his influence and reputation grew. In two of the books he advanced two different major theories. (In another he tried to trace, unconvincingly, the links between them.) One of these developed the theory of pattern variables (Parsons 1951), and the other, with Smelser, presented the AGIL theory (Parsons and Smelser 1958). His reputation did not last, however. Some years after his death he was largely forgotten. (When I asked graduate students in the 1990s, many did not know his name. Some did, but few had read any of his books.)

An earlier cultural sociologist, whom Parsons discusses in his first book as an influence on his work, was the Italian Vilfredo Pareto. He is widely known as an economist, because his major publications are in economics, the field in which he made major contributions. The reason he turned to the *Trattato di Sociologia generale* ([1916] 1963) was to explain why people do not always act in terms of the rational principles of economics. He develops his analysis of "non-logical conduct" on distinct levels. The six residues he distinguishes are fundamental drives or sentiments (Parsons, in his interpretation of Pareto, considered "residues" to refer to shared value orientations).

The two most important residues are the "instinct of innovation" and the "persistence of aggregates," seeking new experiences and preferring old-established traditions, respectively. (The other four residues are self-expression, repugnance of suffering, individual integrity, and sex – a strange admixture.) These presumably affect four derivations, all with subtypes. Pareto's economic work continues to enjoy a high reputation, but his later sociological work seems to be nearly as forgotten as Parsons's.

The topics embraced by cultural studies include all research that deals with people's shared values and norms, preferences, and attitudes. Examples of major types are public opinion surveys, including research on religious preferences, political attitudes, tastes in arts and music, and voting studies. Most these are based on interviews, ideally of random samples. A second type are field studies involving direct observations, sometimes supplemented by interviews, which often are studies of people's social relations, or the networks of relations in groups such as factory workers, office employees, or students in school.

The interpretation of results from single surveys may be ambiguous. For example, if a 1960 opinion survey found that a larger proportion of older than younger men are Democrats, the question arises whether this indicates that younger people are more conservative or that people who grew up during Roosevelt's New Deal have remained less conservative. The general problem is whether an apparent age difference results from the current stage in a person's life or from the attitudes acquired in the distinct past experiences of older people. This question cannot be answered by a one-time survey but only by repeated interviews with the same persons – called a panel design.

The panel design was invented by Lazarsfeld for voting studies to learn how voters make up their minds in the last months before an election (see Lazarsfeld, Berelson, and Gaudet 1944). Most panel studies involve only short time-periods, as Lazarsfeld's did, but there are some that trace the development of youngsters into adulthood for twenty years or more. In principle, the panel design can be used to study changes in people's attitudes, knowledge, or behavior for any period, but the costs for studies lasting years or decades are naturally very high.

In concluding this section on the cultural perspective in sociology, I want to make a personal comment. My own recent work has been structural, but this was not the case for my earlier work. Yet I consider cultural theories to be capable of being more profound than structural ones, though structural theories can be more easily formulated rigorously than cultural ones. I also think that testability is an essential requirement of both cultural and structural theories. Despite my preference for structural theories, my favorite theory, an imaginative gem, is a cultural one and one that cannot be tested to boot – not because it is cultural but because it deals with a unique historical development – Weber's *Protestant Ethic*.

Social Structure

The classic symbol of the structural perspective in sociology is Émile Durkheim, who defined social facts as "ways of acting, thinking and feeling external to the individual and endowed with a power of coercion by reason of which they control him [*sic*]" (Durkheim [1895] 1938: 3). In contrast to Weber's (idealistic) focus on internalized social values and norms as motivating individuals, Durkheim's truly sociological view stresses the external constraints of objective social conditions that delimit conduct. He early received renown for his *De La Division du Travail Social* (*The Division of Labor in*

Society; [1893] 1938), in which he introduced the contrast between mechanical and organic solidarity.

Durkheim ([1893] 1938) suggests in this important book that the division of labor greatly contributes to industrialization and, by implication, to progress and human welfare. Despite this emphasis on its important contributions, Durkheim does not present a functional explanation of the division of labor. Indeed, he explicitly rejects functionalism and advances a causal explanation instead. Population growth and the increasing density often accompanying it intensify the struggle for existence and undermine mechanical solidarity. The continuing progress of subdivision of labor strengthens organic solidarity by engendering the interdependence on which it rests.

Three great contributions were made by Durkheim in this path-breaking book. First, he substituted a causal for the prevailing teleological explanation of social conditions. Second, he demonstrated the significance of the subdivision of work for the interdependence that holds industrial society together (organic solidarity), not despite but because of its very diversity. Third, he provided a superior foundation for structural sociology than Marx's market distinction between employers and employees, which no longer distinguishes, as Marx intended it to do, a ruling class from others.

Durkheim divided people not by market position – employer and employee – but by position in the structure of work relations, the division of labor, which is generally considered to refer to occupations. A detailed division of labor would consist of very narrow occupational specialties, such as chief executives of large corporations and many other specific occupations. This would distinguish the ruling class in today's advanced capitalism, whereas the division by market position no longer does.

This book's significance is thought by many to have been over-shadowed by *Le Suicide* (*Suicide*). I once thought so, too, but my admiration for *De La Division du Travail Social*, and its author, have much increased, and I consider it to be emblematic of structural sociology, the only truly sociological approach.

In *Suicide* (1951), Durkheim presents the first sociological theory that is based on quantitative research, making another great contribution (particularly because he did not consider this to validate the theory, as we shall see). He compares suicide *rates* in different countries and at different times, and makes many internal comparisons (by sex, religion, marital status, and in other ways). This focus enables him to treat the phenomenon of suicide not psychologically as a tragic individual event – why individuals take their own lives – but as a recurrent occurrence in sociological terms – what social conditions affect the likelihood of suicide. After deciding that not all rate differences can be explained by a single principle, he distinguished three types and explained them by different principles.

Egoistic suicide rates, exemplified by the higher rates of Protestants than those of Catholics, are explained by Durkheim in terms of two social differences. One, Protestants have greater freedom of inquiry, symbolized by the vernacular Bible they can read and interpret themselves. Catholics, in contrast, are duty-bound to conform to the strict rules laid down by the priesthood who interpret the Latin Bible that common people cannot read. Two, all Catholics are integrated in their all-embracing Church, whereas Protestants belong to diverse denominations. These two differences are responsible for the higher Protestant than Catholic suicide rates.

Altruistic suicide has the opposite cause, not insufficient but excessive solidarity in a community that makes its members willing to make sacrifices, including even their lives, for the common good. Soldiers, particularly volunteers, exhibit a stronger patriotism than most civilians. The lesser value soldiers place on their own lives compared to civilians, account, according to Durkheim, for the greater likelihood to commit suicide.

A third type, anomic suicide, is frequent in times of economic crises, which disrupt many lives and engender disorientation and confusion among people. The diversity of modern cities and the frequent economic fluctuation in modern times have made anomic disorientation, or even desperation, more prevalent nowadays than it was in more peaceful past centuries. Pervasive anomie accounts for the higher suicide rates in periods of economic crises, notably by disrupting many lives, particularly in modern times, owing to their hectic pace.

What makes this theory particularly impressive is that Durkheim must have implicitly realized that his interpretations of empirical data inferred from them may be invalid. This was a great insight at the time he wrote *Suicide*, which was long before Popper ([1935] 1959) first demonstrated that interpretations of empirical findings inferred from them cannot be considered valid unless new predictions they imply have been repeatedly proved to be valid, or even probably valid. Durkheim consequently deduced additional predictions from his major theoretical hypotheses to test them.

If the spirit of free inquiry of Protestants is responsible for their higher suicide rates, it implies that other differences in inquisitiveness generally would have the same effect. Highly educated persons may be assumed to have more inquisitive minds than those with little education, and thus are expected to be more prone to commit suicide than poorly educated ones. This is the case. If the stronger integration of Catholics in their all-embracing Church is responsible for their low suicide rates, compared to those of Protestants who belong to diverse denominations, the integrative bond of marriage that single adults lack should be reflected in higher single than married suicide rates. This is also the case.

An alternative to Durkheim's interpretation of the higher suicide rates in military than civilian life in terms of altruism might be that the hardships of military duties make life hardly worth living and escape from it a relief, which is reflected in high suicide rates. If this were the case, officers, whose life is surely less hard than that of common soldiers, should have lower suicide rates. But if Durkheim's hypothesis that altruistic identification with the country's welfare is responsible, officers' greater commitment to the army and the country should raise their suicide rates above those of other soldiers. Officers to have higher suicide rates, in accordance with the implication of Durkheim's theory.

Finally, the higher suicide rates in periods of strong economic fluctuations and recurring crises are explained by Durkheim by anomie. If anomic feelings of confusion and desperation are aroused by the disruptions in life in economic crises, the disruption of marital bonds by divorce should also result in feelings of anomie and thus higher chances of suicide. Indeed, divorced persons are more likely to commit suicide than married ones.

Karl Marx was an earlier representative of the materialist or structural perspective. Indeed, he coined the term *materialism*, and his theory centered attention on class structure and conflict (see Marx [1867–79] 1925–6). In my judgment, his theory has a great theses, but his major political prediction violates its implications. Marx's important contribution was the thesis (while "inverting" Hegel's ideas) that history is governed by a *material* dialectical development manifest in recurrent class struggles. His favorite example is the 1789 bourgeois French Revolution in which common people overthrew the Bourbon absolute monarchy.

In due course, the most successful heirs of this middle-class uprising became the capitalist ruling class which exploited the workers ("wage slavery"). One would expect, in accordance with the principles of dialectical materialism, another revolution by the working class, and this is, indeed, what Marx predicted. His theory leads to the further expectation that the dominant leaders of this revolution (1917) would also become a ruling class in Russia exploiting the rest of the country's population. This, indeed, seems to have been what did happen, if not already under Lenin then surely under Stalin, but it was not what Marx predicted. He predicted – wish being father of the thought – the proletarian revolution to be the end of the dialectical course of history and of all class differences.

I consider Marx and Durkheim to be the classic representative of the structural approach in sociology. Their structural conception is, in my opinion, the proper approach for sociology. Neither was a pure structuralist, however; both introduced some cultural elements into structuralism that enriched their theories. Durkheim, in particular, often complemented his structural analysis with cultural insights, notably in his later life. But already in his first book he analyzed how the structural changes of the progressing division of labor affect cultural common solidarity.

Culture is more prominent in Durkheim's later work. In *Suicide*, the basic distinction of the three types is in terms of three cultural orientations, and his last book is an analysis of religion (Durkheim [1915] 1947). Marx proudly emphasizes that his approach is materialistic and not idealistic, but his analysis also employs cultural terms, notably "class-conscious" and "false consciousness," not to mention "ideology," even in the title of his and Engels's book, *The German Ideology* ([1845/6] 1939).

A Theory of Structural Sociology

To formulate a structural theory of sociology, I first specify precisely the distinctive nature of the discipline. I begin by raising and answering simple questions: what is sociology's task? The study of society. But what is society? It is composed of people. People are individuals, who are studied by psychologists, and even the influence of social conditions on people is studied by a subgroup of them – social psychologists. Is there anything left that is distinctly structural to be studied by sociologists? Defining sociology in structural terms requires doing so in terms of attributes of a population that are not attributes of its individual members.

A society's (or other collectivity's) population has two such attributes: the differences among its members and the relations between them. Isolated persons have a body and, unless they have always been isolated, a personality, but social differences and relations cannot be ascribed to them. I conclude that the differences and relations of the members of any collectivity are its defining criteria and the distinctive subject matter of sociology.

What follows is an outline of a structural theory of sociology in accordance with this conception of structure as referring to the differences among and the relations between the members of a population. For these are structural attributes in the sense that they characterize the population without characterizing its individual members.

The definition of social structure in abstract terms is that it is a multidimensional space of social positions among which a population is distributed. I use the term "abstract" simply to refer to generic concepts in theory, as distinguished from their empirical implications with which theory is tested. Thus, heterogeneity and inequality are abstract concepts of my theory, and a population's ethnic heterogeneity and income inequality exemplify empirical variables representing them. That heterogeneity promotes intergroup relations is an abstract theorem, and that a community's ethnic heterogeneity promotes interethnic relations is one of its empirical implications that would test the theory. I consider this distinction between abstract theorems and the empirical tests they imply to reflect Simmel's ([1908] 1923) contrast of form and their contents of social life.

The theory's basic assumption is that social relations depend on opportunities for contact. Putting it in terms of the definition of social structure: it is assumed that social relations depend on proximity in the multidimensional space of social positions.

Three major theorems in abstract terms can be derived from the assumption and the abstract definitions of the three structural dimensions. One, heterogeneity increases the chances of intergroup relations. Two, inequality increases the average status distance between persons. (To be sure, inequality increases the salience of status, which reduces the likelihood of status-distant relations. But the direct, positive *structural effect* of inequality outweighs this indirect negative effect.) Three, intersection increases intergroup relations.

A parallel set of theorems with the same independent variables is stipulated for conflict as the dependent variable. Another such set is stipulated for social mobility as the dependent variable.

The theory formulated in abstract terms has been tested by its implications for empirical relations between variables. The "population" for the tests that were conducted were all SMSAs (Standard Metropolitan Statistical Areas) in the United States in 1970 with a population of more than 250,000. The number of these metropolitan areas was 125. The independent variables were six forms of heterogeneity (of race, nativity, birth region, industry, major occupation, and detailed occupation); three forms of inequality (in years of education, earnings, and socioeconomic status, and eight forms of intersection (all of the above variables except detailed occupation).

A brief summary of results is found in Blau (1994) and fully reported in Blau and Schwartz ([1984] 1997). Tests on five of six forms of heterogeneity (in race, nativity, birth region, industry, and detailed occupation) supported the theory. Heterogeneity in major occupational groups did not, possibly because the differences in major groupings of occupation have no significance for interpersonal relations once the more specific difference in detailed occupations are taken into account (controlled). The tests on all three forms of inequality (in education, earnings, and socioeconomic status) supported the theory. All tests on intersection (race, nativity, birth region, industry, major occupation, education, earnings, socioeconomic status) support the theory.

In short, 15 of 16 tests support the theory. Those in all but one forms of heterogeneity, in all forms of inequality, and in all forms of intersection. The only test that failed to support it was that for major occupational groups, when the specific occupations composing them are controlled, probably because grouping different items creates no new distinctions.

References

Blau, Peter M. 1994. *Structural Contexts of Opportunities*. Chicago: University of Chicago Press.

Blau, Peter M. and Joseph E. Schwartz. [1984] 1997. *Crosscutting Social Circles*. New Brunswick, NJ: Transaction.

Durkheim, Émile. [1893] 1933. *The Division of Labor in Society*. New York: Free Press.

——. [1895] 1938. *The Rules of Sociological Methods*. Chicago: University of Chicago Press.

——. [1915] 1947. *The Elementary Forms of Religious Life*. Glencoe: Free Press.

——. 1951. *Suicide*. Glencoe: Free Press.

Franklin, Benjamin. 1748. *Advice to a Young Tradesman*. New York: Sparks.

Lazarsfeld, Paul F., Bernard Berelson, and Hazel Gaudet. 1944. *The People's Choice*. New York: Duell, Sloan, & Pearce.

Marx, Karl. [1867–79] 1925–6. *Capital*. 3 vols. Chicago: Kerr.

Marx, Karl and Friedrich Engels. [1845/6] 1939. *The German Ideology*. New York: International Publishers.

Mills, C. Wright. 1961. *The Sociological Imagination*. New York: Grove Press.

Pareto, Vilfredo. [1916] 1963. *The Mind and Society: A Treatise on General Sociology*. New York: Dover.

Parsons, Talcott. 1937. *The Structure of Social Action*. New York: McGraw Hill.

———. 1951. *The Social System*. Glencoe: Free Press.

Parsons, Talcott. and Neil J. Smelser. 1958. *Economy and Society*. Glencoe: Free Press.

Popper, Karl R. [1935] 1959. *The Logic of Scientific Discovery*. New York: Basic Books.

Simmel, Georg. [1908] 1923. *Soziologie*. Munich and Leipzig: Duncker & Humblot.

Sumner, William G. 1934. *Folkways*. Boston: Ginn.

Weber, Max. [1922] 1978. *Economy and Society*. Berkeley: University of California Press.

———. [1904–5] 1930. *The Protestant Ethic and the Spirit of Capitalism*. London: Allen & Unwin.

Name Index

Abbot, Pamela, 149
Adam, Barbara, 163, 164, 165, 166
Addelson, Kathryn P., 167
Ainslie, George, 102
Albert, Michal, 29
Alchian, Armen, 226
Alcoff, Linda, 164
Alexander, Jeffrey C., 17, 195
Alexander, R., 219, 230
Allison, P., 230
Althusser, Louis, 27, 37
Amassari, Paulo, 177
Ambrose, Alice, 133
Amin, Ash, 55
Anderson, Perry, 46
Antonio, Robert J., 11, 12, 17, 26, 30,
    56, 61
Archer, Margaret S., 6
Arendt, Hannah, 6
Aristotle, 98
Aschheim, Steven, 26
Ashley, David, 50, 55, 61
Augustine, St, 98, 99
Austin, John, 126, 127
Averroes, 98, 99
Axelrod, Robert, 222, 223, 224, 227
Axtell, Robert, 223, 227

Babich, Babette, 26
Bainbridge, W., 224
Bandura, Albert, 228
Barker, Pat, 77
Barnes, Barry, 154, 157, 159, 161
Bartky, Sandra Lee, 13, 76, 79, 83, 89

Bat-Ami, Bar On, 32, 33
Baudrillard, Jean, 12, 35, 37, 39, 41, 44,
    45, 47, 52, 53, 57, 59
Bauman, Zygmunt, 43, 48, 49, 53
Baym, Nina, 148
Beauvoir, Simone de, 6, 15, 150
Beck, Ulrich, 47, 50
Beck-Gernsheim, Elisabeth, 47
Becker, Gary, 225, 226
Becker, Howard S., 166, 179
Beeker, Carolyn, 244
Bell, Daniel, 22, 41, 42, 43, 45, 47, 48,
    49, 54, 57, 58
Bellah, Robert N., 43
Benhabib, Seyla, 32
Bentham, Jeremy, 50, 52, 59, 112
Berelson, Bernard, 268
Berger, Joseph, 261
Berger, Peter L., 78
Bertens, Hans, 24
Best, Steve, 22, 24, 61
Bienenstock, E., 222
Billig, Michael, 17
Blackstone, William, 111, 112
Blau, Peter M., 10, 11, 15, 18, 19, 20, 211,
    238, 243, 244, 246–8, 250, 254, 274
Bloor, David, 107, 154, 155, 159, 162
Blum, Terry, 244, 246
Blumer, Herbert, 106, 107
Bogard, William, 52, 53, 54
Bohman, James, 6
Bologh, Roslyn, 8, 147
Bonacich, Philip, 222
Bonnano, Alessandro, 22, 56

Boorman, Scott, 229, 230
Bordo, Susan, 13, 32, 76, 79, 89
Boulding, Kenneth, 226
Bourdieu, Pierre, 22
Bové, Paul, 6
Boyd, R., 230
Braithwaite, Richard, 250
Brandom, Robert, 14, 118–25, 131–42
Brown, Richard H., 17, 61
Burns, Tom, 5
Burton, Robert, 13, 77
Butler, Judith, 76, 87, 89
Byrne, R., 99

Calhoun, Craig, 36, 148
Calinescu, Matei, 23
Camiller, Patrick, 46
Campbell, Joseph, 1, 2
Carmichael, Thomas, 7
Carnap, Rudolph, 9, 253
Carroll, Berenice A., 166
Cerullo, John J., 46
Chandler, Alfred D., 58
Chase, Susan E., 76
Chatterjee, R., 260
Chodorow, Nancy, 22
Clawson, Dan, 23, 24
Clough, Patricia, 32, 35
Code, Lorraine, 155, 170
Cohen, I. Bernard, 101
Cohn, Carol, 171
Coleman, James S., 11
Collingwood, Robin, 96
Collini, Stefan, 109
Collins, H. M., 155, 162
Collins, Patricia Hill, 76, 80, 82, 89, 149
Collins, Randall, 19, 240, 241, 242, 253
Comte, Auguste, 26, 132, 265
Condorcet, Marie Jean Antoine, 1
Connell, R. W., 13, 76, 87, 89
Constant, Edward W. 145
Cooley, Charles Horton, 219
Croissant, Jennifer, 15, 145
Crompton, Thomas, 4
Culler, Jonathan, 152
Cushing, F. H., 2

Darwin, Charles, 13, 99
Davidson, Donald, 100, 140
Davis, Mike, 53, 54
Dawkins, Richard, 18, 219, 228, 230, 231
Deane, P., 103

Debord, Guy, 27
De Lauretis, Teresa, 146, 158, 171
Delphy, Christine, 169
Demerath, Nicholas J., 24
Denzin, Norman K., 24, 35, 37, 163
Derrida, Jacques, 6, 9, 23, 31, 152
Descartes, René, 8, 99
Dewey, John, 32, 33, 38, 39, 51, 60, 64
Deweyisn, 37, 39
Dews, Peter, 39
Diaconis, Persi, 260
Dickens, R. David, 61
Dilthey, Wilhelm, 3, 265
Dostoevsky, Fyodor, 171
Durkheim, Emile, 1, 2, 9, 20, 36, 43, 51,
    92, 104, 126, 127, 128, 129, 147,
    265, 267–72

Ebert, Teresa L., 32
Edmondson, Ricca, 17
Einstein, Albert, 113, 216
Ekeh, Peter, 232
Ellis, Sir Henry, 5
Elster, Jon, 13, 102, 227
Emerson, Ralph Waldo, 32
Emirbayer, Mustafa, 201
Emmet, Dorothy, 5, 6
Engels, Friedrich, 42, 204
Epstein, J., 223, 227
Erickson, Victoria Lee, 8
Etzioni, Amitai, 43, 210, 224

Factor, Regis, 4, 126, 131
Fararo, Thomas J., 19, 239, 244, 250, 251
Farganis, Sondra, 32, 61
Fay, Brian, 6
Feenberg, Andrew, 6
Ferguson, Kathy E., 171
Ferry, Luc, 27, 39
Feuerbach, Ludwig, 2
Feyerabend, Paul, 113
Fichte, Johann Gottlieb, 2, 3
Figert, Anne, 154, 155
Fish, Stanley, 30
Fisher, Walter R., 6, 8
Fitzpatrick, Kevin, 244
Forman, Paul, 153
Foucault, Michel, 6, 9, 22, 23, 26, 31,
    51, 52, 77, 156, 159, 160, 161, 162
Frank, Arthur W., 76, 80, 88
Frank, R., 229, 232
Frank, Tom, 29

Franklin, Benjamin, 266
Fraser, Nancy, 23, 24, 32, 36, 46, 61,
    147, 167
Freedman, D., 253
Frege, Gottlob, 119
Freire, Paulo, 76
French, Peter A., 6
Frickers, Miranda, 169
Friedman, M., 225, 255
Fukuyama, Francis, 57, 58, 59
Fuller, Steve, 2, 13, 14, 16, 17, 94, 98,
    100, 109, 113, 114

Gabel, Joseph, 18
Gadamer, Hans-Georg, 9, 163
Garfinkel, Harold, 156
Gaudet, Hazel, 268
Geertz, Clifford, 22
Gellner, Ernest, 5
Gennep, Arnold van, 132
Gergen, Kenneth, 168
Gerth, Hans, 8
Gibson, William, 53
Giddens, Anthony, 13, 46, 47, 50, 51,
    92, 93, 98, 99, 100, 113, 114, 200
Gieryn, Thomas, 154–5
Gilman, Sander, 147
Gitlin, Todd, 48
Glassman, Ronald, 11
Gödel, Kurt, 209, 253, 254
Godwin, Mary, 219
Goethe, Johann Wolfgang, 3
Goffman, Erving, 37, 81
Goldman, Alvin I., 7
Good, J. M. M., 7
Goodman, Robert F., 6, 8
Goodwin, Jeff, 201
Gordon, David, 56
Gordon, Scott, 7
Gottdiener, Mark, 61
Gould, Stephen Jay, 18
Gouldner, Alvin, 17, 95, 96
Grant, Judith, 151
Greenhalgh, John, 4
Gross, A. G., 17
Gutmann, Amy, 36

Haas, Michael, 7
Habermas, Jürgen, 5, 6, 9, 23, 24, 27,
    60, 97, 200
Hacking, Ian, 250
Hägerström, Axel, 131, 132, 138

Hamilton, W., 230, 232
Hamlet, 122
Hannan, Michael, 225
Hanson, F. Allan, 52
Haraway, Donna, 15, 33, 35, 150, 151,
    161, 169
Harding, Sandra, 15, 32, 150, 152, 156,
    158, 159, 162, 163, 171
Harré, Rom, 250
Harrison, Bennett, 56
Hartsock, Nancy M., 15, 33, 147, 150,
    159–61, 169
Harvey, David, 55, 56
Hassan, Ihab, 24
Hawkesworth, Mary, 169
Hayek, Friedrich, 6, 51, 221, 228
Heap, Hargraves, S., 223
Hechter, Michael, 227, 243
Heckathorn, David, 222
Hedstrom, Peter, 224, 225
Heelas, Paul, 46
Hegel, G. W. F., 1, 2, 3, 4, 6, 16, 112,
    265, 272
Heidegger, Martin, 12, 23, 26
Heims, Steven J., 166
Heise, David, 221
Hempel, Carl G. 250, 254
Henderson, David K., 7
Hernstein, Richard J., 18
Hess, David, 160
Hetherington, Stephen, 157
Hintikka, Merrill, 152, 163, 171
Hirsh, Arthur, 27
Hobbes, Thomas, 1, 96, 125, 215
Hochschild, Arlie R., 164
Hodgson, Godfrey, 58, 64
Hollinger, Robert, 61
Hollis, Martin, 7, 157
Homans, George, 11
Homer, 1
hooks, bell, 76, 80, 83, 87, 89
Horwich, Paul, 105
Huber, Joan, 24
Hughes, H. Stuart, 26, 61
Hume, David, 147, 196
Humphreys, Paul, 11, 19, 20, 253
Hurvicz, Leonid, 258
Husserl, Edmund, 4, 9, 12, 13
Huyssen, Andreas, 22, 24

Ihering, Rudolph von, 125, 126, 141
Im Hoff, Ulrich, 193

Ingram, Paul, 228
Iverson, Gregory, 260

Jackson, Norman, 156
James, William, 220
Jameson, Fredric, 12, 22, 23, 24, 27, 40,
    43, 44, 45, 49, 54, 57
Jaspers, Karl, 197
Joas, Hans, 13, 105
Johnson, C., 101

Kalmijn, Matthijs, 242
Kandal, Terry R., 157, 149
Kant, Immanuel, 1, 2, 3, 7, 8, 14, 16, 17,
    100, 101, 118, 196, 197, 198, 202
Kanter, Rosabeth Moss, 165
Kaplan, David, 148
Kaufman, Cynthia, 32, 34
Keller, Evelyn Fox, 29, 76, 86, 89
Keller, J., 260
Kelley, D., 111, 113
Kellner, Doug, 22, 24, 61
Kelsen, Hans, 123, 131
Keynes, John Maynard, 104, 109, 110,
    111
Kiser, E., 227
Kitcher, Patricia, 255
Kitts, James, 219
Kline, Morris, 209
Kloppenberg, James T., 61
Knies, Karl, 3
Knorr-Cetina, Karin, 29, 107, 154–5,
    161
Koelb, Clayton, 26
Kohnke, Klaus C., 3
Kramarae, Cheris, 149
Kreisworth, Martin, 7
Kripke, Saul A., 14, 120, 124, 128
Kuhn, Thomas, 13, 101, 114, 115
Kumar, Krishan, 55, 60

Laclau, Ernesto, 37
Laibach (musician), 57
Lasch, Christopher, 48
Lash, Scott, 60
Latour, Bruno, 29, 154, 159, 160, 162,
    163, 167
Lave, Charles, 220, 223
Laymon, R., 254
Lazarsfeld, Paul, 268
Lefebvre, Henri, 27
Leinberger, Paul, 50

Lenin, Vladimir, 272
Lenski, Gerhard, 213
Leplin, Jarrett, 250
Lerner, Gerda, 150
Levine, George, 29, 61
Levitt, Paul R., 229, 230
Lieberson, Stanley, 15, 16, 178, 183,
    184, 189
Lloyd, Genevieve, 7
Locke, John, 8
Logan, John Allan, 239, 249
Long, Elizabeth, 7
Longino, Helen, 155, 159, 168
Lorde, Audre, 149, 160
Loughlin, J., 147
Loyola, St Ignatius, 64
Luckmann, Thomas, 78
Lukes, Steven, 5, 157
Lyman, Stanford, 106
Lyotard, Jean-François, 12, 23, 24, 26,
    27, 28, 31, 37, 39, 64

Machiavelli, Niccolo, 1, 7
MacIntyre, Alasdair, 5, 6, 100
Macy, Michael, 11, 17, 18, 221, 224, 234
Mandel, Ernst, 43
Manners, Robert A., 148
Mannheim, Karl, 14, 168
March, James, 220, 223
Marschak, Jakob, 258
Marshall, Alfred, 104, 108, 109, 110,
    266
Martin, JoAnn, 32, 34
Martin, Michael, 7, 179
Martineau, Harriet, 147
Marx, Karl, 2, 3, 6, 11, 20, 27, 42, 92,
    98, 104, 112, 147, 161, 204, 265,
    266, 269, 271, 272
Mason, Jeff, 17
Mauss, Marcel, 132
Maynard-Smith, John, 230
McCall, Michal M., 173
McCloskey, Donald [Deirdre], 17
McDonalds (restaurant), 215
McIntyre, Lee C., 7, 179
McLuhan, Marshall, 129, 130, 131, 134
Mead, George Herbert, 4, 6, 36, 38
Mellucci, Alberto, 47, 48, 50
Michnik, Adam, 60
Miele, Maria, 22
Milbank, J., 95
Mill, John Stuart, 108

Miller, Connie, 162
Mills, C. Wright, 8, 147, 156, 165, 267
Morris, Meaghan, 29
Mouffe, Chantal, 37
Mulkay, Michael, 155, 161
Münch, Richard, 197
Murray, Charles, 18
Myles, John, 56

Nash, J., 222
Natanson, Maurice, 13, 77–89
Nee, Victor, 219, 228
Nelson, J. S., 17
Newcombe, Theodore, 201
Newton, Isaac, 101, 196
Nicholson, Linda, 24, 32, 33, 37, 45
Nietzsche, Friedrich, 9, 12, 13, 23, 25,
    26, 27, 33, 52, 64, 125, 129, 131,
    132, 133, 137, 197
Nye, Andrea, 147

Oakeshott, Michael, 51
Oakley, Ann, 149
Offe, Claus, 59
Olivecrona, Knut Hans Karl, 123, 131
Ornstein, D. S., 260

Pareto, Vilfredo, 20, 266, 267
Parsons, Talcott, 13, 16, 17, 51, 92, 104,
    107, 108, 110, 111, 118, 142, 197,
    198, 214, 215, 223, 266, 267
Passmore, John, 132
Pasteur, Louis, 159–160
Pearl, J., 262
Peirce, Charles Sanders, 221
Piccolomini, Michele, 47
Piccone, Paul, 48
Pinker, Steven, 18
Plant, Sadie, 27
Plato, 6, 9, 12, 13, 14, 94, 95, 96
Pluhar, Werner, 16
Pocock, John, 114, 115
Poisson, Nicolas-Joseph, 242
Polanyi, Michael, 263
Popper, Karl, 254, 270
Prelli, Lawrence J., 17
Proudhon, Pierre Joseph, 2
Pufendorf, Samuel, 14, 122, 125
Putnam, Hilary, 253

Rabinow, Paul, 7
Rabinowitz, Nancy Sorkin, 8

Ragin, Charles C., 179
Rawls, John, 97, 100, 113
Reinharz, Shulamit, 76
Remmling, Gunter W., 161
Renaut, Alain, 27, 39
Restivo, Sal, 156, 162
Ricardo, David, 108
Richardson, Laurel, 34, 35
Richerson, Peter, 230
Richlin, Amy, 8
Rickert, Heinrich, 3, 265
Rickman, H. P., 7
Ricoeur, Paul, 13
Riessman, Catherine Kohler, 76
Ritzer, George, 98, 104
Robbins, Bruce, 29
Roberts, R. H., 7
Robinson, W. S., 189
Rogers, Mary, 12, 13, 17, 83
Rorty, Richard, 9, 32, 37, 38, 39, 64
Rose, Gillian, 7
Rosenau, Pauline Marie, 23, 24
Ross, Andrew, 29
Ross, Dorothy, 28, 64
Rousseau, Jean-Jacques, 1
Runciman, W. G., 228
Ruse, Michael, 219, 230
Russell, Bertrand, 201, 210
Ryle, Gilbert, 190
Rytina, Steven, 11, 16, 17, 18, 214, 244

Saatkamp, Herman, 39
Sacks, Karen, B., 164
Said, Edward, 22
Sandel, Michael, 48
Sartre, Jean-Paul, 171
Savigny, Friedrich Karl von, 3, 111, 112
Scarry, Elaine, 171
Schatzki, Theodore, R., 7, 133
Scheff, Thomas, 107
Scheler, Max, 12
Schleifer, Ronald, 7
Schmitt, Carl, 14, 123, 124, 141
Schmitt, Frederick F., 7
Schott, Robin May, 8
Schrift, Alan, 26
Schull, J., 220
Schutz, Alfred, 4, 5, 9, 13, 81, 82, 105,
    156
Schwartz, Joseph E., 244, 246, 274
Scott, Joan W., 153, 154, 158, 159, 164
Searle, John, 13, 100

Secord, Paul, 250
Sedgwick, Eve Kosofsky, 13, 76, 79, 84
Seidman, Steven, 24, 32, 34, 35, 37, 45,
    46, 51, 52, 64
Sennett, Richard, 48
Serres, Michel, 160
Shakespeare, William, 93, 94
Shapin, Steven, 160
Shiva, Vandana, 162
Sica, Alan, 92, 145
Simmel, Georg, 4, 9, 82, 92, 107, 273
Simon, Herbert, 206, 207, 221, 220, 224,
    225
Simons, Herbert W., 17
Sismondo, Sergio, 153
Skinner, Quentin, 7
Skocpol, Theda, 22
Skvoretz, John, 11, 18, 19, 211, 222,
    244, 246, 247, 250, 254
Small, Albion, 112
Smelser, Neil, 234, 267
Smith, Adam, 109, 224
Smith, Dorothy E., 13, 15, 33, 76, 89,
    149, 152, 156, 165, 168, 172
Smith, Maynard, 222
Smith, Norman Kemp, 16
Socrates, 25, 95
Sokal, Alan, 28, 29, 30
Spencer, Herbert, 26, 108, 109
Spender, Dale, 149
Spinoza, Baruch, 99
Stabile, Carol, 32
Stalin, Joseph, 272
Stammler, Rudolph, 3
Stanley, Liz, 149
Staples, William, 22, 52
Stehr, Nico, 108, 109
Stinchcombe, Arthur, 195, 225
Strauss, Leo, 95, 96
Sullivan, William, 7
Sumner, William Graham, 266
Suppes, Patrick, 254
Sztompka, Piotr, 7

Tarski, Alfred, 261
Thales, 1
Thucydides, 95
Tilly, Charles, 211
Tolman, E. C., 111
Tönnies, Ferdinand, 126–9
Toulmin, Stephen, 8, 99
Touraine, Alain, 47

Traweek, Sharon, 160
Treichler, Paula A., 149
Treitel, Corinna, 162
Tucker, Robert C., 50
Turner, Jonathan, 64, 106
Turner, Ralph H., 189
Turner, Stephen, 4, 14, 106
Turner, Victor, 5
Tyler, Stephen, 17

Vanberg, Viktor, 228
Van den Berg, Axel, 24
Varoufakis, Yanis, 223
Vidich, Arthur, 106
Voltaire, F.-M. A. de, 98
Von Mises, Ludwig, 51

Waithe, Mary Ellen, 163, 165
Walby, Sylvia, 165
Wallace, Clair, 149
Wallerstein, Immanuel, 22, 37, 64, 93
Walton, Douglas, 178
Weber, Max, 3, 11, 14, 20, 31, 33, 37,
    61, 62, 65, 92, 101, 104, 125, 126,
    129, 130–3, 147, 188, 225, 266, 268
Weedon, Chris, 151
Wells, Susan, 17
West, Cornel, 23, 31, 32, 34, 35, 36, 46
Willer, David, 222
Willey, Thomas, 3
Williams, Patricia J., 76, 80, 82, 84, 88
Willmott, Hugh, 156
Wilson, E. O., 219, 230
Wilson, John, 148, 160, 167
Winch, Peter, 201, 207, 216
Windelband, Wilhelm, 3, 265, 266
Wise, Sue, 149
Wittgenstein, Ludwig, 14, 112, 118,
    133, 134, 137, 200, 201, 207
Wittig, Monique, 158
Wolfe, Alan, 201
Wollstonecraft, Mary, 6
Wood, Ellen, 32
Woods, John, 178
Woolgar, Steve, 29, 154, 159
Wright, Crispin, 124
Wright, Will, 167
Wynne-Edwards, Vero, 229

Ziman, John, 153
Znaniecki, Florian, 189
Zuni, 2

Subject Index

accounts, 167
accumulation, 55
action theory, 18
adaptation, 220
advantaged life, 87
agency, 46, 48
agency/structure, 103
AIDs, 81, 82, 84, 189
altruism, 17, 18, 230–2, 271
analytic induction, 189
anomie, 270–1
antifoundationalism, 35, 37
antirationalism, 24
articulations, 154
asceticism, 4, 266
"a-sociology," 167
assumptions, 181, 188, 197
Athenians, 96, 97

bad faith, 86
Bayesian causal inference, 262
Bayes's rule, 222
Benthamites, 112
biased net theory, 19, 244
Binomial models, 259
bourgeois moralism, 42

camera obscura, 8
Candide, 98
canon, 15, 94, 147
capitalism, new forms of, 43
Capuchin monks, 4
Cartesianism, 26, 61

Catholics, 270, 271
causal models, 262
causality, 182, 195
charisma, 132, 139, 141
civitas, 43
classics, rediscovery of, 9
coalitions, 48
Code Napoléon, 111
codes, 35
cognitive mapping, 44
commodification, 2
common sense, 153
communal assessment, 124–5
communism, 42
communitarianism, 39
compatibilism, 99
computational template, 257, 259
consciousness, forms of, 127
consensus, 40
consequentialism, 35
constitutionalism, 96, 97
constitutive principle, 101
constructionism, 29, 41, 107
counterculture, 41
creationism, 96
cultural autonomy, 49
cultural exhaustion, 42
cultural expansion, 45
cultural revolution, 5
cultural studies, 23
cultural theory, 20, 60
culture, 157, 266ff
culture vs. structure, 265ff
culture wars, 48

Darwinism, 220
decadence, 25
decentered agency, 50, 51
deduction, 198
democracy, 39, 40
democratization, 51
Democrats, 268
deontic status, 126
depthlessness, 52
de-sedimentation, 89
determinism, 99, 180–1
detraditionalization, 46, 49, 113
difference, 36
discovery, 162
disembedding, 55
Doctor's Club, 3
domain assumptions, 17
domination, 32
Dunkirk, 4
Durkheimianism, 107
dynamic objectivity, 86
dystopias, 58

economic equilibrium, 108
emancipatory knowledge, 169
emergent rationality, 18
empathy, 86
enclave theory, 81, 82, 87
endings, 57–8
Enlightenment, 8, 27, 61, 111, 193
Entzauberung, 138, 139
epistemic relativity, 29
epistemological perspectivism, 31ff
epistemology, 176ff
error, 136
ethnomethodology, 118, 166
ethnos, 38
everyday life, 150, 151, 152
evidence, 180
evolution, biological, 228, 233
evolutionary epistemology, 220
evolutionary theory, 18
examples, 179ff
   technical use of, 16
exchange theory, 10
experience, 149
experiential turn, 76

fact/value, 119
false consciousness, 18, 272
feminism, 8, 15
feminist epistemology, 146ff

folkways, 266
Fordism, 55, 56, 57
formal modeling, 11, 19
formal theory, 255
"fortress LA," 53–4
Foucaultianism, 35, 39, 53, 54
free will, 98
futurology, 206

game theory, 222
Gemein-/Gesellschaft, 105
gender, 164–5
genealogy of morals, 129
generative mechanisms, 251
gerrymandering, 120, 136
grammatical rules, 129
granularity, 17, 193, 203ff
Grundnorm, 131
gynocentricity, 155

habit, 130
"hedons," 108
Hegelianism, 42, 112
hegemonic aesthetic, 45
herd behavior, 129
hermeneutics, 88
hierarchy, 50
historicism, 48
Hobbesian, 102, 223
horizon, 82, 83
hydraulic metaphor, 160
hyperreality, 54
hypothetico-deductive models, 254

ideal type, 266
idealization, 261
identity, 36, 46
immanent critique, 27
implicit norms, 14, 131, 138
implicit rules, 120
incentives, 210
inequality, 243
instrumentalism, 28
intentional states, 140
intentionality, 13, 78
interdependence, 51
intergroup relations, 238ff
intermarriage, 244
interpretation, 49, 118
interracial marriage, 19
intertextuality, 44
invisible hand, 109

inwardness, 25
irony, 3, 28
irrationalism, 26
irrationality, 11

Jews, 37
judgments, 97
jurisprudence, 4
juristic theory, 111, 112
justice, 97, 99

Kantian categories, 196
Kantian pyramid, 16, 196, 202, 213
Kantianism, 4, 9, 102, 119, 130, 197, 200, 202, 213
Keynesianism, 104, 109, 110
knowledge/power, 25
knowledge, sociology of, 156
Kodificationstreit, 111, 112

laissez-faire economics, 108
language, 200
language games, 33, 134
language habits, 133
learning, 134, 135
Left, 59
legal theory, 102, 149
legal validity, 122ff
legislative reason, 49
legitimation, 26, 27
life-world, 200
linguistic turn, 76
literature and science, 171
local knowledge, 28, 79
Lockean political tradition, 112
logical positivism, 9, 19
logocentrism, 17

madness, 85ff
magic, 132, 141
marginal utility, 11
market seduction, 49
markets, 226
Marxian analysis, 5, 16, 23, 26, 27, 28, 31, 32, 33, 36, 37, 41, 42, 44, 45, 50–4, 58, 170, 171
Marxism, 28
Marxist feminism, 32
masculinist reading, 7, 8
materialism, 44, 271
meaning, 77, 81, 201, 208
"melting pot," 106

mental constructs, 200
mental entropy, 161
mercantilism, 110
metanarratives, 27, 39
Methodenstreit, 265
methods, 177
microsociology, 106–7
models, 238ff, 253ff
    definitions of, 255
modernism, exhaustion of, 42
moral education, 128
moral order, 216
multiculturalism, 46
mundanity, 79

natural right, 112
nature/nurture, 219
necessity, 196
neoconservatism, 59
Neo-Kantianism, 5
neoliberalism, 39
neo-Marxism, 55, 56, 59
nestedness, 17
nesting, 205
network analysis, 202
new class, 41
Newtonian, 113, 153
Newton's Second Law, 19, 257, 259
Nietzschianism, 28, 35, 42, 48
nihilism, 26
nomothetic versus ideographic, 3
non-logical action, 267
normal science, 101
normative assertion, 118
normative justification, 122
normative perspectivism, 36
normativity, 14, 118ff, 128, 148
NRA, 208

objectivity, 11, 28, 33, 62, 172
ontology, 158
ordinary language, 80
otherness, 81
Ottoman empire, 188
outsider theory, 84
overdetermination, 77

panoptical regime, 52
paradigms, 114
Parsonian theory, 166
patriarchy, 34, 50
perspectivism, 26, 28, 29, 38, 39

phenomenology, 9, 12–13, 77ff
philosophical puzzles, 201–2
philosophy of law, 131
philosophy of nature, 2
philosophy versus social theory, 192
police brutality, 54
political economy, 55
political power, 158
post-Fordism, 56
postmaterialism, 47
postmodern aesthetics, 56
postmodern science, 27
postmodernism, 12, 22–65
   types of, 30ff
poststructuralism, 23
power and feminism, 163
power/knowledge, 48, 159–60
practices, 119, 124
pragmatism, 37
predicates, 194, 200, 202
prediction, 240
preferences, 215
prejudice, 34
Presburger arithmetic, 254
privileged position, 34
probability, 184
probability theory, 20
proceduralism, 61
professionalization of science, 28
profit making, 55
promises, 132
proofs, 189
Protestant ethic thesis, 268
Protestants, 270, 271
Puritanism, 41
purposive behavior, 111

queer theory, 34

racism, 106
randomness, 19
RAT vs RCT, 233
rational action 11, 224ff
rational choice, 17
rationalism, 220
rationality, 99, 111, 223
rationalization, 50, 112
reciprocity, 232
reflexivity, 46, 47, 50, 148
regress argument, 121
regulative principle, 100
reinforcement, 227

relativism, 39
representationalism, 26, 32, 35
resource allocation, 225
ressentiment, 25
rhetoric, 95, 211–12
   economic, 110
risk, 47
ritual, 132
Roosevelt's New Deal, 268
rule-utilitarianism, 101
rules, 100–1, 230

sample size, 185
science, assumptions of, 170
science, sociology of, 154ff
secularization, 100
sedimentation, 78, 86
selectionism, 215
self, 8, 49
"selfish gene," 230
self-objectivization, 161
shopping, 84
signs, 43
simulacra, 41
simulation, 52
social change, 104
Social Darwinism, 109
social epistemology, 13, 93
social functionality, 45
social order, 219ff
social research, goals of, 178–9
social/sociological theory, 63–4
social structure, 214, 260, 269, 273
social theory and philosophy, 6–7, 10
socialization, 126, 134
society, definitions of, 194, 198
sociological laws, 262
sociology of knowledge, 14
Sophists, 9
spectator theory, 32
speech acts, 140
SSK, 162
starving bell, 4, 5
statistical reasoning, 242
stealing, 126
stranger, 107
structural analysis, 265
structural effects, 273
structuralism, 20
structuration, 113
structure/agency debate, 13, 93ff
STS theory, 15, 145

subjectivity, 13
submerged statements, 186ff
subpolity, 50
suicide, 270
surveillance, 41, 52, 53
symbolic interactionism, 104
symmetry principle, 107

tastes, 243, 247, 248
telematic order, 53
teleology, social, 220
testability, 20
tests, 183
theodicy, 98, 99
theorizing, 147
theory and data, 239
theory, definitions of, 148ff

theory-driven models, 19, 254
theory models, 5
total institutions, 81
tradition, 115
translation, theory as, 94
truth claims, 145
two-sided logit model, 249
typifications, 105

Ur-difference, 101–2
utopias, 58

Verstehen, 265
verstehende Soziologie, 3
voting studies, 268

Weberianism, 51